IMPOSING POWER-

To the memory of Andrina Mitchel,
to Robert and Valerie,
and to Daniel

IMPOSING POWER-SHARING

Conflict and Coexistence in Northern Ireland and Lebanon

MICHAEL KERR

Foreword by Brendan O'Leary

IRISH ACADEMIC PRESS

DUBLIN • PORTLAND, OR

First published in 2006 by
IRISH ACADEMIC PRESS
44 Northumberland Road, Dublin 4, Ireland

and in the United States of America by
IRISH ACADEMIC PRESS
c/o ISBS, Suite 300
920 NE 58th Avenue
Portland, Oregon 97213-3786

Website: www.iap.ie

Michael Kerr © 2005

British Library Cataloguing in Publication Data
An entry can be found on request

ISBN 0-7165-3384-7 (cloth)
ISBN 0-7165-3383-9 (paper)

Library of Congress Cataloging-in-Publication Data
An entry can be found on request

Typeset by FiSH Books, Enfield, Middx.
Printed by Creative Print and Design, Gwent, Wales

Contents

LIST OF TABLES, CHARTS AND MAPS   vi

LIST OF ABBREVIATIONS   vii

CHRONOLOGY OF KEY EVENTS IN NORTHERN IRELAND, 1920–2005   ix

CHRONOLOGY OF KEY EVENTS IN LEBANON, 1920–2005   xi

ACKNOWLEDGEMENTS   xiii

NOTE ON TRANSLITERATION   xv

FOREWORD BY BRENDAN O'LEARY   xvii

INTRODUCTION   1

1. Consociation   26

2. Sunningdale   41

3. From Containment to Regulation   73

4. The Good Friday Agreement   87

5. A National Pact   112

6. Lebanisation   141

7. The Ta'if Agreement   159

8. Imposing Power-Sharing   179

CONCLUSION   198

ENDNOTES   201

BIBLIOGRAPHY   220

    NORTHERN IRELAND   220

    LEBANON   226

    CONSOCIATIONAL THEORY   234

INDEX   235

List of Tables, Charts and Maps

1 Public attitudes to Northern Ireland's constitutional position 54
2 Public attitudes to the White Paper 55
3 Public attitudes to executive power-sharing 55
4 Public attitudes to the Northern Ireland Assembly 56
5 Public acceptance to power-sharing in Northern Ireland in the 1970s 56
6 Issues Fuelling anti-Agreement Unionists' Opposition to the GFA in 2001 105
7 Unionist support for power-sharing 106
8 Public attitudes to the power-sharing Executive 107
9 Protestant acceptance of power-sharing, 1973–2002 107
10 Religious Communities as a percentage of the 1932 Census 137
11 Estimated changes in resident citizens, by religious affiliation 1932–73 137
12 Confessional representation in the Lebanese Parliament, 1972–92 161
13 Parliamentary confessional distribution of seats in 1992 173

List of Maps

1 Northern Ireland 8

2 Lebanon after 1920 17

Abbreviations

AIA	Anglo-Irish Agreement
ANP	Arab National Party
APNI	Alliance Party of Northern Ireland
BBC	British Broadcasting Corporation
CLMC	Combined Loyalist Military Command
DSD	Downing Street Declaration
DULC	Democratic Unionist Loyalist Coalition
DUP	Democratic Unionist Party
EU	European Union
GFA	Good Friday Agreement
HMSO	Her Majesty's Stationery Office
IRA	Irish Republican Army
LF	Lebanese Forces
LNM	Lebanese National Movement
MLA	Member of the Legislative Assembly (Northern Ireland)
MP	Member of Parliament
NILP	Northern Ireland Labour Party
PLO	Palestine Liberation Organisation
PR	Proportional Representation
PSP	Progressive Socialist Party
PUP	Progressive Unionist Party
RTÉ	Radio Telefís Éireann
RUC	Royal Ulster Constabulary
SDLP	Social Democratic and Labour Party
STV	Single Transferable Vote
TD	Teachta Dála (Member of the Lower House of the Irish Parliament)
UDA	Ulster Defence Association
UDP	Ulster Democratic Party

UDR	Ulster Defence Regiment
UK	United Kingdom
UKUP	United Kingdom Unionist Party
UN	United Nations
UNIFIL	United Nations Interim Force in Lebanon
US	United States
UUC	Ulster Unionist Council
UUP	Ulster Unionist Party
UUUC	United Ulster Unionist Council
UVF	Ulster Volunteer Force
UWC	Ulster Workers' Council
VULC	Vanguard Unionist Loyalist Coalition
VUPP	Vanguard Unionist Progressive Party
WBLC	West Belfast Loyalist Coalition

Chronology of Key Events in Northern Ireland, 1920–2005

1920		Government of Ireland Act
1921		First Northern Ireland Parliament opened
1921–23		Irish Civil War
1922		Six of the nine counties of Ulster opt out of Irish Free State
1949		Republic of Ireland established, leaving the Commonwealth
1967		Northern Ireland Civil Rights Association formed
1972	(January)	Bloody Sunday
	(March)	Direct rule from Westminster imposed
1973	(March)	White Paper published on constitutional proposals, including Irish dimension
	(June)	Elections for Northern Ireland Assembly
	(November)	Agreement reached between parties on the formation of a Northern Ireland power-sharing Executive
	(December)	Intergovernmental Sunningdale Conference
1974	(1 January)	Northern Ireland Executive takes office at Stormont
	(4 January)	Ulster Unionist Council rejects Council of Ireland proposals
	(7 January)	Brian Faulkner resigns as Official Unionist Party leader
	(February)	Westminster general election – 11 seats won by UUUC
	(14 May)	Executive carries Assembly vote on Sunningdale; UWC strike begins
	(17 May)	Dublin and Monaghan bombings
	(28 May)	Direct rule resumed after Executive collapses
1975–76		Constitutional Convention fails to regulate the conflict

1979 (May)	Margaret Thatcher becomes Prime Minister of UK
1981 (March)	IRA man, Bobby Sands, refuses food at the Maze Prison
(April)	Sands wins Fermanagh and South Tyrone by-election
(May)	Sands dies on 66th day of his hunger strike
1985	Margaret Thatcher and Garret FitzGerald sign the AIA
1988	SDLP opens dialogue with Sinn Féin
1989	Peter Brooke becomes Secretary of State for Northern Ireland
1991	British reopen secret back channel with the IRA; Irish government steps up back channel contact with Sinn Féin
1993	Political Process culminates in DSD
1994 (January)	Bill Clinton grants Gerry Adams US visa
(August)	IRA ceasefire announced
(October)	CLMC ceasefire announced
1995	Framework Documents produced by British and Irish Governments
1996 (February)	IRA ceasefire breaks down
(May)	Elections to the Northern Ireland Forum
(June)	Talks process begins
1997 (May)	Tony Blair becomes British Prime Minister
(June)	Bertie Ahern becomes Taoiseach
(July)	IRA ceasefire reinstated; DUP and UKUP withdraw from talks
1998 (April)	GFA signed
(May)	Referendums held in Northern Ireland and the Republic approving the GFA
2005 (May)	Trimble's UUP lose Westminister general election
(July)	IRA instructs its units to dump arms

Chronology of Key Events
in Lebanon, 1920–2005

1920 (April)		France entrusted at San Remo with League of Nations Mandate for Lebanon and Syria
	(September)	Creation of the State of Greater Lebanon
1926		Lebanon receives its first constitution
1932		Last official Lebanese census conducted
1936		Franco-Lebanese Treaty negotiated but unratified in Paris
1940		France defeated; pro-Vichy government installed in Beirut
1941 (June)		Britain and Free French regain the Levant
	(September)	General Catroux declares Lebanon's independence
1942		Edward Louis Spears becomes British Minister to the Levant
1943 (August)		Lebanese Parliamentary elections held
	(September)	President Beshara al-Khoury appoints Riad Solh Prime Minister, sparking a Christian-Muslim push for independence
	(11 November)	Free French arrest Khoury, Solh and their government
	(22 November)	British force their release, marking Lebanon's independence
1948		First influx of Palestinian refugees following the creation of Israel
1957		President Chamoun announces Lebanon's acceptence of the Eisenhower Doctrine
1958		First civil war breaks out
1969		Lebanon signs the Cairo Agreement
1975 (April)		Lebanon divides over Palestinian question – civil war breaks out; National Dialogue Committee meets to discuss Syrian-sponsored reforms

1976	Constitutional Document enshrines compromise backed by Syria and US
1978	First Israeli invasion
1982 (June)	Second Israeli invasion culminates in the siege of Beirut
(August)	Bashir Gemayel elected President
(September)	President Gemayel assassinated
1983 (17 May)	Lebanese-Israeli Agreement signed
1985	Tripartite Agreement signed by militia leaders through Syria
1988	Constitutional crisis engulfs Lebanon, with two rival governments being formed at the end of Amin Gemayel's presidency
1989 (March)	General Aoun declares war of liberation against Syria
(May)	Casablanca Summit on Lebanese crisis
(October)	Lebanese deputies reach constitutional agreement at Ta'if in Saudi Arabia
(5 November)	Ta'if Agreement ratified by Parliament and René Moawad elected President of the Second Republic
(22 November)	President Moawad assassinated
1990 (August)	Iraq invades Kuwait
(October)	Syria shells Aoun out of office
1992	Lebanese elections take place with Christian boycott
2000	Israel ends its occupation of southern Lebanon
2005	Assassination of Rafic Hariri – North Syria withdraws from Lebanon

Acknowledgements

I began research for this book as a PhD student at the Government Department of the London School of Economics and Political Science (LSE) in October 1999, and completed it at the International History Department. Interviews and archival work were conducted in the UK, Ireland and Lebanon between 2000 and 2005. Over 125 political actors – people who had taken part in the making or breaking of power-sharing accords in Northern Ireland and Lebanon – were generous enough to grant me lengthy on-the-record interviews. They included members of political parties, the security services, civil service administrations, academic institutions and paramilitary organisations. I am extremely grateful to all of them for their time, patience and goodwill.

Having completed this research, I owe a debt of gratitude to many friends and colleagues who helped and encouraged me along the way, both from an intellectual perspective and, equally, in a personal capacity. I must first thank Dr Kirsten Schulze of the LSE's International History Department. Without her support, guidance and friendship, completing this work would have been a lonely and infinitely more difficult task. I would like to thank Professor Brendan O'Leary, who was Convenor of the LSE's Government Department when I began my research under his supervision and who has provided an insightful Foreword. The important people in one's life are those who have confidence in you and then make you prove to them that their confidence was justified.

Thanks, and much credit for this work, must go to Robert, Valerie, Richard, Gillian, Julia and Fred. This work is dedicated to Andrina Mitchel, who quietly passed away before it was completed.

Special thanks must go to David McClay, for keeping me on the right path, from start to finish, on many of the finer technicalities of writing.

I would like to thank Era Gjurgjeala, Ross Jordan, Claire Kirk, Justin Lowry, Owen McEldowney, Geoff McGimpsey, Simon McWhirter, Scott Mackenzie, Rebecca Newton, Ronan Smyth, Paul Wilmshurst and Leslie Zachary for their friendship and support. I must also thank Dr Sarah Birch, Dr Shelley Deane, Dr Mark Devenney, Professor Adrian Guelke, Lord Kilclooney, Professor Antony King, Dr Bill Kissane, Dr Brendan O'Duffy, Farid Salman and Dr Chris Van-Stolk.

Special thanks to Lisa Hyde of Irish Academic Press for all her efforts and enthusiasm. Thanks also to Mick Alabaster, Frank Cass, Toby Harris and Rosa El-Eini.

I wish to thank the Ulster Unionist Party for all their help, especially Alderman Roy Beggs for his friendship and guidance over the years.

Thanks must go to Nadim Shehadi for giving me the perfect start to my research in Beirut. Also in Lebanon, I would especially like to thank the Housseini family, whose patience and hospitality, like their excellent coffee, never ran out. Warmest appreciation must go to Jeanine El Jalakh, who inspired, encouraged and looked after me tirelessly on both my fieldwork trips in Lebanon. Without her expertise and energetic intellectual stimulation my research would have been even more modest.

I would like to thank the LSE's Government and International History Departments and the University of London's Central Research Fund, which helped me conduct my major fieldwork trip to Lebanon in 2002. I would like also to thank the LSE Student Support Fund, the LSE Student's Union and especially the Reeves Foundation, which consistently financed my endeavours with equal doses of kindness and enthusiasm.

Finally, I would like to thank Sarah, who looked after the most important things in life while I wrote this book.

Note on Transliteration

Arabic words other than personal and place-names have been transliterated in accordance with the standard applied by *The International Journal of Middle East Studies*. The spelling of Arabic personal and place-names has been based on the most prevalent practice used in books. As far as interviewees are concerned, the transliteration of their names is based on how the individuals in question spell them themselves.

Foreword

The Realism of Power-Sharing

Brendan O'Leary
Lauder Professor of Political Science
Director of the Solomon Asch Center
University of Pennsylvania

Belfast and Beirut are twins. I am old enough to have known both cities in my childhood, before they become synonyms for urban communal violence, paramilitaries and 'sectarian' killing. The car bomb was invented, accidentally, in Belfast, and used to even more devastating effect in Beirut. The depth of ethnic and religious antagonisms on display in these cities from the 1970s startled many outside observers who usually saw them as atavistic throwbacks, resisting the progressive thrust of enlightenment. Little did they realize that they were better understood as portents for other late-twentieth century and contemporary conflicts.

The two cities other, and more prosaic, histories were rapidly wiped from the world's memory-banks. Both had once been major centres of industry and commerce, innovators in their regions, sites of proper and proud bourgeois development. Dr Michael Kerr's fascinating study offers hope that both port cities, and the polities of which they are the capitals, Northern Ireland and Lebanon, may recover more civil reputations in the early twenty-first century. I had the privilege of witnessing the start of this research when Michael Kerr came from Belfast to the London School of Economics and Political Science just before I left that great institution for another equally great one in another land. In a small way our relationship shows what may be possible again in Northern Ireland – civil and warm inter-personal engagements despite differences in national allegiance, political formation, party membership, and the religions of our ancestors. Dr Kerr has advised Ulster Unionists; I have advised others not known to share their core beliefs. It is an honour that he has asked me to preface his careful, deeply informed comparative analysis that is rooted in fluent Belfast argot, French, Arabic, intimate familiarity with the local power players, history and political science.

I shall not use this opportunity to scoop what is to follow. Readers should make their own précis of Dr Kerr's sober grasp of what was, is and may be possible for coexistence in Lebanon and Northern Ireland – including his belief that external forces are necessary to stabilize their consociational prospects. Instead, I would like to sketch for the novice reader key elements of the intellectual tradition within which both Dr Kerr and I have worked, namely consociational thinking, and to defend it against some misconceptions as this tradition is frequently misunderstood, sometimes wilfully so. I shall not provide a narrative of the antecedents of consociational practices, or their intellectual distillation, or a comprehensive guide to the debates that surround the work of the leading contemporary pioneer in this field, the Dutch political scientist Arend Lijphart, now the holder of an honorary PhD from the Queen's University of Belfast. Others, including me, have executed such enterprises elsewhere.[1] Rather, I shall portray consociational thinking as a form of pragmatic realism, one with a distinctive logic, the logic of 'political triage': deciding what institutions need political treatment first, according to how seriously defective they are. This political triage developed as a response to the inadequate institutions of the liberal democratic nation-state in the presence of two or more peoples mobilized behind rival conceptions of nationality or religious allegiance.

Consociation sounds a technical term. Indeed, it is expressed in technical and sometimes highly complex institutional forms. Consociational institutions have three essential features, and a fourth that frequently accompanies them. First, executive political power is *jointly* shared across the representatives of rival peoples. Second, rules of proportionality are used to share power, express representation, and to allocate resources. Third, each people to the partnership is an equal, entitled to self-rule in matters of profound cultural consequence, with the institutional recognition that principle entails. The fourth and more contingent feature is the existence of veto-powers, which stop one people unilaterally changing the rules of the game at the expense of others.

But consociation is also known, non-technically, as 'power-sharing', and for good reasons. Yet there is more to power-sharing than the sharing of power. Consociationalists are not, generally, emotional. They do not plead for sibling or puppy or conjugal love in politics. Consociation is not the injunction to say prayers together. Consociation has tougher mental lineages. No sensible advocate of power-sharing assumes it is a universal panacea. Commending power-sharing has to be appropriate and feasible as well as desirable. It is vital to distinguish three logics of political power: 'the division of power', 'competition for power', and 'power-sharing'. The third logic builds on the others and, contrary to what its critics say or imagine, need not displace them.

The division of power is at the heart of the liberal tradition. Strongly present in American federalism, and influenced by the arguments of Montesquieu and Madison, the belief is that dividing power is critical to preventing despotism. This tradition seeks to formalize separate executive, legislative and judicial institutions. By inhibiting a monopoly of power, especially in the executive, dictatorship can be avoided. A legislature comprised of a dominant faction that judges in its own interest is not one from which much justice for others can be expected. The separation of civilian from military power, the separation of nomination from appointment, the separation of police powers to arrest and interrogate from the judicial power to prosecute, the separation of local governments from central governments, are less recognized, but equally critical parts of the same logic of dividing power. To divide power is to prevent its abuse; to check power with power controls public officials, elected and appointed.

Some, mistakenly, think that properly organizing the division of power is what really matters in the stabilization of deeply divided territories, such as those of Lebanon and Northern Ireland. A well-structured division of power, they say, will inhibit the prospects of national, ethnic or communal majorities – or minorities – tyrannizing over others. Proponents of integration and assimilation are strongly inclined to this claim. They deny that they are against power-sharing as such. They say that they are supporters of sharing power, but just among the individual citizens (of a unified democratic nation state) rather than among communities. For them, the standard systems of representative government, either based on executive presidencies and congresses, or on the parliamentary fusion of executive and legislative power, are modes of power-sharing because they oblige power-holders to account to the public and to work in anticipation of the checking and balancing capacities of the others.

The logic of the 'competition for power' is at the core of the democratic tradition. It focuses on how officials 'win' positions, be they executive, legislative, judicial or bureaucratic. In the democratic tradition executive and legislative power should be competed for through elections;[2] liberals are, however, more doubtful about elections to judicial and administrative positions, where they tend to favour meritocratic appointment. The minimal definitional standard of liberal democracy, or representative government, is a political system in which officials compete for authoritative positions in free and fair elections for citizens' votes; and in which those officials hold office for limited terms, and make laws, and give orders to unelected officials, within constitutional norms that ensure that the officials can be held accountable by voters for their actions – both through the ballot box and recourse to the courts. The competition for power, it is hoped, socializes politicians to offer both popular and responsible policies, and socializes voters to punish incompetent, irresponsible or corrupt politicians by ejecting them from office. The 'vote motive' will encourage politicians to build winning coalitions, and therefore soften ideological programs.

The division of power, and competition for power, are 'undoubtedly' – the phrase is often used in Belfast where political phrasing is rarely shy – good and intelligent principles, widely envied in the authoritarian states that still blot large parts of our world. But, consociationalists claim, that on their own, or combined, dividing power and the competition for power are most unlikely to calm deeply divided territories. Indeed, we claim that the combination of the division of power and the competition for power in certain conditions may be highly conducive toward the oppression of some national, ethnic and religious communities. The competition for power expresses or creates 'majorities' – and such majorities may be built on or reinforce deep national, ethnic or communal cleavages. Majorities from the same community may win complete control over all major offices and governments, even if the powers of those offices and governments are divided and checked. They can then propose public policy and conceptions of merit that are entirely group-centred. Such conduct, unless it ruthlessly disorganizes the 'minority' or 'minorities', will generate insurgents who seek their own states – or to usurp power and create a new regime. Where winning in a democratic contest signals singular national, ethnic or religious regime definition and the existential victory of one community over another or others, it may usher in or confirm a collective despotism.

Integrationists and assimilationists too easily presume that a nation of individuals is in existence, or that one should be built. Their principles for managing difference are recipes for conflict in deeply divided territories, even when motivated by high-minded considerations, and however desirable they seem in the abstract, or however vindicated they may seem elsewhere. Faced with states or regions with rival national self-determination claims (for Ireland or Britain), or rival allegiances to wider civilizations (for the West or the Arab world), advocacy of integration, and especially of assimilation, is partisan and provocative.

It is especially partisan when the triumph of one community's claims to nationalize the state or region in its image is commended on no better claim than might (numbers) makes right. It is dangerously transformative and dystopian when antagonistic communities are instructed to fuse. Partisans and transformative racial and ethnic engineers succeeded many times in winning control of government in the last two centuries in many parts of Europe and the lands that surround the Mediterranean, generating bloodbaths.

That is why Dr Kerr rightly commends a distinctive form of power-sharing as a supplementary approach to avoiding the worst in modern politics, namely consociation. Power-sharing in democracies commends the sharing of power between communities, *as well as* the division of power and the competition for power. It commends 'coalition' as a considered way of doing things, but not as a substitute for the division of power or the competition for power. Advocates of power-sharing may personally prefer an integrationist or assimilationist outcome – a British Ulster, an Irish Ireland, an Arab Lebanon, a Christian Lebanon – in which all citizens have a primary loyalty to a culturally sharply resonant nation-state. But, as realists, they know that they cannot guarantee their preferred outcome – at least not without risking 'internal' war – I don't understand why we still call such wars 'civil' – which their side may lose, or may be unable to win. Consociational realists may prefer a strong programmatic government organized by a single-minded party with common values, but know that the costs of coherence may be too high if an insurgent opposition or a tyrannical government is the consequence. Consociationalists smile wryly and agree that it would be better if their polity had a 'normal' set of institutions for dividing and competing for power. But experience has taught them that deep and protracted conflicts between national, ethnic and religious communities requires that power be systematically shared, as well as divided and subject to competition.

Proponents of consociation start from the recognition that political or cultural homogenization has been associated with genocide, ethnic expulsion, imposed partition, and coercive assimilation. Their trump argument is very simple. The alternatives are worse. Power-holders and their challengers have often pursued extremist and exterminist strategies. In a little known aside in *The Communist Manifesto* Karl Marx and Friedrich Engels treated the 'mutual ruin of the contending classes' as one possible outcome of class struggle. Over one hundred and fifty years later we are generally more worried by the prospect of the mutual ruin of contending nations, ethnic groups and communal protagonists. Rudolf Rummel's calculations in *Death by Government* suggest that the last century was absolutely and proportionately the most lethal in human history. Consociation is intended to stop governments from being ethnic cleansers. What cannot be won on the battlefield is best resolved through a political settlement.

Power-sharers wish to share political power between communities without dissolving them into one. They follow Rousseau's declared method in *The Social Contract* that commends taking 'men as they are, and laws as they might be'. But, because they do not seek to create or recognize just one community they reject Rousseau's infamous proposals: inalienable, indivisible, and absolute sovereignty of 'the people', his rejection of partial associations, and his support for a vigorous homogenizing civic religion.

Consociational politics begins with the full appreciation that there is more than one people with reasonable claims. I am writing this Foreword in Iraq, on 12 August 2005, as an advisor to the Kurdistan government. Three days ago I was asked to comment on a paper, written as an advisory note to the United Iraqi Alliance. The relevant advisor, a distinguished constitutional lawyer, was trying to nudge the Shi'a dominated alliance from a strongly majoritarian conception of who constitutes the Iraqi people, and argued instead for a widely shared vision of an Iraqi nation. To a consociationalist the first part of this advisor's intention was sound, but the second ridiculous and dangerous. Consociational politics is, after all, politics without 'shared vision'; it is a politics of shared accommodation, of shared fears, but not one in which an imagined or visionary unity can or should be presented. At most, consociation is a politics with a shared vision of catastrophe.

Power-sharers seek social contracts between two or more peoples, or between two or more territorial governments. The first of these possibilities leads in properly 'consociational' directions; the second in the direction of pluralist federation – what would best suit contemporary Iraq if it is to remain a state. Both consociations and pluralist federations have much to commend them in circumstances of deep national, ethnic or religious division. The first is necessary triage where peoples are extensively inter-connected if not intermingled; the second is easier where peoples are extensively demographically, geographically and commercially separated. If Northern Ireland and the Lebanon, as a result of their wars and local residential choices, become ever more spatially segregated on wider and wider scales then a shift to pluralist federal ways of coexistence may become feasible. But, for the present, the relevant peoples are too close, especially in Belfast and Beirut, to make that formula possible. Even though both cities and their surrounding polities are segregated residentially and territorially they are not segregated at a level of aggregation that makes territorial federalism an option.

Consociational and pluralist federal possibilities can be combined in complex forms, where the complexity refers both to their institutional formats and their contexts. Northern Ireland since 1998 has had a consociational settlement that may stabilize within unfolding federal possibilities – within the previously centralized United Kingdom, across the island of Ireland, and within the confederalizing European Union. By contrast, Lebanon, is unlikely to develop formal federal forms without ceasing to be the Lebanon.

Ulster Unionists who care about theology will learn that the concept of consociation is traceable to the Protestant Johannes Althusius (1557-1638), a German jurist, a magistrate, and the author of *Politica* (1603 and 1614). He coined the formula *consociatio consociationum* for his vision of a co-operative commonwealth. The etymology is suggestive: 'con', from *cum*, Latin for 'with', and '*societas*', society. A consociation therefore is a society of societies, or, a people of peoples. The word's roots imply separate societies that nevertheless co-operate in peaceful coexistence. A political consociation, it follows, exists in a state or region within which two or more peoples peaceably coexist, with none being institutionally superior to the others, and in which the relevant leaders co-operate politically through both self-government and shared government. Equality between the consociational partners is supposed; and elements of both autonomy (self-government for each community) and of integration (joint or shared government of all the partner communities). This conception precludes any endorsement of caste, colonial or racist relations between the partner peoples. In the case of Lebanon and Northern Ireland, two formerly dominant groups, Ulster Protestants and Christian Maronites, must accept a loss of status to live with consociation. In the case of Northern Ireland's Irish nationalists and Lebanon's Shi'a full consociation marks an uplift in the status of their communities – although it falls short of their preferred reconstruction of the future.

The consociational idea has been invented and re-invented by politicians and peoples on many occasions. It did not need philosophers to create it; it only needs philosophers to justify it, to discourage its premature dissolution, and to respond to bad arguments about it. Reformers in the Habsburg Empire thought each nationality should be treated as a full cultural equal (as autonomous *Kulturgemeinschafte*, cultural communities), and that each citizen, on the basis of 'the personality principle', should be able to declare to which nationality or linguistic community they belonged, and enjoy rights (including voting rights) wherever they lived. 'Nations', Karl Renner argued, should be constituted as 'associations of persons instead of as areas of domination'. Arend Lijphart's *The Politics of Accommodation: Pluralism and Democracy in the Netherlands* defined accommodation as the 'settlement of divisive issues and conflict, where only a minimal consensus exists'. He thought that the secret of Dutch political stability – after a history of religious disputes – was a spirit of accommodation amongst its political elites, who co-operated to avoid violent conflict in a benign self-denying prophecy. Its political leaders developed key capacities: the ability to accommodate the divergent interests and demands of their respective collective communities; to transcend cleavages to create common interests [note 'interests', rather than 'vision' or 'identity']; to commit to maintain and improve the system; and, lastly, a prudent appreciation of the perils of fragmentation.

Lijphart went on to reason that democracies could be differentiated by the style of their political elites, which could be competitive or collaborative, and by their overall political culture, (fragmented, or divided). These dimensions generate four types of democracy:

1. Centripetal democracy, in which politicians compete within a homogeneous national culture (the received image of how liberal democracies work in the Anglo-American world);

2. Centrifugal democracy, in which politicians compete within a fragmented multi-cultural environment, threatening system-breakdown (the experience of Lebanon after 1975, and Northern Ireland between 1974 and 1998);
3. Cartel democracy, in which politicians collaborate within a homogeneous and depoliticized national culture; and
4. Consociational democracy, in which political elites co-operate within a heterogeneous political culture, and sustain a politics of accommodation (the politics that Lebanon and Northern Ireland require if they are to be democracies).

This typology is not quite right, for it suggests that consociation must be anti-competitive. But co-operation need not preclude political competition for power (elections), and forms of co-operation may encompass the division (of executive, legislative and judiciary) as well as the sharing of power. Unfortunately, Lijphart once declared that consociational democracy means government by 'elite cartel' (Lijphart 1969, *World Politics*, 216), a statement he has regretted. A cartel, in normal definitions, is anti-competitive, and the outlawing of competition (and opposition) cannot be part of any consociation that is democratic.

There can, of course, be non-democratic consociations – when political leaders co-operate and conduct themselves according to consociational but not democratic practices. Elements of pre-democratic consociational styles were present in the Ottoman Levant. Power was shared among the élites of different communities with little or no reference to their blocs, and religious institutions governed personal law. But that there can be undemocratic consociations does not mean that consociation is inherently undemocratic. There can be democratic and undemocratic consociations.

A 'grand', 'total' or 'all-encompassing' coalition is not essential for consociation to work, because what matters is meaningful, cross-community, joint decision-making: 'jointness' is more critical than comprehensive inclusion. A concurrent consociational executive is one in which each significant community has over half of its voters supporting parties in the government, and acting on their behalf. Consociation does not, in other words, require the absence of opposition (or competition), as critics wrongly suggest.

A related false belief is that consociations stop free electoral competition by forcing voters to vote for national, ethic, religious or tribal candidates. Not necessarily so. Where a political system deliberately obliges voters to vote only within their own community for their own leaders then to that degree the system is *corporately* consociational: separate electoral registers would do that. Requiring voters to choose among a restricted group of religiously or ethnically defined candidates, as in Lebanon's electoral law, has a differently constraining character –

though in this case its curious feature in some constituencies is that it obliges people to choose only from candidates from other communities. But in *liberal* consociational arrangements, as in Northern Ireland, all voters are on a common electoral register, and they are not required to vote for leaders from their own community of origin, and they are free to vote for parties which present themselves as neither nationalist nor unionist. The distinction between corporate and liberal consociational practice corresponds to that between 'pre-determined' and 'self-determined' identity. The distinction is vital because it is untrue that consociation necessarily privileges, institutionalizes and reinforces prior collective identities. It can do; it need not do so.

It is usually a distinguishing feature of consociational cabinets that they will be 'over-sized', i.e. there are either more parties in the executive and/or more legislators supporting those parties than would be needed to control the legislature with a minimum winning coalition. An example of the former is the Northern Ireland Executive (1999-2002) in which, under the d'Hondt allocation rule, four parties were in the cabinet, even though only three parties would have been required to have majority control within the assembly.[3] This, however, was a matter of choice for each of the four parties – none of them was obliged to take up its entitlements to ministries.

Let me summarize my rebuttal of some initial misconceptions. Rather than requiring a grand coalition government, a democratic consociation necessarily has an executive in which there is significant cross-community representation and support, though the levels of representation and support may range from complete, through concurrent, to weak support across the included communities. Consociations vary in the extent to which communities are included and in the degree of opposition to the governing coalition in the executive. Consociations vary in the degree to which they are liberal or corporate in their popular and assembly voting systems. Lastly, consociational arrangements may co-exist with non-ethnic and inter-ethnic parties.

Power is shared in consociations where it must be, i.e. on matters of cross-community concern. In independent sovereign consociations, as Lebanon will be when the Syrians leave fully, key policies and positions in security institutions (the armed forces, intelligence organizations, and central policing services) and in economic institutions (such as central banks) are integrated. But it is a hallmark of successful consociations that they delegate decision-making or grant autonomy (self-government) to communities on matters that are deemed appropriate. They work with their own distinct principle of 'subsidiarity', making it inappropriate to seek autonomy over what are matters of common concern, and equally inappropriate to try to make a matter of common concern what has been decreed to be within a segment's autonomous rights.

The core idea of autonomy from the perspective of minorities, according to Lijphart, is 'rule by the minority over itself in the area of the minority's exclusive concern'. But the idea applies to all communities, including majorities, that have autonomy. Autonomy is not the same as independence or sovereignty. Autonomy requires minimally constitutionalized (or statutory or normative) arrangements, which regulate the level of discretion enjoyed by the relevant authorities.

The key contrast in types of autonomy differentiates territorial and non-territorial forms. Non-territorial autonomy is distinctively consociational. It may seem a puzzling notion. Must not all powers or rights be exercised within a territory? Yes, and for this reason the idea is best understood as personal and/or group autonomy – sometimes both notions are subsumed under the notion of 'functional autonomy'. Under the provisions of group autonomy members of communities may exercise these rights wherever they reside – i.e. irrespective of the specific territory within which they live or commute. So, for example, they may publicly profess their religious beliefs and hold religious meetings in public no matter wherever they happen to be. Under personal autonomy each person may opt to be recognized, or to receive services, in accordance with their group membership. A modern example of community autonomy is the provision of separate broadcasting networks for different linguistic users throughout the entirety of a state, especially if each network is run by its own community's political institutions or civil society. Striking examples of corporate legal autonomy are the separate civil law and personal status arrangements of the ethno-religious communities of the Lebanon. Less startling but no less consociational are the now fully funded and separate primary and secondary educational systems of Northern Ireland. Equality with difference is the motto of this type of autonomy.

These principles, like all principles, are not without their difficulties. While ethnic, religious and linguistic associational life is *prima facie* unproblematic, modern states cannot dispense with common territorial jurisdiction, either within a state, or within a region. In some matters – the usual examples given are criminal or business law – a single code of behaviour and a single regime of sanctions will usually be sought and be rational in at least some domains of public and private life, if only to avoid perverse incentives. The idea of people changing their ethnic, religious or linguistic identity just to avoid criminal sanctions is not appealing. Meaningful community autonomy has one legal consequence. Authentic consociational systems necessarily generate a complex jurisprudence in which courts and other authorities have to regulate potentially conflictual territorial, corporate and personal principles.

The feasibility or coherence of the idea of proportionality is not an issue in disputes over consociation, unlike the ideas of grand coalition and non-territorial autonomy. The idea is that each community expects to be represented (either descriptively or through choice) in political bodies in at least rough accordance with its demographic, or electoral share of the citizenry or population. The representation may be either descriptive, mirroring appropriately shares of groups, or substantive, with persons expected to act for the interests of their groups. There may, of course, be differences between the demographic and electoral shares of communities, and this may be a source of political controversy and fear, as Dr Kerr shows in the history of the Lebanon. Proportionality can be partially applied, just to formal political institutions, or it can be applied to all common institutions in a state and civil society (excluding perhaps those in which each community has autonomy).[4]

Proportionality may be underpinned by electoral systems. Whole families of such systems ensure that legislative bodies are composed so that parties are represented in proportion to their vote-share. The most commonly used are closed and open party list systems, and hybrid or mixed systems (which generally combine winner-take-all systems at the district level with compensatory proportional allocations of top-up seats for parties). There cannot be any uncontroversial notion of proportionality, given that human beings do not come in fractions, that voters are very unlikely to divide their votes in neat easily convertible shares, and that each method for achieving proportionality is now known to 'minimize disproportionality according to the way it defines disproportionality' as Professor Michael Gallagher of Trinity College, Dublin has put it. All proportionality systems necessarily require mathematical rules to deal with the necessary 'rounding off' or 'sequencing' of votes into seats. Each rule has an explicit or tacit notion of what minimizing disproportionality involves. These rules or formulae, however, may be rank-ordered as to whether, when bias is inevitable, they favour larger parties over smaller ones.

It is no surprise that d'Hondt or STV (Droop) are the commonly used formulae since larger parties are likely to be the key co-architects of electoral institutions, including within consociations. The merits of using PR systems to achieve proportional outcomes are obvious. Provided district magnitudes are not too small and relatively evenly sized, and provided that there has not been significant gerrymandering of electoral districts, PR methods will produce outcomes that are usually seen as technically fair and consistent, even though each may each have distinct quirks of their own. Using such systems on a common roll has the merit of enabling voters to decide whether they want to be represented by ethnic, trans-ethnic or non-ethnic parties, i.e. voters enjoy self-determination.

The Lebanon remains unusual is trying to achieve proportionality by organizing quotas by seats, rather than by leaving voters to exercise full freedom. After 1943 seats in the Lebanese chamber of deputies were divided in the ratio of six Christians to five Muslims, or 54.5: 46.5, which supposedly reflected the shares of the two communities in the 1932 census. Constituencies, of differing magnitude, were mandated to produce specific numbers of Christian and Muslim deputies to achieve this effect. In fact, the census of 1932 suggested a Christian: Muslim ratio of residents of 50: 49, and of 52: 47 among registered citizens. So the fixed ratio of 6: 5 was not very proportionate. Parity, or a ratio of 9:8, would have been more just. The ratio of 6: 5 was also, by definition, inflexible – unless, of course, it could be agreed to vary the ratio in accordance with changing census returns. But, in Lebanese politics it gradually became impossible to hold a fresh census. When Muslims, presumed to be expanding demographically,[5] demanded a fresh census, Christians riposted by demanding that the Lebanese diaspora, presumed disproportionately Christian, be included in any count. This led to a stalemate and was one of the grievances that provoked the outbreak of Lebanon's internal war.

Systems of reserved seats, or systems that rely on informal norms, are less likely to achieve proportionality smoothly than proportional electoral formulae. They may also involve pre-empting people's identities and preferences, or adopting corporate (pre-determined) rather than liberal (self-determined) principles of representation. Fixed quotas create obvious difficulties, as seen in Lebanon. Much the least controversial quota allocation is to give a community a guaranteed share of positions in the executive or legislature that is broadly proportional to its demographic or electoral weight. By contrast, the over-representation of significant minorities automatically creates serious tensions, especially if the over-represented minority already has other protections or has historically been privileged. This situation should be distinguished from one in which positive preferential or affirmative action is required to rectify historical imbalances (usually the result of historic discrimination, as for example experienced by Northern Ireland Catholics). Positive preferential or affirmative action policies may temporarily over-represent the under-represented in new cohorts of appointees, but these policies are intended to achieve overall proportionality, not to deliver net over-representation in the long-run.

Parity of representation amongst demographic unequals creates predictable objections amongst majority communities who, correctly, argue that proportionality is a different principle from parity. The post-Agreement Northern Ireland executive (1999–2002) had equal numbers of unionist and nationalist ministers, but this was a result of parties agreeing that there should be ten ministries and the subsequent result of the application of the d'Hondt formula. With the same number of ministries and a different distribution of seats among parties there is no guarantee of parity of representation – as demonstrated by the outcome of the 2003 Assembly elections.

Lijphart, at various times, has described both the over-representation of minorities and parity of representation of unequals, as 'extensions of the proportionality rule' even though he accurately regards them as methods of 'disproportional representation'. It is plain that Lijphart's intentions have been to counsel against over-representation of minorities. Disproportional representation may well be conceived of as a method of minority protection, and may be demanded by minorities on various grounds, but such representation may be, and is legitimately, criticized as departing from the norm of proportionality (to each according to their numbers) and therefore from strict consociational logic. The conjunction of over-representation or parity among unequals with minority veto rights (see below) creates obvious problems for majorities. Majorities may well accept veto rights on matters or national, ethnic, cultural or religious significance for minorities, but they do not appreciate why they additionally have to endure under-representation or parity when they comprise the largest community.

The idea of proportionality also serves as a standard for the disbursement of public funds. Indeed departures from proportionality may occasion dissatisfaction, unless one community is demonstrably poorer than another. Proportional allocation of public expenditure is relatively easy to achieve technically among groups that are sharply differentiated and relatively equal in endowments, though the politics of such allocation cannot be presumed to be unproblematic.

In consociations, proportionality is used as a standard for the allocation of positions throughout the state or region, especially in its public (and sometimes in its private) sector. In 1958 in the Lebanon President Chehab proclaimed the introduction of the principle of strict parity between Christian and Muslim appointees to the civil service. This calmed communal relations though tensions remained because of Maronite 'preserves' in the security sector; later, Muslims, convinced of their increased numbers and educational uplift, started to demand the end of the quota and the proportionality principle. Examples of the use of proportionality rules or quotas to allocate administrative and judicial positions abound: Northern Ireland is now, at last, a region with rigorous and fair employment laws, including the use of affirmative action, and in some cases quotas, to achieve proportionality in public life.

Proportionality, in short, does not occasion any fundamental operational difficulties. There may be practical difficulties in some cases in implementing the principle, e.g. difficulties occasioned by shortages of appropriately qualified people in historically under-represented communities, but there is no fundamental conceptual difficulty. The same cannot be said, of course, of its political and moral evaluation.

When there is cross-community executive power-sharing each community has at least weak and perhaps vigorous protection against executive discretion and legislative agenda-setting. When there is consociational autonomy then minorities can stop other minorities or majorities from exercising dominance over them within the functions and spaces where autonomy applies. When there is proportional representation then the capacity of each group to block dominance by the others is enhanced – though not guaranteed. These three arrangements may still not be enough, however, to assure minorities (or disappearing majorities) when there are histories of antagonism. That is when 'veto rights' are demanded.

Formal mutual veto rights may exist within the constitution. Within the executive collective presidents or dual premiers may share agenda-setting and agenda-blocking powers. Within the legislature the consent of all the affected communities may be required before constitutional change can take place. This can take the form of requiring unanimity within the executive, a concurrent majority within the legislature, or a weighted or super-majority that ensures concurrent or weak cross-community support – as in the 'cross-community consent provisions' of the 1998 agreement in Northern Ireland. Similar restrictions to standard majority rule in the legislature may apply to ordinary legislation if minorities have the right to petition that such matters be deemed of national, ethnic or communal significance. Courts may be charged with protecting group autonomy in bills of rights and charters that effectively place constitutional constraints on majorities that are equivalent to entrenched veto rights; ombudsmen may be given similar quasi-judicial roles.

Veto-rights create obvious difficulties for standard democratic theory: minority 'tyrannies' may block change; deadlock, immobilism, or policy stagnation can flow from the deployment of vetoes by all groups; and minorities that over-use their veto rights may de-stabilise a consociational settlement. That said, these difficulties should not be exaggerated. In consociational systems formal veto rights tend to apply in the domains of the politics of identity, i.e. in ethnic, religious or national domains, and not to every policy sector. In effect, in these domains groups have parity of power, rather than proportional power.

Consociational political settlements are therefore very demanding. They demand political and intellectual patience and restraint – and these are often lacking as Dr Kerr shows in his accounts of past consociational failures in Northern Ireland and the Lebanon. The new experiments in both polities try, with difficulty, institutionally to recognize more than one people and attempt to provide constitutional architecture within which they can durably co-exist. These political settlements simultaneously have come after or during peace processes – mechanisms, confidence-building measures and institutional and policy transformations intended to halt conflict and to terminate future violent recurrences. They therefore involve both the reform and the restructuring of security systems, and measures intended to end paramilitarism, as well as new human rights protection mechanisms. They necessarily involve the restructuring of security policies and institutions. Spoilers of all kinds have sought to destabilize the fragile new systems, which are not (yet?) stable.

Consociations have further institutional complexities. They may have arbitration mechanisms for resolving disputes between the partners – impartial courts, commissions, international judges, international commissions. Consociations may have elements of integration – citizenship equality provisions – including constitutional and institutional designs that permit the voluntary integration of communities: some hope that the Shi'a of Lebanon are becoming Lebanese Shi'a. Consociations may have mechanisms that enable the secession of the relevant unit. Northern Ireland illustrates the point.

The international and external involvement in the making, ratification and maintenance of consociational settlements is Dr Kerr's distinctive angle in this book and I shall not pre-empt or abbreviate his discussion, merely add to it. He may have provided the initial evidence for a possible wider truth: viable consociations that address ethno-national disputes may have to be the de facto or de jure protectorates of external powers. International involvement in consociations may involve neighbouring states, regional powers, great powers, regional organizations (e.g. the OSCE or the EU), or international organizations (e.g. the UN). It is obvious that international involvement may be critical in organizing and monitoring cease-fires, in providing good offices for the making of settlements, in designing implementation arrangements, and providing default mechanisms to arbitrate disputes. Domestic incorporation of international human and minority rights standards does not necessarily challenge the sovereignty of the state or the autonomy of a region. Institutionalized cross-border co-operation and the formation of bodies with executive powers in more than one formally sovereign jurisdiction, by contrast, entail at least a pooling if not necessarily a diminution of sovereignty. High commissioners appointed by great powers, as in Bosnia and Herzegovina, are indistinguishable from the prefects of protectorates.

Dr Kerr's analysis suggests that Northern Ireland and the Lebananon's may indicate relatively novel configurations, precarious consociational protectorates. These may be likely to proliferate from now on, in a range of crisis zones. That is not to suggest that they completely lack precedents, e.g. the failed Cypriot Constitution of 1960. Two reasons have been suggested to explain why such consociational protectorates may be emerging: the small polity effect, and changes in the international order.

Size is a variable regularly invoked as facilitating consociation. Small size and consociations are correlated, where size is defined as small demographic size: Lebanon, Austria, the Netherlands, Belgium, Switzerland, Suriname and the Netherlands Antilles (and some would now add Luxembourg, Lichtenstein, South Tyrol) are past cases. Northern Ireland, Bosnia Herzegovina and Macedonia also fit this picture.

Lijphart has distinguished four possible effects of small size that may explain the correlation between size and consociation:

1 *The direct internal effect*: political elites all know one another, interact regularly, and thereby negotiate more easily without too much constituency pressure;
2 *The direct external effect*: small states are likely to feel externally threatened and therefore more induced towards internal accommodation;
3 *The indirect internal effect*: smaller states are easier to govern; and
4 *The indirect external effect*: the country's low international salience creates a lighter foreign policy load.

These hypothesised effects, however, do not withstand scrutiny. What matters, presumably, for successful elite interaction is psychological and political closeness rather than geographical distance or interpersonal ignorance or impersonality. 'Great hatreds, little room' was Yeats' memorable line about intra-Irish ethno-religious relations. It still applies. Lijphart and others have sometimes speculated that there may be directly negative effects from too small a population: a dearth of political talent is more likely. But, this too seems unwarranted. Political talent has existed in abundance in Lebanon and Northern Ireland. It has just not been deployed until recently in a sustained politics of accommodation. The hypothesis of the greater governability of the small is also surely not obvious. Governing Lebanon is surely more daunting than governing France.

The alleged external effects of small size seem better warranted, but even here there are plausible counter-hypotheses. The direct effect surely operates independently of size. That is because shared external threats give domestic elites significant incentives to accommodate one another's communities whatever size the state's population happens to be. The direct effect surely also requires that the threats are shared – only in that way can the fact that my internal rival is my external enemy's enemy generate the appropriate dispositions for coalition and accommodation. The formation of the Lebanese *pacte nationale* in 1943 is a case in point. It was formed largely by Maronite and Sunni elites in opposition to the (Free) French mandatory authorities' attempt to avoid decolonisation. In the 1970s Lebanese elites certainly did not share a common perspective on external threats, and today they differ over the Syrian withdrawal.

As for the indirect effect, it might as plausibly be suggested that small states experience foreign policy overload, and, conversely, that a light foreign policy load might make the domestic indulgence of political antagonism easier. Within regional consociations, as opposed to sovereign states, local elites have blocked power-sharing deals even though when they have had no serious international responsibilities, e.g. Ulster Unionists in Northern Ireland between 1974 and 1998.

A last sceptical word on the treatment of size is in order. No theorist maintains a small population size is a necessary condition of consociational success. Consociational transitional arrangements arguably worked in South Africa between 1993 and 1996, despite a population of nearly 40 million. Canada, the second largest territorial state in the world, has been seen as having had at least a semi-consociational past and possible future. The European Union, on target to encompass 400 million people, arguably has consociational and confederal practices.

There are perhaps better ways to express the intuition behind the apparent correlation between consociational protectorates, small size, and international politics. A realist would predict that the elites of great powers are more likely to be reluctant to embrace consociational style decision-making because their security imperatives allegedly call for less consensual decision-making and energetic discretionary executive power. In his essay, 'Between Two Laws' Max Weber, famously argued that Germany could not govern itself like Switzerland if it wished to be a great power (*Political Writings*, eds. P. Lassman and R. Speirs, Cambridge University Press, 1994: 75–80). This reasoning is shared by those who want to create a vigorous and energetic apparatus for the foreign and security policy-making of the European Union. But there is a related point: great and regional powers may be more willing to impose on small powers domestic arrangements they would not dream of implementing themselves. The USA and the European powers have used vigorous coercion and inducements to promote consociational settlements in Bosnia Herzegovina and Macedonia, and in the nineteenth century the European powers intervened to create autonomy and rights packages for Christian minorities within many of the provinces of the Ottoman empire – packages that they did not always or even generally apply to their own religious minorities. Likewise, the centres of sovereign unitary states may be willing to induce local elites to agree consociational settlements in small localised regions without re-engineering their core states, e.g. Great Britain and Northern Ireland, and Italy and South Tyrol. Neighbouring great or even medium-sized powers may act as protectors of their national minorities or near kin or co-believers – and this very support may make it more feasible for such groups to bid for a full consociational settlement.

There is a more idealist way of appreciating why external relations may matter in explaining the emergence of consociational protectorates. The direct and indirect effects of international norms may matter. The received understanding of the Westphalian system is that sovereign states left one another alone in their domestic cultural zones. Sovereignty enabled them coercively to assimilate or integrate minorities within their borders – on some interpretations sovereignty even included the right to commit genocide.

This reading of the Westphalian system and its practices was, however, never entirely without challengers. The original treaty, after all, protected some religious power-sharing within the Holy Roman Empire. In the 1920s (after the collapse of the Habsburg, Ottoman and Czarist empires) the new European states recognised at Versailles signed minority rights treaties that in principle could be regulated by the League of Nations. The treaties bound these states not to abuse their minorities, and in some cases required them to maintain or develop semi-consociational practices (notably in religious, educational and linguistic autonomy). The inter-war story was hardly an overall success in achieving protection and avoiding abuses – and indeed the United Nations was partly constructed in a deliberate rejection of these experiments. But the post de-colonisation international law of self-determination, the politics of recognition of the post-communist successors, and the principles attached to the expansion of the European Union have seen a revival of efforts to lock new states into systems of minority protection – and that has provided some external shield for minorities that advance consociational demands.

Indirect effects of international norms and interventions exist. There are international proscriptions against genocide and expulsion. There are norms of some significance that reward states that are democratic – and which make control regimes potential pariahs. There are additional proscriptions against coercive assimilation. There remain strong biases against secessions and partitions. The conjunction of these norms leave international organizations and great powers, when they intervene in national, ethnic, and communal conflicts, in practice confined to promoting one of three repertoires of domestic conflict regulation (or permutations of them): (i) integration; (ii) territorial autonomy (including federacies and federations); and (iii) consociation. In some scenarios to prescribe integration — Northern Ireland, or Lebanon — is to prescribe the partisan victory of one community over another. The upshot is that the normative prohibition, if not factual exclusion, of certain options that were once available to all states, has created some incentives in favour of consociational arrangements in small political systems.

Consociations may be the most benign political forms possible after serious internal identity-based wars, and the best formats to prevent serious or recurrent wars. They are more likely to emerge than to be planned. They may, just may, be best when they facilitate transitions to other integrative arrangements. They are difficult to love and celebrate – even if their makers often fully merit intellectual, moral and political admiration. They are usually cold bargains, even if they display admirable political imagination and compromise. But consociational thinking as this book demonstrates still has a role in staunching the wounds of war.

Brendan O'Leary
Salahaddin, Kurdistan
12 August 2005

Notes

1   My latest effort to survey these matters can be found in Brendan O'Leary, 'Debating Consociation: Normative and Explanatory Arguments', in *From Power-Sharing to Democracy: Post-Conflict Institutions in Ethnically Divided Societies*, S.J.R. Noel (ed.) (Toronto: McGill-Queens University Press, 2005).
2   Archaic conservativism, by contrast, sees a role for hereditary – traditional – leadership in the executive (monarchs or chiefs), or in a senate (a house of elders). This form of thinking is, fortunately, nearly extinguished in Northern Ireland and the Lebanon. Ulster unionists are loyal to the Crown of the UK but are not literal monarchists.
3   For a technical discussion of d'Hondt and similar rules see Brendan O'Leary, Bernard Grofman and Jorgen Elklit, 2005. Divisor Methods for Sequential Portfolio Allocation in Multi-Party Executive Bodies: Evidence from Northern Ireland and Denmark. *American Journal of Political Science* 2005, 49 (1 (January)):198–211.
4   For example, the appointment of Protestants to Catholic school boards would be against the spirit of consociational accommodation if education is supposed to be a domain of community autonomy.
5   The presumed Muslim demographic expansion had two causes: a higher birth-rate, and Muslim over-representation amongst the Palestinian refugee population – from the 1948 war accompanying the formation of Israel, and from the 'Black September' massacre in Jordan in 1970.

'So we beat on, boats against the current, borne back ceaselessly into the past'. F. Scott Fitzgerald, *The Great Gatsby*

Introduction

During the twentieth century different models of consociational democracy were applied to Northern Ireland and Lebanon in efforts to regulate ethno-national conflict and establish power-sharing governments. In Lebanon the system was internally reformulated in 1943 as Christian and Muslim leaders pushed for independence under a National Pact. In Northern Ireland power-sharing was imposed, in an attempt to stem escalating violence, under the 1973 Sunningdale Agreement. Power-sharing accords collapsed in both cases, due to internal and external pressures. This resulted in the outbreak of civil war in Lebanon and the continuation of protracted ethno-national violence in Northern Ireland. In 1989, Lebanon reconstructed its power-sharing arrangements under the Ta'if Accords; Northern Ireland returned to the Sunningdale model on Good Friday 1998. In both cases complex conflict regulation strategies were externally facilitated and implemented through coercive consociational engineering. In Northern Ireland's case these were brokered through an agreement between the British and Irish governments, whereas in Lebanon they were imposed through Syrian political and military intervention under the auspices of a US-Saudi regional deal.

The central questions this book addresses in its comparative analysis of power-sharing in Northern Ireland and Lebanon are:

1) Why did consociation fail in Northern Ireland and Lebanon?
2) Was the failure of consociation inevitable in these two divided societies?
3) If so, why, then, did post-war conflict regulation mark a return to the models that had previously collapsed, in both cases?
4) What impact did external pressures have on creating an environment where consociation could be successfully employed to re-regulate ethnic conflict?
5) Can consociation be successfully used to regulate ethno-national conflict in the absence of positive external pressures?

Through addressing these questions this book seeks to provide an evaluation of how internal and external elite relations influenced the chances of a successful regulation of ethnic conflict through power-sharing. It also provides an analysis for academics and policy-makers of the limitations of imposing consociation in divided societies in the post-Cold War world. In comparing and contrasting power-sharing agreements in two territories, it examines the changing internal and external circumstances that brought about these settlements, and questions whether consociation is a viable mechanism with which to secure the peaceful regulation of ethnic conflict. The central argument propounded in this book is that, in both the cases studied, the relationships between the internal and external elites determined the prospects for successful conflict regulation. It highlights the importance of external forces in the creation of power-sharing agreements in Northern Ireland and Lebanon, and concludes that their success or failure was dependent on the maintenance of positive exogenous pressures.

An adequate comparative analysis of these agreements does not exist in the current literature, nor has a book-length comparative analysis of power-sharing in Northern Ireland and Lebanon been undertaken.[1] This book thus contributes to and elaborates on the literature concerning consociational democratic theory and comparative politics. It adds a new dimension to the theories of Arend Lijphart, and the subsequent theory-building approaches to conflict regulation of John McGarry and Brendan O'Leary.[2] It provides a new analytical approach to thinking about the factors that contribute to the successful establishment of consociation, highlighting the prominence and essential influence of external actors in the regulation of ethno-national conflict in both Northern Ireland and Lebanon. Through addressing these questions it illustrates the extent to which consociational theorists and other commentators have underestimated the importance of external variables in making or breaking power-sharing agreements.

The aim of this book is, then, to access the record of consociational democracy when used as a tool for conflict regulation in Northern Ireland and Lebanon. The main hypothesis argues that the consociational model cannot provide long-term conflict regulation of the ethno-national conflicts of Northern Ireland and Lebanon in the absence of coercive positive exogenous pressures. It analyses the role played by external elites and the influence they brought to bear on their internal counterparts. It argues that the external actors in these conflicts largely determined whether power-sharing could be successfully established. Without such proactive exogenous variables the power-sharing agreements reached in both cases would not have occurred; moreover, these agreements remained reliant upon external forces for both the successful implementation of their consociational provisions and the stability of their power-sharing administrations. Consequently, consociational government is not a model for long-term ethnic conflict resolution but, rather, should be viewed as a tool for conflict regulation, provided that a stable external political environment exists to guarantee the political structures. Power-sharing agreements were brokered in Northern Ireland and Lebanon, not just on the strength and balance of the divided communities that engaged in them, but equally on the strength and interests of the regional and international actors that agreed them. For the continuity of their power-sharing arrangements the internal elites were reliant on the balance that existed between internal and external forces at the time of each agreement. It is these relationships that this book attempts to explain.

This book also questions whether the imposition of consociation in these divided societies is actually democratic, or whether democratic transition is a secondary concern for those attempting coercive consociationalism. Consociation is essentially reliant upon extra-democratic methods and externally driven constitutional engineering if it is to be successfully implemented. The power-sharing experiences of Northern Ireland and Lebanon are analysed to illustrate the limitations and costs of imposing consociation in ethnically divided societies, in both democratic and non-democratic environments.

WHY NORTHERN IRELAND AND LEBANON?

Northern Ireland and Lebanon were chosen for case studies primarily because of the similarity of their ethno-national conflicts and the stark contrast between their regional situations. Both conflicts emanated from colonial state-building failures and were regulated (in different periods) through consociation. As political entities Northern Ireland and Lebanon were divided between religious or ethno-national groups, some of which gave little or no allegiance to the state. Moreover, in both cases, the irredentist claims of countries bordering the territory in question fuelled inter-ethnic tensions.

As a colonial power Britain failed to integrate Ireland into the United Kingdom (UK), while Ireland subsequently failed to incorporate six of the nine counties of the province of Ulster within its republic. Consequently, Northern Ireland became a devolved region of the UK, divided on national grounds between Ulster Unionists, who wished to maintain their British connection, and Irish nationalists, who aspired to unite the two parts of Ireland. Likewise, France failed in its nation-state-building ventures in the Middle East, in what became Lebanon and Syria. Through the partition of the Levant France significantly expanded Lebanese territory at the behest of the Maronite Christian community, but failed to nurture corresponding national identities in the two new states. As a result Lebanon was left divided between Lebanese nationalists, who were mostly Christian, and Greater Syrian or Arab nationalists, who were mostly Muslim. Accordingly, the danger of the emergence, or re-emergence, of ethno-national conflict over the formation of governments and the nature of the state existed in both Northern Ireland and Lebanon. Both societies contained ethnic groups that had actively partitioned the country in the past and would be likely to promote a similar strategy in the context of any future civil war.

Consociational government was used in both cases to regulate the conflicts and broker political coexistence within the internationally recognised political boundaries of Northern Ireland and Lebanon. However, consociation was not successful in either case, as power-sharing collapsed in the 1970s, resulting in civil war in Lebanon and continued intercommunal violence in Northern Ireland. Yet what makes this comparison interesting is that a return to consociation was the way in which both conflicts were eventually re-regulated. While the new power-sharing arrangements were different in their intercommunal construction and implementation, they were both directed and underpinned by external forces. The key differences between the two cases are largely attributable to their strategic importance, the stability of their regional environment, and the positive and negative external forces supporting or undermining conflict regulation between their elites. As the comparative analysis in this book will illustrate, the long-term prospects for successfully maintaining consociational democracy are very different in Northern Ireland and Lebanon.

CHAPTER STRUCTURE

This introduction reviews the relevant literature on Northern Ireland and Lebanon, and situates this book with reference to historiography.

Chapter 1 highlights where this book differs from, and adds to, the existing literature on consociational theory, bringing to the fore the focus on external variables in the implementation of consociation in societies divided by ethno-national conflict and illustrating how major consociational theorists have underestimated these factors. The chapter draws attention to the overemphasis in consociational debates on the internal variables that make the successful implementation of power-sharing more or less likely. It concludes that, in both Northern Ireland and Lebanon, it was the exogenous forces that were the key factors in the formulation of their consociational constructs, underpinning constitutional engineering and holding the balance in determining their future success or failure.

Chapter 2 analyses the Sunningdale Agreement of 1973, explaining why it collapsed five months later. The chapter demonstrates the embryonic nature of Anglo-Irish relations in the early 1970s, highlighting how the agreement was undermined by both internal and external variables. It concludes that Sunningdale failed primarily due to the inability of the

British and Irish governments to provide the motivations and incentives for the Northern Ireland parties to successfully engage in consociation.

Chapter 3 illustrates how the modalities of direct rule changed in Northern Ireland over the course of the conflict – fundamentally, how a steady process of strengthening Anglo-Irish relations, culminating in the Downing Street Declaration (DSD) and the Framework Documents, established a structure for conflict regulation through a return to the consociational model. It argues that the Good Friday Agreement (GFA) of 1998 was the result of an incremental diplomatic process, beginning at Sunningdale, which saw the British and Irish governments finally deal with Northern Ireland's constitutional issues on an inclusive basis, having developed a unity of purpose in order to regulate the conflict as an interest in itself.

Chapter 4 analyses the GFA, and its negotiation process in comparison to Sunningdale. It examines the pivotal role that the British and Irish governments played in brokering the accord, with the support of the United States (US), and illustrates how they worked in unison to ensure that a settlement was finalised in 1998. It was these positive exogenous variables that provided the incentive and motivation for the majority of Northern Ireland's elites to engage in an inclusive devolved power-sharing government, despite the absence of intra-elite stability.

Chapter 5 accounts for the fall of the Free French in Lebanon during the Second World War, and the emergence of a power-sharing compromise between Christian and Muslim leaders in 1943, which became known as the National Pact. The chapter focuses on the local, regional and international political dynamics that converged and provided the incentive and motivation for the Lebanese to engage in power-sharing within the borders of the Greater Lebanese state. It concludes that this combination of internal and external variables facilitated Lebanon's independence through consociation.

Chapter 6 details the collapse of the Lebanese political system during and after 1975, highlighting the attempts at conflict regulation during the course of the war. It illustrates that the essence of the Ta'if compromise was largely present throughout the conflict, but that a combination of local, regional and international factors prevented the internal equilibrium between Christians and Muslims from being re-established before 1989.

Chapter 7 evaluates the Ta'if Agreement brokered by the US and Saudi Arabia. It concludes that Ta'if succeeded in 1989 due to the convergence of international and regional interests in regulating the Lebanese conflict, granting the internal traditional elites an opportunity to re-establish their position in power through consociation. It argues, further, that the Syrian interpretation and implementation of the agreement undermined the long-term prospects for conflict regulation and power-sharing in Lebanon. In fact, Ta'if lacked any of the core consociational variables (as well as the external stability) that theorists view as fundamental to the successful regulation of ethnic conflict under this model.

Through comparative analysis Chapter 8 draws together the lessons learned from consociational experimentation in Northern Ireland and Lebanon. It evaluates the prospects for the successful regulation of both ethno-national conflicts under power-sharing. It concludes that, while Lebanon has a history of power-sharing and its leaders possess the will to re-engage in consociation, the successful adoption of power-sharing is more likely in Northern Ireland, given its geographical proximity to democratic regimes and the stability of its regional environment. This is in spite of Northern Ireland's elites having no great enthusiasm for the idea of power-sharing. On the other hand, while traditional Lebanese political leaders possess the will to engage in peaceful coexistence, its prospects are undermined by their proximity to the Arab-Israeli and intra-Arab conflicts: they remain as much at the mercy of the Middle East state system as they did before and during the civil war. Ironically, the very nature of their power-sharing deal, guaranteed by external powers, locks them into this position. Lacking the ability to shape their regional environment, their prospects for successfully implementing and stabilising a democratic consociational deal remain slim.

The book concludes that consociation can successfully regulate ethnic conflict in Northern Ireland and Lebanon, in the short to medium term, but only if external powers actively support this form of government. This presupposes that those powers holding an interest in the conflict provide positive incentives and motives for the internal elites to engage in power-sharing. There remains the question of the long-term viability of applying consociation as a means of stabilising and regulating these divided societies. It will be argued that this is possible only if the external pressures remain constant and the environment is conducive to the maintenance of this model of government. In the case of Northern Ireland with the British and Irish governments acting as stanchions between the two communities, and politically underpinning the GFA, the long-term prospects appear good. On the other hand, while Lebanon was under *de facto* Syrian control, with its consociational arrangements enforced by this non-democratic participant in the Arab-Israeli conflict, there seems little cause for any optimism. Syria's departure in 2005 has not removed the uncertainty that has prevailed over the future of power-sharing in Lebanon since the outbreak of civil war. Any attempt by the Lebanese to re-engage in power-sharing will be heavily dependent on positive external support for its success. Where those positive structures may come from is unclear.

The academic literature addressing the solutions, possible regulation or resolution, and causes and consequences of the breakdown of the previous systems in Northern Ireland and Lebanon is vast. So too is the number of solutions and theses aimed at explaining why so many attempts at regulation failed, resulting in civil war, military intervention and political stalemate. This book refutes the integrationist or civic society model of conflict regulation, arguing that positive coercive consociational government is the only feasible means of conflict regulation, short of repartition, in Lebanon and Northern Ireland. Further, it highlights the futility and shortcomings of the integrationist model and its inability to forge any form of stable or overarching syncretistic nationalism.

As far as the consociational literature and the use of power-sharing as a model of conflict regulation are concerned, this book picks up where most consociational theorists stop. It examines the impact and influence that external actors have upon internal elites in ethnically divided societies. It highlights their ability to provide the motivation and incentives for internal elites to engage in consociation, to create the conditions for the implementation of power-sharing arrangements, and to engage in coercive consociational state-building itself. Too much emphasis has been placed on the internal variables that are necessary for power-sharing to succeed in ethnically divided societies. If it is used to regulate ethno-national conflict then consociation is exactly that: a tool for the implementation of a political system that facilitates accommodation between ethno-national groups.

LITERATURE REVIEW: NORTHERN IRELAND

The Irish and the Lebanese have been as divided over their rival interpretations of history as over their incompatible ethno-national aspirations. The historical debates can therefore be viewed as microcosms of their ethnic conflicts. For nationalists the root cause of conflict in Ireland is British colonialism and the continued British presence on Irish soil. Nationalists argue that a resolution of the conflict, in which Ireland would be reunified, can only be brought about by the removal of this political and military presence. They point to the abject failure of British policy in Ireland over the centuries, arguing that the only course of action that remains to be tried is unconditional withdrawal. Anthony Coughlan contends that, if Britain realised that it was not the Irish Republican Army (IRA) but 'their own government's insistence on maintaining sovereignty which was the real root of the problem, it would be a major step towards a united Ireland'.[3] Irish nationalism is based on a claim to territorial national self-determination – one people in one state – and aims to cast off the yoke of centuries of British colonial rule. Such thinking has led Irish nationalists to view Protestant unionists as a minority group within the Irish nation and, as such, one that has no right to prevent Irish

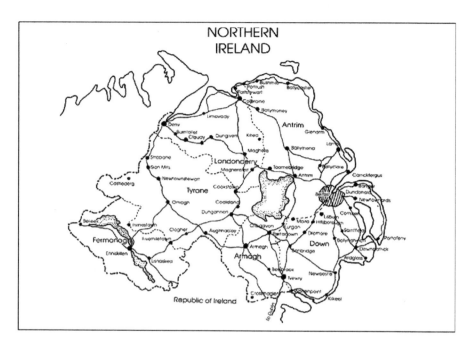

territorial self-determination. Yet nationalism remains divided over what strategy is best suited to achieving a united Ireland. Constitutional nationalists, such as the members of the Social Democratic Labour Party (SDLP), have worked for political reform within Northern Ireland, whereas the militant Republicans of the IRA developed an armed campaign to remove the British presence.

For their part, the unionist community have sought to maintain Northern Ireland's position within the UK. They see themselves as neither an independent nation nor a part of the Irish one and, while they were rigidly opposed to any form of Irish home rule, faced with a *fait accompli* in 1920, they opted for partition.[4] Viewing themselves as British, and the province of Ulster an integral part of the UK, they chose to retain six of its nine counties and abandon their kin in the remaining three. They took partition to be the final settlement of the Irish question and blamed Irish irredentism for fuelling Republican violence against the British state. The importance of this issue to the unionist community was illustrated when two figures in the Ulster Unionist Party (UUP), Dr Chris McGimpsey and his brother Michael, took the Irish government to court over the territorial claim to Northern Ireland that used to appear in Articles Two and Three of the Irish Constitution.[5] Ironically, the failure of their case deepened the constitutional imperative of Irish unification in Republican hearts, and consequently, the siege mentality in unionist minds.

As unionist divisions intensified, some began to favour independence for Northern Ireland after 1972, in preference to relying on the British state to preserve their position within the UK. While this was inherently contradictory to unionism itself, such aspirations derived from a perception among some unionists that a future British government might attempt to remove Northern Ireland from the UK. Most unionists, however, fell into two other categories: integrationists, wanting full administrative integration with the rest of the UK; and devolutionists, those wanting some form of devolved government at Stormont. These groups cross-cut the two main unionist parties, the UUP and the Democratic Unionist Party (DUP).

After Northern Ireland's government at Stormont was prorogued in 1972, integrationists argued for the full incorporation of Northern Ireland within the UK and were therefore content with direct rule. Consequently, they viewed any departure from this position as itself an attack on the union. They believed that full integration within the UK would have dampened nationalist aspirations for a united Ireland and removed any uncertainty over the future constitutional position of Northern Ireland. Conversely, devolutionists favoured self-government within the UK as a buffer against any British ambitions to push them towards some form of a united Ireland or any power-sharing government with nationalists.

While a historical sense of grievance over partition and anti-colonial sentiment formed the backbone of nationalist discourse, Irish irredentism and British lack of interest reinforced a sense of siege mentality within unionism. Such colonial thinking led Republicans, for the best part of the twentieth century, to misread British intentions in Ireland. Their belief that Britain was a colonial power, which would only leave Ireland if forced to, proved false. They ignored Britain's inherent desire to be rid of Ireland, and the fact that it had partitioned the country to avoid a conflict over Ulster, which might have led to civil war. When the conflict erupted in 1969, the British were badly informed as to what was going on, having allowed the unionists to govern from Stormont since 1922 and, in effect, provide a check on any Northern Irish business ever reaching Westminster.

There were also those on both sides of the divide who viewed the conflict from the perspective of Marxist notions of class struggle.[6] For Marxist nationalists colonialism was the key, the root cause of the conflict being imperial capitalism, which suppressed the Irish and kept their economy in subordination to the British. Such discourse had an impact on Republican thinking during the phase of the conflict with which this book is concerned. Conversely, there were Protestant socialists who offered a different Marxist interpretation of the conflict, in defence of the union. Rejecting Marxist nationalist theories, many Protestant socialists argued that 'Protestant working-class resistance to a united Ireland was and is autonomous of ruling class suasion'.[7]

Another school of thought viewed Northern Ireland's divisions in religious terms and, since this book deals primarily with ethno-national conflict regulation, it must be addressed.[8] The importance of religion in Northern Ireland is illustrated in Richard Rose's monolithic survey of its population at the beginning of the recent outbreak of violence.[9] His work demonstrated the high level of regular church attendance among both of Northern Ireland's communities in comparison with most other European countries. The popular perception that religious tension was at the heart of the conflict is understandable given the importance of the church to both communities, and the fact that Protestants and Catholics are identified through their religious denominations.[10] However, belonging to either the Protestant or the Catholic community is actually an ethnic marker, used to identify which ethno-national group a person comes from. In strictly religious terms, being a practising Protestant or Catholic has had very little to do with being a unionist or a nationalist. It is a person's allegiance to one of the two national communities that is important, rather than theological beliefs. In fact, the issue of religion *per se* in both Northern Ireland and Lebanon is of much less significance than ethno-national identity.

In reference to the war over Irish history, Brendan O'Leary and Paul Arthur have argued that Northern Ireland can only be understood from the premise that it is a site of failures in both state-building and nation-building.[11] They divide modern Irish history into three phases of Anglo-Irish failure. The first period, 1801–1922, saw the failure of British state-builders to forge a pan-British identity in the two islands, and equally, the failure of Irish state-builders to build a pan-Irish identity in the island of Ireland. The second period, 1920–72, saw the dissolution of Stormont as a direct result of these previous state-building failures. The third period was that of protracted ethno-national conflict in Northern Ireland following the abolition of Stormont in 1972. It is the third period, with its Anglo-Irish attempts to address the failures of the past, with which this book is concerned.

It is, however, beyond the scope of this book to assess all the various propositions and models for resolution or regulation that have been developed over the years.[12] Instead, it will focus on those that have been seriously tried and tested, contrasting the 'top down' and 'bottom up' strategies that have been hotly debated within the literature over the course of the conflict. There are essentially two schools of thought regarding which direction conflict regulation strategies should take in Northern Ireland. On the one hand, there are those who argue that it must be a top-down-elite, driven process, such as implementing democratic consociation.[13] On the other hand, there are those who argue that democratic coexistence based on consensus can emerge from within society or from intercommunal 'grass roots' through an essentially non-elite -driven process, by tackling socio-economic issues, addressing political inequality and promoting social integration.[14] The latter model will be evaluated first.

THE INTEGRATIONIST MODEL

Integrationist or civic society theorists argue that, by reforming Northern Ireland through addressing socio-economic issues rather than practising constitutional engineering, Britain and, subsequently, the Republic of Ireland had a better chance of bringing about a successful regulation of the conflict. Integrationists contend that intercommunal reconciliation can be encouraged through the promotion of interethnic contact. In their view this is more conducive to the expansion of a democratic basis for peaceful coexistence than the imposition of consociation.[15] While many of them recognise the ethno-national nature of the conflict, they maintain that it is socio-economic issues that must be addressed, rather than the constitutional issues regarding Northern Ireland's sovereignty.[16]

Paul Bew and Henry Patterson argue that the British government should have focused on creating a 'set of Anglo-Irish institutions', within which they would have been committed to the promotion of 'real moves to substantive equality between Protestants and Catholics economically and before the law', while 'leaving the ultimate constitutional aspirations untouched'.[17] In other words, they contend that there is actually no need to pursue the core constitutional causes from which the ethnic conflict emanates, for regulation could be achieved by addressing the key socio-economic issues that have marked political inequality in Northern Ireland since partition. In line with such thinking, Paul Dixon argues that consociational theorists such as Lijphart, McGarry and O'Leary are unduly pessimistic in their analysis of the conflict. He maintains that there appears to be 'no conclusive evidence to suggest whether the consociational or civil society theories offer a better opportunity for promoting peace'.[18] Yet the weakness of this approach was apparent even before Sunningdale. A strong moderate political centre ground was not forthcoming in Northern Ireland, as the collapse of the Northern Ireland Labour Party (NILP) and the poor performance of the intercommunal Alliance Party of Northern Ireland (APNI) in the Assembly election in 1973 illustrates. This remained the case in the Assembly election in 1998: if the Alliance Party had been functioning successfully, a party such as the Women's Coalition would never have come into existence, nevermind won Assembly seats. In sum, Dixon's overall analysis ignores the fact that the origins of the conflict are ethno-national, and that any attempt at regulation – never mind resolution – must recognise these defining parameters and address the unionist–nationalist constitutional antagonisms that fuelled its violence.

Rick Wilford challenges the norms of the political debate by suggesting that opening the corridors of power to more women might increase some politicians' tendency to compromise. He contends that women's propensity to be motivated by communitarianism, their tendency to be 'more inclined to compromise' and the public's desire to see 'more women in public office' offer a challenging vision to Northern Ireland's society.[19] However, female leaders such as Margaret Thatcher, Golda Meir and Benazir Bhutto illustrate clearly that, even in democratic politics, women behave no differently than their male counterparts. The existence of the Women's Coalition highlights this point. Rather than aiding conflict regulation, they have actually fragmented the moderate unionist/nationalist bloc and undermined the centre ground they claim to represent.

Rupert Taylor strongly criticises the consociational model and questions whether the 'institutionalisation of ethno-nationalism', solidified into governmental structures by consociation, is the best way to regulate the conflict.[20] He argues that a better way forward would be to take exactly the opposite course to that advocated by consociational theorists, suggesting that Northern Ireland can undergo a reconciliation process similar to that of South Africa. He contests that theorists and social engineers should be focusing on transforming the conflict and challenging ethnicity, rather than attempting to actually regulate it.[21] Like other integration theorists, Taylor argues for the creation of a strong democratic centre ground that would supersede ethno-national identities, overcome intercommunal antagonisms and 'cross-cut social divisions'.[22] As with his optimistic reading of events in South Africa, Taylor remains sanguine about the prospects of transcending conflict in Northern Ireland.

Joseph Ruane and Jennifer Todd also emphasise the multifaceted dimensions of conflict regulation in Northern Ireland and the importance of the role played by civic society in founding any settlement.[23] However, Brendan O'Duffy contends that their focus on the 'emancipation through reform of the economic, social and political structures underemphasises the agenda-setting and frame-working of the negotiations and the structure of the settlement' through the two governments since the Anglo-Irish Agreement (AIA) of 1985.[24] Ruane and Todd's subsequent analysis of the GFA pays closer attention to these constitutional variables.[25]

The obvious problem with integration strategies is that over the course of the conflict they failed to muster any significant degree of cross-communal support.[26] The idea of creating a moderate centre ground in Northern Ireland, one that excludes the extremists, has become politically redundant. The problem with the idea of moving away from the ethno-national aspect of the conflict is exemplified by the fact that, even from the outset, the APNI 'took their unionist position on the chin'.[27] From its very inception the APNI was a party exclusive to Northern Ireland, which accepted that there could be no sidestepping the ethno-national dynamics of the Irish question. It is through addressing this point – the ethno-national nature of the conflict – that the potential for conflict regulation can be realised, as consociational theorists argue.

THE CONSOCIATIONAL MODEL

Consociational theorists claim that conflict regulation must emerge from within the existing elite structures and, in turn, be managed through the political situation's present parameters. The most serious proponents of consociation are Lijphart, McGarry and O'Leary. These theorists have highlighted and debated the different factors and variables conducive to the implementation of the consociational model, and their analyses will be evaluated in Chapter 1. In sum, they argue that consociation can be used to regulate the Northern Ireland conflict through power-sharing, electoral proportional representation, maximising communal autonomy and providing minority veto rights.[28] O'Leary asserts that, through coercive constitutional engineering, a form of consociation can be imposed on Northern Ireland's parties through the provision of sufficient incentives and motivations for elite engagement.[29]

O'Leary's original analysis of the prospects of coercive consociationalism concluded that the AIA was the first British attempt at coercive consociationalism, coming as a direct result of the failure of voluntary power-sharing in the 1970s. While one could argue over just how voluntary these consociational attempts were, as Sunningdale was largely imposed,[30] his conclusion that such constitutional engineering is the only viable solution, short of joint sovereignty or repartition, has been borne out. O'Leary highlights the confederal and federal elements of the GFA, which were absent from Sunningdale, illustrating how the confederal all-Ireland provisions provide incentives and motivations for the Northern Ireland parties to work the agreement.[31] Yet Lijphart, McGarry and O'Leary have all paid too much attention to the architectural constructs of consociation, and thus do not fully account for the external pressures that are required to impose, implement and regulate such administrative structures.

Paul Mitchell applies Nordlinger's conflict regulation theory to Northern Ireland.[32] He questions whether the basic environment 'for conciliatory action actually exists in the first place'.[33] Mitchell argues that political scientists spend too much time weighing up internal variables

when assessing the prospects of consociation in divided societies. He concludes that the 'key to an acceptable consociational formula is the balance
which is struck between the internal and external dimensions of the problem'.[34] He maintains that regulation of the conflict in Northern Ireland
could be forthcoming if the external powers clear up the confusion
between the internal elites over what is and is not 'constitutionally possible'.[35] What Mitchell falls short of saying is that it is up to the external
forces to create and maintain the equilibrium necessary for the internal
elites to compromise, and to provide the incentives and motives for them
to reach a constitutional settlement.

O'Duffy follows on from such thinking in his interesting comparative
analysis of Sunningdale and the GFA. He argues that only by 'addressing
the competing claims to sovereignty' can the British and Irish governments regulate Northern Ireland's ethno-national conflict.[36] He concludes that: 'The key to cultivating a ripe moment for a constitutional
settlement was based on the process of self-determination needed to
address and modify constitutive aspects of sovereignty that preceded partition, as well as regulative aspects that have evolved since the Anglo-Irish
Agreement in 1985'.[37] O'Duffy correctly focuses on the contradictory
claims to sovereignty over Northern Ireland as being central to the conflict, and thus intrinsic to its regulation, but he somewhat overestimates
the relative weight of the Irish government in this equation. He argues
that what has changed most fundamentally is 'the relative equalisation of
the status of the opposing sovereigns (the UK and the Irish Republic),
with regard to *de jure* and *de facto* authority in Northern Ireland'.[38]
However, the political situation in Northern Ireland since the signing of
the GFA has not borne out this analysis. While the British government
has worked in partnership with its Irish counterpart, it has remained
responsible for sovereign decisions reflecting Northern Ireland's constitutional position within the UK. In fact, it decisively exercised its power
during the implementation process, as the multiple suspensions of the
Northern Ireland Assembly illustrate.

Henry Cox has argued that the AIA failed due to its inability to address
the long-term issues of sovereignty and contrary constitutional claims.[39]
He concluded that, while they were attempting an imaginative enterprise,
the two governments were 'too much in thrall to their own inheritance of
simplistic concepts of sovereignty and territoriality', 'out of which the two
regimes had done far too little in the past to educate their respective
Northern Irish clients'.[40] While this rings true, the external elites were
themselves going through a slow learning process. In essence, the underlying historical issues and antagonisms between the two states had to be
addressed before successful conflict regulation became possible.

Adrian Guelke argues that Northern Ireland's lack of international
legitimacy played 'an important role in the legitimisation of political vio-

lence'.[41] He points out that the external parties to the conflict 'tended to favour the nationalist case in Northern Ireland', and that this was largely a consequence of Northern Ireland's constitutional ambiguities.[42] Guelke concludes that 'internationalisation has made the conflict more intractable because of the role that external factors have played in the legitimisation of violence', as it did in Lebanon.[43] It is themes such as Guelke's that this book will focus on in its evaluation of the international facets of Northern Ireland's conflict. There is, of course, no guarantee that consociation will succeed: therefore, alternative forms of conflict resolution must be considered.

WORST-CASE SCENARIOS

There are other political options that Britain or the two governments might impose on Northern Ireland if the consociational model fails. The most obvious worst-case scenario is a repartition of Northern Ireland. While such an action would not match unionist or nationalist aspirations, Kennedy argues that 'there is no solution to the Ulster question' and suggests that a repartition of Northern Ireland would offer two Ulsters. [44] This is likely to strike horror into the hearts and minds of anyone who has ever visited Northern Ireland, but Kennedy contends that each one would be 'largely homogenous in terms of political composition'.[45] Therefore it would gain its legitimacy from the fact that the inhabitants of the two new political entities would have chosen them in preference to the constitutional packages offered by the two governments.

The problem with this argument is that it is unlikely that either community would be prepared to support repartition. To be successful such a venture would require cross-communal legitimacy, something that would be difficult to come by following the failure of whatever more moderate arrangements the two governments had previously supported. Other than the obvious logistical difficulties, it is hard to see how the motivation and incentives could be galvanised to force the two ethnic blocs to engage in population exchanges. Kennedy's argument is based on the premise that there is no solution to the conflict in Northern Ireland. This, along with much of the integrationist and civic society arguments, misses the point of conflict regulation through consociation. No ultimate solution to the conflict is necessary to actually regulate it. Consociation is like a plaster stabilising a broken bone: the plaster will not heal or fix the wound, but it may create the conditions whereby the break can, at best, be healed or, at worst, be prevented from splintering further. Thus, while constitutional packages are on offer from the governments, albeit ones that entail many impalpable things for many parties, they must be tried and tested before policy-makers retreat to such doomsday scenarios as repartition.

If consociation were to fail, some form of joint sovereignty might be imposed along federal or confederal lines, as envisaged by Claire Palley.[46] Of course, the possibility that the two governments might actually adopt some form of joint sovereignty over Northern Ireland is, in itself, a major incentive for the unionist elites to engage in consociation. Palley argues that a confederal structure is something that the unionists should look towards while they still have strong bargaining power vis-à-vis the British government. Conversely, O'Leary argues that joint authority over Northern Ireland would not work, as it would further destabilise the unionist community and offer nationalists no incentive to share power with them.[47] However, O'Leary and McGarry later concluded that joint authority, taking the form of 'a democratised condominium', would be the most viable option given the outright failure of power-sharing.[48]

Following this brief review of the opposing themes, currents and other options debated in the literature, this book finds its place in the consociational theorists' camp, building upon the works of Lijphart, McGarry and O'Leary. With the benefit of hindsight, it is clear that the integrationist themes hold little potential in the search for a viable conflict regulation strategy in Northern Ireland. The various attempts to forge a centre ground in Northern Ireland have all failed to address the core issues of sovereignty and self-determination, and are now widely recognised as having no stable institutionalised foundations. It has proved impossible to build a syncretistic intercommunal or national identity in Northern Ireland, an identity that could overarch and supersede ethno-national allegiances.

LEBANON

This section briefly reviews the literature concerning power-sharing in Lebanon, dealing with it in three strands: the debate over the National Pact; the breakdown of the state and the consequent outbreak of civil war in 1975; and finally, the return to power-sharing under the Ta'if Agreement of 1989. Different ethno-national groups, largely Christian and Muslim, which held contradictory national aspirations and adverse views on what form the state should take, divided Lebanon's society. In his seminal work, *A House of Many Mansions*, Kemal Salibi dissects Lebanese history by cutting through the conflicting images of national identity and imagined communities.[49] He traces the roots of Christian–Muslim conflict back through Mount Lebanon's different colonial phases, from the days of ancient Phoenicia to the Christian–Druze autonomous rule of the *Règlement* under the Ottoman *millet* system.[50] Salibi argues that the conflict over history has blurred the realities of coexistence on Mount Lebanon and, quoting the Druze

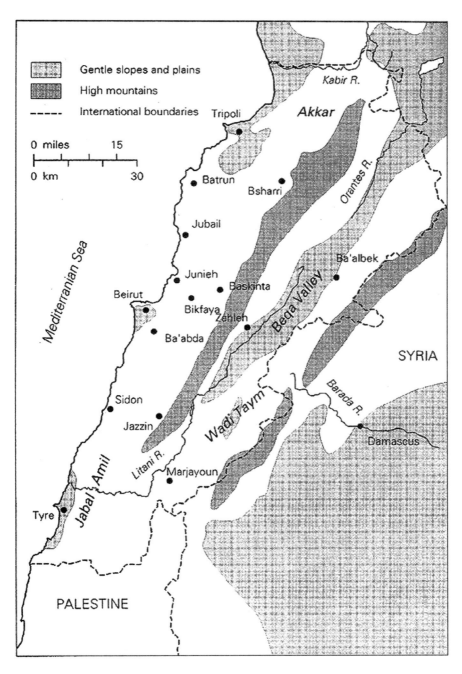

Lebanon after 1920

leader, Walid Jumblat, he argues that the 'rewriting of the Lebanese history textbook [is] a necessary precondition for any lasting political settlement in Lebanon, if not the primary one'.[51]

The Christian Maronites and the Druze were the two main groups that settled on Mount Lebanon, but alongside them were Greek Catholics, Greek Orthodox, Armenian Christians, Shi'a Muslims and a handful of other small religious communities. As Mount Lebanon was an extremely difficult place to govern and collect taxes from, it became a safe haven for religious minority groups that wanted to maintain their religious independence without antagonising the Islamic Ottoman Empire.

Alongside many other communities, the Maronites trace their lineage back to the Phoenicians, believing them to be the 'ancient Lebanese people' that inhabited the coastal cities of Byblos, Tyre and Sidon.[52] W. Phares argues that by the seventh century the Maronites were a mix of 'predominantly Aramaic ethnicity, with a Greco-Roman cultural influence and Christian religious inclinations'.[53] This reading of history and ethnicity places the Maronites among the oldest non-Arab communities in the Middle East. Yet, while the Maronites view themselves as a religious community, Salibi argues that this is exaggerated, and that they actually have been held together by a strong sense of group solidarity, rather than any devotion to religious creed or custom.[54] As in Northern Ireland, while the modern conflict has been shrouded in the cloak of conflicting religious beliefs, identity politics is at the root of Lebanon's ethnic tension. The Christian communities that coexisted on Mount Lebanon have sought to preserve their ethnic difference, both in the past, from the Sunni-dominated empires, and in the present, through Maronite rejection of Arab nationalism.

Regarding modern Lebanon, much of the debate over the National Pact, the civil war and the return to power-sharing has revolved around the question of nation-building. Was Lebanon's ethno-national conflict resolvable through political reform after 1943? Seven years before the outbreak of the civil war, Michael Hudson argued that civil strife in Lebanon was in fact inevitable.[55] Following the constitutional crisis that Lebanon faced over Camille Chamoun's government in the 1950s, it is surprising that many other commentators were not as forthcoming in their analysis. Hudson was as much speaking with hindsight as he was predicting future trends, for those who brokered the deal in 1943 seemed well aware of the potential for ethnic strife.[56] Hudson argued that the lack of strong national institutions of government was responsible for Lebanon's inability to cope with the sort of socio-economic challenges that immobilised President Suleiman Frangieh's government before 1975. He concluded that Lebanon's political system prevented the development of the sort of opposition politics that allowed western democracies to cope with processes of political reform and modernisation. For

Hudson the weak consociational state was the problem and the creation of strong central state institutions was the only solution.

In general, Israeli scholars, such as Meir Zamir, came out heavily against the consociational model in Lebanon, pinning much of the country's misfortunes on the nature of this political system. This probably had more to do with a desire to see it fail than it had to do with academic conviction, such was their fear that the international community might once again promote some form of power-sharing to regulate the Palestinian–Israeli conflict. However, Lebanon's ability to survive these turbulent times had at least as much to do with the regional balance between Egypt, on the one hand, and Syria, Iraq and Saudi Arabia on the other. These external forces were instrumental in preventing its collapse and without their positive contribution Lebanon could well have been consumed long before 1975. Farid el-Khazen concludes that the resuscitation of the National Pact after 1958 was facilitated by 'a political arrangement involving internal and external actors', as opposed to any resolution of the socio-political tensions that emanated from the deal.[57]

Regarding the internal dynamics of the National Pact after 1958, the socio-economic gap between the 'haves' and the 'have nots' significantly increased. This heightened demands for broad-based political, social and economic reform. L. Abul-Husn highlights the growing discontent within the Shi'a community in particular, stemming from their proportional under-representation in the National Pact.[58] By the 1970s, this had manifested itself in a formidable left-wing opposition, made up of all the excluded or disenfranchised elements of Lebanese society. After this movement was given military prowess by the presence of the PLO, it presented the government with a challenge that rendered the National Pact unworkable. It was the destabilisation of the external balance that denied the Lebanese their traditional mechanisms for reconstituting the consociational arrangements in order to meet such political challenges. While the PLO was to some extent restrained by other Arab states after the erosion of Lebanese sovereignty under the Cairo Agreement of 1969, its presence as a military force in Lebanon crippled the National Pact system. Crucially, none of the external powers with influence saw it as being in their vital interest to rescue the Lebanese government. For example, even if Syria could have suppressed the PLO militarily, the regional and domestic cost of such action would have been severe. Therefore, while the regional balance in 1958 facilitated a reconstructed National Pact, under President Chehab the consensus among Arab states that the PLO could operate from Lebanese territory heralded the end of Lebanon's First Republic.

Evaluating the prospects for peaceful coexistence, Theodor Hanf quotes one of the National Pact's founding fathers, Henri Pharaon, who wrote: 'Perhaps it is true that not all our countrymen are Lebanese in their hearts, but sensible policies can ensure that they are Lebanese in their minds'.[59] The pact's internal and external dynamics, however, prevented the Lebanese from fulfilling such 'convivialist' aspirations. Hanf argued that the foundations of state collapse were grounded in this internal and external balance. While Lebanon's intercommunal tensions were largely regulated peacefully through the National Pact system between 1943 and 1975, 'conflict regulation broke down when one of the Lebanese communities or actors operated their strategy in an attempt to get more than a relative advantage'.[60] This was possible when one group saw an opportunity that might elevate its political position through external support. Such options were regularly open to the Lebanese. As Guelke points out, one stark difference between Northern Ireland and Lebanon was 'the relative absence of external intervention in the Northern Ireland conflict'.[61]

DEBATE OVER THE NATIONAL PACT

There are many rival interpretations of the meaning, causes and consequences of Lebanon's National Pact. According to some historians it defined national unity and interconfessional harmonisation.[62] For others it marked the convergence of intercommunal economic interests, which allowed a deal to be brokered that favoured certain communities and delivered independence.[63] The internal and external contradictions of the pact were, arguably, the root causes of Lebanon's power-sharing conflicts throughout the remainder of the twentieth century, as the pact was a device of its time. According to Farid el-Khazen the National Pact was a 'quintessential example of political pragmatism: the lowest common denominator shared by the independence leaders'.[64] Khazen's unsentimental analysis of the pact provides a clear picture of the Lebanese situation in 1943, accounting for the regional and international dynamics that hastened independence. For him the pact primarily offered the Lebanese the 'most effective way of ridding the country of the French Mandate – a desire shared by many Muslim and Christian leaders'.[65]

As for the eminent political scientist, Theodor Hanf, the pact was taken to mean proportionality, and he credits Michel Chiha and other convivialist thinkers for its technical formulation.[66] He argues that the pact was meant to be only a temporary agreement and that its founders did not envisage proportionality rigidly underpinning the future administration of the new republic. However, Hanf illustrates how the pact set the parameters of Lebanese government, in that it 'institutionalised consociational democracy as constitutional reality: important decisions cannot be taken by simple majority; they require consensus and compromise'.[67]

Elizabeth Picard also situates the pact in relation to the joint

Muslim–Christian struggle for independence. She argues that for a brief period in 1943 'exemplary coordination took place between the two rival political forces' to rid Lebanon of the French when the external regional and international situation proved favourable at the end of the Second World War.[68] However, highlighting the proportional rigidity spelt out by Hanf, Picard describes the Lebanese compromise as a 'precarious and dangerously static pact'.[69] She argues that it was these features that led directly to the Lebanese constitutional crisis of 1958. On the question of democracy, Picard contends that Lebanon only 'approached' being a liberal democracy, primarily because the pact's 'chief defect' was that it secured the benefits that the elites could gain from their positions in power.[70] This is in stark contrast to European consociational systems, where power-sharing is not strictly a top-down process. Thus, the inherent weakness in the National Pact was that, while it was meant to be only a temporary mechanism to achieve independence, those who brokered it, and their successors, became completely reliant on its consociational framework for the fulfilment of their economic interests and positions of power.

The pact can be seen as a benchmark in Lebanese politics and the foundation on which the new Republic of Lebanon was successfully governed. However, as Eyal Zisser correctly emphasises, most historians also derive its origins from the *Règlement* during the Ottoman period of interethnic coexistence under the *millet* system.[71] There can be little doubt that the pact was a renewal of the traditional principles of cohabitation that existed between different religious groups on Mount Lebanon: only in 1943 were they extended to the Greater Lebanese state.[72] Zisser argues that the 'eminence of the pact lay precisely in its sophisticated combination of innovative and old elements for bridging the communal gaps'.[73] Its innovation was that it brought forth the consociational tools of the colonial periods, while readjusting them to suit the political realities of the new state. Again, the salience of the static nature of the pact is apparent – this renewal was in tune with the local, regional and international politics of 1943, but it left Lebanon ill equipped to deal with future socio-economic or political changes, or the ever-shifting dynamics of a volatile region.

Zisser evaluates the demerits of the pact emanating from the debate in the literature. First, he argues that a system of interconfessional elite power-sharing, based on the premise that no single group could dominate the others, was bound to result in 'immobility, if not paralysis'.[74] Second, while basing the system of government on the confessional consociational grounds of 'pluralism and openness' ensured a certain level of democracy, it also 'produced a weak state structure'.[75] Finally, lacking any mechanism for constitutional change and reflecting the intercommunal balance of power as of 1943, the pact led inevitably to a crisis that challenged the Lebanese state.

THE COLLAPSE OF THE NATIONAL PACT

In contrast to the creation of the Lebanese state, a plethora of work has been written on its collapse in 1975, and this section will review the most notable of those works.[76] First, in attempting to explain why consociational government failed, Michael Hudson's modernisation approach questioned Lebanon's ability to adapt to external and internal pressures and shifts. He argued that, if Lebanon was 'essentially consociational' between 1943 and 1975, then 'it has not been clearly established that its consociational devices significantly accounted for such democratic stability'.[77] He makes the case that consociational engineering 'induced a degree of immobilism that prevented government from dealing with socio-economic and ideological challenges'.[78] He argues that the elites not only failed to meet these challenges, but became deeply divided by them under the power-sharing system. In response to this, consociational theorists point to the defects in the Lebanese model. Some suggest that this might not have been the case if a true consociational democracy had been applied strictly along European lines.[79]

Hudson highlights the fact that one of the major defects of Lebanese consociationalism was the exclusive nature of the National Pact. Most notably, it significantly underrepresented the Shi'a community in its coalitions. Further, elite accommodation broke down regularly over foreign policy, counter-elites challenged the state's legitimacy, and elites were unable to lead and control their masses.[80] He succinctly concludes by suggesting that, if a 'withered state' needs the consociational model to 'perform its basic function of lubricating communal relations', while the consociational benefits in conflict regulation can only be delivered through a strong state, 'then the positive synthesis is impossible to achieve and Lebanon's dilemma is inescapable'.[81] Hudson's analysis primarily rests on an examination of the internal political system in Lebanon and he blames the confessional system for much of the shortcomings of successive administrations. As a result he does not fully account for the external regional constraints placed upon Lebanon's institutions and governments, although he does question its ability to deal with such factors.[82]

Farid el-Khazen takes the view that the radicalisation of Arab politics through Nasserism threatened the National Pact. He argues that the pact 'presupposed a non-ideological scene', with moderate accommodationist Arab leaders prevailing, but instead the Arab world became politically charged and Lebanon virtually remained static under its confessional system.[83] Of course, the Arab–Israeli conflict fed into and exacerbated this problem. Joseph Maila contends that the pact could not survive such a regional atmosphere forever, as 'a culture of political neutrality between Israel and Syria within the context of the Arab–Israeli conflict is impossible'.[84] In his important work on the breakdown of the Lebanese state

Khazen surveys the various multidimensional internal and external variables that led to the pact's collapse and the outbreak of civil war. He argues that the central problem with Hudson's modernisation approach lies in its inability to 'explain the causes of political instability and periodic crises as well as the occurrence of conflicts of the magnitude and duration of those witnessed in post-1975 Lebanon'.[85] Khazen questions whether an 'open and democratic state in Lebanon' can survive and maintain its character 'in crisis situations involving contested issues related to pan-Arab politics whilst interacting with a regional system composed of states that lack both democracy and openness'.[86] He argues convincingly that it was Lebanon's failure to deal with the internal and external dynamics that largely accounted for the breakdown of the state. In a region dominated by dictatorships and itself fundamentally divided by ethno-national conflict, Lebanon's consociational system became a source of weakness and, in effect, 'a liability for stability'.[87] Khazen concludes that the National Pact handicapped Lebanon in relation to international and regional politics, in the sense that, after 1943, it lacked the 'instruments of control that are at the disposal of other Arab states'.[88] Lebanon was unable to maintain its open democratic system and deal with such pressures at the same time. The emergence of the PLO as a major non-state actor in Lebanon in the early 1970s illustrates the dynamics of this dilemma.[89]

Marius Deeb's analysis of the outbreak of civil war in Lebanon concludes that it had three major facets. First, Lebanon's sovereignty was undermined by the presence of the PLO, the growth of private militias, the disintegration of the army and the government's growing dependence on Syria. Second, there was growing tension over demands to reform the pact and their consequences for the traditional leaders. Finally, the ever-present intercommunal divide over Lebanese identity threatened to rip the country apart.[90] Yet many of the compromises proposed at the beginning of the war were identical to what was actually achieved under the Ta'if Agreement.

THE RETURN TO THE NATIONAL PACT

For some Lebanon's return to power-sharing after Ta'if spelt a positive re-engagement of intercommunal democracy and a resuscitation of peaceful coexistence.[91] Others remained more sceptical as to the extent to which reconciliation had occurred and exactly what form of power-sharing Syrian-controlled Lebanon would adopt, concluding that it certainly would not reflect the pre-war model.[92] It was in fact clear that there was scant possibility of a return to the pre-war status quo without a significant realignment within Middle Eastern politics. Until then power-sharing in Lebanon would remain a fig leaf for Syrian control.

Abul-Husn describes the Ta'if Accords as 'conflict resolution', and views the new power-sharing dispensation as having provided 'social engineers and decision-makers with an instrument for nation-building'.[93] He argues that a 'resolution of the conflict became possible when the problems of power and authority in the social structure were addressed, when balance to communal entitlement was restored, and the deep cleavages ... were recognised. This was achieved through a revived consociational remedy to a multicommunal social structure'.[94] Where previous attempts at reconciliation had failed, Abul-Husn hailed Ta'if as a success, since it addressed the underlying causes of state collapse and the outbreak of civil war. He did not, however, critically analyse the context in which Ta'if was imposed, or the stark non-implementation of its consociational variables.

Theodor Hanf addresses these issues in full and concludes that Ta'if was a *realpolitik* agreement cast in the mould of the National Pact. He argues that the Lebanese 'foxes' seized the moment to end the war and stage a return to power at the expense of the militia forces on the ground in Lebanon, albeit under Syrian hegemony.[95] Hanf details the 'dereliction' of Ta'if through its perverse interpretation and non-implementation under Syrian supervision.[96] He argues that the cost of ending the civil war and the 'restoration of the Lebanese state' amounted to restrictions being placed on Lebanon's sovereignty, followed by 'restrictions on democracy and on the rule of law'.[97] Hanf puts Ta'if in its correct context, concluding that: 'As so often in the history of independent Lebanon, dereliction of the agreement arose not so much from the Lebanese as from the regional developments'.[98] He stops short of adding that the same thing could be said for the achievement of the agreement, as it was brokered and subsequently broken due to the changing dynamics of Arab politics and regional geopolitical relations.

Likewise, Elizabeth Picard views Ta'if through the prism of its internal and external variables. She highlights the fact that, instead of abolishing or diluting 'political communitarianism', the new accord not only reinforced but enshrined these principles and, while aspiring to abolish them one day, made such an abolition 'most improbable'.[99] She argues that this is explained, internally, by the traditional elites' obvious eagerness to return to power in Beirut, having been ousted and discredited during the war, and, externally, by Syrian and Saudi engagement. Both states favoured the maintenance of the confessional system, as it enabled Syria to consolidate its control over Lebanon and allowed Saudi Arabia to maintain its influence in the Sunni community. More importantly, by 1989 the US had finally accepted the Syrian position in Lebanon. Accordingly the internal and external dynamics were largely harmonious at the time the agreement was signed. In contrast to Abul-Husn's assertion that Ta'if provided the Lebanese with the mechanics for nation-building, Picard argues that: 'The new constitution reflected the resilience of the communal groups as the most immediately operative part of the Lebanese social structure and thus codified the elements of communal group interaction'.[100]

Joseph Maila joins the Ta'if sceptics in his detailed and disparaging evaluation of the accord, and its endogenous and exogenous implications for Lebanon. He argues that the Ta'if document 'is nothing new', as it merely builds on and confirms many of the compromises agreed by the elites and the Lebanese equilibrium that had been established during the war.[101] He reminds us that Ta'if was not really about systemic 'reforms' in the true sense of the word; rather, it reflected 'new communal accommodations' in the light of political and social changes. Intuitively, he points out that strict attachment to the text of the agreement 'is liable to make one forget that, whatever the new arrangements, the Lebanese political system will continue to function within the spirit of communal participation'.[102]

Maila provides a useful framework for analysing Ta'if's political reforms from the perspective of confessionalism and constitutional law. Ta'if, for Maila, was simply an '*aggiornamento* of the 1943 National Pact', as 'confessionalism dictated the remodelling of the institutions', while a realignment of constitutional responsibilities marked 'an end to the presidential system that had prevailed in Lebanon'.[103] He concludes that the new Ta'if institutions 'have become nothing more than pawns of a confessional structure, dressed up as constitutional authorities',[104] while ominously questioning why an agreement aimed at resolving 'constitutional and political misunderstandings' contains a whole chapter on the 'nature of relations between Lebanon and Syria'.[105] He argues that Ta'if is not workable without changes in the regional political environment, as 'stability is one of the utmost factors that makes consociationalism work'. Maila contends that it has failed in Lebanon because all the different communities follow external 'linkage policies': 'every community has links and privileged links with a foreign power' just as they did under Ottoman rule.[106] As Malcolm Kerr aptly concludes, 'confessional democracy will collapse if outside pressures make it impossible for politicians to compromise'.[107]

CHAPTER ONE

Consociation

> Lebanese woman: 'It is our capacity to adapt (*musayara*) which led us to where we are'.
> Companion: 'Without this capacity, things would have been worse'.[1]

At the beginning of the twenty-first century reformulated consociational agreements were regulating both Northern Ireland and Lebanon's ethno-national conflicts. The external powers with influence over these divided societies had concluded that a return to a power-sharing model of government was the best way to manage their historic disputes. The successful implementation of consociational government in Northern Ireland and Lebanon was thus largely dependent on the external actors that had an interest in regulating the conflicts. After protracted civil wars it was clear that power-sharing could be established, or re-established, only by exogenous pressures. External forces either positively regulated political divisions or provided the incentives and motives necessary to bring the internal elites to engage in consociation. As Eric Nordlinger suggests, 'successful or unsuccessful regulation will be largely dependent on the purposeful behaviour of political elites'.[2]

WHAT IS CONSOCIATION?

The Oxford English Dictionary defines consociation as 'a political system formed by the cooperation of different social groups on the basis of shared power'.[3] Elaborating on this, Brendan O'Leary provides a general definition of 'political consociation' as 'a state or region within which two or more cultural or ethnic or national communities peaceably coexist, with none being institutionally superior to the others, and in which the relevant communities cooperate politically through self-government and shared government'.[4] O'Leary's definition is most suitable for democratically consolidated consociations, where the emphasis is on 'self-government', that is, regions or states where government is not externally imposed or regulated, but is established and maintained through internal political cooperation, as opposed to external coercion. Therefore this definition does not fit easily with either of Northern Ireland's previous consociations, or Lebanon's since 1989. Questions of self-governance and institutional superiority in Northern Ireland and Lebanon have never been sufficiently resolved to fit such a general definition. However, granted that such a thing is possible in states or regions divided by ethno-national conflict, O'Leary's definition is something to which they can aspire.

According to Arend Lijphart, a complete democratic consociational government must have a grand coalition of the political leaders of all significant segments of the plural society, a high degree of autonomy for each segment, the use of proportionality principles and the existence of mutual vetoes.[5] Lijphart argues that the success or failure of consociational democracy is dependent on the presence or absence of a number of political variables. There is no concrete general rule as to which of these are the most important, as all ethnic conflicts have idiosyncratic dynamics and need to be addressed by particularistic methods.[6] Debate therefore continues over which variables are the most important, alongside criticism of the consociational approach in general.[7]
The most prominent of Lijphart's favourable factors for consociation are as follows:

1) segmental isolation of the ethnic communities;
2) a multiple balance of power between the ethnic communities;
3) external threats common to the ethnic communities;
4) overarching national loyalties to the state;
5) a tradition of elite accommodation;
6) socio-economic equality;
7) small population size, providing small government workload;
8) a moderate multi-party system with segmental parties.

As with democratic theory itself, there is no universally applicable consociational formula suitable for all divided societies. Therefore these consociational variables all have different values under different political circumstances. The absence of some variables, as opposed to others, can help to explain the failure of power-sharing under consociational government. However, the consociational debate has largely revolved around the comparison of established democracies that use the consociational model in the absence of ethno-national conflict, in other words, in states where the maintenance of the consociational system was not the only thing preventing state collapse and the outbreak of civil war.

O'Leary builds on Lijphart's theory by offering definitions of three different types of consociational democracy. He argues that in democratic consociations: 'There must be executives which enjoy cross-community support: support from all significant elements of the electorate (complete), majorities within each segment (concurrent), or a plurality of all significant segments (weak or virtual)'.[8] He restates the need for communal autonomy and the use of proportional representation in the electoral system and that, additionally, but not necessarily, rigid consociations need parity of veto rights. In line with Nordlinger and Adriano Pappalardo,[9] O'Leary's focus is largely directed at the inter- and intrasegmental dynamics of the domestic elites in plural societies. There is consequently a need to refocus the debate towards the influence that non-domestic elites bring to bear on consociation on the one hand, the 'carrots' – incentives and political rewards for domestic compliance – and on the other the 'sticks' – various pressures and political or military sanctions designed to punish domestic elites when they fail to comply. Those who forward the power-sharing agenda often owe their positions to the external power that brought about political change. As both Northern Ireland and Lebanon were totally dependent on their regional environments and all questions of foreign policy were either dictated or heavily influenced by exogenous forces, the concept of 'external carrots and sticks' in coercive consociationalism must be fully addressed.

John McGarry and Brendan O'Leary highlight three conditions that are crucial to the establishment of a democratic consociational government:

1) elites require sufficient motivation to engage in power-sharing and to take the tough decisions conducive to inter-ethnic political accommodation;
2) elites must be free to negotiate and to lead their electorates where they might not want to go;
3) there must be a multiple balance of power among the subcultures and those subcultures must be stable within society.[10]

This study contributes a fourth criterion to McGarry and O'Leary's conditions, which adds to the first, regarding Northern Ireland and Lebanon, and in these cases interconnects with the others: the existence of positive external regulating pressures, from state and non-state actors, which provide the internal elites with sufficient incentives and motives for their acceptance of, and support for, consociation.

McGarry and O'Leary's first criterion highlights the need for 'sufficient motivation' to engage elites in power-sharing, but it is the necessity that this pressure should come in the form of coercive external forces that is often underestimated.[11] Coercive external forces are state actors that bring an influence to bear on the domestic elites, prompting them to take actions that they were not previously predisposed to take. Coercion does not necessarily mean physical pressure, but, in effect, the provision of political motives and incentives that prompt domestic elites to engage in power-sharing.

In 1973 British and Irish elites failed to provide such coercive pressure, to the extent that their failure largely undermined their power-sharing experiment. Conversely, it was the presence of positive external and internal motivating pressures that allowed the consociational model to become the mode of government adopted by a majority of Lebanon's elites in 1943. In 1998 the dynamics of the exogenous influences over the Northern Ireland parties had changed to the extent that the British and Irish governments were able to provide the motivation and incentives for a majority of the domestic elites to fully engage in consociation. This was largely in the absence of McGarry and O'Leary's second and third variables: elites were not free to lead their electorates where they might not want to go, nor was there stability between the subcultures within society at that time. Finally, when Lebanese power-sharing was restored in 1989 the external forces created the circumstances and the environment for its return.

Thus, in these four cases the defining political factors in the success, implementation, maintenance and failure of consociation were external pressures. The fact that Lebanon's exogenous influences were not entirely positive in 1989, nor indeed democratic, is irrelevant in the short term, as they achieved a regulation of that phase of the conflict regardless of whose interests were best served.

As for the second criterion, elites' freedom to negotiate and to lead their followers where they might not otherwise go, the inability of the external elites at Sunningdale to create the circumstances where the majority of the domestic elites were capable of doing this, or had enough incentive to do so, largely contributed to the collapse of the power-sharing experiment. They failed to provide the majority of the local elites with the confidence they required to lead their constituencies towards compromise. However, the opposite was true for Lebanon in 1943, as Anglo-French rivalry and regional Arab independence movements created a favourable environment for consociation. Regarding Lebanon in 1989 and Northern Ireland in 1998, elites were certainly not free to negotiate or to lead their communities unhindered, but the external forces coerced and supported them, most notably the Maronite Christians and the Ulster Unionists.

Finally, while a balance of power was certainly lacking between Northern Ireland's subcultures in 1973, demographic changes had actually furthered the prospects of agreement by 1998. However, stability within these subcultures had not been established in 1998, as the unionist community remained divided by UUP–DUP rivalry in a similar sense to 1973, something that the external powers largely failed to influence. Conversely, such an intercommunal balance existed at the time Lebanon attained its independence, adding a level of stability to the accord that was significantly absent in 1989. The Christian community had decreased considerably in demographic terms by 1989, but parity of political representation was agreed and imposed at Ta'if anyway, with a semblance of the old equilibrium being recast, regardless of segmental imbalance and intrasegmental instability.

THE INFLUENCE OF EXTERNAL PRESSURES ON INTERNAL ELITES

All of McGarry and O'Leary's variables interconnect with, and are influenced by, external pressures. In Northern Ireland and Lebanon the external forces were paramount in the brokering of the power-sharing agreements. This illustrates how external actors can facilitate accommodation between domestic elites and establish power-sharing. Equally, if it does not suit their interests or they lack the ability to act, they can prevent consociation or simply fail in their attempts to initiate it. However, if the internal variables are not present – such as the lack of intrasegmental stability within the unionist bloc during the GFA negotiations – then considerable constraints are placed on the external actors' ability to regulate the conflict through consociation. On the other hand, domestic elites can significantly affect the external equilibrium. For example, the former SDLP leader, John Hume, influenced the Irish government during the Sunningdale period and, subsequently, both governments in the late 1980s and early 1990s. On the unionists side it was partly their opposition to any form of agreement with nationalism that led the British government to sign the AIA without consulting them.

If external forces have a positive interest in consociation – an interest that is not wholly selfish and accounts for the interests of the different domestic elites – then they can create the motives and incentives for them to engage in consociation. Of course, it helps enormously if they are not hindered by other regional actors who hold a conflicting interest in the divided society, and if the internal elites are prepared to work the consociation of their own accord. The case of Lebanon illustrates the fact that these exogenous pressures do not have to be unselfish to impose consociation. The Ta'if Accords were brokered exactly because of the convergence of the selfish interests of external actors. While these interests coincided with those of the traditional Lebanese elites, the external elites were not entirely dependent on the internal elites to reach agreement. Complying with the external powers offered the old Lebanese elites a chance of regaining power. Refusal would have led to their exclusion from any post-war consociational settlement or simply a continuation of the conflict. This was typical of the regional dilemma facing the Lebanese. Antoine Messarra argues that, as with the Cairo Agreement of 1969, the presidential election crisis over Mikhail Daher in 1988 and the parliamentary election boycott in 1992, for the Lebanese, 'in all cases, the alternative was either acceptance or chaos'.[12]

In both Northern Ireland and Lebanon it was largely this regional environment and its colonial legacy that defined the ethno-national conflict, the intensity and protracted nature of the divide, and the potential for its regulation through power-sharing. While the interests of the local elites may not cross-cut, if the interests of external forces coincide, then they can successfully create an environment within which the interests of the domestic elites converge to some extent. This was certainly the case in Northern Ireland in 1998, and the enormous amount of energy spent on the local elites by the British and Irish governments illustrates this point. This does not primarily have to be for the benefit of the divided society, as the Ta'if Agreement exemplified. The fact that an end to the war suited the Lebanese themselves was actually secondary to the regulation of the conflict at that time. External forces imposed the consociational model when it suited their interests and when they were capable of doing so.

Therefore, in all four cases – Northern Ireland in 1973 and 1998, and Lebanon in 1943 and 1989 – the actual timing of the agreement was dictated by the agendas of the external powers. Whatever arguments can be raised against this point, the internal elites would never have come to such agreements by themselves, nor would they have had the power to implement them. External elites are, however, susceptible to changes of government and foreign policy interests. Such changes can therefore have both positive and negative influences on consociation.

Lijphart argues that 'elite cooperation is the primary distinguishing feature of consociational democracy', adding that 'conflict management by cooperation and agreement amongst the different elites rather than by majority and competition is the second feature of consociationalism'.[13] Neither of these two features has proved possible in the long term in Northern Ireland and Lebanon, as the variables that might provide elite cooperation or conflict management are highly dependent on the exogenous regional environment and have not proved static or consistently positive. This is highlighted by the implementation of consociation in all four agreements. An environment of elite cooperation came about in Northern Ireland only when the British and Irish governments began practising coercive consociationalism, which culminated in the reimposition of power-sharing in 1998. Conversely, it was the changing regional environment and the shifting dynamics of the Arab–Israeli conflict that largely contributed to the collapse of power-sharing in Lebanon in 1975, and brought about its reconstruction in 1989.

Lijphart goes on to argue that 'the consociational model is an intermediate model that stands between the unitary British model and the model of international diplomacy'.[14] While he does not sufficiently elaborate on the theme of international diplomacy, this point is pivotal to the adoption of consociation in societies divided by ethno-national conflict.

The consociational model is not a self-sufficient model for the regulation of societies divided by ethnic conflict. The inherent weakness of such political entities leaves them reliant on international diplomacy to support and stabilise their governments. Conversely, if the neighbouring states or regional powers have no interest in stabilising the consociation, then it is likely that they may have a negative effect. The phrase 'good social fences may make good political neighbours' is often cited in this debate.[15] Societies weakened and divided by ethno-national conflict are, however, often incapable of building fences or competing with neighbouring states. This poses the question as to how sovereign ethnically divided societies regulated by consociation can be. Lebanon is a classic example of this, as its first consociational agreement was founded on the premise that it would have a foreign policy based on neutrality. Thus, Lebanon's political dependence on the external status quo illustrated both the potential and the limitations of its consociational framework, as exogenous forces influenced not only its system of government, but its different communities as well. In 2003–5 the inability of the US-led forces in Iraq to secure an environment that was conducive to the imposition of some form of stable consociation highlighted the limitations of external intervention in the absence of both international and domestic legitimacy.

The central problem here is one of establishing cooperation and agreement between elites – but which elites: the internal ones, the external ones, or both? Clearly, Lijphart was talking about the internal elites in general, but an evaluation of their behaviour cannot be made in Northern Ireland or Lebanon independently of other state actors, as they are interdependent. Ghassan Tuéni suggests that 'the reality of sovereignty' in Lebanon 'is itself a function of external coercive forces and their interests'.[16] A distinction must be made between domestic and external sovereignty in countries divided by ethno-national conflict. Only through an analysis of regional power plays – the means by which external powers pursue their interests in a divided society and their subsequent interaction with domestic elites – can any comprehensive evaluation of the situation be made. This is the purpose of the comparative analysis in this book. Only within such a framework can consociation as a mode of ethnic conflict regulation in such societies be properly assessed.

POSITIVE AND NEGATIVE EXTERNAL PRESSURES

Consociation in societies divided by ethno-national conflict can be influenced in different ways by external forces. Positive exogenous pressures influence the likelihood of successful conflict regulation when the regional powers have an interest in that regulation itself, or cross-cutting interests, in implementing or preserving consociational government in an ethnically divided society. Under such circumstances the chances for successful short-to-medium-term conflict regulation dramatically increase. Such an interest, however, must not be primarily strategic or economic. Of course, external forces may also have an interest in regulating the conflict by consociation when it suits them to do so. While this might be positive for the internal elites or the establishment of consociation, it is an unstable basis for conflict regulation, as the interests of the external powers supersede those of the internal elites. They are primarily strategic or economic interests, as they have no primary concern with conflict regulation or consociation, other than what they can gain from its implementation or preservation. A negative external influence would be one where the regional powers have a direct interest in destabilising the consociation, and have the ability and desire to do so.

Thus, the external elite influences do not have to be strictly positive, in the sense that they are conducive to producing democratic political consociation, as defined by O'Leary.[17] Non-democratic exogenous pressures can regulate ethno-national conflict under a form of weak or virtual consociation, as Lebanon's Ta'if Agreement demonstrates. Farid el-Khazen argues that 'Lebanon has been interdependent on the negative aspects of the regional system of security and not on the positive aspects'.[18] However, this, of course, raises the question of just how long such consociations can last. The outcome is an obvious one, and one that the internal elites have little power to influence. It can last as long as the regional status quo allows the consociation to regulate the conflict under the parameters that they implemented in the first place. That is not to say that a slight change or shift in power or interests will result in collapse, but if there is a major change the plaster of consociation may begin to crack. A consociation in an unstable region may well appear fairly static, yet political changes in that regional environment, which the consociation is reliant on for its continuity, can fracture its internal and external balance.

O'Leary reminds us that consociationalism is fundamentally a bargain, and nowhere is this more evident than in societies where it is used to regulate ethno-national conflict.[19] The apparent deep-rooted traditions of democracy and consociation among the Lebanese failed to prevent any community from retreating to its confessional bunker, or opening up age-old ethno-national sores that were bandaged over by the establishment of the state. Nor did the fact of Lebanon's small size, or the high degree of familiarity and continuity among its elites, prevent them from reopening ethnic hostilities in 1975.

Lijphart argues that the 'consociational model requires the leaders to have at least some commitment to the maintenance of the state as well as to democratic practice'.[20] Again, this misses the point of using consociation as a means of regulating ethnic conflict. First, commitment to democratic practice in societies divided by ethno-national conflict is not such a significant factor when evaluating whether the consociational model can be used as a regulatory tool. When an ethnic conflict is exacerbated by internal or external factors, the democratic values that domestic elites may hold are largely overruled by their contradictory national aspirations and their analysis of the political situation in zero-sum terms. Therefore, commitment to democratic practice remains secondary to national identity politics, and this is borne out when external variables weaken the equilibrium within which the consociation exists.

Second, even a high level of commitment to democratic practice will do little to stabilise consociation in an ethnically divided society in a region where democracy is not valued or practised. Further, the commitment to the state is often lacking in at least one of the different groups in an ethno-national conflict, yet this does not mean that consociational democracy cannot be established. Lijphart's analysis is drawn largely from a western democratic perspective and fits into a theoretical framework of democratic transition and democratisation. The Lebanese case illustrates the point that the environment where consociation is used or most needed is not always democratic. In fact, in Lebanon's first power-sharing agreement and Northern Ireland's second the commitment to the state or region in question on the part of some of the internal elites was consolidated largely by the motives and incentives provided by external powers.

It is therefore possible that exogenous pressures influencing different internal elites can establish and maintain a commitment to the idea of the state and to democratic practice, which may be required for consociational government to function. They do not, however, have to be democratic practices in all cases, but merely support the ideal of democracy in itself. The US-led coalition's handover of sovereignty to the Iraqis in 2004 illustrates this point. In circumstances where consociationalism is externally imposed by powers that hold ultimate sovereignty over the state or region, the democratic foundations underpinning the consociation are often very thin, or merely a fig leaf. In such cases the democratic ideal lends itself to the elites' need to publicly legitimise the consociation into which they are entering. Such exogenous pressures can take the form either of positive stabilising forces, such as the British and Irish governments' role in brokering the GFA, or of negative ones, as with the Syrian influence after Ta'if. On the other hand, alternating positive and negative external variables can either maintain or destabilise the internal elite balance through their influence, as was the case in Lebanon between 1943 and 1975.

Too much emphasis has been placed on the importance of democratisation and the democratic structures used to regulate conflict under the consociational model. Such focus tends to miss the point of power-sharing in societies divided by ethno-national conflict: it is the regulation of the conflict that is important in the short term, not, essentially, democratisation or democratic transition. If consociation can be replaced in plural societies as a process of democratisation develops[21] and, equally, if consociation can be abandoned in societies divided by ethno-national conflict when civil war breaks out, then maintaining the internal/external equilibrium that sustains consociation is crucial. The pressures that allow the conflict to be regulated successfully under the consociational model must initially be preserved. Only through this can a process of democratic transition take place.

The fact that a power-sharing government's integrity and continuity is largely dependent on its relationship with external powers is one of the main dilemmas of consociation in ethnically divided societies. The internal elites often have little influence over this political equation, hence the need for coercive or supportive consociational engineering. The paradox is that, even if the internal elites do not really favour consociation, having had it implicitly or explicitly imposed upon them by external forces they are then largely reliant on the good will of those forces to maintain the internal balance. Further, they are also totally reliant on their ability and inclination to preserve the external status quo. In other words, the external elites must at least have an interest in keeping the internal and external equilibrium. For example, even if Lebanon met all Lijphart's different criteria for the successful implementation of consociation, such ventures could still fail every time if the external variables were non-conducive, or coercive in a purely negative fashion, to the implementation and maintenance of this system. The role played in Lebanon's civil war by Syria and Israel illustrates this point. So, while it is clear that the influences that external factors have on consociational agreements may largely determine their success in such cases, does this mean that exogenous forces have the ability to establish consociation?

Imposing consociation

Lijphart argues that consociationalism 'cannot be imposed against one of the segments, especially if it is the majority'. He points to the failure of consociationalism in Northern Ireland in the early 1970s to illustrate this point, concluding that 'most of the Protestant leaders as well as the rank and file remain opposed to power-sharing with the Catholics'.[22] Lijphart's assertion that most of the Protestant elites were opposed to power-sharing is correct, but there is less evidence to suggest that Protestants in general were also against the idea in principle (see Chapter 2, Table 8). They may not have favoured or supported consociation as their first choice of government in Northern Ireland, but that is not the same as being opposed to power-sharing with Catholics in principle. Further, for most of those Protestants who did oppose power-sharing, it was power-sharing with nationalists or republicans that they rejected, not power-sharing with Catholics. Lijphart's view that the consociational model cannot be imposed on one of the segments, let alone the majority one, is also questionable, as both Northern Ireland and Lebanon's experiences suggest.

Of the four power-sharing agreements in question, only for Lebanon's National Pact of 1943 could a serious argument be constructed that the local elites established a form of consociational government themselves. Even then, the different communities did not endorse it, and it was established primarily due to a coincidence of positive internal and external cross-cutting factors that heavily favoured that outcome. Lebanon's Ta'if Agreement was actually imposed on all of its communities and, as the nature of its external interpretation and implementation became clear, against the Christian segment. The fact that none of the elites were in any position to reject this imposition, regardless of how undemocratic it was, made it no less imposed. The pre-war fractures were set and recast in an internally modified, externally regulated consociational mould.

While referendums were held in Northern Ireland and the Republic of Ireland endorsing the 1998 Good Friday Agreement, the unionist community supported it by the slenderest of margins, and it could never have come about in the first place without the coercive pressures brought to bear by London and Dublin. Coercion thus remains the determining feature of power-sharing in Northern Ireland. Every time the model has broken down or begun to crack, the sovereign power has intervened to re-straighten the parameters of power-sharing and reinterpret the agreement to accommodate changes to the political environment or its own interests. Lebanon's problem after 1969 was that when political, economic and demographic pressures challenged the state, the government lacked the positive external support needed to preserve its intercommunal balance.

Ultimately, consociations that rely on external imposition, and especially those imposed against one or more of the segments, will be reliant on consistent international, regional and domestic pressures to maintain their administration. Realistically, only positive exogenous forces are likely to win broad-based domestic legitimacy and support for imposed consociational settlements if they are to prove workable. Instead of gaining legitimacy and domestic support, selfish or negative externally imposed consociations are far more likely to slip backwards to renewed ethnic conflict or some form of authoritarian government. Here, the divided society's proximity to democracy and the stability of the region are crucial.

THE EXTERNAL DEBATE

Concerning the external relations of political regimes, and their prospects for implementing and maintaining consociational practices, O'Leary highlights and criticises three factors identified in the literature – size, shared threats and foreign policy – adding a fourth, 'international norms'.[23] According to Lijphart, size does matter. He argues that small states are more likely to feel externally threatened, so that elites are more inclined to enter into consociational practices to protect themselves.[24] Conversely, O'Leary argues that the direct effect of external threats 'surely operates independently of size', because 'shared external threats give domestic elites significant incentives to accommodate', regardless of size.[25]

In fact, shared external threats did not always prompt Lebanon's elites to maintain their consociational alliances, as the Palestinian issue in the 1970s indicates. Lebanese Muslims were prepared to place pan-Arab causes above their coexistence pact and, as a direct consequence, concede state sovereignty to a foreign force. To what extent, then, were Lebanon's domestic elites to blame for this dilemma? Antoine Messarra contends that the collapse of the National Pact in 1975 was 'certainly not caused by the failure of the consociational system, but rather because of regional and international implications, and, of course, the incapacity of the Lebanese state to struggle against foreign pressure and interventions'. He argues that, despite all of this, 'the regime's structures remained almost intact'.[26]

So, while they operate independently of size, the proximity of the state or region to an unstable political environment and/or the exposure of its elites to destabilising exogenous influences are far more important than size. O'Leary contends that small states are no easier to govern in all cases than large ones are. He argues that running Lebanon would be more daunting than governing France.[27] In the same sense, if a consociational democracy the size of France existed in the Middle East, for example, perhaps between Syria and Saudi Arabia, as opposed to the stable democratic environment of Western Europe, it would be open to much the same external manipulation that Lebanon has endured since it achieved its independence.

The fact that the level of violence in Northern Ireland did not fluctuate greatly after the initial years of its recent conflict[28] was largely due to the stability of its regional environment and the ability of the British government to contain the conflict. While the promotion of power-sharing was not a policy that was consistently pursued by London and Dublin, the containment of violence within Northern Ireland was.[29] If the exogenous actors had had an interest in high-intensity conflict by proxy in this region, its civil war would have been more like Lebanon's. It was Northern Ireland's position within the UK, its proximity to Western

Europe and Anglo-American relations that prevented further escalation of the violence. Equally, while Northern Ireland has no history of power-sharing, its potential for successfully adopting consociation in the long term is better than Lebanon's, as the regional environment is more conducive to domestic stability than the chaotic unpredictability of the Middle East is.

History does matter regarding the question of regulating ethnic conflict by consociation. It is highly beneficial for political continuity if elites have previously chosen to engage in power-sharing. However, if a consociation is reliant on the regional equilibrium within which it exists, then history cannot offer much protection from the destabilising impact that external forces can have. While Lebanon's elites have repeatedly chosen to engage in power-sharing, the fact that each community looked to foreign backers to guarantee their position within the consociation was an enduring weakness.

In the post-Cold War era consociation has become the tool of choice for conflict regulation and the reconstitution of states in insecure regions by the West. In many ways consociation offers the world's power brokers a means of providing security where insecurity would otherwise prevail. It allows powerful states to maintain a dominant role within regions where they have an interest, as any new consociation is almost entirely reliant on those who brought it into being. Thus, in the post-colonial world the use of consociation can actually enable superpowers to exercise a form of territorial political and military control without physically acting in a traditionally colonial manner. Further, the use of consociation by post-colonial powers is rather reflective of the sort of cultural imperialism that accompanied European territorial expansion in the nineteenth and twentieth centuries. It is therefore not surprising that in the twenty-first century western ideals of democracy and transition have not been met with universal popular support in the Middle East. Its peoples have, after all, had a great deal of experience of foreign rulers.

O'Leary highlights the modern phenomenon of externally imposed consociation, pointing out that 'great and regional powers may be more willing to impose on small powers domestic arrangements they would not dream of implementing themselves', citing the western refragmentation of Bosnia–Herzegovina and Macedonia in the consociational mould as an example.[30] Again, these polities would probably not be consociations without the external forces that brokered and imposed their agreements. It was the pursuit of western foreign policy goals in the region that led to the implementation of power-sharing agreements to regulate their ethno-national conflicts. It suited the interests of the external actors to use the consociational tool. Once this had been done, the internal elites were, in turn, reliant on the external actors for the continuation of their regime and their positions in power.

Thus, the imposition of semi-democratic or virtual consociations, using coercive consociational engineering, has become a useful method for western intervention or limited control in a similar sense to that of the *millet* system under the Ottoman Empire. While traditional territorial imperialism looks likely to remain largely redundant in the twenty-first century, the dependence of consociational regimes in their post-conflict phase on the external powers allows great powers to exercise *de facto* control by proxy, in tune with their strategic, political and economic interests.

To take this point one step further, it is quite possible that post-Saddam Iraq may have a consociational system imposed on it by the US with the support of the UK. If this happens, the new Shi'a, Sunni and Kurdish elites will be highly reliant on the members of the US-led coalition, because it would be these powers that provided the incentives, motives and political power for them to engage in power-sharing. Therefore, while their interests and those of the external powers coincide, the exogenous pressures would supersede and overarch those of the domestic elites in the creation of consociation. The impact of Turkey's attempts to join the EU, and of Cyprus's accession to that body, on the Turkish and Greek Cypriots'attitudes towards power-sharing in Cyprus is another example of this external dynamic. In such cases consociation would lead the domestic elites that engaged in it to be dependent on the internal/external equilibrium that established their form of government. Moreover, the greater the regime's proximity to undemocratic states or regional instability, the more dependent it would be on its powerful foreign allies. Thus, any new consociation in the Middle East would be utterly dependent on the powers that established it, at least in the short to medium term. Consociation could not operate without stable external powers supporting it.

To the same extent, if the Lebanese Christians had been successful in their attempts in the 1980s to establish a largely Christian state in Beirut and its mountainous hinterland, they would have been totally dependent on external support, at least in the short to medium term. This highlights the difference, or potential difference, between regional and sovereign consociations or repartitions as a result of consociational failure. In the case of Northern Ireland, one of the 'external' forces, if Britain may be called external at all, is sovereign, while the other, the Republic of Ireland, has a national minority in the terrritory. O'Leary argues that such external players acting as protectors of their respective minorities, or even being rather neutral, as in Britain's case in Northern Ireland, makes a consociational outcome more probable. This is certainly true in the short to medium term in stable environments such as the UK or Italy, as in the case of South Tyrol. This is because the external powers have an interest in regulating the conflict, not only for themselves, but also for their national minorities. On the other hand, unitary consociations in states or regions that are divided by ethno-national conflict, in non-democratic environments where external actors may use national minorities to undermine the regime, are far more susceptible to exogenous destabilising forces. However, if they are consociations that are set up by exogenous forces, such as Bosnia–Herzegovina after Dayton and Macedonia after Ohrid, then this raises questions over the extent to which they are actually sovereign.

While the state system has never been more interdependent, if a state is fully dependent on a great power, or powers, for its *de jure* sovereignty, should it really be classed as sovereign at all? For example, the different levels of sovereignty between states such as Austria and the Netherlands, and externally sponsored states such as Bosnia–Herzegovina or provinces such as Kosovo, are obvious. Thus, there is a correlation between the proximity of the ethno-nationally divided consociation to destabilising forces, and the determination of what level of sovereignty it enjoys vis-à-vis the external powers that imposed and regulated its government. Therefore, the debate over consociation has changed in the post-Cold War world. Consociation has become a tool favoured by the west for intervention in regions where its interests are threatened.

CONCLUSION

As far as consociation in Northern Ireland and Lebanon is concerned, exogenous pressures have been the determining factors when evaluating consociation's chances of long-term success. However, power-sharing has not been used in the past to try to resolve conflict in these areas. Such an interpretation misunderstands the nature of the ethnic conflict in both regions. It has been and can be used as an externally coordinated mode of conflict regulation, given positive external variables in the short to medium term. Of course, proximity to democracy and/or a regional environment conducive to the maintenance of stable democratic systems primarily enhances the chance of its success. The external dynamic remains key to peaceful coexistence in both these regions. Many conflict regulation theorists, including Lijphart, argue that consociationalism cannot succeed unless the elites desire it.[31] The wishes of domestic elites are not always enough in these cases, as they are often secondary to the desires of the externally involved state actors.[32] As O'Leary suggests, if the variables for consociation are unfavourable, the policy-makers must then consider if it is possible to engineer such conditions.[33]

CHAPTER TWO

Sunningdale

Michael Kerr: 'Did Edward Heath tell Brian Faulkner that power-sharing with a Council of Ireland was the price to be paid for the maintenance of the union with Britain?'
Sir Ken Bloomfield: 'Yes, I wouldn't be at all surprised ... and even if he didn't, as it were, threaten to chuck them out of the union, there was no doubt that if the whole thing broke down in the face of what could be characterised as Unionist obduracy, the blame for the whole situation would be laid at Faulkner's door. So he was in a most unenviable position'.[1]

Northern Ireland's first power-sharing government, established following the Sunningdale Agreement in 1973, collapsed after only a few months in office. Sunningdale itself, however, was the beginning of an Anglo-Irish political process that culminated in 1998 with Britain and Ireland regulating the conflict under the GFA. The fact that Anglo-Irish relations regarding Northern Ireland were at an embryonic stage in the early 1970s partly accounts for the brevity of the first power-sharing experiment. The two governments' inability to act in unison to promote and consolidate an agreement, along with the unwillingness of some unionist and nationalist leaders to support a power-sharing formula, ensured Sunningdale's collapse. While Northern Ireland lacked the external pillars of strong Anglo-Irish relations, internal intra-elite stability, based on an acceptance of Northern Ireland's new political situation, was also missing.

If such external forces had existed in Britain and Ireland at that time – with an interest in regulating the conflict, as opposed to merely containing the violence within Northern Ireland – then Sunningdale might have at least established the idea that power-sharing was the only viable method of regulating the situation. Without such support it took the two governments two-and-a-half decades to successfully return to this model. The Unionist elites did not lack the ability to share power with nationalists at that time, but the majority simply lacked the will to do so. Some believed that there was a workable political alternative open to them and therefore used the Council of Ireland to bring Sunningdale down. Such opposition firmly tested the resolve, commitment and capability of the two governments in their attempt to impose power-sharing on Northern Ireland – a test they both failed.

THE SUNNINGDALE AGREEMENT

The Sunningdale Agreement itself stemmed from a reform of the Government of Ireland Act, 1920, as set out in the White Paper of March 1973.[2] It comprised a devolved unicameral assembly, an 'Irish Dimension', an executive committee structure, and anti-discrimination and human rights provisions. It provided for a devolved power-sharing government, whereby the British Secretary of State for Northern Ireland would enact a programme of 'rolling devolution', relinquishing his powers in accordance with the performance of the executive and the ability of its parties to work together. The Assembly was to have real powers to legislate on most regional matters, while Westminster would retain ultimate control over security and foreign affairs.

Although the White Paper began with a renewal of Northern Ireland's constitutional guarantee, in the same breath it emphasised the need for a developed 'Irish Dimension' in its political affairs. Section 12.1 stated that: 'Northern Ireland must and will remain part of the United Kingdom for as long as that is the wish of a majority of the people; but that status does not preclude the necessary taking into account of what has been described in this paper as the Irish dimension'. Through this Irish Dimension a 'ministerial council' was envisaged within which the two parts of Ireland would 'consult and coordinate' on issues of obvious mutual interest, such as agriculture, tourism and transport. This dimension was clearly open-ended, with the potential to be developed and expanded once devolution had taken place.

The Northern Ireland Assembly Act of 1973 provided that: 'A Northern Ireland executive authority may consult on any matter with any authority of the Republic of Ireland [and] enter into agreements or arrangements with any authority of the Republic of Ireland in respect of any transferred matter'. This Council of Ireland was to consist of seven members of the Northern Ireland Executive and seven members of the Irish government with a rotating chairmanship. The layer beneath the Council would be a consultative forum consisting of thirty members of the Northern Ireland Assembly and thirty members of the Dáil Éireann, who would be elected by single transferable vote (STV) from their respective legislatures. Further, there was to be a mutual veto on the council's decision-making process and all its decisions had to be unanimous to be enacted. Therefore any integration or moves toward unification could only be developed or passed if all seven Northern Ireland Executive delegates *and* their southern counterparts voted for them. Consequently, from a unionist perspective signing up to the Council of Ireland involved a constitutional guarantee from Britain and Ireland that Dublin's influence would be as limited as the northern executive allowed it to become. In short, the relationship envisaged was devolved institutionalised cooperation with mutual vetoes on any evolution of this process.

The Executive was to be a power-sharing body made up from the respective parties, with the implicit exclusion of anti-Agreement unionists and republicans, based upon their representation within the Assembly. Section 52 of the White Paper stipulated that Northern Ireland's government could no longer be based on a single party that drew its support 'virtually entirely from only one section of a divided community'.[3] However, as will be seen, its exclusive nature substantially weakened its consociational aspirations. It was to consist of eleven members and each member would head but not control a department, as had been the case under the old Stormont regime. Eight to ten inter-communal departmental committees were to be set up consisting of Assembly members on a proportional representation basis, headed either by a minister or by one of the non-voting members of the Executive nominated by the Secretary of State. The fullest consultation was required between the head of the department and the committee during the formulation of any new policy, thereby creating a strong link between the Executive and the Assembly. Initially, the Secretary of State was to play a very significant role in overseeing the government's administration. If devolution had been successful, he would have loosened the reins of power, allowing ministers more leeway and control over departmental affairs.

The Northern Ireland Assembly itself was to be a unicameral parliament with around eighty members that would sit for four-year periods. This number was deemed suitable as it would involve maximum participation in the committees between the Executive and all the Assembly members, given the number of departments. Election to the Assembly was conducted under the STV system, and in order to get the Assembly up and running as soon as possible the twelve Westminster constituencies were used instead of drawing up fresh electoral boundaries.

The White Paper included a charter of human rights that safeguarded freedoms of political and religious conscience, enshrining rights to equal benefit and opportunity within society. This aimed to fill the gaps in the Government of Ireland Act of 1920, which legislated against discrimination on religious grounds but failed to protect against discrimination on grounds of political affiliation, and it did not extend to all public bodies, let alone private ones. Under the legislation of 1973, every public authority was required to operate a fair employment policy, and it also offered protection against religious or political discrimination in the use of the Assembly's law-making powers. However, the government stopped short of delivering a formal bill of rights for Northern Ireland, thinking that it might precipitate a call for similar legislation for the rest of the UK.

How close was Sunningdale to the consociational model? The final agreement did contain most of the main elements of Arend Lijphart's consociational model:

1) a power-sharing government with very strong links with its legislature;
2) proportional representation for the Assembly and its respective committees;
3) a mutual veto on the Council of Ireland, and;
4) provisions against political and religious discrimination.

It lacked official provisions for segmental autonomy, proportional representation in the public sector, and security and police reform. More importantly, it was an exclusive accord. Sunningdale was not a precise piece of consociational constitutional engineering. It was a power-sharing agreement designed to create a moderate political centre ground through the isolation of political extremists and the destruction of the old unionist mould.

A BRIDGE TOO FAR?

This section explains how the two governments came to sign the Sunningdale Agreement and how Protestant opposition succeeded in bringing about its collapse through the Ulster Workers' Council (UWC) strike.

Towards agreement

In October 1972 the British government published a document called *The Future of Northern Ireland*.[4] This discussion paper set out its position on Northern Ireland and served as a precursor to the White Paper and the Northern Ireland Assembly Act, 1973.[5] London thereby signalled to Dublin that it was prepared to legislate for a Council of Ireland and had come to recognise the Republic's right to have a formal political role in the affairs of Northern Ireland, with a power-sharing formula based on the Lebanese model.[6] The deteriorating security situation marked a turning point for the two states and the British Prime Minister Edward Heath's stipulation that 'the quicker we get [Jack] Lynch here, the better' was a far cry from his earlier position that Northern Ireland was none of the Irish Taoiseach's business.[7] Lynch responded positively by closing down Provisional Sinn Féin's headquarters in Dublin, arresting some of its leaders and introducing tough security measures to combat terrorism. Subsequently, on 24 November, Lynch met Heath in London to voice his approval for the British government's constitutional proposals.

However, Lynch's government soon collapsed and, after a general election on 28 February, Fine Gael's leader, Liam Cosgrave, formed a Fine Gael/Labour coalition with a cabinet including Garret FitzGerald, Conor Cruise O'Brien and Brendan Corish. Days later, in a symbolic attempt to ease the unionist community's anxiety over Irish involvement, Heath held a 'border poll', offering a straight choice between the maintenance of the union and a united Ireland (unlike in 1998, no subsequent referendum took place in the Republic). Of the 57 per cent of voters who turned out, 97.8 per cent favoured the maintenance of Northern Ireland's constitutional position within the UK. The low turnout was due to the SDLP's boycott of the referendum, on the grounds that it was not on an all-Ireland basis.

The British government then released its White Paper, which met with the cautious support of Brian Faulkner and other moderate Unionists politicians. However, Vanguard leader William Craig, Ian Paisley and other Unionist leaders immediately rejected the proposals, in the firm belief that their resistance could force a return to the old Stormont government.[8] The jostling for position had begun within the Unionist camp, and the fate of former Unionist Prime Minister of Northern Ireland, Captain Terence O'Neill,[9] was fresh in the minds of all those who had a stake in the upcoming Assembly elections. However, against the advice of many in the pro-Agreement camp, the British government first held district council elections by STV, in which anti-Agreement Unionists performed particularly well. The old Unionist Party of the Stormont era had fragmented into factions (and also spawned independents).[10] The majority of these could not be counted upon by Faulkner to back a deal that included a strong Council of Ireland and lacked tough security powers. Regaining security provisions was as important to many Unionist leaders as was their rejection of a Council of Ireland.[11] However, before the 1973 Assembly elections Faulkner had asked all Official Unionist candidates to sign up to his policies, unnecessarily forcing a *de facto* split into two camps of 'pledged' and 'unpledged' Unionists.[12]

On 30 May the district council elections saw the anti-White Paper Unionists perform very well, while the NILP was obliterated as a result of the SDLP's strong performance. In the Assembly elections, which followed on 28 June, the STV system again failed to facilitate cross-community support for the centrist pro-Agreement parties, the anti-Agreement Unionists picked up twenty-six seats to Faulkner's twenty-four. The spread of anti-Agreement Unionism harmed the STV system, as the list of Unionists could not have been more confusing and many voters failed to award pro-Agreement candidates their lower-preference votes. The APNI and the NILP again performed poorly, whereas the SDLP firmly established itself as the main nationalist party, winning nineteen seats with 22.1 per cent of the poll.[13]

Heath misinterpreted Unionist fragmentation as Unionist weakness, while correctly viewing the SDLP's huge vote as offering a chance to marginalise the influence of the IRA, as nationalist intra-elite competition was weak in comparison to Faulkner's predicament. In meeting most of the SDLP's demands over the Council of Ireland, Heath hoped that it would accept tough security measures against terrorism. Further, Heath's plans were democratically exclusive, as the White Paper aimed to coerce moderate unionism into a power-sharing deal with constitutional nationalists at the expense of all opposition.

Faulkner's position within the unionist community was far from concrete, being dependent upon three things: the British government's capacity to improve the security situation; the issue of 'status' vis-à-vis the Republic; and the creation of a soft landing for the idea of a Council of Ireland. The pro-Agreement parties thus depended on strong support from the British government to sell the accord to their constituencies. However, Heath had made it clear to Faulkner that power-sharing with an Irish dimension was the price that had to be paid to maintain the union.[14] Ironically, support for Faulkner, and the acceptance of a political settlement with nationalists, *was* available from within the Protestant electorate (see Table 5). Yet with the range of anti-Agreement forces pitted against him, Faulkner desperately needed the support of both governments if he was to get it. Given these opinion poll results, the pro-Agreement parties should have pushed for a referendum on power-sharing with an Irish dimension, but the British were not keen on the idea, considering the uncertainty of the result and the complexity of the issue. However, a positive response from the electorate would have considerably strengthened Sunningdale.

The Irish government strongly favoured the proposed power-sharing deal, yet the only voice urging caution regarding the unionist position was Conor Cruise O'Brien's. He argued that shutting the anti-Agreement parties out of the political process would lead to serious political unrest and stressed the dangers of pressing for a strong Irish dimension. However, the Irish government saw no advantage in entering into an agreement that left it with little or no executive power.[15] Cosgrave also understood the danger of excluding the anti-Agreement Unionists, but agreed with Heath that they should not attend Sunningdale. The dominant figure in the cabinet was FitzGerald, who, in line with the SDLP's deputy leader, John Hume, stuck firmly to the nationalist position that they should only support a strong Council of Ireland with executive powers. With hindsight, FitzGerald concedes that O'Brien was 'more nearly right' than the rest of the Irish Cabinet in the run up to, and during, the Sunningdale talks.[16]

The Sunningdale Executive was actually formed only after negotiations at Stormont Castle over the exact nature of its makeup.[17] It was agreed that the Executive would be confirmed before and established after

Sunningdale,[18] but this took place only after Faulkner narrowly won two crucial votes on power-sharing: first within the Unionist Party's Standing Committee, and then in the Ulster Unionist Council (UUC). In the subsequent talks the Secretary of State for Northern Ireland, William Whitelaw, broke the stalemate by devising an executive compromise that gave the Unionists a majority of the eleven ministries, while 'overall domination was negated by the addition of three non-voting departmental heads', two SDLP and one Alliance.[19] The agreed template consisted of six Ulster Unionists, four SDLP members, and one Alliance member, with Faulkner and the SDLP's leader, Gerry Fitt, as Chief and Deputy Chief Executive respectively. These figures bore no proportional relation to the parties' first-preference votes in the Assembly elections, which would have allocated Faulkner's Unionists and the SDLP no more than three seats each.

Faulkner could hardly have entered government in a weaker position: his party was split down the middle and the anti-Agreement Unionists raged at their exclusion from the talks.[20] Critically, Westminster and Dublin failed to shore up strength on the Unionist side of the executive. Consequently, the centre parties were unable to unite the two communities and the bulk of the Unionist elite was poised to oppose any deal before it was even agreed. Whitelaw came to view the divisions within Unionism as the crux of the matter and, with hindsight, admitted that he did not give enough thought to helping Faulkner.[21]

BEFORE THE POINT OF NO RETURN

On 22 November 1973, Northern Ireland's first power-sharing government was formed, and tripartite talks on the Council of Ireland were set to take place on 6 December at Sunningdale in Berkshire. The anti-Agreement Unionist alliance of Craig, Paisley and Harry West had gained momentum, and the exclusive nature of the process handed them the moral high ground to foster Protestant opposition to the Executive. On 29 November Faulkner tried to reassure his supporters by stating that an end to the Republic's territorial claim was a 'prerequisite' to power-sharing,[22] but the anti-Agreement Unionists were in a win-win situation. If they had been invited to Sunningdale, they could have disclosed the nature of the Council of Ireland or disrupted the negotiations. Whitelaw conceded that their exclusion was a mistake and at the last minute invited them to put their arguments to the conference and then leave. They refused, relishing the opportunity to return the government's snub. Thus Paisley's argument that only 'the conference' was inviting them, and that 'constitutionalists who opposed the British government' were shut out of the democratic process, was reinforced.[23]

While the British and Irish governments were attempting to practise a form of coercive consociationalism, they had unwittingly excluded what was to become the majority of Protestant opinion. Before the conference got under way anti-Agreement Unionists voiced their anger, with Vanguard and DUP members launching a physical assault on the pledged Unionists in the chamber.[24]

Against a backdrop of increasing IRA violence and Unionist opposition, the negotiations took place between the British and Irish governments and the three pro-Agreement parties over the weekend of 6–9 December. On the first day of the plenary session Faulkner made it clear that he was going to have trouble selling the Council of Ireland as it stood, only to be reminded by the SDLP that he and the British had already agreed to it.[25] It was the Council's finer details that remained open for discussion. There have been retrospective claims from the SDLP negotiators, Paddy Devlin and Gerry Fitt, that they helped the Unionists to substantially reduce the Irish dimension. However, while Devlin did shorten and compress the list of executive functions from thirteen to eight,[26] the Irish subsequently produced a detailed study on 'the number of civil servants that would have been needed to carry out the list of things in the Sunningdale Agreement, and it ran into thousands', with executive powers that were 'colossal'.[27] By this stage Hume had the support of Cosgrave and FitzGerald who, unopposed by Heath, held that the Council must have significant executive powers. For Faulkner to sell such a deal he needed some trade-off from Dublin on Northern Ireland's constitutional status. The two governments, however, could agree only on parallel statements, beginning with the Republic's position, so that Britain's constitutional declaration on Northern Ireland's status could not be read as implying Dublin's *de jure* constitutional acceptance.

Heath made matters worse by applying pressure on the Unionists at the talks to reach a settlement, having made the mistake of replacing the veteran Whitelaw with a novice in Northern Ireland's affairs, Francis Pym. Initially, it was obvious that the British and Irish governments intended the power-sharing executive to govern Northern Ireland over the heads of the opposition. Therefore the talks went ahead without any last-minute representation from the anti-Agreement unionists, while John Laird and three Assembly members protested outside.[28] Faulkner then pressed for Articles Two and Three of the Irish Constitution to be removed, but this would have required a referendum in the Republic. Further, the British government might have offered concessions to the SDLP over internment and security measures, against the Council of Ireland, yet this would have been unacceptable to all parties. London and Dublin were not prepared for radical security reforms, so there could be no relaxation of internment until republican violence was curbed, while the SDLP could not concede due to pressure from these same republican elements and its own manifesto's commitments on internment.[29]

The talks dragged on, not over the Council of Ireland, but over whether security powers and policing would be tied to it. The SDLP demanded a major policing role for the Council, with Hume arguing that if the SDLP could not support the police it could not sit in government. Countering this, Faulkner claimed that he could not sell an executive without control of policing powers, while Heath remained adamant that he would not devolve security to either body.[30] FitzGerald maintains that the conference ended in agreement only after the SDLP was forced to back down on this, as there was a general consensus at this stage that Faulkner had gained the least from the talks vis-à-vis his constituency.[31]

Sunningdale with its Council of Ireland was agreed and the parties returned to Northern Ireland, with the Executive due to take office at Stormont on New Year's Day 1974. Cracks were appearing in Dublin's bipartisan approach to Sunningdale, however, as Cosgrave came under pressure in the Dáil from Lynch to 'clarify' the Irish government's stance on Northern Ireland's status.[32] Lynch subsequently backed down, giving Sunningdale 'moderate' support, and the Agreement was ratified by a majority of five votes in the Dáil.[33] The Irish government then stated that no change could take place to the status of Northern Ireland without the consent of its majority. This made little impression on the unionist community, as the anti-Agreement leaders declared Sunningdale a Lundy-style sell-out.[34] Hume summed up the atmosphere in the Assembly, pointing out that the opposition had rejected Sunningdale 'out of hand' before it had even been made public.[35] By then the Official Unionist Party had split beyond Faulkner's control and he consequently resigned as leader, having lost, by fifty-three votes, on a crucial motion in the UUC, proposed by West and John Taylor, to reject the proposed all-Ireland Council settlement on 4 January.

On 16 January Faulkner's position in the Executive was further weakened by the Irish Supreme Court's ruling that the government's statement that: 'Northern Ireland could not be reintegrated into the national territory until and unless a majority of the people of Northern Ireland indicated a wish to become part of a united Ireland [was] no more than a statement of policy' (*Boland* v. *An Taoiseach*). The Irish government's stance in the Sunningdale Communiqué merely recognised Northern Ireland's *de facto* position within the UK and therefore did not contradict its *de jure* status as written in the Irish Constitution.[36] Faulkner stated that there could be no ratification of Sunningdale until Dublin publicly cleared up the status issue, but again Cosgrave's weakness was exemplified by his inability to act until Boland's appeal took place.[37]

Heath's decision to hold a general election on 28 February 1974, and Cosgrave's inability to resolve the status issue, indicated that, while the power-sharing executive was a high priority for both governments, the inherent instability of their domestic positions underscored the loose foundations upon which Sunningdale stood. The election handed Faulkner's opposition an excellent opportunity, and the electorate voiced their disdain at both the Council of Ireland and the manner in which Sunningdale had been imposed, thoroughly routing the pro-Agreement candidates at the polls.[38] The anti-Agreement candidates, standing under the rubric of the United Ulster Unionist Council (UUUC) and the slogan 'Dublin is just a Sunningdale away', took eleven of the twelve seats with just over 51 per cent of the vote, and claimed a popular mandate for the rejection of the agreement.[39] Fitt was the only pro-Agreement candidate to hold his seat, as the plurality rule inflicted a humiliating defeat upon the new executive. Moreover, Heath's early election backfired and Harold Wilson formed a Labour government, with Merlyn Rees replacing Pym as Secretary of State for Northern Ireland.

On 4 March Faulkner tried to put Sunningdale on hold by ruling out any further cooperation with Dublin until the status issue had been resolved, while a debate on the 'renegotiation'[40] of the agreement raged on in the Assembly. Consequently, Cosgrave's belated attempt to ease tensions by announcing in the Dáil that 'the factual position of Northern Ireland is that it is within the United Kingdom and my government accepts this as a fact' fell on deaf ears north of the border.[41] Faced with the worst violence in months, Wilson promised tighter security and increases in troop numbers, while Rees embarked upon his 'detention sponsorship scheme', legalising Sinn Féin and the Ulster Volunteer Force (UVF).[42] If Heath's government had sent the terrorists mixed messages, Wilson's looked set to emulate its mistakes. It was short-sighted to legalise these groups after the previous government had excluded constitutional opposition parties from the talks and negotiations. Moreover, while the SDLP welcomed these moves, cracks were appearing within the Executive, as the pledged Unionist, Roy Bradford, opposed the ratification of Sunningdale before an improvement in the security situation.

Then a major challenge to Sunningdale emerged from the unlikely source of the UWC,[43] a twenty-one-man executive under the control of the Ulster Defence Association (UDA) with largely overlapping membership.[44] Paisley, West and Craig were co-opted onto this committee by its leaders to provide political legitimacy to a UDA-based organisation, but only when it looked as if it would become a vehicle of popular Protestant opinion did they throw their full weight behind it.[45] The Council of Ireland still had to be ratified within the Assembly and the UWC leaders told their UUUC representatives that a strike would begin at 6 pm on 14 May to coincide with this crucial vote. If the Executive was to be saved at this late stage, Wilson's government had to back up its rhetoric with action. This meant meeting the anti-Agreement opposition head on and ostensibly taking military action against British strikers – action that a weak Labour government was not well disposed to take. Heath and Cosgrave's governments had failed to manage the transition smoothly, so the strikers' challenge fell to Wilson.

THE ULSTER WORKERS' COUNCIL STRIKE AND THE COLLAPSE OF SUNNINGDALE

Before the strike began the new British government's position on Sunningdale was very unclear. Wilson stated publicly that there would be no negotiation with the UWC and that the Executive was not to be allowed to collapse, in spite of the loyalist extremists.[46] Yet on 25 April the Defence Secretary, Roy Mason, subsequently made a speech suggesting that the troops might be withdrawn due to 'increasing pressure'.[47] On 12 May Wilson made matters worse, announcing to the House of Commons that the security forces had uncovered the IRA's 'scorched earth' doomsday plans concerning Belfast, again heightening tension within the unionist community. Coinciding with this, the IRA released a letter that it claimed had been written by Rees when he was Labour Opposition Spokesman,[48] stating: 'frankly, we have not the faintest desire to stay in Ireland, and the quicker we are out the better'.[49] His government's contradictory messages were not matched with any action that might have broken the anti-Agreement coalition once the strike was under way. The stoppage began with the reduction of electricity output just after the Assembly had passed an amendment endorsing Sunningdale by forty-four votes to twenty-eight. On 15 May the UWC declared a provisional government, stepping up its campaign of roadblocks and widespread disruption across Northern Ireland, with a mixture of blatant intimidation and grass-roots support. Faulkner was powerless to act as all security powers lay with Rees, but it was not obvious from the beginning of the strike exactly how the British Army or the Royal Ulster Constabulary (RUC) had been instructed to act. Rees failed to order them to dismantle the barricades, seeking to avoid confrontation between the security forces and a Protestant population towards whom they clearly felt a good deal of empathy.[50] There is much debate over how the security forces could have tackled the strikers, but almost all political actors agree that if the army and the RUC had been deployed in the first few days, they would have carried out their duties and the strike might well have collapsed.[51]

On 17 May, as the strike was gaining momentum, Craig, West and Barr met Rees at Stormont to warn him that the strike could bring Northern Ireland to its knees if the government did not negotiate with the UWC, but Rees would not budge.[52] This day was to prove the worst in the conflict's history, as bombs exploded in Dublin and Monaghan, causing widespread carnage and a final death toll of 33. The extremely guarded response of the Irish government, blaming republican violence, increased suspicions of Protestant paramilitary involvement.[53] By the end of the first week, with the exception of essential services Northern Ireland had largely ceased to function. With a free hand from the security forces and widespread intimidation, power in Northern Ireland lay firmly in the hands of the UWC. As the strike gripped Northern Ireland support for its political aims grew.

Making matters worse for the Executive, divisions increased, with Bradford calling for a scaling down of the Council of Ireland and the opening of negotiations with the strikers. Some argue that Bradford was already in contact with the UWC,[54] while others insist that the strikers did not trust him enough to accept his overtures.[55] While the SDLP wanted to see tough action taken by the army to break the anti-Agreement alliance, Bradford presented parallels with the civil rights movement, and Paddy Devlin threatened resignation over a Unionist proposal to penalise all Catholics remaining on the 'rent and rates' strike in opposition to internment. Until then the Executive had been relatively stable, the only clashes being over personality between Bradford and Devlin. The government and opposition at Westminster were also at odds, with Wilson coming under fire for being seen on the one hand to have supported the strikes that brought down Heath's government, while on the other claiming that the UWC were fascists.[56] Wilson retorted that the UWC strike belonged in the seventeenth century and that not only was it 'a political strike, it was a sectarian strike'.[57]

The next day Faulkner attempted to renegotiate the Agreement with a watering down of the Council of Ireland and a delay in its executive functions until after Northern Ireland's next Assembly elections. While some SDLP leaders had joined the Executive only because it entailed power-sharing with an Irish dimension, the Unionists managed to persuade them to weaken its powers and announce a 're-phasing' of the Council, which Dublin also accepted.[58] The SDLP Assembly members rejected this by eleven votes before Rees's deputy, Stanley Orme, convinced them that without this concession there would be no Council of Ireland at all.[59] The Executive hung on, but the UWC, whose power was now indisputable, rejected re-phasing, with Paisley contemptuously labelling it Sunningdale 'in two spoonfuls' rather than one.[60]

In another series of counter-productive moves the British published the *Law Commission Report*, at a time when its impact would be negligible, and Rees launched a strong attack on Paisley at Westminster, labelling him 'a democrat here, but a demagogue in Northern Ireland'.[61] Meanwhile, Cosgrave urged London to act with the army to break the strikers as soon as possible, while Wilson and Rees issued confused and contradictory statements about what they were doing to restore services and security. Heath said that he would have acted early to break the strike, but, given Wilson's stalling and confusion, it seems likely that he never intended to attempt military action against the UWC.[62]

On 24 May Faulkner, Fitt and APNI's leader, Oliver Napier, met Wilson, Rees and Mason at Chequers to plead that decisive action against the strike was the only way to save the Sunningdale Agreement. Wilson sensed the desperation of the three party leaders and, having questioned them about internal executive splits, sent them back to Belfast reassured that the government should, and would, use force to protect essential services and break the strike.[63] However, this interpretation of the meeting was not shared at Westminster, where civil servants stated that Wilson merely said that the army should be used to protect essential services 'if necessary'.[64] Faulkner, Fitt and Napier had failed to notice Wilson's questioning over internal splits and, as they waited for action to be taken, Rees informed Wilson that without it the Executive would collapse during the next couple of days.[65] Misled by Wilson, the party leaders returned to the Executive cheered by his pledges, but the Prime Minister had decided it should be left to its fate, as the strength of the UWC made its collapse inevitable.[66] If the strikers lacked political or moral support by this stage, from any section of the Protestant population, Wilson's 'arrogant and self-indulgent'[67] speech the following day delivered it when he accused the loyalist population of 'sponging on Westminster and British democracy'.[68] Barr remarked sardonically that Wilson should be made an honorary member of the UWC.[69]

Many argue that the Executive constantly threatened to implode,[70] yet it remained very stable up until the strike when SDLP ministers John Hume and Austin Currie threatened to resign if the army did not wrest oil depots and petrol points from the UWC.[71] They got their way, but on 28 May Faulkner's backbenchers informed him that he could no longer rely on their support, handing those opposed to the Executive a majority in the Assembly. Inevitably, Faulkner told the Executive that the only option left was to negotiate with the strikers, as Bradford had been arguing. The two Assembly members from the Alliance Party backed him, but the SDLP, who could not, refused, and Faulkner tendered his resignation as Chief Executive to Rees, having also failed to convince him to negotiate with the strikers. The unionist movement against the Council of Ireland had brought Northern Ireland to its knees, humiliating the British government and consigning the Sunningdale Agreement to history.

THE CASE FOR POWER-SHARING

As should be clear from the preceding summary, conditions for power-sharing in Northern Ireland were less than favourable in the early 1970s.

However, an assessment of survey data available from the time points strongly to the possibility of a positive outcome. The data are unfortunately limited by size and reliability, but merging the sources provides a useful framework for an overall analysis.

Opinion in the nationalist community in 1973 on Northern Ireland's future constitutional position was far more divided than within unionism (see Table 1). An amalgamation of responses from a *Fortnight* opinion poll conducted in April shows 55 per cent of Catholics favoured 'some' form of an Irish dimension in government with their first preferences, and 50 per cent with their second.[72] While only 12 per cent of Catholics expressed a preference for integration with the Republic as their first choice, with 36 per cent opting for a 'New Ireland' as their first preference and 15 per cent as their second, some substantial Irish dimension was clearly necessary if the SDLP was to deliver on its manifesto pledges.[73] However, it was certainly not in a position where it had to appear ultra-nationalist in order to electorally outflank militant republicanism within the Catholic community.[74] Only 3 per cent more Catholics polled expressed a first preference for integration with the Republic than they did with Britain. Furthermore, a very large number of Catholics chose 'don't know' – 18 per cent and 28 per cent – with their first and second choices, respectively.

On the unionist side, the Protestant population was very clear about its constitutional aspirations, with almost no preference being shown for any direct Irish influence in the government of Northern Ireland. Naturally, this constrained unionist leaders where the Irish dimension was concerned, as 39 per cent of Protestant first and second preferences opted for full integration within the UK, preferring to be governed completely by Westminster rather than have any influence from Dublin or regional autonomy. However, 45 per cent and 41 per cent expressed a preference for regional government within the UK, and only 6 per cent and 5 per cent, for an independent dominion of Ulster, with their first and second choices respectively. This suggests that a majority might have

TABLE 1: PUBLIC ATTITUDES TO NORTHERN IRELAND'S CONSTITUTIONAL POSITION
Question: if you had been given more choice in the border poll, what would your preferences have been from the following? (%)

Northern Ireland's constitutional status	All		Protestants		Catholics	
	1st	2nd	1st	2nd	1st	2nd
Regional government within the UK	35	30	45	41	17	10
Integration with Britain	28	28	39	39	9	8
New Ireland	14	7	2	2	36	15
Integration with the Republic	4	6	0	1	12	15
Independent dominion of Ulster	4	4	6	5	1	2
Joint rule by Britain and the Republic	3	8	0	1	7	20
Don't know	11	17	7	10	18	28

Source: Poll conducted by CJMR between 2 and 14 May 1973

TABLE 2: Public attitudes to the White Paper
Question: Which attitude to the White Paper would you support? (%)

Attitude	All	Protestants	Catholics
Try to make them work	17	13	23
Give them a try	39	37	41
Try and get them changed a bit and then make them work	28	36	14
Don't mind whether they succeed or fail	10	9	11
Try to make them fail	5	5	5
Try to make them fail by strikes and violence	3	2	4

Source: Poll conducted by CJMR between 2 and 14 May 1973

TABLE 3: Public attitudes to Executive Power-Sharimg
Question: do you approve of power within the Executive being shared by parties representing the Protestant and Catholic communities? (%)

	Protestants	Catholics	Others
Approve strongly	28	78	33
Just approve	38	16	67
Neither/Don't know	13	5	0
Just disapprove	9	1	11
Disapprove strongly	13	1	0

Source: NOP survey conducted between 31 March and 7 April from a random sample of the Northern Ireland electoral register, which proved to be quite unreliable, with only 979 of 2000 interviews completed (49 per cent). Of those interviewed 68 per cent were Protestant and 31 per cent were Catholic, thus slightly over-representing Protestant adults. Results were published in the *Belfast Telegraph*, 18 May 1974.

accepted some Irish dimension in a devolved government in order to maintain the union. Yet, in the absence of a clear unionist component for a concurrent majority supporting power-sharing, exactly how much influence they would be prepared to accept was the question every unionist leader had to consider during the Sunningdale negotiations.

Table 5 illustrates the attitudes of the population towards power-sharing. Unfortunately, this was the only relevant survey conducted at the time and it was heavily loaded in favour of a positive response. It shows only 7 per cent of Protestants wishing for the failure of the White Paper in comparison with 76 per cent, who were at least prepared to negotiate and try to make it work. However, the Assembly elections suggest that more than three quarters of Protestant voters did not support Faulkner or the White Paper's proposals at that time. Further, from this survey it appears that the only major difference of opinion on the White Paper between the two communities was that a lot more Protestants (36 per cent) than Catholics (14 per cent) preferred to have it altered and then try to make it work.

However, the results of an NOP survey conducted shortly before the collapse of the Executive are more evenly balanced (see Table 3). This showed a majority in both communities approving of executive power-sharing, with Protestant and Catholic approval rates of 66 per cent and

TABLE 4: Public attitudes to the Northern Ireland Assembly
Question: Do you agree or disagree that the present Northern Ireland Assembly should be given a chance
to govern Northern Ireland? (%)

	Protestants	Catholics	Others
Agree strongly	27	67	33
Just agree	32	23	33
Neither/don't know	17	5	22
Just disagree	7	1	11
Disagree strongly	17	3	11

Source: NOP survey conducted between 31 March and 7 April 1974.

94 per cent respectively, giving an overall approval rate of 80 per cent
The high Protestant approval rate here is also interesting, as the inclusion
of parties representing Catholic communities implicitly acknowledges
some acceptance of anti-union parties such as the SDLP. Further, 69 per
cent of respondents thought that Northern Ireland's Assembly should be
given a chance to govern, with just 24 per cent of Protestants and 4 per
cent of Catholics disagreeing (see Table 4). This gives the impression that
a solid majority of Protestants – around 60 per cent – found power-
sharing and the Executive acceptable. Interestingly, east of the Bann only
33 per cent 'agreed strongly' that the Executive should be given a chance
to govern compared with 50 per cent in the west, underlining the thesis

TABLE 5
Public Acceptance of Power-Sharing in Northern Ireland in the 1970s (%)

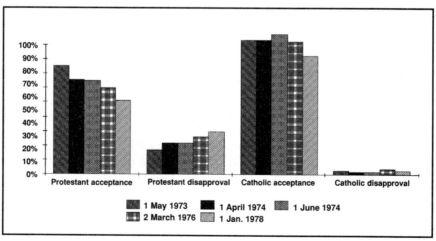

Source: 2–14 May 1973, CJMR; 30 March–7 April 1974, NOP Market Research; 1–4 June,
         ORC quota sample with 640 respondents for ITN; 4–10 March 1976, NOP Market
         Research survey for the BBC (quota sample with 1,007 respondents used, as random
         electoral sample in 1974 proved unreliable), *Belfast Telegraph*, 19 March 1976;
         3–10 January 1978, ORC quota sample with 1,009 respondents conducted for Ulster
         Television.

that the redoubts of majority rule or anti-Agreement unionism were found in Antrim, North Down and North Armagh.[75]

Weight is added to these figures by looking at public attitudes to power-sharing throughout the 1970s (see Table 5). From the three surveys conducted before, during and after Sunningdale, there was a median of 69 per cent of Protestants accepting some form of power-sharing, and there was an overall average of 63.5 per cent throughout the 1970s. Catholic attitudes to power-sharing were almost static during that decade, with a median acceptance rate of 92.4 per cent. It appears from these figures that less than a quarter of Protestants disapproved of power-sharing in principle, a median of 23.4 per cent. However, a rather high average of around 13 per cent replied 'don't know'.

Accordingly, while the statistical data from this period are far from perfect, it is safe to conclude that there was a majority in both communities, before and after the Sunningdale Agreement, that accepted the concept of some form of power-sharing. This adds considerable weight to the argument that Protestant intransigence was top-heavy and that the unionist elite was not proportionately representative of its electorate.

In stark contrast was the level of Protestant support for a Council of Ireland: a clear majority of Protestants thought it a bad idea. With only 26 per cent regarding it as a good idea and 19 per cent unsure, it was always going to be difficult to sell such an idea to the unionist electorate as part of a power-sharing deal.[76] Overall, there was no concurrent majority in Northern Ireland supporting the whole of the power-sharing arrangement, but there were consistent majorities in both communities that at least accepted some form of power-sharing government between Protestants and Catholics.

To conclude, there was a political elite in the nationalist community that was insistent on a strong Council of Ireland, while there was a majority of the unionist political elite that was largely opposed to power-sharing, some of whom were convinced they could win Stormont back with concessions. Both were well ahead of their constituencies in terms of what they could or could not accept, and their actions and motives tipped the internal balance of the power-sharing experiment. It was the rejection of Sunningdale on these terms that drew the public's attitudes closer to theirs and consequently made any future deal even harder to come by. In 1974 the bulk of the unionist elite, believing that it could regain Stormont, was well ahead of its constituency in terms of its opposition to accepting the concept of power-sharing with constitutional nationalists. There was, however, far from sufficient anti-power-sharing sentiment in the unionist or nationalist communities in 1974 to guarantee the outright failure of the Agreement (see Table 3). The Protestant elite's and the loyalist paramilitary leaders' resistance to power-sharing was not matched by their electorate's: this is borne out

by the polling data showing a concurrent majority of Protestants accepting the concept of power-sharing throughout the 1970s (see Table 5). The
irony of this is that, twenty-five years later, the bulk of the unionist elite,
including most of those purporting to be opposed, accepted that power-
sharing with constitutional nationalists and republicans was unavoidable,
while a majority of its constituency did not.

EXPLAINING THE FAILURE OF SUNNINGDALE

Anglo-Irish frailties

Sunningdale has been both historically neglected and viewed somewhat
in isolation from events in Northern Ireland over the past thirty years.
Sunningdale was viewed as being fatally flawed and doomed to failure.
Because of the failure of power-sharing in 1974, many British and Irish
historians have overlooked Sunningdale's significance as the event that
marked the first step in the current Anglo-Irish peace process.

One school of thought, 'civic society' or 'integrationist', questions the
suitability of the consociational agreements such as Sunningdale for conflict regulation in Northern Ireland. Paul Dixon argues that Northern
Ireland's political elites 'generally lack the ability to bring their supporters with them towards a political settlement'; that 'there is little evidence
to suggest that on constitutional questions the political elites are unrepresentative of their voters'; and that 'the reformist civic society approach
appears to offer a way out of the current impasse by creating an environment in which accommodation might be possible'.[77] This thesis is
incorrect on three counts. First, Sunningdale collapsed because a significant element of the unionist elite lacked the will, rather than the ability,
to negotiate a political settlement with nationalists. Second, the majority
of the unionist elite was quite significantly unrepresentative of its electorate in 1973–74 on the constitutional issue of power-sharing (see Table
5). Third, it was because the civic society model, and all other prescrip-
tions, had failed to offer any credible solution to the conflict that the
Sunningdale model came to be tried again in the 1990s.

Others criticise Sunningdale for its inherent ambiguities, which
enabled the participating political parties to make paradoxical interpretations of the agreement and thereby sell it to their respective electorates.[78] Yet if the White Paper had not been composed in such a way,
the Sunningdale talks would never even have occurred. In fact, it is taken
for granted today that constructive ambiguities are a prerequisite for the
successful negotiation of consociational agreements in divided societies.
Brendan O'Duffy argues that the Sunningdale Agreement was 'fundamentally flawed because it did not address the competing claims to sovereignty by the British and Irish states'.[79] However, while Articles Two

and Three of the Irish Constitution, and Section 75 of the Government of Ireland Act, 1920, were not up for negotiation, it was the Sunningdale period that saw both the British and the Irish governments come out of their mutual constitutional denial and begin working together towards regulating Northern Ireland's conflict, with an emphasis on consent.[80] While little time had passed since Heath told Lynch that the North was none of his business, enough violence had occurred by the time of the implementation of direct rule in 1972 to alert British minds to the gravity of the security situation and the necessity of Irish assistance in containing the conflict.

This was when the principle of consent first came to be recognised by both governments as the key to any regulation. It has remained so until today. Britain realised that it needed the consent of the nationalist community, with the backing of Dublin, to stabilise government in Northern Ireland. For its part, the Irish government recognised that the consent of the unionists would be required for any change in Northern Ireland's constitutional status. Thus, Britain was recognising that Dublin had a role to play in Northern Ireland, while, in contradiction to its Constitution, Ireland was accepting its status as part of the UK until a majority there wished otherwise. The problem was that neither government was politically strong enough to act on such thinking at that time. An agreement such as Sunningdale needed intergovernmental political synchronisation, a deep understanding of the issues and subtleties of the situation, and time. Critically, Anglo-Irish relations in the early 1970s lacked all three things. First, Northern Ireland looked to be on the brink of civil war in 1973–74 and, given that both governments' primary concern was security, time was simply not available. In essence, the Sunningdale Agreement was rushed, leaving nobody prepared for, or even knowing what to expect from, its political fallout. Second, Anglo-Irish relations were at a rudimentary stage, and their political coordination lacked focus, unity of purpose and direction. Third, an advanced understanding of the complexities of the conflict was not reached by either administration. On the contrary, both Dublin and London had been relatively isolated from Northern Ireland's politics until the rise of the civil rights movement in 1969.

Sunningdale was nonetheless necessary for an Anglo-Irish conditioning of opinion on the issues of consent, status and power-sharing, in both the nationalist and unionist populations. It is often said that it was before its time, but it had to happen before things could progress between Britain and Ireland. So, in many ways, Sunningdale was the beginning of a new Anglo-Irish relationship, which began to deal with the bitterness emanating from British withdrawal, the Irish Civil War and Irish neutrality in the Second World War. While Sunningdale failed, it illustrated the potential for something to be done within an Anglo-Irish framework and laid the foundations for any future settlement. In this it highlighted what the Taoiseach, Albert Reynolds, and the British Prime Minister, John Major, came to realise in the 1990s: that such an agreement could not easily be created and maintained in the face of both loyalist and republican violence. While the 'ceasefires first' mentality was still a long way off, it indicated the long-term problems of imposing an exclusive settlement within a democracy. The security-centred view of bolstering the moderates and isolating the extremists, from both London and Dublin, meant that such thinking and policy were well ahead of Sunningdale.

The 'status' issue further exemplified the precarious nature of Brian Faulkner's position. The incapability of the governments to even come up with a set of ambiguous words that they could both put their names to and issue as a joint statement illustrated their inability to fully engage in this process together at such a time. Consequently, it proved very difficult for Faulkner to tell unionists that the Irish government recognised Northern Ireland as part of the UK when it failed to make any movement on Articles Two and Three. Such questions needed to be addressed well in advance of negotiations. This highlights the rushed nature of Sunningdale and the weakness of Anglo-Irish relations.

Just as the Irish government failed to offer Faulkner a *quid pro quo* on these issues vis-à-vis the Council of Ireland, Edward Heath could not grant the Executive the security provisions it needed to consolidate its position at home. The Irish view was that its acceptance of the issue of consent was implicit in Sunningdale – this was its *quid pro quo* – whereas Heath's primary focus was on maintaining security and protecting Britain's international reputation. This amounted to keeping all security powers from any devolved government, certainly in the short to medium term. It should be remembered that direct rule in 1972 had partly been a consequence of Faulkner's refusal to carry on governing without security powers. This issue remained the main sticking point between the Official Unionist leader and Heath at Sunningdale, not the all-Ireland institutions. Faulkner, correctly, viewed the devolution of security provisions as fundamental to Sunningdale's survival, for his Executive appeared politically lame from the start of the strike, as it had no power whatsoever to deal with the crisis. It was Heath's intransigence on this issue, combined with Hume's untimely pressure for a joint policing authority, that led Sunningdale to drag on for so long.

Heath's overconfidence was exemplified by his removal of Whitelaw to London before the Sunningdale conference began. Whitelaw's mediation had been crucial to the process. He of all people had a handle on where the equilibrium lay and replacing him was like switching jockeys in the middle of a race. The direct consequence of Whitelaw's removal was that Heath took full control at Sunningdale, with the Permanent Under-Secretary, Sir Frank Cooper, at his side, leaving Francis Pym a mere bystander. Sir Ken Bloomfield contends that Whitelaw was 'just the man to realise that Northern Ireland situations were not black and white, they were often rather grey, but on the other hand, if ever there was a black-and-white man, it was Heath'.[81]

Despite the collapse of Sunningdale it was this agreement, and not the AIA, that was the first signal to both communities that the British were prepared to regulate Northern Ireland over the heads of unionists and to create an all-Ireland framework within which to do so. The success of the UWC strike prevented many Unionists from seeing that until after 1985. On the Irish side, Liam Cosgrave had managed to establish a joint approach with Fianna Fáil towards the Sunningdale negotiations, securing Jack Lynch's full understanding and support for what he was trying to achieve.[82] The question was to what extent the rest of Lynch's party accepted the consent principle, and whether any movement or commitment could be expected from them regarding Articles Two and Three. Like the British Conservative Party, Fianna Fáil was the party best placed to deliver constitutional changes. Moreover, Cosgrave's coalition made no serious moves on the issue for fear of losing a referendum and then office.

While Garrett FitzGerald contends that he was unsure of whether Lynch could have delivered constitutional change, he claims that the Fianna Fáil leader did offer to support the government on such action, so the Irish 'may have missed an opportunity there'.[83] Further, Heath maintains that when he met Cosgrave at Baldonnell in September 1973 the Taoiseach was prepared to change the Irish Constitution, only to subsequently 'come back and withdraw his agreement'.[84] It may well have been considered, but the outcome of a constitutional referendum would have been very uncertain for Cosgrave, as would the strength of the opposition from some quarters of Fianna Fáil. It would have been high-risk politics for Lynch if he had still been Taoiseach, never mind Cosgrave, but this issue ultimately had the potential to take the wind out of the UUUC's sails. As on so many other critical issues at Sunningdale, the choreography was misjudged. In a survey of the Republic's electorate, conducted for Radio Telefís Éireann (RTÉ) by the Market Research Bureau of Ireland in October 1974, only 11 per cent said that they would vote to 'delete' Articles Two and Three of the Constitution. The word 'delete', however, was never going to be on anyone's lips in the Republic.

The Irish delegates at Sunningdale, especially FitzGerald, seemed to totally underestimate the weakness of Faulkner's position; if they did not, they certainly failed to act on it. Some of the blame here lies with Faulkner and Cosgrave, as they had excellent relations, and thus many opportunities to assess and clarify their respective positions. Crucially, the Irish stance on a Council of Ireland with executive functions was non-negotiable at Sunningdale,[85] since the Irish cabinet had agreed in advance on exactly what it was going to accept on the main issues, leaving no leeway for further negotiation on extradition, status or the all-Ireland executive powers. It appeared that its bottom line was the SDLP's bottom line, which was a very unsatisfactory position for a sovereign government to be in, especially since power-sharing itself was such a leap forward for nationalism and, in fact, security was their primary concern. Instead of attempting to moderate the SDLP's position to achieve a balance that could be acceptable to both nationalism and unionism, the Irish government simply accepted it. If it had not taken its cue from Hume, it would have done well to accept an advisory council, granting Dublin an initially limited role in Northern Ireland's affairs. FitzGerald readily admits that he and his colleagues 'pushed for too much' and 'underestimated the unionist negative position'.[86] Hume contends that the SDLP's influence over Dublin's policy on the North 'in those days was total'.[87] This was almost the opposite of the British government's position, as the last group Heath took his cues from was the Unionist politicians. It was very clear that Heath was negotiating primarily for British interests and, if those did not coincide with Unionist interests, then the Unionists would have to move. Lord Butler recalls that 'the real negotiations were much more between Heath and Hume than they were with Cosgrave', as the Prime Minister was very much 'beguiled' by the young SDLP men.[88]

Negotiations

Sunningdale is remembered as the moment when some of Northern Ireland's parties agreed to form a power-sharing government, yet almost all the substantial issues had been agreed in principle during Whitelaw's 'castle talks'. One reason for this was the SDLP's need for the Unionists to commit themselves to an internal settlement with an Irish dimension. Another was Faulkner's requirement for a Unionist majority on the executive. It was at these talks that the Unionist leader hastily made the historic decision to accept the idea of a Council of Ireland with executive functions. This left him unable to fully negotiate the issue with the Irish government at Sunningdale. Crucially, this was not seen as 'a very big issue' by Faulkner or his liberal team at this stage, so instead of pushing for it to be a consultative advisory body, at least in the short to medium term, they accepted it with executive powers.[89] Faulkner may well have thought at the time that the Irish would deliver something tangible on consent or status in return. Yet accept it he did, correctly believing that it needed a unionist mandate to function and was consequently under their decisive influence.

Instead, Faulkner's fixation in the Castle Talks was on achieving a Unionist majority of one on the executive. On the strength of their performance in the Assembly election, Faulkner's Unionists did not deserve anything like this proportion. He was consequently pushed to concede many of the SDLP's demands on the Council of Ireland in return.

However, such a concession on executive functions was avoidable, as the SDLP and the Alliance Party were well compensated with non-voting ministers in the government. Moreover, Faulkner could not have faced the UUC without a Unionist majority and, as he saw it, the issue of a Council of Ireland was a red herring, since its executive decision-making powers were subject to a fail-safe dual North–South veto, while his majority on the Executive gave the unionists a further *de facto* veto on domestic decisions. With this internal and external safety net, Faulkner felt confident that the unionist population would accept it. In fairness to Faulkner, if he had accepted anything less than a majority on the Executive and managed to restrain the Council of Ireland to advisory functions, the issue of an assembly with 'no unionist majority', or a possible 'nationalist majority' or 'nationalist Chief Executive', would probably have become the tool that the anti-Agreement Unionists used to break the accord. No Unionist leader could have agreed this anyway, but would such an argument have been as emotive or as successful in rousing the Protestant population against the Executive as the 'Dublin is just a Sunningdale away' rhetoric? There is little doubt that it was the all-Ireland framework of an unknown quantity that unionists were most frightened of, certainly compared to the concept of accepting power-sharing with nationalists.

Yet on the question of intercommunal power-sharing Whitelaw's proposals were ill conceived, in that they failed to provide any political re-entry point for anti-Agreement Unionists. There was no empty seat on the Executive for the likes of Craig, Paisley or West, seats that unionism demographically deserved. Arguably, this stemmed from the fear that Craig or Paisley might win a general election and take power, something the British government was not prepared to contemplate.[90] This policy did not just exclude unionists, as neither government envisaged bringing on board the IRA, which firmly believed that it could remove the British by force: bringing down Sunningdale was also the main aim of the IRA at the time.[91]

This left Sunningdale a constitutionally exclusive agreement, and not particularly democratic or consociational. At the castle talks, when proposals to allow a way back for the other parties were floated by Sir Ken Bloomfield, the pro-Agreement parties rejected them outright.[92] Consequently, after the general election in February 1974 the anti-Agreement Unionists could convincingly argue that the majority of voters in Northern Ireland were electorally excluded from its democratic government. While it was a Westminster election, it was widely perceived as a referendum on the Agreement and its results severely undermined the Executive's legitimacy.

For unionists the problem with the Council of Ireland was not the Council itself, it was the symbolism of the remaining six counties of

Ulster being drawn back into the all-Ireland framework of 1920, and the negative effect to which the anti-Agreement Unionists were able to successfully wield this psychological threat. Ironically, while this was seen as being a vehicle towards a united Ireland, constitutionally it was nothing of the sort and, as it stood, it could become no such thing. Unanimity on the council was a prerequisite for executive decisions to be enacted on an all-Ireland basis, since a dual veto underpinned the body's functions. However, the Council could travel in only one direction, and would ultimately have brought Northern Ireland and the Republic much closer on many issues. Unlike the the Council of the Isles under the GFA it contained no British involvement, furthering the argument that it was a one-way street. The British Foreign Office was keen to cautiously explore the idea of a tripartite council, something similar to the GFA's Council of the Isles, but Northern Ireland's top civil servants dismissed it, arguing that it was not the right time and work was already being done in this direction.[93] Undoubtedly this could have helped in the wrangle over the Council of Ireland and it remains unclear as to why it was not pursued.

The leaders of the UWC believed that if the Irish and the SDLP had not pushed so hard for the Council of Ireland, their campaign might not have had the emotional impact necessary to carry off the strike and cause the Agreement to collapse.[94] The Council consequently became their emotional trump card. In addition, while this Irish dimension was essential for the SDLP, that party's subsequent triumphalism, with Hugh Logue talking about the Council being a vehicle trundling through to a united Ireland, damaged the Agreement.[95] On the other hand, the IRA, encouraged by the mixed messages it received from the British, would have rejected any settlement that the SDLP could deliver.[96]

Faulkner's Unionists

Faulkner's unusual decision to demand public 'pledging' to his policies left him with a weak mandate for power-sharing, a party split ahead of the Assembly elections and no strong base from which to promote his strategy.[97] Until then Faulkner had held the centre ground of unionism and was in a strong position vis-à-vis his party. Like David Trimble in 1995, he had taken control of the party as a hardliner and thus initially had the leeway to forge ahead with radical change. However, the former UUP leader, James Molyneaux, contends that Faulkner was a 'new political convert' to the concept of power-sharing, having been convinced by Heath that it was the only way to secure the union.[98] This argument is supported by the fact that in 1971 Faulkner told Heath he would resign before allowing even Gerry Fitt to take a seat in his cabinet.[99] In this conversion he failed to bring the bulk of the Official Unionist Party's hierarchy with him, and who then in turn viewed his weakness as an opportunity to rise to the top of the party.[100] Having brought about the split, Faulkner was forced to proceed with a weakened Assembly team, as many influential Unionist politicians declared themselves 'unpledged'. Bradford was the exception, but his commitment to Faulkner and the Executive was, at best, uncertain.

One of the obvious problems that Faulkner had at Sunningdale was that while he was there on his own, making up around one tenth of the entire delegation, the SDLP and the Irish government accounted for about half of the delegates and were functioning as one negotiating team. To make matters worse for the Unionists, rather than act as a counter-weight to the Irish government Heath in fact pressured and bullied Faulkner's delegation into accepting what was being proposed. While Heath had little time for the Unionists, instead of seeing the weakness of Faulkner's position and bolstering it he took advantage of it and coerced them to concede.

Faulkner's Unionists could have gained advantage at the beginning of the Sunningdale talks by walking out after the Irish broke ranks and informed the media that they had secured the Council of Ireland in advance of any agreement. Faulkner decided against this for three reasons. First, he had already agreed to the Council of Ireland. Second, Heath pressured him into thinking that there was no alternative to the deal being offered. Third, the Irish government had made it clear before the talks that its stance on a Council of Ireland with executive powers was non-negotiable. If Faulkner and his team had walked out pending a renegotiation of some of the agreed issues, then the British and Irish governments would have been left with two options. They could have let the talks collapse, and continued with direct rule and increasing violence, or they could have reconvened the conference, having broken for separate cabinet consultations on a new way forward. The Irish maintain that this was not a possibility, but it is not clear why it was not. The Unionists would also have been supported in this by the Alliance Party, which was deeply sceptical about accepting an agreement with no extradition provisions or legal recognition of Northern Ireland's status from Dublin. Again, Heath bullied the Alliance into submission on these issues, threatening that if it held out it would go down in history as the tiny non-sectarian party that broke the Agreement.[101]

The SDLP

The SDLP were also significantly split at the time of Sunningdale. The division could be seen as being between those more concerned with achieving participation in government and power-sharing – the Belfast labourite socialists such as Fitt and Devlin – and those for whom an Irish dimension with executive powers was a prerequisite for going into a devolved UK assembly – the ideological nationalists such as Hume and

Seamus Mallon. In retrospect the crucial question was whether a Council of Ireland with only advisory or consultative functions would have been acceptable to the SDLP's constituency. Electorally the republican movement offered absolutely no threat to the SDLP's position, which was concrete following its triumph in the Assembly elections.[102] Further, the SDLP had already accepted partition and, while a Council of Ireland was one of its Assembly manifesto commitments, it was not the biggest issue for nationalist voters. Power-sharing was. If it had survived, all the issues that the IRA had hijacked from the civil rights movement could have been addressed, partially undermining support and legitimacy for republican violence within the nationalist community. While republicans argue that the British presence would have ensured the continuation of the armed struggle,[103] its endurance and resilience against a joint Anglo-Irish security policy with SDLP support would have been questionable, as the republicans 'were on their knees in 1976–77', even after the failure of Sunningdale.[104] The SDLP probably could therefore have sold an agreement with no executive powers for the Council of Ireland.

From a historical perspective unionists are likely to ask themselves why the SDLP was not asked to do so. Nationalists would no doubt respond that the SDLP, the Irish and the British must have taken it for granted that Faulkner, having bought into the deal on behalf of unionism, was the man best placed to know whether he could sell it to his constituency. Yet if it had been asked, the SDLP could have sold such an agreement to its constituency without executive powers for the Council of Ireland. Why? First, the agreement provided the SDLP with a role in government that exceeded what many nationalists expected. Second, the SDLP was not restrained by any electoral challenge. Third, given the ideological U-turns that Sinn Féin successfully sold to its constituency in 1998, it seems inconceivable that Sunningdale with a strictly advisory Council of Ireland would have provoked a nationalist backlash strong enough to undermine it. The pressures on the SDLP during the Sunningdale period came from within the party, as opposed to its electoral constituency. The question of whether it was fundamentally a socialist party or a nationalist party had not been fully resolved in 1973, but while the socialists still led the SDLP it was clear that the nationalists drove the political agenda. It was these nationalists who directed Dublin to take such a hard line over the Council of Ireland. However, while the Irish misread the level of unionist opposition on the issue and pushed for too much, they saw no great problem with the all-Ireland bodies, as they were reliant on mutual consent.[105] While Fitt was still the leader of the SDLP, Hume had negotiated strongly, convincing both FitzGerald and Heath of the necessity of a Council of Ireland with executive functions as a prerequisite to any agreement. By the time the SDLP was finally forced to accept a postponement of those functions, the Executive was days away from collapse anyway.

Anti-Agreement unionists

There has been much conjecture over whether the anti-Agreement unionists were against power-sharing with nationalists in principle, a Council of
Ireland or both. T. Hennessy argues that Ian Paisley rejected talks with
Whitelaw because the anti-Agreement unionists were not going to be invited to Sunningdale.[106] While Paisley's DUP was foolish enough to think that
Stormont could be revived and was certainly against power-sharing in
principle, their exclusion overshadowed the impact of their rejection of
the talks. Anti-Agreement unionism in 1998 was full of many of the same
figures who thought that they could regain Stormont and were opposed to
power-sharing with nationalists in principle. In stark contrast, many of
those who opposed Sunningdale because of its all-Ireland provisions were
the same unionists promoting the GFA under David Trimble in 1998, having learned the lessons of Sunningdale.[107] The question of whether
Faulkner could have converted some of the anti-Agreement unionists or
even included some of the Westminster MPs in his team requires reflection. As far as his own party was concerned, Faulkner actually felt that he
had to split the UUP in order to proceed, and in such circumstances he
proved far too willing to allow those with doubts to turn out against him
and his proposals.[108] Unfortunately, no attempt was made to bring the
robust Westminster team on board to strengthen his hand.[109] As for
Vanguard and the DUP, Craig could never have supported Faulkner without Paisley stealing his mantle as the leader of right-wing unionism. The
UUUC was at times tense,[110] but neither the pro-Agreement parties nor the
British government took advantage of their splits. There was a three-way
struggle going on between Craig, Paisley and West over the heart of unionism and which party would emerge victorious. There was always 'a two
and one' situation among them and when the three met talks always broke
down, with each side trying to outwit the others.[111]

The circumstances of Craig's demise at the hands of Paisley in 1977
suggest that he was not against power-sharing in principle.[112] However,
by then it was clear to most unionists that they were not going to get
Stormont back with soft compromises, whereas three years earlier, for
many, it was not. In 1974 the only alternative they saw to Stormont was
a united Ireland, so most of them felt that regaining Stormont was an
imperative.[113] Crucially, unlike Faulkner, unionists such as Craig were not
convinced that the British government had the determination, or the constitutional right under the Act of Union, to replace Stormont. In fact,
both Craig and Paisley even toyed with the idea of independence when
faced with this challenge, so it is safe to conclude that any participation
the anti-Agreement unionists might have had would have been a destructive participation, as their conduct in the Assembly indicated.

Their exclusion was a 'Catch 22' situation for the British government.

It was damned if it let them come on board, as they undoubtedly would have rendered it a farce, and damned if it did not, as it was then essentially saying that a large section of the electorate's opinion was invalid because it constituted an opinion that the government did not share. Crucially, Heath mistakenly believed that if the British could break the unionist mould, create a political centre ground and proceed without the anti-Agreement unionists, then they would be marginalised.[114] This strategy was foolhardy, as eventually it would have to stand the test of an election. When this happened Heath's agreement appeared doomed, with only Fitt holding his seat from the pro-Sunningdale camp. When the politicians returned to Northern Ireland after Sunningdale, Faulkner's Unionists struggled to get their message across, whereas the UUUC, under the charismatic leadership of Craig and Paisley, fought a brilliant campaign. Faulkner did not have their public appeal and failed to convince the unionist electorate of the merits of Sunningdale. The intra-communal elite tensions within unionism were simply far too divisive for him to sell it. Further, many of the events and issues went in the anti-Agreement camp's favour, from the Boland case to the general election in February 1974, from the UWC strike to Wilson's 'spongers' speech. This all took place against a background of consistent IRA bombing and violence, which added strength to the anti-Agreement unionists' argument that the Irish government was fickle on security and constitutionally irredentist. The reason for Heath's rashness was that he saw Sunningdale primarily as a quick fix for the security situation, and as an opportunity to isolate the IRA by joining forces with Dublin and the SDLP, stopping Craig and Paisley in their tracks. Some also question whether Heath, Whitelaw or the British government had any great confidence in the whole power-sharing idea anyway, as they had to be seen to be doing something to quell the upsurge in violence.[115]

The strike

One of the oddest things about the UWC strike was that, while it was a successful coup against Northern Ireland's government, its leaders made no subsequent attempt to replace that government or take any position of power. Moreover, it was not that the British were incapable of successfully taking on the strikers, or that they had lost control over the army: they simply chose not to act. If they had done so, the strike could have been broken in the first couple of days, and if Heath had remained Prime Minister he would certainly have acted. Whitelaw had successfully faced down the republicans with Operation Motorman, while avoiding the dire consequences that were widely predicted, and would readily have done the same against the UWC. The strikers themselves certainly held that opinion and expected a similar response. In forcing the strike they made a desperate effort to bring down an Executive that they feared was becoming established. In fact the strike, and support for it, were only consolidated when no response came to it.

There was precious little support for the strike on 14 May, especially among the Protestant middle classes, but after a week of total political inertia from the British government and paralysis in the Executive the unionist community realised that they might not have to accept Sunningdale after all. Consequently, support for the strike, or at least acceptance of it, rapidly increased. The key historical lesson to be learned here is that the big sea change in unionist opinion came during the strike, not before it, for the reasons outlined above. This is why the strike was called at that time. The vote on Sunningdale was about to be held in the Assembly, its result a foregone conclusion in favour, and the strikers saw their action as a last-ditch attempt to wreck the Executive before it became politically entrenched in both communities' minds.[116]

Merlyn Rees had the power to tackle the strike and, in what many observers regarded as a gross dereliction of duty, totally failed the Executive by not using it. While the army, under Sir Frank King, was anxious not to get involved against the Protestant community, there is no doubt that it would have acted if the government had ordered it to do so. It was, however, 'told not to interfere' – the message was simply: 'Hands off, boys'.[117] If a decisive Secretary of State like Whitelaw, or a tough one like Roy Mason, had acted in the early days, 'then the stoppage would have collapsed'.[118]

However, the strike was not the only event that finished Sunningdale: the general election in February 1974 also played a major role. Wilson taking office did not bode well for the Sunningdale Agreement. With the UUUC sweeping to victory across Northern Ireland, the prospect of Labour maintaining the Executive diminished. After Heath's 'winter of discontent' the new government was even more concerned with security than its predecessor had been. It opted to abandon the Executive when faced with the prospect of taking military action against the strikers.

Wilson had no desire to use the Queen's troops against 'workers' or 'strikers' when his own domestic problems were boiling over. He was also unsure of his ability to deal with the strike, as the British Army, the Ulster Defence Regiment (UDR), the RUC and the civil service in Northern Ireland were as divided over the issues of Sunningdale and its Irish dimension as the politicians and the public were. While they were certainly not all working against the Executive, what they were prepared to do to save it under a Labour government was uncertain. If security powers had been devolved to the Executive, the RUC would have obeyed its orders and the politicians would not have looked so hapless when confronted with disorder. However, even if Wilson or the Executive had attempted to reimpose control over essential services, a few acts of sabotage by the UWC could have rendered all the technicians and soldiers in the country use-less.[119] Ironically, the government had been forewarned by Northern Ireland's top civil servants about the potential disaster of electricity plant sabotage and the need for stand-by generators.[120] Further, Robert Fisk argues that since Ballylumford power station was new the army did know how to run it, as it subsequently ran power stations in Great Britain when there were strikes.[121] Fisk's view, however, is strongly contested by army sources.[122]

It is clear that Wilson felt no great attachment to Sunningdale, as it was not his construction. Whether he confused an insurrection with workers striking is immaterial: he did not see it as being in his vital interests to save the Executive. Instead, he misled it with regard to his intentions and allowed it to collapse of its own accord. He suffered little damage from its collapse, as Sunningdale was Heath's agreement, but if he had supported it and it had subsequently fallen his government's position would have been weakened. He had no personal interest in Northern Ireland and the Anglo-Irish relations that Sunningdale created were frozen until he left office. In terms of the government and the army, Wilson's actions were arguably a dereliction of duty. However, that is a moral judgement, and one that had little impact on events in May 1974. There is of course one question that remains for historians to ponder regarding the UWC strike. It is uncertain what action anti-Agreement unionists would have taken if their strike had been broken by the British state, or even the Northern Ireland Executive.

CONCLUSION

On practical issues the Executive worked very well and, by all accounts, would have succeeded if it had been given time to develop. The strains became apparent when Faulkner lost the UUC vote on the Agreement and resigned his leadership. Without the power of the Official Unionist Party behind him, his position from then on was permanently undermined. Crucially, when it came to the question of suspending the Council of Ireland's functions, the Executive met a serious challenge. While the SDLP members of the Executive realised that it was necessary, they had great trouble convincing the other SDLP members in the Assembly to agree to it. This exemplified one of the core problems of power-sharing in ethnically divided societies. The Executive's members knew what was possible and necessary, having been privy to every stage of the decision-making process, while the Assembly parties were not part of that process, and keeping them on board became extremely difficult in times of crisis. So, while Faulkner had his majority on the Executive, he really could not use the implicit veto anyway, for when a crisis arose consensus was always going to be required as a prerequisite to continuing power-sharing. Ken Bloomfield argues that, even with this veto on the Executive, 'when during the strike it came to a voting situation the very fact that they were divided on the fundamental issue [negotiation with the strikers] meant that the underlying consensus for power-sharing was not there any more'.[123]

There was not a sufficiently strong element of the unionist elite available to support a power-sharing agreement in 1973–74 and the relative disengagement of both the British and Irish governments made it extremely difficult to sustain the Executive's momentum, for it needed consistent and synchronised external support to survive. If there had been a steady engagement between the two governments since 1969, buffered by broad domestic support, then perhaps Sunningdale might have lasted long enough for some of its ideas to become established. The sudden defeat of Sunningdale was a setback for the consociational model as a means of regulating the conflict in the 1970s. Such steady engagement did not really begin until 1973, and the weakness of Anglo-Irish relations, and the security-centred focus of the two governments' approach to conflict regulation, undermined power-sharing from the start. As a majority of Protestants accepted the principle of power-sharing with Catholics, if the British had made a concerted commitment to sustaining it, its chances of survival would have been higher. In the same respect, if the Irish political establishment had successfully engaged itself on the issues of consent, status and constitutional reform, this would have provided a Sunningdale with the balance and structure it required. The parameters of the Agreement were faulty, but Sunningdale provided a learning curve for the two governments to realise that the next agreement had to be constructed from the outside in, in order to prevent the insides from falling out.

In terms of the political climate, the Agreement did not fail due to implementation difficulties or the strength of the anti-Agreement coalition. Its collapse was the result of internal and external elite instability, which enabled unionist intransigence, and republican and loyalist violence, to undermine the peace process. The key difference between 1998 and 1973–74 amounted to coercive inclusive consociationalism and exogenous incentives, as the intra-communal competition was greater within both subcultures in 1998 than it was in 1973–74. In 1998 the British and Irish governments, buffered by paramilitary ceasefires, worked in tandem, making sure that no political segment was excluded from the Agreement in order to square the circle. This was not possible in 1973–74 since the republican movement had barely begun to organise politically, and the anti-Agreement unionists allowed Heath to exclude them by making it obvious that if they had participated in the negotiations they would have disrupted them.

The tools of conflict regulation and the rules of political engagement changed over the following twenty-five years. Preoccupied with marginalising the IRA, Heath used summitry and bullying to coerce Faulkner into an agreement that it should have been clear he could not sell. In 1998 the British and Irish governments used spin-doctoring, joint referendums, public personalities, the media, the civil service and international pressure to sell the GFA to the public. With more than 70 per cent of the North's electorate voting 'Yes' in the referendum, the task of destroying it was considerably tougher for GFA anti-Agreement unionists. The opponents of Sunningdale were in a far stronger position, as their political exclusion granted them the moral high ground and almost every political event worked in their favour. When the Executive's inability to tackle the strike signalled its collapse, many Protestants, who would not usually have supported undemocratic methods, came either to accept, or at least to acquiesce in, the actions of the UWC.

CHAPTER THREE

From containment
to regulation

Question: 'What do Northern Ireland's politicians do when they see light at the end of the tunnel?'
Answer: 'Build more tunnel'.

Anon.

Michael Kerr: 'How did you perceive Thatcher's instincts on Northern Ireland in 1985?'
Lord Butler (Robin Butler): 'Well, her instincts were not to be on the side of the doves, basically. I think she undoubtedly had in her mind the memory of the Sunningdale Agreement and Ted Heath having gone further than the unionists would want. She had to be, as it were, persuaded into the Anglo-Irish Agreement. I think she did accept that some political advance had to be made and, in particular, she felt that getting the cooperation of the Irish government was utterly important to the security operations against terrorism. So she was, as it were, prepared to make some concessions to that, but you could not say that she was enthusiastic about the AIA, she acquiesced in it'.[1]

Following the failure of the Sunningdale Agreement of 1973, Anglo-Irish relations took a downturn and little successful cooperation was achieved between the two governments until Margaret Thatcher's second term as British Prime Minister, which began in 1983. Following the failure of the Constitutional Convention of 1975, the all-party talks in 1979–80, Secretary of State Jim Prior's 'rolling devolution' programme[2] and continued IRA violence, Thatcher signed the AIA[3] with the Taoiseach, Garret FitzGerald, in 1985. Essentially the AIA formally re-engaged the two governments in a process of conflict regulation in Northern Ireland.

This chapter describes how the arduous journey that Britain and Ireland embarked upon in the mid-1980s led to a joint declaration on a framework for a negotiated settlement, which culminated in the signing of the GFA in 1998.[4] While there were many problems and diplomatic slumps between the two states, a concentrated effort developed between London and Dublin, focusing on the need to work together to regulate the conflict. This resulted in an evolving unity of purpose, creating the motivation and incentive for the engagement of the Northern Ireland parties in consociation, and, in turn, an intergovernmental interest in establishing peace in itself. By the time the DSD was signed in 1993[5] the exogenous variables influencing it had finally created an environment where conflict could be successfully managed through a return to the consociational model of government, as envisaged at Sunningdale. In order to illustrate these developments this chapter provides an overview of the AIA, the DSD, the achievement of the republican and loyalist ceasefires, and the three-strand talks process that led to substantive negotiations in October 1997.

RE-ENGAGEMENT: THE ANGLO-IRISH AGREEMENT

On 15 November 1985 Thatcher and FitzGerald signed the AIA, committing their two governments to work closely together on Northern Ireland through a joint ministerial council, with a permanent secretariat at Maryfield, to focus on issues of concern to the nationalist community. This marked a major turning point in British thinking on the conflict, as they returned to accepting the Irish dimension without unionist consent, the constitutional issue that had undermined Sunningdale. While the AIA offered the Irish less influence in the affairs of Northern Ireland than Sunningdale had, the big difference in 1985 was that the British excluded the entire unionist elite from the negotiations.[6]

The agreement formalised the Republic's role in Northern Ireland's affairs, signalling that the two governments could and would work together to regulate the conflict, with or without the consent of Northern Ireland's parties. This Anglo-Irish approach, however, got off to a very poor start. In the Republic Fianna Fáil's leader, Charles Haughey, accused FitzGerald of having a 'pro-partitionist' stance on the North,[7] while in Britain Enoch Powell charged Thatcher with treachery over the agreement.[8] In Northern Ireland the Unionist parties' response was to end all cooperation with the British government, while Sinn Féin also vehemently opposed it. Compared with the strong domestic approval that the AIA gained in Britain and Ireland, it received little support in Northern Ireland outside the SDLP and the Alliance Party.

The AIA sought to develop a framework for the regulation of Northern Ireland's ethnic conflict through what Brendan O'Leary and John McGarry have described as an 'experiment in coercive consociationalism',[9] yet from its outset the accord was beset by a variety of rival interpretations.[10] Some saw it as a minimalist agreement, with the primary purpose of containing conflict to Northern Ireland. Others saw it as the first step towards a spectrum of different significant constitutional possibilities, such as a united Ireland with federal structures, joint sovereignty and, more realistically, an attempt to push the parties towards power-sharing.[11] Whatever their initial intentions, both governments underestimated unionist opposition to it. Thatcher subsequently retreated from its political commitments and viewed it primarily from a security- centred orientation.[12]

When Thatcher began her second term of office in 1983 she displayed a new-found determination to do something about Northern Ireland in the wake of the hunger strikes and continued violence, which had much to do with US perceptions of Britain's mishandling of direct rule.[13] Consequently, serious diplomatic engagement was reopened through the British and Irish civil servants who had kept in regular contact since Sunningdale. Yet the strength of the unionist backlash seriously reduced whatever political reforms Thatcher had envisaged undertaking. She assumed that if Britain conceded a limited role for Dublin in Northern Ireland's affairs, the security situation in the North could be improved through close border cooperation with the Republic.[14] She made the mistake of thinking that unionists would be reassured by the Irish government's concession on 'consent' and its recognition of Northern Ireland's status, which had both been key issues at Sunningdale.[15] While Thatcher clearly wanted to address the conflict in Northern Ireland with the Irish by the mid-1980s, 'the real question now was whether the agreement would result in better security'. In fact, she was pleased that international opinion was very favourable concerning the UK's efforts to broker the agreement, 'most importantly American'.[16] It was clear from 1986 that Thatcher was interested only in the security side of the agreement and in damage limitation vis-à-vis the unionists. From this perspective the AIA was a failure, as the Irish were unable and unwilling to provide the sort of cooperation, in the absence of political reform, that she had envisaged.[17]

Since her negotiation of the AIA was security-based, with the failure of Sunningdale very much in mind, her engagement after the unionist protests lacked enthusiasm from the perspective of conflict regulation: she merely 'acquiesced in it'.[18] However, in signing the AIA the two governments emerged from the mutual denial over Northern Ireland that had shrouded relations in the wake of Sunningdale and, in effect, again began to pool their resources.

Fundamentally, Thatcher's outlook on Northern Ireland was minimalist, in the sense that she was reluctant to engage in a political treaty after having withstood the hunger strikes. However, facing an resurgent IRA terrorist campaign, British civil servants and the Irish government convinced her that the problem could not be solved by security means alone and that some political initiative had to be forthcoming.[19] For the British the *quid pro quo* with the Irish was that they would coordinate security policies, while holding out the future possibility of changing Articles Two and Three of the Irish Constitution, in return for a formal

British declaration that, if a majority of the people of Northern Ireland wished to join the Republic at some future date, then Britain would accept their choice. Therefore, in that sense, the Irish government viewed it as a 'minimalist agreement' as well.[20]

From FitzGerald's perspective, his concern regarding Northern Ireland before the AIA was that Sinn Féin would break through politically as an electoral force and challenge the SDLP, creating a situation that could 'get out of control and threaten the whole island'.[21] The Irish had come to share Thatcher's view that 'it might now be more dangerous to do nothing than to attempt an initiative aimed at stabilising the situation'.[22] On the question of Articles Two and Three, FitzGerald signalled his willingness to push for amendments, having made a linkage between them and 'a substantial package that seemed likely to secure political acceptance by the northern minority, ending the problem of alienation'.[23] He claims, however, that Thatcher ruled out any notion of joint authority or anything that could be construed as a derogation of British sovereignty in Northern Ireland.[24] He argues that the British were actually cool on the idea of changes to the Republic's Constitution and that the 'political problem was being sidelined by an exclusively security-orientated approach'.[25]

The Irish held the same false assumption that bedevilled their predecessors at Sunningdale, believing that if they 'delivered' the nationalists then the British would 'deliver' the unionists. In fact, Dick Spring, who was leader of the Irish Labour Party and a minister in FitzGerald's government at the time of the AIA, now contends that he realised afterwards that the UUP learned more about the formulation of the AIA from the Irish government than they did from the British.[26] Contrary to other unionist sources, Molyneaux claims that he had known about it for the best part of a year, but that he was powerless to do anything about it.[27] Ironically, in brokering the AIA, one of the main problems faced by both the British and the Irish administrations was convincing Thatcher to sign it.[28] In that sense the AIA was a reconstruction of Anglo-Irish relations, something to be built upon that recognised that there would be a return to the Sunningdale approach at some future date. It reset the regional parameters for future Anglo-Irish engagement.

OPENING DIALOGUE

Anglo-Irish relations cooled off considerably when Haughey became Taoiseach for the third time in March 1987, as a result of the bad relations between the two premiers during his previous term in office. Yet much was going on behind the scenes, as both governments slowly responded to the changes occurring within republicanism. There had been a shift in republican tactics emanating from the political victories that Sinn Féin had enjoyed as a result of the hunger strikes. Its leadership began to realise that the IRA's campaign was stunting Sinn Féin's electoral potential and was incapable of achieving a united Ireland. Sinn Féin's leaders, Gerry Adams and Martin McGuinness, then consolidated the new political orientation of the movement by ending its policy of abstention from taking seats in the Dáil, in November 1986.[29] Republicans started to engage politically and this was borne out by their joint strategy of 'the Armalite and the ballot box'.[30]

Sinn Féin's emergence from the cold began in earnest when John Hume started secret talks with Adams. This dialogue eventually resulted in a framework for agreement between the SDLP, Sinn Féin and the Irish government in 1993, and the formation of a pan-nationalist alliance that included Irish America. Much credit must go to Hume for kick-starting a broad process of engagement with republicans at a time when talking to Sinn Féin was publicly off everyone's agenda. In fact, he was also briefly engaged in dialogue with a senior UDA figure, John McMichael, at around the same time, after he had persuaded the UDA that power-sharing was the most realistic way of removing the AIA.[31] O'Leary argues that the AIA had a 'built-in carrot' in that a 'devolved consociational government would reduce the importance of the Intergovernmental Conference and the direct influence of the Irish Government on British policy-making in Northern Ireland'.[32]

Hume began his dialogue with Adams in an attempt to convince him and his colleagues that the traditional reasons for IRA violence, regardless of the past, no longer existed. He put it to Adams that the British no longer held an interest in Ireland and that it was actually IRA violence itself that was impeding their departure.[33] During 1988, Hume and Adams had several meetings, which were subsequently widened to include a number of other Sinn Féin and SDLP leaders. Adams asked Hume to prove what he was saying, and there began a slow process of engagement between Hume and the two governments, and, in turn, Sinn Féin.

By the late 1980s it had become clear to the SDLP leadership that there was a great debate going on within republicanism, stimulated by IRA prisoners, as to the direction the movement should be taking. The IRA itself had realised that it could not deliver 'the knockout punch to the British Army'[34] and consequently had become 'open to persuasion' that its strategy ought to change.[35] Nothing actually came of this initial dialogue but the Hume–Adams channel remained open and by 1990–91 the two leaders were again meeting regularly, with Hume keeping both governments informed of developments.

On the British side the Secretary of State for Northern Ireland, Peter Brooke, attempted to break the AIA stalemate in 1989 by creating a political talks process that included all the constitutional parties. In his public addresses he signalled to the IRA that Britain foresaw no military solution to the conflict, and indicated that it would be 'flexible and imaginative' if the IRA ended its campaign of violence.[36] More significantly, he declared that the government he represented had 'no selfish strategic or economic interest in Northern Ireland'.[37] Adrian Guelke argues that these two speeches 'underlined the significance of external dimensions of the conflict in the formulation of British policy in Northern Ireland'.[38] They led directly to a process where Brooke reopened an existing line of contact between the British government and the IRA. It was widely believed that the British government reactivated the back channel in 1990, as reported by Martin McGuinness when the story broke in 1993.[39] However, a decade later Brooke contests this claim, arguing that he did not actually reopen the back channel until 1991.[40] He claims that he accepted the assertion made by McGuinness at the time of the exposure, but, having subsequently gone through the relevant documentation, realised that it was actually reopened the following year. This suggests that it was not in fact Thatcher who authorised these contacts, as was widely believed,[41] but Major, who had become Prime Minister in November 1990. Major does not allude to this in his autobiography, merely stating that Brooke 'reopened the channel in 1990'.[42]

Haughey had also authorised talks with Sinn Féin in 1988, through his adviser, Martin Mansergh, but broke them off when they failed to make progress.[43] After Reynolds became Taoiseach on 6 February 1992 he quickly picked up the process where Haughey had left off.[44] Dialogue with Sinn Féin was resumed in 1992, by which time republicans were becoming increasingly convinced of Hume's analysis of the conflict: that violence was an impediment to a united Ireland, which in itself could only be brought about through a process of dialogue.[45] Reynolds seized on this initiative, and brought to the process a dynamic of urgency and a willingness to take risks for peace. His instinct was to drag the process out into the open, cutting a very different style from his predecessor, who had been content to take a back seat and let Hume deal with the republicans. Reynolds nurtured the process Hume had started, pushing it forward on the British agenda through his strong relationship with Major, in what led to the DSD.

THE DOWNING STREET DECLARATION

The DSD, signed by Major and Reynolds on 15 December 1993, marked a huge shift in official British policy, from one based on the primacy of exclusive talks aimed at isolating the republican movement to an inclusive process that recognised its potential role in any settlement once it had renounced violence.[46] Such thinking was in direct contrast to the Thatcher years, when Conservative Party policy on Northern Ireland 'probably didn't get much beyond containment of the military threat'.[47] It marked the coming together of the two governments on a path where they began to co-manage a serious attempt to regulate the divide. As O'Leary argues, 'by the end of Thatcher's premiership, and throughout Major's, it had become unthinkable to consider managing Northern Ireland except through the cooperation of the two governments'.[48]

The actual negotiating process began in June 1993, when Reynolds gave the British a document that had many elements of what Hume and Adams had agreed upon during their dialogue. The British refused to negotiate on that basis, as any initiative emanating from the republican camp would have provoked a further unionist backlash.[49] Regarding a joint declaration, the British had already seen documents through Hume and Haughey, and this one was very much along the same lines.[50] While showing interest in this process, Major still preferred to keep the talks going in Northern Ireland at the expense of bringing in Sinn Féin, as he was highly sceptical of Dublin's ability to deliver an IRA ceasefire and of the republican movement's intentions. Reynolds's commitment to this process and the level of trust that developed between the two leaders helped to keep Major on board. The draft thus became a basis for discussion rather than negotiation. Major was certainly as keen to do something about Northern Ireland as his Irish counterpart was, but only if the political circumstances proved favourable.[51] While Hume had been convincing the British that he could lead the nationalist community away from supporting the IRA,[52] Reynolds saw clear potential stemming from his dialogue with republicans. He firmly believed that if they could get a ceasefire first, then they would have the foundations to reignite the flagging all-party talks with the inclusion of Sinn Féin.[53] What he was attempting to do was to convince Sinn Féin that, while the Conservative Party itself was not neutral, the government or state of the Conservatives was, as O'Leary succinctly put it.[54]

The Irish talks with Sinn Féin had been taking place through the mediation of Father Alex Reid from Clonard Monastery on the Falls Road in Belfast. It was around this time that the Catholic Church felt a shift in Sinn Féin's position towards accepting Hume's analysis. Working with Reid was Father Gerry Reynolds, who stressed that by September 1990 'there seemed to be quite a different approach from the republican people'.[55] The IRA was still far from convinced of British neutrality, yet this process was greatly furthered by the internationalisation of the dialogue through the Irish-American lobby and the contacts that it built up with Sinn Féin.[56] It is very difficult to ascertain when or if some seismic shift took place in republican thinking, but around 1993 an obvious change in direction occurred that transformed the dialogue into a vehicle for significant political progress.

The Irish government had begun to convince nationalist leaders that they could change the situation to their advantage from a perspective of political equality within the framework of Northern Ireland. The prospect of political equality was paramount in bringing republicans around to the idea of accepting some form of an internal settlement, as this opened up the whole spectrum of political incentives for them to do so.[57] As a consequence of this republican input the first draft received by the British asserted that they should become persuaders for a united Ireland, a proposition that was swiftly rejected by Major. While the draft was very similar to the one that Hume had previously shown the British, and was very 'green' in political orientation, it became a basis for future negotiation and a position from which the two governments could move forward.[58]

While this was taking place, parallel processes of dialogue between loyalists and the British and Irish governments were developing, aimed at achieving ceasefires and reassuring the paramilitary leaders that no deal had being struck with the IRA behind their backs. However, the politicisation of the loyalist paramilitary groups took a very different form from that of republicanism, as there was no potential for them to become a major political threat to mainstream unionism. The influence of political activists was not pivotal within either the UDA's or the UVF's leadership.[59] In fact, while the IRA had realised that it could not force a British withdrawal from Northern Ireland, the loyalist paramilitaries had successfully stepped up their campaign in the early 1990s and a youthful leadership had taken control of the UDA – one that had very little interest in politics.[60]

Nevertheless, a process developed whereby loyalism came to have confidence in, and offer a contribution to, the DSD. This emerged through the engagement of senior church figures from the unionist community in talks with the British and Irish governments. The Irish government, again through Mansergh, contacted the Reverend Dr Roy Magee, a Presbyterian minister with close contacts to the UDA's inner Ruling Council. They began to discuss how the loyalist community could be brought into the political process and what potential there was for achieving UDA/UVF ceasefires. It was through this channel that loyalists became convinced that the 'consent principle' would be fundamental to any future change in Northern Ireland's constitutional status and would be central in any forthcoming agreement between the two governments.[61]

Six proposals concerning a bill of rights were drafted by the loyalists and became incorporated into the DSD through this channel. Reynolds actually mistook these as conditions that the loyalists were demanding, when in fact they represented what they were willing to concede to nationalism.[62] However, a level of trust developed between the parties to such an extent that members of the Combined Loyalist Military

Command (CLMC) actually went to Dublin for a secret meeting with Reynolds to put their concerns to him in person and, in turn, received his reassurances over consent.[63] Reynolds convinced them that there was going to be an IRA ceasefire and that a parallel place for them existed in the peace process. This mediation lent both symmetry and broad confidence to a process that had very 'green' origins.

Working in the same direction was the Aglican Archbishop, Robin Eames, who delivered assurances to the unionist community from the British and Irish governments that no secret deal had been done with the IRA. He reinforced the significance of the consent principle to Reynolds, and drafted it into the declaration himself.[64] Eames's role also entailed keeping the Ulster Unionists abreast of developments between London and Dublin. This proved crucial to ensuring their silence over the whole process and garnered their implicit approval. The Taoiseach had given Eames the task of weaving unionist passages and language into the first draft of the declaration, thereby providing unionists with some access to the process by properly addressing their positions.

The British Secretary of State for Northern Ireland, Patrick Mayhew, highlighted the UUP leader James Molyneaux's constructive role in the process. He remarked that the highest sign of approval the UUP leader ever gave the government on the joint declaration was to say that 'it would not cause him to expostulate'.[65] This was a UUP that had not found a way out of the cul-de-sac of its anti-AIA campaign, and Molyneaux's leadership epitomised this. In fact, Major was extremely anxious about taking Molyneaux into his confidence over the document, but once he had done so he realised that the UUP leader did not intend to break it. Yet, while Major did keep Molyneaux informed to a certain extent, it appears that he divulged to him as little information as he thought he could get away with.[66]

Major, unlike the Taoiseach, had no leeway or appetite for the sort of risk-taking that Reynolds was suggesting: he was constrained by a weakening domestic position and a cabinet that was extremely sceptical of any agreement that brought about the inclusion of Sinn Féin.[67] However, a level of trust had developed between Major and Reynolds, and their respective governmental apparatuses, to such an extent that it has been suggested that 'their preoccupation was peace in Northern Ireland at almost any cost'.[68] This overestimates the British position. Major often felt that Dublin and Washington were so eager to engage Sinn Féin that 'both sometimes seemed to overlook the existence of the Unionists'.[69] Yet it was this overarching objective that drove Major in particular to switch tracks from the talks process in Northern Ireland to the DSD, in spite of his sceptical cabinet.[70] Whether he truly believed that it would work is something only he knows, but, even with his slim majority in the House of Commons, he was prepared to proceed. While the DSD process complemented the three-stranded talks approach, Major accepted that the two tracks could merge only after ceasefires emanated from the former. Further, the negotiating process over the drafts was not without its difficulties, and British procedure and policy very much favoured a 'slow bicycle race', as opposed to rushing into a situation without a Plan B.[71]

To speed along the process Reynolds was determined to draw in US President Bill Clinton, on the basis of his election pledge regarding a visa for Adams.[72] He saw this as a means of granting Sinn Féin the legitimacy and trust they needed to deliver a ceasefire and bring the republican constituency with them.[73] Reynolds convinced Clinton that if he gave Adams a visa it would rapidly help create the circumstances in which a ceasefire would be forthcoming.[74] This, of course, damaged and changed the dynamics of Anglo-Irish relations somewhat, as did other incidents, such as the exposure of the British back channel with the IRA.[75] Yet, while these incidents added to the considerable suspicion that still existed between the British and Irish governments, they did not divert their focus from the task in hand for long. There is no doubt that the Irish felt that finding a role for the US in the peace process could act as a constraining force on the British, or a form of guarantee on their position. Further, the effect that the pan-nationalist alliance had on Sinn Féin was that when the DSD was finally signed Adams, while refusing to accept it, was very careful not to reject it outright. This marked a firm shift in the republican analysis of British intentions.[76]

The negotiations leading up to the signing of the DSD in December were arduous and fraught with difficulties.[77] The British tried to place an entirely new document on the table for renegotiation at the last minute, while the Irish Department of Foreign Affairs leaked details of a secret plan regarding the future of Northern Ireland to the Irish press,[78] which entailed Britain becoming 'persuaders' for a united Ireland and expanding the AIA.[79] This was largely the British testing how far they could pull the whole agreement back but, equally, it indicated their continuing nervousness over the whole agenda. If it was not a negotiating tactic, as the British claim,[80] then perhaps they truly believed that a lower level of accommodation could actually be reached. Such thinking stemmed from the British view that the Irish were driving the process too fast, expecting Britain to take all the risks,[81] and from the fact that Major needed the UUP to maintain his position as Prime Minister. The UUP's failure to support the government might have resulted in a Labour administration, more predisposed to reach agreement with Dublin, a point that was not lost on the UUP's leadership.[82]

Once signed, the DSD marked a turning point in the political process and established an internationally legitimised political platform for moving Northern Ireland towards a constitutional settlement. While the DSD was a terribly convoluted document and could be interpreted as meaning any number of things to any number of parties, it laid down the parameters and foundations for any future agreement. It compartmentalised the core issues of self-determination, consent and North–South relations, so that when it came to the actual substantive negotiations between the parties they could negotiate the practical issues at hand. Most importantly, the DSD locked the two governments into a process where an interest in the regulation of the conflict had become a defining dynamic in itself. In addition, from a consociational perspective it provided another positive exogenous variable, in the form of the US government, which brought balance and stability to the process.

CEASEFIRES AND FRAMEWORK DOCUMENTS

On 31 August 1994 the IRA announced its ceasefire and Major immediately called for the clarification of its 'permanence' as a precondition for Sinn Féin's entry into talks.[83] Tellingly, John Taylor helped the process by stating that his 'gut reaction' was that this ceasefire was 'for real', broadening Major's leeway for moving towards the possibility of Sinn Féin's future inclusion in the talks process.[84] The IRA had stepped into the political arena largely due to the confidence that the pan-nationalist alliance had provided to the republican movement, and on the premise that Sinn Féin would be included in the talks process. The force of Sinn Féin, the SDLP, the Irish government, and the Irish-American lobby all working in tandem gave Adams the motives and incentives he needed to convince the bulk of the IRA that accepting a transitional internal solution was in its interests. While this fell well short of republican national aspirations, it could further their long-term goals and deliver political benefits that a semi-constitutional nationalist party wedded to violence could never achieve.

Six weeks later, on 13 October,[85] the IRA's ceasefire was matched by the CLMC's cessation, following assurances by UUP spokesman, Michael McGimpsey, that the DSD was not a sell-out.[86] The CLMC had become convinced that the DSD secured the union and that it offered loyalists the prospect of becoming involved in the political process.[87] Once trust had been established through Eames and Magee, it created a balance in the process that might even have culminated in loyalists pre-empting the republican move by declaring their ceasefire first, although this seems unlikely. However, the murders of two leading loyalists, Ray Smallwoods and Trevor King, in the weeks preceding the IRA's declaration prevented any such move.[88] The CLMC presumed that the republicans had stepped up their campaign against senior loyalist figures in the run-up to their declaration in order to ensure that loyalists did not steal the IRA's limelight.[89] Like the British government, the loyalists were in no way convinced that Sinn Féin was sincere about achieving peace, but saw the DSD as a means of putting republicans to the test, with the support of mainstream Irish nationalism.

London was very slow to respond to the IRA's move and Sinn Féin's inclusion was delayed. British suspicions concerning the IRA's intentions, emanating from British intelligence and Major's increasing domestic frailties, raised the question of the permanence of the ceasefire and the spectre of decommissioning. There were also clashes between the British and Irish governments over the constitutional issues, with Mayhew calling for the Republic to drop its constitutional claim,[90] which was clearly something that the Irish were keeping for future negotiations when Sinn Féin was at the table.[91] On 15 December 1994 John Bruton of Fine Gael was elected Taoiseach, a month after Reynolds had been forced out of office over a controversial Supreme Court appointment and replaced as Fianna Fáil's leader by Bertie Ahern. Although Bruton endorsed the DSD and subsequently released the Framework Documents with Major on 22 February 1995, he was very uncomfortable dealing with Sinn Féin, while Reynolds's departure deeply troubled republicans.

The Framework Documents detailed possible arrangements for a Northern Ireland Assembly to be elected by proportional representation, with an all-party committee system of government overseen by a panel of three elected figures to complement the Assembly's functions.[92] O'Leary and McGarry assert that the immediate goals of the Framework Documents were to reinvigorate the three-strand talks process, and to build peace by bringing republicans and loyalists into constitutional politics.[93] Brendan O'Duffy highlights their proposal to 'adjust constitutive sovereignty claims', the Irish marking a recognition of 'consent' with promises to change Articles Two and Three, and the British undertaking to amend the Government of Ireland Act, 1920.[94]

The Documents showed the two governments' sophisticated commitment to regulating the conflict, but by 1996 it had become increasingly clear that Major's administration was not capable of directing the process any more. The momentum of the Major–Reynolds days had been temporarily lost, resulting in the subsequent breakdown of the IRA ceasefire on 9 February 1996, when it exploded a large bomb at the Canary Wharf Tower in London. In that sense, the Framework Documents failed in their objectives. However, despite unionist rejection of them they remained as a basis for future talks between the parties, or at least as something for unionists to work away from during substantive negotiations.

SUBSTANTIVE NEGOTIATIONS

Little change occurred in the flagging peace process until Tony Blair carried the Labour Party to a general election victory on 1 May 1997 and then appointed Mo Mowlam as the new Secretary of State for Northern Ireland. The following month saw the arrival of Ahern as Taoiseach, at the head of a coalition between Fianna Fáil and the Progressive Democrats. On 6 June, the British and Irish governments appointed the former US Senator, George Mitchell, as chairman of the plenary talks, alongside the Canadian General, John de Chastelain, and the former Prime Minister of Finland, Harri Holkeri. Progress in the talks was slow due to unionist opposition to the appointment of a US chairman and pro-cedural arguments between the different parties. Ironically, Mitchell's diplomacy proved a major catalyst in the formulation and success of the substantive negotiations. These took place under a 'sufficient consensus' mechanism, which meant concurrent majority support from the unionist and nationalist representatives chosen in the Forum elections in 1996.

On 25 June Blair spelled out his timetable for agreement to the par-ties, with substantive negotiations to begin by September and an overall settlement to be reached by May 1998. Here he signalled his intention to push the process forward with Dublin and assured republicans that an unequivocal ceasefire would lead to their immediate inclusion in the talks process.[95] Prompted by Blair's assertion that they could join the talks if they signed up to the Mitchell principles of democracy,[96] the IRA swiftly reinstated their ceasefire on 19 July. Their subsequent inclusion days later resulted in the permanent withdrawal from the talks of the DUP and the United Kingdom Unionist Party (UKUP). This proved a defining moment, and not just for republicans. David Trimble's decision to re-enter the talks with loyalist paramilitary representatives from the Progressive Unionist Party (PUP) and the Ulster Democratic Party (UDP) signalled that the positive force that he brought to Unionism had taken root. Trimble's UUP was there to cut a deal on behalf of the unionist commu-nity, with or without the DUP and the UKUP.[97] George Mitchell argued, however, that if Ian Paisley and the UKUP leader, Robert McCartney, had stayed, there could have been no agreement, and that their departure and the development of a sub-committee to deal with decommissioning freed the UUP to negotiate.[98] When questioned six years on, Mitchell suggest-ed that if the DUP and the UKUP had 'engaged' and 'positively negotiat-ed' alongside Trimble's UUP, a rather different agreement might have been presented to the public on Good Friday.[99]

In the New Year the two governments presented the Northern Ireland parties with 'Propositions on Heads of Agreement' for negotiation.[100] These concerned the constitutional changes envisaged between the UK and Ireland regarding the Government of Ireland Act, 1920, and Articles Two and Three; the North–South bodies; the Intergovernmental Conference; and a new Anglo-Irish agreement to replace the existing AIA. The main purpose was to outline the issues that would become the core components of the GFA. Once the substantive negotiations had commenced all the parties – with the exception of Sinn Féin, which was unhappy with the document – were fully engaged in the process. Momentum gathered as Mitchell gave the parties two weeks to reach agreement before the Easter holiday weekend. He was supposed to deliver the first draft of the agreement to them with a week left open for further negotiation. However, the two governments had not agreed Strand Two and, reluctant to give them a partial document, the chairman was forced to delay it until 6 April. This delay happened at the insistence of the Irish government and left the parties very little time to find accommodation over the remaining areas of conflict when they finally received it.

The draft envisaged strong 'independent authority' for the cross-border bodies, which the UUP could never have accepted.[101] John Taylor proclaimed to the press that he 'wouldn't touch this paper with a forty-foot barge poll'.[102] After a communication breakdown between Blair and Trimble, the document was renegotiated when the two premiers rushed to Belfast to deal with the impending crisis, Ahern coming straight from his mother's funeral. In direct contrast to Sunningdale, the Irish position was renegotiable and the British backed the UUP against the Irish, with a deal being finalised on 10 April 1998. Ironically, when Paisley turned up to protest outside Stormont against the accord, he was heckled and subdued by the very loyalists he had rallied and used twenty-five years earlier to bring the Sunningdale Executive down. If ever there was a sign of the times, this was it.

CONCLUSION

This chapter has described how an incremental process of developing Anglo-Irish relations grew steadily from Sunningdale, despite many setbacks, and culminated in the signing of the GFA in 1998. It was these positive exogenous pressures that provided the incentive and motivation for most of the Northern Ireland parties to accept and support a consociational constitutional settlement, and that held the vital dynamic in the interpretation and implementation of the agreement.

Through a slow process of engagement between the two governments, building on the foundations of the failure of Sunningdale and the mutual learning process it preceded, Anglo-Irish relations had improved to the extent that a unity of purpose to regulate the conflict had developed. It was through such a unity of purpose that Britain and Ireland came to create an environment within which consociation could once again be employed to regulate the conflict. By effectively employing political carrots and sticks, while working in unison to promote consociation, the two governments successfully coerced the majority of Northern Ireland's elites into accepting a conditional settlement within the UK.

CHAPTER FOUR

The Good Friday Agreement

'I think that the governments themselves, and certainly the machinery of state in both countries, have an absolute unity of purpose in relation to the Good Friday Agreement. We have it and we have to make it work'.

Dick Spring[1]

On 10 April 1998 the signing of the GFA brought Northern Ireland's parties and the British and Irish governments back to the Sunningdale model of power-sharing after twenty-five years of ethno-national conflict. This marked an end to a phase in a struggle that many commentators had labelled insoluble.[2] This chapter argues that the defining factor leading to the conclusion of the GFA was an overriding unity of purpose between London and Dublin to regulate power-sharing institutions in Northern Ireland. While Sunningdale had failed due to weak Anglo-Irish relations and the intractable positions taken by some of Northern Ireland's elites, the establishment of strong intergovernmental foundations, with broad political incentives offered to those elites, culminated in the achievement of an inclusive constitutional settlement in 1998. This was not the result of any great shift in public opinion towards favouring a consociational settlement, nor did it provide any resolution of the constitutional paradoxes that divide unionism and nationalism. It was the outcome of a re-engagement process in which the two governments pooled their resources, creating an environment for the implementation of a consociational settlement that could be accepted and supported by the majority of both communities and their elected representatives. Before evaluating the centrifugal nature of the intergovernmental relationships, the three strands, the parties' positions and the legitimisation of Northern Ireland's reformulated consociational arrangement through the referendums, a brief overview of the GFA itself is required.

OVERVIEW OF THE GFA

The initial observation that must be made in comparing the GFA to Sunningdale is that the GFA is not an exclusive accord formulated specifically to deal with an escalating security situation. On the contrary, it is a fully inclusive and refined amalgamation of all the parties' positions and perspectives, accounting for the antagonistic constitutional issues at the heart of the ethnic conflict, which had contributed to a further twenty-five years of violence. The GFA is thus a sophisticated piece of consociational engineering, a long way from the post-Sunningdale experimentation of the AIA. Its intergovernmental structures illustrate just how far the British and Irish governments have come in their handling of the conflict and just how confident they have been in working together to regulate it.

The GFA was broken into three strands. The first dealt with the internal democratic institutions, while the second and third accounted for the external North–South Ministerial Council, the British–Irish Council, and the British–Irish Intergovernmental Conference. It then addressed the contentious issues of decommissioning, security, policing, justice and prisoners. In Annexes A and B of the GFA the British and Irish governments addressed the constitutional questions that had overshadowed Northern Ireland since partition. Both governments recognised the legitimacy of a future change in the status of Northern Ireland, 'subject to the agreement and consent of a majority of the people of Northern Ireland'.[3] The Irish government declared its intention to propose amendments to Articles Two and Three of the Irish Constitution to the people of the Republic in a referendum, while the British repealed the Government of Ireland Act, 1920, notwithstanding any previous enactment and both provided for governments referendums to determine whether a future majority for unification existed.

Strand One provides for a fully devolved 108-member Assembly elected by STV from the existing Westminster constituencies. From this Assembly an Executive was to be chosen through the d'Hondt electoral system,[4] with ten ministers elected on their parties' respective strengths in the Assembly, overseen by a dual premiership of First and Deputy First Ministers. They were to be elected together by the mutual consent of at least 50 per cent of both nationalists and unionists in the Assembly, and were to be reliant on each other for the maintenance of their respective positions, which were to be of equal power. Each Assembly member was to designate his or her identity as Nationalist, Unionist or 'other', and cross-community support was required for all key decisions as well as for the election of the First and Deputy First Ministers. Such support was to be provided by either 'parallel consent' – a majority of those present and voting, including a majority of unionist and nationalist members present and voting – or by a 'weighted majority' – 60 per cent of members present and voting, including at least 40 per cent of each of the nationalist and unionist blocs present and voting.[5] Thus the GFA entails full consociational minority veto rights on all key decision-making in the Assembly.

Strand Two of the GFA details the North–South Ministerial Council. Its aim is to bring together those with executive responsibility in Northern Ireland and the Republic in order to develop 'consultation, cooperation and action within the island of Ireland' as a whole.[6] The GFA provides for each side to take decisions in the Council while both delegations remain accountable to the Assembly and the Oireachtas, respectively, thus being dependent on both institutions for the implementation and ratification of any executive decisions. Brendan O'Leary argues that this solves a dual problem: 'Nationalists were concerned that if the Assembly could outlast the North–South Council, it would provide incentives for unionists to undermine the latter. Unionists, by contrast, worried that if the Council could survive the destruction of the Assembly, nationalists would seek to bring this about'. Therefore 'internal consociation and external confederation go together'.[7] The two elements are mutually interdependent.

While this mutual veto is not unlike the provision in the Sunningdale Agreement that all decisions would have to be taken within the Council of Ireland by unanimity, the list of areas for consideration and the scope for cooperation were considerably trimmed in 1998, and there was to be no 'all-Ireland parliamentary body'.[8] Like Sunningdale, the GFA lists the potential areas where cooperation may take place, but, as O'Leary highlights, the Council is to identify and agree at least six matters for cooperation and implementation 'where existing bodies will be the appropriate mechanisms for cooperation in each separate jurisdiction', and where cooperation is to take place through agreed implementation bodies on a cross-border or all-island basis.[9] Therefore, while the Council is to be limited and dependent on the authority of the respective administrations in Ireland, its programme of cooperation and its framework for institutionalisation are clearly set out.

Strand Three of the GFA provides for a British–Irish Council to promote harmonious and mutually beneficial development of the totality of the relationships among the peoples of the UK and the Republic of Ireland. This idea had been proposed well before the Sunningdale negotiations took place.[10] As mentioned in Chapter 2, ironically, it was dropped in the early 1970s due to fears of a unionist backlash, whereas in 1998 unionists pushed for it, as it provided a balance to the British position. This illustrates the fact that the GFA is not a one-way street that envisages no furthering of the UK dimension in the new set of relations that it entails. It also provides for a British-Irish Intergovernmental Conference, which promised a new Anglo–Irish Agreement that would bring together the two governments, promoting bilateral cooperation at all levels on matters of mutual interest, including cooperation on security matters.

For the first time the GFA provides Northern Ireland with a bill of rights that aims to safeguard the political, national and religious liberties of all. Further, it promises an Equality Commission, pledges economic, social and cultural inclusion, and speaks of intercommunal reconciliation and assistance for victims of violence. On the difficult issue of decommissioning, the GFA is vague and contains no linkage between the handing-over of paramilitary arms, the release of paramilitary prisoners and the holding of executive office. It merely states that all participants must reaffirm their commitment to 'use any influence they may have to achieve decommissioning of all paramilitary arms' within two years of the endorsement of the GFA by referendums North and South. As far as security and policing are concerned, 'normalisation' was desired with the removal of security installations. The GFA also provides an opportunity for a fresh start to policing, with a force capable of attracting and sustaining support from the community as a whole. Finally, the GFA entails a review of the criminal justice system, and has provisions for the early release of prisoners affiliated to organisations maintaining complete and unequivocal ceasefires.

THE HIGH TIDE OF ANGLO-IRISH RELATIONS

While Anglo-Irish relations saw many vicissitudes, bitter rows and periods of cooling off, the ties established at Sunningdale were kept up at official level and consistently built upon, as politicians lacking the baggage of Anglo-Irish animosity came into office. In fact, even politicians who were not predisposed to compromise, such as Margaret Thatcher or Charles Haughey, found themselves moved along by the process that had been started in the early 1970s. By the time John Major and Albert Reynolds took office, the British and Irish civil servants who had charted the turbulent waters of Sunningdale and the AIA had well established relationships and a very clear idea of where they should be directing their masters, given favourable political circumstances. This side of the process has often been overlooked. Yet it was diplomats with, in many cases, a quarter of a century's experience working on the Anglo-Irish dilemma who in many ways guided and underpinned long-term political developments in Northern Ireland. Joint membership of the EU also gave the two governments a commonality on many issues and granted their successive leaders meetings on the sidelines of summits that they would not otherwise have had.

As Major and Reynolds negotiated what was to become the DSD, a unity of approach began to emerge between their governments over securing peace in Northern Ireland. While Reynolds wholeheartedly embraced the political process that he had inherited from John Hume, Major had no overwhelming interest in doing so, given his weak domestic position. Yet he placed Northern Ireland fairly close to the top of the British government's political agenda, which was something no other British Premier had done since the outbreak of violence in 1969. Consequently, by the mid-1990s the relationship between the two governments had changed, in the sense that their primary interest in Northern Ireland no longer revolved around security. Seriously attempting political regulation and establishing peace in Northern Ireland had become an interest in itself.

The two premiers' determination to stick together over the Hume–Adams document exemplifies this. Not only did Reynolds pick up the process from Hume and make it his own, but both governments were happy to let Hume become a 'lightning conductor' and break the taboo on talking to Sinn Féin. This happened at a time when both administrations were secretly engaged in separate contacts with republicans. Hume took the risks involved in granting political legitimacy to Adams, and then weathered a public and media onslaught for having done so. Major and Reynolds subsequently abandoned Hume, yet they simply carried on the process from where he left off. Further, when the British dialogue with the IRA was exposed in the media in 1993 there was a major public row over the breach of trust between London and Dublin. However, this merely followed the serious behind-the-scenes quarrel that the governments had had a couple of months earlier, when the Irish first found out about the contacts.[11] Crucially, high-level diplomatic problems like this did not distract them from their overarching commitment to the project of securing peace in Northern Ireland. Much was made of the good political partnership between Major and Reynolds, and their behaviour said a lot about Anglo-Irish relations at the time. This was exemplified by the fact that Britain and Ireland could have such a public row, a disagreement that might have wilted diplomatic relations between most countries for some time, and quickly come back to the table and negotiate, from exactly where they left off.

Another example of this was the Adams visa crisis in the US, which culminated in an Anglo-American rift. While this caused animosity, someone had to legitimise Adams on the international stage, and it certainly could not have been Major. The British were genuinely upset by this move, but most would admit with hindsight that, somehow, it had to happen. The real issue here was that the internationalisation of the political process brought in a US influence that went some way towards narrowing the gulf between British and Irish negotiating strengths, and further heightened British nervousness over political developments in Northern Ireland. It seems far more likely that Major was upset about being snubbed by Bill Clinton, over what would previously have been a British- influenced decision vis-à-vis the US State Department, than about Adams actually getting the visa to visit the US.

While the end of the Cold War freed the US Presidency from non-interference in Britain's handling of Northern Ireland,[12] 1992 saw a President enter the White House with a long-term personal interest in doing something to help to regulate the conflict, while getting a minimum-risk foreign policy 'bounce' from his involvement.[13] What Clinton initially brought to the process was the trust- and confidence-building measures that the republican movement needed to engage with the British and move towards a ceasefire. Clinton became the international guarantor of the political process and Conor O'Clery, Washington Correspondent of the *Irish Times*, credits him with bringing the ceasefire forward by at least a year.[14] Clinton brought a clear and deep analysis of the difficulties involved to the process and, from an Irish perspective, acted as an honest broker between the British and Irish governments. The Clinton factor enabled the Irish to harness a certain balance with London that they would not otherwise have had.[15] Fundamentally, the President ensured that Northern Ireland remained high up on the British government's agenda, while granting Adams a visa convinced the republican movement that US policy on Ireland was no longer dictated by the pro-British US State Department.[16] This, and the mediation and interaction of the Irish-American lobby, proved crucial in bringing forward the IRA's ceasefire.[17]

Clinton had initially made the mistake of focusing on strengthening nationalism, in moves that consistently appeared to be at unionism's expense, but he subsequently rectified this short-sightedness by creating an open door policy to the unionist and loyalist parties. While Clinton's actual influence in brokering the accord was minimal, the pressure brought to bear on the parties from London and Dublin being highly effective in itself, his role in kick-starting the process and smoothing the way for Sinn Féin and the loyalists to bring their constituencies towards a ceasefire has been seriously underestimated.

George Mitchell's diplomacy also brought a positive external influence to the process. Once all the parties had established trust in him, he proved to be a very fair and skilful mediator, and highly adept at overseeing the negotiations. The parties that remained in the talks came to view his role in a positive light, as the even-handedness of his diplomacy became apparent.

THE THREE STRANDS

Most of the negotiations were conducted on an individual basis concerning the different heads of agreement, under the premise that nothing was agreed until everything was agreed. Strand One was left for the parties to negotiate themselves, which largely meant the UUP and the SDLP, as Sinn Féin would not countenance negotiating the internal aspects of devolution. The SDLP strongly favoured an executive with the d'Hondt system,[18] the UUP held out for a committee system of government and the Alliance Party opposed the consociational model, as it enshrined sectarianism and intercommunal division.[19]

As at Sunningdale, on the Strand Two section of the GFA the Irish government wanted very significant North–South bodies.[20] However, this time the Irish were mindful of creating institutions that both nationalists and unionists could live with. When the Mitchell document was released, in order to avoid a unionist backlash, the British government had allowed the Irish to negotiate on Strand Two. In doing this the British provided the UUP with something to negotiate away from, correctly thinking that an overtly 'green' Strand Two would focus the UUP delegates' minds on the deal and at the same time enable them to claim a victory over the renegotiation of the Irish position. Well aware of this, Dublin applied this hardball-negotiating tactic in the full knowledge that the UUP could never accept the document that was on the table.[21] Candidly, Mansergh has described the crisis at the end of the negotiations as 'not entirely unpredictable'.[22]

When the parties received the draft Strand One it had many different possible options for each section written in italics, whereas Strand Two had no negotiating options whatsoever. This created the impression that Strand One was wholly negotiable while Strand Two was not. As far as the all-Ireland bodies were concerned, it appeared to be 'Sunningdale mark two', only this time there was actually room for renegotiation. Strand Two determined whether the parties were really prepared to cut a deal: it gave the nationalists something to work towards and the unionists something to work against. Where they met in the middle was the only piece of ground where agreement could realistically be reached.[23]

While the two strands were negotiated separately, there was also an obvious linkage between them. This entailed a UUP–SDLP *quid pro quo* over the issues that mattered most to them. David Trimble had put all his energy and talent into two things: the negotiation of his party's constitutional imperative of securing the union between Great Britain and Northern Ireland with the British government; and hollowing out the North–South bodies envisaged in the Framework Documents with the Irish government and ensuring that they were fully tied to any future Northern Ireland Assembly. After the Mitchell draft was released, agreement on Strand One was achieved between the two parties in a matter of hours. Trimble accepted much of the SDLP's proposals on legislative devolution, but pushed hard on Strand Two, on which he satisfied most unionist expectations. The fact that the SDLP relied on the Irish to negotiate Strand Two and the Irish left the SDLP to work on Strand One meant that they were far more focused on it than the UUP and got most of what they bargained for.[24] In comparison to Sunningdale, the SDLP was actually more engaged in the dynamics of the internal consociational mechanisms than on the North–South bodies. This time around all the parties, including Sinn Féin implicitly, had recognised that the UUP had to score constitutionally on Strand Two for any deal to be forthcoming.

It became clear at the last minute where the UUP delegates stood. They were prepared to abandon their committee system proposals on Strand One, provided that they successfully limited Strand Two's all-Ireland provisions. Aside from the fact that they would have preferred no North–South bodies, they were reasonably satisfied with the outcome after the Mitchell draft was renegotiated.[25] Trimble's focus on Strand Two is exemplified by the ministerial choices the UUP eventually made when d'Hondt was activated on 19 November 1999.[26] So preoccupied was the UUP with the North–South bodies that it picked two of the ministries that were most concerned with cross-border issues, Environment and Culture, Arts and Leisure, thereby allowing Sinn Féin to take the two high-profile and high-budget departments of Education and Health.

While the North–South dimension was not nearly as robust as the Council of Ireland proposed at Sunningdale, and the SDLP did not feel it was particularly well defined, it was happy with the Executive and the Assembly.[27] Further, to convince Trimble of it the SDLP argued that an executive form of government would strengthen Northern Ireland's position vis-à-vis the Republic, in that it would have ministers going to North–South meetings, as opposed to committee chairpersons.[28] Reinforcing this point was the fact that the Scottish Parliament would have a cabinet while Northern Ireland would only have committees. These arguments were not lost on the UUP.

Keeping Sinn Féin on board concerning Strand Two was the British revocation of Section 75 of the Government of Ireland Act, 1920, which Reynolds had insisted on since the beginning of the DSD process.[29] While it did not have the same weight as the major Irish constitutional changes envisaged over Articles Two and Three, Section 75 was of huge symbolic importance to the republican movement, while the Irish government felt that removing it added legitimacy to their position.[30] Therefore, while the UUP and the SDLP focused on the internal political and constitutional issues, Sinn Féin concentrated on the security agenda, which their constituency would be most concerned about in the short term. Again, there was a balance in the equation. As the UUP focused on renegotiating the Mitchell draft, it was unable to pay as much attention to the issues of prisoners, decommissioning and police reform as it would have liked.[31]

Strand Three of the GFA provided for a British–Irish Council, which made the deal more attractive to those unionists who had viewed Sunningdale as a one-way street and strengthened the GFA as an inter-governmental package. Further, legislative devolution in the UK was another incentive for unionists to accept the Assembly, while the

British–Irish Council strengthened the GFA in the sense that the UUP could argue that the border between Britain and Ireland was weakening due to their common interests, so there was little to be feared from the North–South linkage. During the negotiations the UUP had pushed for the North–South institutions to be tied to these bodies in a subsidiary position, but had failed to achieve this. Many unionists, however, saw this strand as the most important from a long-term perspective, believing that it might eventually subsume the North–South bodies as Britain and Ireland became increasingly interdependent.[32] The closeness of Anglo-Irish relations in 1998 had again worked to take the sting out of the constitutional difficulties that had undermined Sunningdale.

THE ARRIVAL OF NATIONALISM

The GFA marked an acceptance by almost all strands of Irish nationalism of an internal framework for agreement within Northern Ireland and commitment by republicans to pursue their national agenda by political means alone. The SDLP had paved the way for Sinn Féin's entry into the political arena as a potentially serious constitutional party, and an inclusive process offered it a prominent role in working Northern Ireland's administration. The SDLP and the Irish government had learned the lessons of Sunningdale regarding the Council of Ireland, and were happy to settle for North–South bodies that the UUP could live with, provided that full legislative devolution with executive power-sharing was on offer. This was something that the UUP had wanted to avoid, primarily because it had been rejected in 1974 and the committee system would have offered unionists a greater degree of control as the majority community. The fact that the Irish government was negotiating with the British and the UUP left the SDLP free to concentrate on pushing executive power-sharing through. This enabled the SDLP's negotiators, Seamus Mallon and Mark Durkan, to be largely successful on their Strand One proposals, as the UUP had no draft documents other than its position on the committee system. Thus, during the final days the SDLP's draft was the paper that was negotiated, with final agreement being reached by Mallon and Trimble on that basis.[33]

For its part Sinn Féin focused on security issues in the talks, as this was where it would be able to sell the agreement to the republican community. If the DUP and the UKUP had remained in the talks, it would have made Sinn Féin's task considerably more difficult. Without them, Sinn Féin was able to disguise the serious constitutional defeats the agreement entailed for republicanism and thereby conceal the ideological U-turns the movement was being forced into making. The republican leadership had accepted that, in the short term, an internal settlement with a devolved assembly at Stormont was necessary to further its long-term goals. What it got in return for its concessions was the promise of the early release of prisoners, police reform, demilitarisation and a last-minute fudge on decommissioning.

The positive symbolic impact of these issues on the republican community was as great as it was negative within unionism, hugely assisting Sinn Féin in publicly accepting devolution. Yet, while Gerry Adams and Martin McGuinness enjoyed the comfort zone of these short-term symbolic victories, Trimble was forced to absorb heavy political defeats on these issues in return for securing unionism's long-term constitutional imperatives. To a large extent this explains why Sinn Féin had little trouble selling the deal to its constituency in comparison to the UUP leader. It was these symbolic victories that carried the republican movement through the turbulent years of political adjustment that followed the signing of the GFA and, at the same time, slowly undermined Trimble's electoral position. Sinn Féin was successful on the issue of decommissioning, having convinced Tony Blair and Bertie Ahern that their needs were greater than Trimble's on this matter. As a result it turned out to be the one major piece of the Agreement where the governments failed to push nationalism and unionism onto common ground. Here Blair failed to heed Edward Heath's mistakes at Sunningdale and maintain the unionist segment of the equilibrium. This was an error that would both undermine the moderate parties and scupper Blair's attempts to implement power-sharing over the following five years. With hindsight it seems possible that Sinn Féin could have delivered Republicanism without such huge incentives, but this was a view held by few commentators in 1998.[34]

Republican gains were not altogether symbolic either. Sinn Féin's assessment was that the GFA was not 'a military strategy clothed in politics ... [but] properly implemented created a level playing field within which nationalists have access to all the levers of power'.[35] While this is what attracted Sinn Féin to the GFA, it sold it to its constituency by convincing them that, demographically, Northern Ireland was merely years away from a Catholic majority, so the GFA was a politically transitional phase necessary on the road to a united Ireland.[36] Again, there was little that Sinn Féin negotiated other than these symbolic victories, as it did not want to be tainted with Strand One, nor could it be seen to be conceding Strand Two, and it obviously had very little interest in Strand Three. The problem that republicans had with Strands One and Two was that any public approval of the British and Irish governments' interpretation of consent would reinforce their acceptance of a partitionist settlement in the eyes of the republican community. Sinn Féin even considered running a two-pronged campaign of 'support for the agreement in the North' and a 'very sceptical one against in the South', such were its fears over endorsing Strand Two.[37] There had been no ideological shift within republicanism on the crucial consent principle – or at least this was the official line from Sinn Féin.[38] In that sense republicans were suffering from the same dilemma the DUP were to encounter in 2004/2005. They both had the dilemma of having to recast their ideological positions to reflect political realities while disguising the constitutional U-turns they had made from their constituencies. Yet, of all the parties, Sinn Féin kept in touch with its grassroots and was meticulous in carrying the republican movement with it into the process. Sinn Féin was able to come to the GFA and convince the IRA of its value due to the internationalisation of the process before 1998.[39] This provided republicans with the confidence to politically engage. In sum, the political initiatives, constitutional and symbolic, provided the motivation for the republican elite to finally support a consociational settlement.

DIVIDED THEY STOOD

By re-entering the talks with the two small loyalist parties, the UDP and the PUP, Trimble had marked his intention to engage in an inclusive process with republicans and signalled his determination to reach some form of accommodation over Northern Ireland's future. Yet, while he led a unified team into these talks and the subsequent substantive negotiations, as Good Friday 1998 approached cracks began to appear within his party. These divisions reflected the uneasy position Trimble held in brokering a deal on behalf of unionism while representing just less than half of its electorate.

The UUP negotiated on the basis of the Mitchell document, as opposed to rejecting it, which was what it told the media it had done.[40] As the deadline drew closer, Jeffery Donaldson, among others, argued that the UUP should reject the document as a basis for negotiation, as it was obviously a ploy to draw the party into conceding more than it otherwise would.[41] In spite of this Trimble was convinced that he had secured the best deal available to his party. So why did Donaldson walk out and create a fracture within the UUP that would both hamper the implementation of the GFA and undermine his party's position as the champion of any future power-sharing government? First, Trimble had not kept anyone in his team, never mind his party, fully informed as to where the negotiations were going. Second, he sidetracked Donaldson, who was one of his senior negotiators on Strand One, excluding him from the decision-making process that finalised the deal with the SDLP. Finally, the UUP leader would not lightly consider walking out on Blair.[42] Trimble felt that, in stark contrast to Heath's handling of Sunningdale, the British

Prime Minister had kept the overall balance for unionism within the negotiations when it really mattered. Therefore, given John Taylor's support, Trimble felt that he had the momentum and strength to carry his party forward.[43]

The final negotiations had taken place between Blair and Ahern, with a couple of key advisers, and then between the parties. Of his original team Trimble had kept only his senior negotiator, Sir Reg Empey, largely informed of everything that was going on, but even then Trimble himself was not party to every negotiation between the two governments. At the final meeting, on Good Friday morning, John Taylor listed eighteen issues that he was unhappy with in the draft. Trimble then argued that they should address only two – decommissioning and Maryfield – as they could not get concessions on all of them. The UUP leader then received two letters from Blair, one stating that Maryfield would be closed by the end of the year, the other that decommissioning was a prerequisite for participation in the Executive.[44] With Taylor's support, Trimble announced that he 'didn't think there was anything more to negotiate',[45] he was 'going upstairs' and 'we are going with this'.[46] The UUP had come under enormous pressure to reach an agreement and Trimble had felt obliged to concede on issues that were of symbolic rather than constitutional importance to his constituency, since Blair had supported him at the crucial stages of the negotiations on Strand Two.

It was at this stage that Donaldson informed the UUP Chairman, Denis Rogan, that he could not accept this and could not agree it.[47] He did so for three reasons. First, he believed that the UUP could walk away and negotiate a better agreement on the issues of decommissioning and prisoners,[48] not sharing Trimble's loyalty and commitment to Blair. Second, Trimble's leadership in the final week had excluded some of his negotiating team from a decision-making process that they felt required unanimity.[49] Third, and more importantly, this was Donaldson's moment to mount a challenge to Trimble's leadership and build his own support base from within the divided UUP. Nearly all those involved in the negotiations were surprised when Donaldson came out against the GFA.[50] Having been a key negotiator and a trusted member of Trimble's team, he cannot have been greatly suprised by anything in the GFA even the potential inclusion of Sinn Féin in any future Northern Ireland Executive.

The big problem facing Trimble was that the unionist population was not prepared for many of the GFA's reforms. It was one thing for the UUP leader to sell his constitutional achievements to the UUC and his party officers, but his constituency was psychologically unprepared for Sinn Féin taking up ministries, a fact that was not lost on Donaldson and his supporters. As the UUP was reliant on the two loyalist parties to make up the unionist part of the equation in the talks, prisoners and decommissioning were issues where it knew it would have to concede. If the DUP or the UKUP had remained in the talks, then these issues and policing would have faced an entirely more robust unionist challenge. In fact, the whole balance of the GFA would have shifted if they had participated, undoubtedly making unionism a much stronger force, but, in turn, making agreement more difficult to come by. Just as it is clear that their political exclusion in 1973 allowed a deal to be done by a weakened unionist Party, so, ironically, their self-exclusion severely weakened the unionist hand in the 1998 negotiations and resulted in the subsequent crisis within unionism over the GFA. On the other hand, while the exclusion of the anti-Agreement unionists in 1973 had aided the UWC strike, the inclusion of the small loyalist parties in 1998, with their desire to work alongside the UUP, ruled out the prospect of a similar anti-Agreement campaign.

Blair's role was pivotal to this process. As at Sunningdale, the Irish and the SDLP made up one negotiating team, while unionists were significantly underrepresented due to the self-exclusion of the DUP and the UKUP. However, unlike Heath, Blair was guided by an acute sense of fairness over the constitutional issues and stabilised the negotiation process in its final stages. Fundamentally, the UUP, especially Trimble and Taylor, trusted him to honour his commitments, and this was key to their agreement on Good Friday morning.[51] They knew the issue of decommissioning had been fudged at the last minute, but they had faith in Blair's commitment to keep his side of the bargain on the issues where he had promised his support.

The UUP faced the same dilemma in 1998 as they had in 1973: could unionists walk away from an agreement and come back at a later stage to negotiate a better deal? For their part Trimble, Taylor and Empey all felt that they had negotiated the best possible deal available on all the long-term issues that really mattered to unionists, and therefore could sell it as a package to their constituency. Further, issues such as prisoners, police reform and decommissioning could be dealt with by the British government independently of any agreement, and with or without the consent of the UUP or, in fact, any of the Northern Ireland parties. This well worn question of whether there would be more or less bread at the table on another occasion has, however, finally been answered by the opponents of Trimble's power-sharing agenda. Alongside his achievements in negotiating the GFA with nationalists, Trimble's legacy must also include carrying unionists to a position where even his sworn enemies came to fully accept his analysis of the conflict. It was no coincidence that those anti-Agreement politicians who had attacked him at every stage of the political process were by December 2004 tripping over themselves to take ownership of the deal that Trimble had negotiated under the two governments' Comprehensive Proposals.[52]

THE FAILURE OF ANTI-AGREEMENT UNIONISM

At Sunningdale the Council of Ireland had been a highly emotive issue
and the majority of the unionist elite was against the Agreement, whereas in 1998 the impact of the North–South bodies on public opinion was
negligible (see Table 6). The UUP had successfully tied them to the
Assembly and, since the AIA, most of the unionist population had
realised that there was no option regarding an Irish dimension of some
form in any future settlement. Compared to their political exclusion by
the British in 1973, the anti-Agreement unionists' opposition campaign
was badly damaged by the fact that they walked away from the talks,
leaving the UUP and the loyalists to fight the unionist corner.

In 1997 Trimble carried a strong united party into the substantive
negotiations, alongside the backbone of hard-line loyalism. This was in
total contrast to 1973, when Brian Faulkner had led a split Unionist Party
with a liberal negotiating team into talks at Sunningdale. The vast majority of unionists had come to recognise that there could be no return to
majority rule, that the British were prepared to work with Dublin over
their heads and that some form of agreement with nationalists was
unavoidable. Leading anti-Agreement unionists admit that it was simply
unrealistic to opt out and expect the British government to create a completely new process that favoured their interests. Outright opposition
meant that the British would simply revert to an AIA-style arrangement.[53]
Anti-Agreement unionists in 1998, therefore, rested their arguments on
short-term emotive issues, as opposed to the long-term constitutional
ones that undermined Sunningdale. As Brendan O'Duffy argues, in comparison to Faulkner, Trimble 'had the clear advantage of having secured
the constitutional recognition of unionist self-determination by the political representatives of Irish nationalism'.[54]

The situation had fundamentally changed since Sunningdale. While
Trimble's UUP had moved well ahead of its constituency, the weakening of
the anti-Agreement unionist leaders' conviction was not reflected in the
segment of the unionist electorate that they represented. While a majority of
unionists were in favour of some form of agreement, the DUP had sown the
seeds of its own dilemma by convincing the public that the GFA was against
their interests. Ironically, the majority of those who opposed Sunningdale so
ferociously in 1973 would have happily accepted it in 1998.

What also hurt anti-Agreement unionism in comparison to 1973–74 was
the lack of widespread violence, as ceasefires facilitated the process and
created an atmosphere conducive to reaching a settlement. There was a deep
well of uncertainty for opponents of the GFA to tap into within the unionist
community, this was somewhat offset by the public expectation of
agreement whipped up by community leaders and the British government's
spin-doctoring machine. The cross-communal momentum that the

intergovernmental apparatus was able to create through the media in anticipation of the GFA counteracted and considerably deflated the anti-Agreement campaign. This, again, was in direct contrast to Sunningdale, where the lack of intergovernmental coordination and Harold Wilson's ambivalence over the fate of the Northern Ireland Executive significantly helped the opposition in bringing about its collapse.

Thus, while the new dynamic that Trimble brought to the UUP in 1995 led his party to proactively engage in the peace process for the first time, Ian Paisley continued to champion the politics of opposition that had been his trademark for more than three decades. The nature of anti-Agreement unionism had, however, fundamentally changed. Many of those politicians who actively opposed the GFA quickly came to accept that this form of political accommodation with nationalism was inevitable. If Robert McCartney had not attempted to outflank Paisley on his right and, in effect, lead the DUP out of the talks process in 1997, many in the DUP's leadership, such as Peter Robinson or Nigel Dodds, might have advocated staying in the talks process with the UUP. These DUP moderates were hampered by both their own fundamentalist religious wing and the rival anti-Agreement movement led by McCartney. The parts of the Agreement that offended anti-Agreement unionists in the DUP and the UUP might not have been so offensive if they had remained united and doubled their negotiating strength. The majority of them were no longer anti-Agreement in principle, but were unprepared to lend public support to the emotive symbolic reforms that were abhorrent to large parts of the unionist electorate as this would have damaged their political position. Paisley knew that the unionist population was psychologically unprepared to see Sinn Féin in government before decommissioning, and the various security reforms the Agreement entailed. His opposition to the Agreement, and Sinn Féin's intransigence over IRA decommissioning negatively affected the electorate's view of the UUP's handling of the peace process. As a result Trimble and the SDLP lost the Assembly election on 26 November 2003, leaving the DUP as Northern Ireland's largest party. Donaldson's subsequent defection to Paisley's team on 5 January 2004 further strengthened his hand. By then, however, anti-Agreement unionism had nowhere else to go politically and Paisley finally dropped his oppositionist rhetoric and began considering his constituency for the quantum leap to pro-Agreement politics.

A UNITY OF PURPOSE

If historians pose the question as to how the GFA was finally agreed, then the short answer is that nothing was agreed until the Prime Minister and the Taoiseach arrived to settle it themselves. The two leaders emerged onto the political scene in Northern Ireland during the culmination of an incremental process that had been maturing for twenty-five years. To their credit, they wasted no time in becoming the driving forces behind the negotiations and the players from whom all the party leaders took their cue. Only the premiers saw the political developments in their entirety, and they managed, shaped and reviewed the negotiating process at all its crucial stages. The date on which agreement was reached had little to do with the parties: it was down to Blair and Ahern's shared determination to build up the momentum, and force the deal through in the final two weeks. They knew exactly where the common ground lay – where the small area available for compromise between the parties existed – and took it as their task to bring the various protagonists to that ultimate position.

Of course, the hardest part was to get the UUP and Sinn Féin to move onto that plateau where accommodation could be brokered, and only the two premiers could have done this. For example, at the last minute, Sinn Féin came up with close to one hundred issues that it was unhappy with and it looked as if no agreement would be forthcoming. Sinn Féin was worried about any backtracking from the Framework Documents on Strand Two and, in fact, that was where the balance had to be kept. While most thought that the Agreement was about to unravel, Ahern assumed that Sinn Féin was just testing the two governments' negotiating positions to destruction. He sat all night with Sinn Féin's negotiators, his officials drafting written answers to all their points, until he had their consent.[55] On the other side, Blair delivered the UUP with a combination of enormous pressure and mutual trust. He convinced them that the other parties were sincere and that this was the best deal that would ever be available to them within the UK. In comparison to the position at Sunningdale, the UUP did not feel isolated.[56] Unlike Heath, Blair was the key figure stabilising the negotiations over the North–South linkages and convincing the leaders that an opportunity to get an agreement like this might not come again for a decade.

In October 2003, when the two governments were finalising the sequencing of a deal between the UUP and Sinn Féin, trust between the UUP leader and the Prime Minister was once again the crucial ingredient. On 21 October Blair announced a date for an Assembly election as a prelude to reinstating the devolved institutions. The IRA carried out an act of decommissioning under the supervision of General de Chastelain. This decommissioning was to have an element of transparency in order to create the confidence in the unionist community that was necessary for the UUP to return to government with Sinn Féin. This transparency had been agreed between Trimble, Adams and McGuinness before the sequencing. The transparent element was, however, missing from de Chastelain's statement, the UUP leader withdrew from the deal and Blair pressed ahead with the election in the absence of agreement. Blair had promised

Trimble, both orally and in writing, that he would not let him down – again, this was a promise that the British Prime Minister failed to honour.[57] With hindsight it seems clear that Blair no longer felt that Trimble had the ability to win the Assembly election and carry the process forward. His refusal to cancel the election signalled the British government's intention to abandon Trimble, and try to force through a deal between the DUP and Sinn Féin at a later date. By December 2004 the two governments had pushed the DUP close to accepting the GFA and the fact that Paisley was publicly negotiating a deal that entailed entering into government with Sinn Féin signalled the likelihood of a slightly modified form of power-sharing being implemented at Stormont under what became known as the Comprehensive Proposals. While the name had changed, no one was in any doubt that it was the GFA in two spoonfuls.

While trust and a unity of purpose had been developing over the previous decade, Anglo-Irish relations were at their zenith in 1998, and the Blair–Ahern partnership gave the process the robustness and legitimacy that it needed to succeed. Martin Mansergh has described the relationship between the two leaders as 'absolutely unprecedented', emphasising the vitality that their 'hands on role' brought to the process.[58] They were so closely involved in the final weeks and days that they created the dynamic and momentum for agreement. Their personal commitment in fastening the 'nuts and bolts' of the GFA provided the trust and confidence that the different parties needed to take a leap of faith and cut a deal in the final hours.[59]

In comparison to their predecessors at Sunningdale, both leaders also had the domestic political power and the international legitimacy to broker and guarantee an intergovernmental constitutional settlement. Most of the elements in the equation that Sunningdale had lacked were in place by 1998: domestic stability, international legitimacy, inclusivity, ceasefires, weakened opposition, an intergovernmental interest in regulating the conflict and, most importantly, a unity of purpose. Peter Mandelson described this strong Anglo-Irish partnership, based on trust, as 'indispensable'.[60]

Further, the demographic balance between the two segments had significantly changed over the course of the conflict. Before Sunningdale the ratio between Protestants and Catholics in the Census of 1971 was 63:37, whereas in the 2001 Census it recorded 53.13 per cent Protestants to 43.76 per cent Catholics with the remainder made up of 'others' and 'non-allocations'.[61] These shifts certainly furthered the possibility of a consociational deal being brokered in the 1990s and buried unionist dreams of a return to Protestant majority rule at Stormont, which had prevented so many of them from supporting Sunningdale. On the other hand, it made political and social equality within an internal context seem more attractive to nationalists, compared to the 1970s, when they were always going to be a weaker political force than unionists.

John McGarry and Brendan O'Leary argue that the consociational model had failed to produce a settlement in Northern Ireland because of the absence of sufficient elite predominance and intrasegmental stability.[62] However, the data in Chapter 2, Table 5, suggests that there *was* sufficient elite predominance in both communities to embark on some form of power-sharing in the 1970s. In fact, the external elites lacked the ability to provide the incentives and motivation for the internal elites to do just that. In 1998 the lack of intrasegmental stability was more salient than in 1973–74, yet agreement was reached precisely because the external elites provided the security for the majority of them to embark on the hazardous enterprise of compromise.

The concessions made by the SDLP, Sinn Féin, the UUP and the two loyalist parties were all underwritten by the dual guardianship of the British and Irish governments. This was based on the premise that no secret deals had been done with the other side and that the consociational model could bring them out of the conflict while addressing the constitutional needs of both sides. There was a guarantee for the nationalists that a united Ireland could come about by democratic means if the majority so wished it, but for the first time unionists had been guaranteed that Northern Ireland's position within the UK was constitutionally secure until the people wished otherwise. Paradoxically, the GFA provided a safeguard for unionists that the consociational model was no Trojan horse for a united Ireland, while for nationalists there was the assurance that consociationalism did not lock them exclusively into UK administration forever.

McGarry and O'Leary argue that the conflict was a result of dual British and Irish failures in nation-building and that the two states' actions often fuelled a conflict that they both wished to resolve.[63] Their successful negotiation in 1998 and their current regulation of the conflict are primarily due to the reversal of formerly antagonistic roles. Both states had emerged from mutual denial, constitutionally and politically addressing the failures in nation-building that perpetuated the conflict, in order to create the conditions for a consociational settlement in Northern Ireland. In sum, it is clear, then, that the endogenous conditions for conflict regulation could be established only when the exogenous variables were in place, acting in concert to create, maintain and manage the endogenous ones.

HEARTS AND MINDS

One of the great myths about the GFA, fuelled by the results of the referendums, notably the one in the North, is that the population had largely come around to the idea of power-sharing, and that there was a much

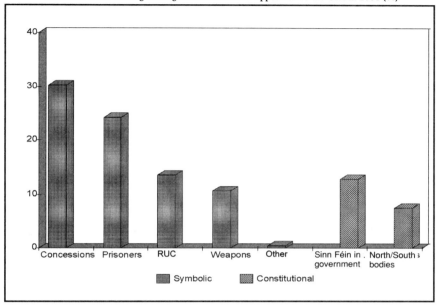

TABLE 6: Issues fuelling anti-Agreement Unionists' opposition to the GFA in 2001 (%)

wider cross-communal endorsement of the overall settlement than there had been in 1973. This was not the case. Cross-communal support for a consociational settlement did not increase at all over the course of the conflict, despite the political growth of Sinn Féin and the weakening of intrasegmental stratification within nationalism. Moreover, on the unionist side support had clearly decreased since the 1970s, as the result of the referendum in the North indicates, with only a marginal majority of Protestants actually supporting the GFA in 1998. While the Council of Ireland was the vehicle for unionist discontent in 1974, it was actually power-sharing with Sinn Féin, and the symbolic political victories that had delivered its acceptance of the GFA, that unionists were opposed to in 1998. However, as in 1974, it was not the actual principle of power-sharing that most unionists opposed, it was the emotive issues and the inclusion of Sinn Féin that they found objectionable (see Table 6).

In a private poll conducted for the UUP in March 2001, anti-Agreement unionist voters were asked: 'What is the single biggest issue which makes you opposed to the Good Friday Agreement?'. Interestingly, only 12.9 per cent chose 'Martin McGuinness/Barbara de Brun in government' compared to 30.2 per cent whose main contention was that, 'all concessions were to nationalists' in the GFA.[64] This gave the impression that the constitutional issues of power-sharing and North–South bodies were not the most salient in post-GFA opposition from anti-Agreement unionists. Again, the misnomer of 'anti-Agreement unionist' seems obvious. What is clear from Table 6 is that for 79.5 per cent of those polled the biggest issues fuelling their opposition were symbolic rather than constitutional. The difference in unionist opposition between 1974 and 1998 was that, during Sunningdale, its focus was predominantly on constitutional issues, whereas after 1998 the emotive issues were symbolic ones, with 'all the concessions going to nationalists' being the most salient.

These figures are not for unionism as a whole, but only for unionists who intended to vote against the GFA in the general election of 2001. Too much could be read into the lack of opposition to the inclusion of Sinn Féin as the symbolic security issues were very much on the DUP's agenda in the run-up to that election. More can be ascertained from looking at how attitudes to power-sharing in both communities have changed since Sunningdale. Unfortunately, questions on 'support' for and 'acceptance' of power-sharing in principle have not been asked in any recent major political survey, as they were in the 1970s.

In October 2002 a poll tested unionist attitudes to 'supporting' power-sharing with nationalists (see Table 7). Again, unfortunately, it was not followed up by a question asking whether they 'accepted' power-sharing with nationalists. The most obvious point here is that outside the UUP there was very little support among unionists for power-sharing

TABLE 7: UNIONIST SUPPORT FOR POWER-SHARING (%)
Who do you 'support' power-sharing with? (%)

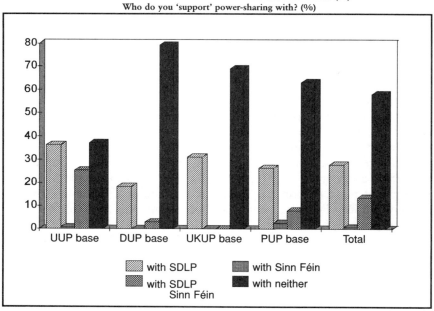

Source: Price WaterhouseCoopers poll of 1,080 people conducted on 15–16 October 2002 for the BBC Television Programme *Hearts and Minds*

TABLE 8: PUBLIC ATTITUDES TO THE POWER-SHARING EXECUTIVE
Looking back on the proposals contained in the GFA, could you tell me how you now feel about the requirement that the new Executive is power-sharing? (%)

	Catholics	Protestants	Secularists	Totals
Strongly support	28	9	21	16
Support	49	31	25	36
Neither	16	33	31	28
Oppose	0	8	9	6
Strongly oppose	1	9	5	6
Can't choose	5	8	7	7
Missing	1	2	2	2

Source: Northern Ireland Life and Times Survey 2000 of 12,390 people, Module: Political Attitudes, Variable: GFAPROP8

with nationalists, with an overall total of only 41.7 per cent in favour. In comparison to the 1970s, the inclusion of Sinn Féin has undoubtedly dragged these figures down dramitically and, given the arduous antagonisms over decommissioning and the other symbolic issues, it is perhaps surprising that they are not even lower (see Table 9). By comparing these attitudes to the answers to a similar question asked two years previously, it is safe to conclude that these issues have continued to weaken support for executive power-sharing (see Table 8). In 2000 only 17 per cent of

TABLE 9:
Protestant acceptance of Power-Sharing 1973–2002. A comparison of Protestant acceptance of the idea of power-sharing in 1973–74 with support for it after the GFA (%)

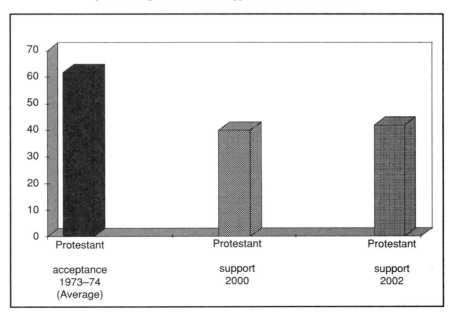

Protestants polled opposed the requirement of executive power-sharing, while 40 per cent actually supported it. These figures still fall far short of the numbers of those accepting the idea before and after Sunningdale.

Comparing the figures for 2000 with those in Chapter 2, Table 5, clearly shows that disapproval rates in the Protestant community have not changed a great deal. However, in 2000 the question implicitly concerned supporting power-sharing with Sinn Féin in the Executive, whereas in 1973–74 it concerned acceptance of power-sharing with constitutional nationalists (see Table 9). In 2000 only 40 per cent supported executive power-sharing, whereas in 1974 more than 60 per cent accepted the concept (see Table 9).

As for the Catholic/nationalist community, there has been a decrease in acceptance/support from an average of 92.4 per cent in the 1970s to 77 per cent in 2000. Unfortunately, the survey data, in the same fashion as in the 1970s, are skewed because the questionnaire offered respondents too many options instead of looking for definitive answers. On judging how attitudes to power-sharing have changed over the course of the conflict, it is probably safe to conclude that acceptance of executive power-sharing has decreased. The inclusion of Sinn Féin and the protracted wrangle over decommissioning has certainly prevented a majority of Protestants from offering the idea support.

Underlining this analysis is the fact that 37 per cent of UUP respondents did not support power-sharing with either nationalist party in 2002 (see Table 7). This strongly indicates that the Protestant community was not psychologically ready for these changes in 1998, in exactly the same way as it was not ready for the Council of Ireland and the loss of Stormont in 1973–74. However, it is unlikely that these are attitudes entirely backed up by principle; rather, they are probably influenced by the symbolic losses incurred by Unionism in the agreement. Ironically, the power-sharing Executive was working so well in 1974 that its success and cross-communal approval spurred on its opponents in their campaign against it, while the failure of the more recent Executive to function coherently after 1998 has added to growing intercommunal disapproval. Support for the GFA dropped in both communities between 1998 and 2002, with a similar margin of decline in support for the GFA among both Protestants and Catholics. This is probably attributable to the failure of the institutions to proceed and govern as expected in 1998, due to the difficulties that the symbolic issues have raised. The big difference from 1974 is that in June 2001 the GFA marginally passed the searing test of a Westminster general election. As in February 1974, the parties and voters in the unionist community treated the election as a collective poll on the GFA and on the UUP's leadership. The 2001 election damaged the UUP, but unlike in 1974, when endorsement of Sunningdale was by proxy of election results until it was re-questioned in February 1974, the collapse of support for UUP candidates and the GFA did not materialise in 2001 as the DUP had predicted. Like Faulkner, Trimble had often gone politically far ahead of his own constituency, but he had kept his party intact, retained the support of the British government and was seen to have secured the constitutional imperatives that his constituency needed to support a deal.

In sum, there was no great seismic shift in public opinion between 1973 and 1998 in favour of power-sharing: in fact, any shift was in the opposite direction. The crucial difference was that, while Trimble was prepared to take calculated leaps of faith in the Faulkner mould, the British and Irish governments provided a strong, balanced approach, enabling the UUP leader to initially sell the GFA to his constituency. However, the fact that Blair reneged on his promises and commitments to Trimble regarding decommissioning largely accounts for the lurch in the unionist electorate towards anti-Agreement candidates, and the decline in the UUP's vote. Ironically, through capitalising on this issue, Peter Robinson saw both a window for his party, the DUP, to enter the political process and a means of overtaking the UUP as the voice of pro-Agreement unionism. If Blair had kept his word to Trimble, this would have meant holding Sinn Féin to their commitment to decommission under the Agreement – something that the Labour government was not prepared to do. This increased the perception within the unionist community that nationalists had gained more from the GFA than they had. It also perpetuated the growing sense of disillusionment among unionists with the political process.

By October 2003 the British government, having failed to implement the GFA through its fear of using sanctions against republicans, had abandoned the UUP leadership and the moderate centre ground it represented, and began to engage with Sinn Féin and the DUP in search for a way forward. Northern Ireland's elites had come full circle. Those who had threatened constitutional change and a devolved power-sharing accord with violence and opposition eagerly sought to do business with each other in order to reap the political benefits that their intracommunal rivals had enjoyed in the years since 1998. Yet their electorates had not, and, in fact, the dominance of the extremists by 2004 illustrated how public opinion on the GFA had moved away from the pluralist ideals of 1998.

On 5 May 2005, Trimble finally lost his seat in Upper Bann as the DUP celebrated a landslide victory over their Unionist rivals in the Westminster general election. In its centenary year the UUP was reduced to just one seat at Westminster with 17.7 per cent of the total vote. While the DUP had failed to alter the fundamentals of the GFA under the Comprehensive Proposals they would have agreed a power-sharing deal with Republicans had it not been for the absence of transparent decommissioning. The UUP had lost the trust of its electorate, and Trimble had paid the price for continuously taking risks to keep the GFA alive in the absence of the support of that electorate, many of his party colleagues and the British government.[65] As in 1974, power-sharing in 1998 was very much an imposed piece of constitutional engineering, rather than a model of government chosen on the basis of any overwhelming sense of popular support. After the republican movement had failed to grant Trimble the transparent decommissioning he required to restart the Assembly in 2003, Blair abandoned the UUP leader, and with him, the political centre ground, turning his attention to finding a way forward that revolved around Northern Ireland's extremes.

CONCLUSION

One could be forgiven for thinking that Northern Ireland had come a long way by 1998 in its efforts to find peace. However, what the GFA actually illustrates is just how far Anglo-Irish relations had travelled from Britain and Ireland's unlikely partnership during the Sunningdale period. The consolidation of Anglo-Irish intergovernmental interests and structures, fortified by a synchronisation of efforts from London and Dublin in regulating the conflict, led directly to the materialisation of a unity of purpose that, by the mid-1990s, had become the driving force behind the peace process.

The DSD and the Framework Documents set the Anglo-Irish agenda, providing the context for substantive negotiations to get under way. These external relations provided the motivation and incentives for the Northern Ireland parties to engage in consociation. They enabled party leaders to go ahead of their constituencies and provided them with the confidence to take the risks that were necessary to conclude a constitutional settlement involving significant U-turns on what both sides would otherwise have viewed as positions contradictory to their ethno-national aspirations. It was these positive external factors that generated the stimulus for internal elites to successfully negotiate the GFA and engage in consociation. While the internal conditions were far from perfect, the British and Irish governments acted as stanchions, overarching and channelling the internal political developments in a fashion that was conducive to compromise. The GFA depended on this external relationship and the intergovernmental structures that established it, and problems concerning these very relationships emerged that resulted in the numerous suspensions of the Executive.

O'Leary's interpretation of the GFA is that the UK government no longer had the power to do 'anything that was not legitimate under the Agreement's procedures'.[66] He argues that 'the central purpose of the UK's agreement to delete Section 75 of the Government of Ireland Act of

1920, and the Irish state's agreement to modify Articles Two and Three
... had been to show that both states were engaged in a balanced constitutional change'.[67] O'Leary appears surprised that the Labour government interpreted the British constitutional change in the equation as
meaningless and that the Irish government understood it to be of equa-
nimity or balance to theirs. This view overestimates Irish expectations
considerably, as many politicians and diplomats realised the purely symbolic nature of the British change, and the fact that the unionists barely
mentioned it illustrates its insignificance. Mansergh described the dele-
tion of Section 75 as 'nothing close to as big a change as the Irish one',
but something that 'gave us symbolic political change, which added legitimacy to our position'.[68]

Annex A of the GFA includes a draft clause for incorporation in
British legislation, declaring that 'Northern Ireland in its entirety remains
part of the United Kingdom and shall not cease to be so without the consent of a majority of the people of Northern Ireland voting in a poll'.
This illustrates exactly how the two governments envisaged the sovereign
position of Northern Ireland after the signing of the GFA. Accordingly,
the external forces, while being partners, are not and will never be, equal
partners in the regulation of Northern Ireland's conflict, unless a new
Agreement establishes some form of co-sovereignty. O'Leary concludes
that 'every aspect of the Agreement is vulnerable to Westminster's doctrine of parliamentary sovereignty'.[69] He is absolutely right, yet the GFA
actually hangs on how the British government exercises its sovereignty in
the interests of preserving consociation in Northern Ireland, as opposed
to supporting idiosyncratic British or unionist interests. The downside of
this, of course, is that, if these external parameters were to shift, to the
detriment of the status quo in Northern Ireland, or the two governments
were to disengage from the process to any significant degree, the GFA
would collapse. This is in fact exactly what happened after the two governments failed to establish the Assembly in 2003. It became clear that
the British government was more concerned with the security aspects of
the GFA with Sinn Féin, than it was in preserving the accord itself. The
British government's failure to act against Sinn Féin and maintain the
spirit of the Agreement seriously undermined the credibility of the accord
in the eyes of the unionist electorate.

CHAPTER FIVE

A National Pact

General de Gaulle told me he had informed the Secretary of State
that he was in fact Joan of Arc, to which I retorted that this was a
rather unfortunate simile, as Joan of Arc had been somewhat
roughly handled by the British soldiery.

Edward Louis Spears[1]

Chapters 2, 3 and 4, have illustrated how consociation can be successfully employed by external powers that provide the incentives and
motives for domestic elites to engage in power-sharing. Having evaluated the British government's failure to impose consociation under
Sunningdale and its more successful reimposition under the GFA, this
chapter and the following two examine the different attempts to regulate
Lebanon's ethnic conflict.

In 1943 leading Lebanese Christian and Muslim politicians, came to
an unwritten agreement that reformulated the country's power-sharing
government and helped to end French colonial rule. The agreement,
which later became known as the National Pact, was primarily a device
to achieve independence, and to regulate conflicting Christian and
Muslim aspirations over Lebanon's national identity and its place in the
Middle East. It was not intended to be a long-term consociational formula for ending interconfessional conflict. Rather, as the political, economic and national interests of many Christian and Muslim leaders coincided, it was in fact a political compromise that temporarily sidestepped
the national question and, in doing so, unintentionally formed the
bedrock of Lebanese political life for the rest of the twentieth century.

This chapter describes how the National Pact developed as a consequence of converging local, regional and international variables that
facilitated the emergence of a power-sharing agreement in 1943. It
argues that the Lebanese seized the moment, as the Second World War
provided an opportunity for them to achieve independence through the
establishment of a Christian–Muslim pact. As the socio-economic interests of Lebanon's political leaders coincided with their desire to break the
yoke of French colonial rule, the regional dynamics of state-centred Arab
nationalism and Anglo-French colonial rivalry facilitated an independence settlement. This arrangement was not meant to permanently struc-

ture Lebanese politics, but, as it established the political positions of those who brokered it, the Pact endured. It was, however, agreed on the basis of the regional political environment as of 1943. When that environment changed, with the creation of Israel in 1948 and the subsequent rise of revolutionary Arab states, the Pact left Lebanon exposed to the instability of Middle Eastern politics.

In order to analyse how and why the National Pact was formed an overview of the events leading up to Lebanon's independence is required. This chapter analyses the intra-elite rivalries that shaped Lebanese politics under the French Mandate and the Anglo-French rivalry that facilitated the compromise of 1943. This historical narrative provides the basis for an evaluation of the internal and external dynamics that converged and culminated in a successful independence movement.

THE FRENCH DILEMMA

In 1915–16, the British began to consolidate their interests in the Middle East through the Hussein–MacMahon Correspondence, between Sharif Hussein in Mecca and the British High Commissioner in Cairo. In anticipation of the collapse of the Ottoman Empire, the British immediately opened talks with the French, which led to the Sykes-Picot Agreement in the spring of 1916.[2] This sought to balance French interests in the Levant with Britain's pledges to Arab nationalist leaders. With the defeat of the Ottomans in 1918 the two western powers divided the Arab lands between them, with Britain appearing to revoke its pledges to further Arab independence under Hussein–MacMahon.[3] On 1 October 1917 the Ottoman administration in Beirut fell and the Maronite leader Habib al-Saad established an Arab government in the name of Sharif Hussein of Mecca. This action directly contradicted the Sykes-Picot Agreement, which had placed Lebanon within the French sphere of influence, prompting a swift response from France.[4] An 'A' Mandate was then entrusted to France by the League of Nations at San Remo on 26 April 1920, granting France the task of nurturing Lebanon (and Syria) towards independence, and providing maximum self-government in religious and secular affairs. Instead, France exploited its position in both countries, furthered its regional interests and failed to build nation states possessing anything close to corresponding national identities in what became Lebanon and Syria.

The French dilemma entailed managing conflicting claims to pan-Arab unity, a Greater Syrian state and an independent Christian Lebanon. The Syrians expected the Maronite Christians to accept some form of autonomous existence on Mount Lebanon within a Greater Syrian state, similar to the position that they had enjoyed under the Ottoman Empire.

On the other hand, the Maronites, most of whom did not see themselves as Arabs at all, incessantly pursued an independent state. They were split, however, over whether there should be a larger independent Lebanon or a smaller, more homogeneous Christian entity tied to France.[5] Most Maronites believed that the Christian community could dominate a new republic, in spite of the fact that the demographic majority they enjoyed on Mount Lebanon would be greatly diminished by the inclusion of the Muslim coastal towns and their hinterlands, which had Sunni majorities, and the Bekaa Valley and Jabal Amel, which were predominantly Shi'a.

There was further division within the broader Christian community and some were, in fact, Arab nationalists. While the Maronites were specific to Mount Lebanon, the Greek Orthodox community had co-religionists spread across the Fertile Crescent and many of them endorsed Greater Syrian nationalism. On 1 September 1920 the French nonetheless created a politically and economically viable 'Greater' Lebanon in order to promote their long-term goals in the region. This marked a major political defeat for Lebanon's Sunni Muslims, as they had gone from being part of the religious majority community under the Ottoman Empire to being just one of many religious minorities in a Christian-dominated and French-controlled state. Most Christians were happy with a Greater Lebanon under the Mandate, even though they made up only 50 per cent of the resident population, according to the census of 1932 (see Table 10).

The mandated territories of Syria and Lebanon came under the control of the French High Commissioner in Beirut, Henri de Jouvenel. Lebanon received its first Constitution in 1926, which provided for an elected Chamber of Deputies and an appointed Senate. A Greek Orthodox politican was elected by Parliament, Charles Dabbas, as Lebanon's first President and the Maronite leader, Auguste Adib Pasha, was nominated to the premiership by de Jouvenel. After much wrangling over proportional representation, positions in the government were distributed along confessional lines, with the Maronites receiving two seats, and the Sunni, Shi'a, Druze, Greek Orthodox and Greek Catholic communities each receiving one.[6] This reinforced political and social confessionalism, and saw the communal system stunt the growth of any serious ideologically based interconfessional party system. The Senate was soon abolished and the presidential term was extended from three years to six with no possibility of re-election. In 1929 further constitutional changes were introduced in an attempt to reduce the scope for political manipulation and prevent anyone from holding power for more than six consecutive years.

The French suspended the Constitution in 1932, maintaining sovereignty through the High Commissioner, and reinstated Dabbas as an appointed President. This situation arose following tension between the rival Christian power blocs or parties. Many of these Lebanese parties were not political groups stemming from modern ideological movements. In fact, they were vehicles for traditional leaders, the *Zu'ama*, who represented the interests and political philosophies of their own religious communities and family clans. These organisations are best categorised as religious and intrareligious blocs, each representing one leader under the guise of a party organisation.[7]

When a presidential election finally took place in 1936 Émile Eddé beat his main rival, Beshara al-Khoury, to the office, which by then was considered a Maronite preserve. A treaty between Lebanon and France was then concluded, but after Léon Blum's government fell in Paris the French Chamber of Deputies and the Senate refused to ratify it.[8] The French thus failed to follow Britain's lead in signing treaties with the Iraqi and Egyptian governments, negotiated on the premise that they would ignore them if they could, but if the circumstances proved positive for the independence movements then they had something substantial to fall back on.

The situation in the Levant changed suddenly when Nazi Germany defeated France in 1940, establishing pro-Vichy rule in the Levant.[9] In June 1941, with the help of General Charles de Gaulle's Free French troops, Britain imposed Allied control over Lebanon and Syria. After much acrimony between Britain and the French Committee, agreements were signed between them concerning the administration of the two states during the war.[10] French control was reinstated after the Free French declared their intention to put an end eventually to the Mandate regime and conclude treaties with two sovereign states.[11] Subsequently de Gaulle resisted British pressure to issue a joint proclamation of independence.[12] Instead, on 26 November 1941 the Free French High Commissioner, General Georges Catroux, pledged Lebanese independence and sovereignty under the presidency of Alfred Naccache.[13] The declaration of independence was subsequently underwritten and guaranteed independently by the British, while the French set about preventing it from coming into force.[14]

The British Prime Minister, Winston Churchill, had wanted a joint declaration, but de Gaulle contended that the 'word of France had no need of a foreign guarantee'.[15] He suspected that the British wanted to position themselves as arbitrators between that the Free French and the Levant states. This would have created the impression that when they actually gained independence, 'they would owe it to England'.[16] Conversely, when tension rose between the allies over the issue de Gaulle argued that Catroux's declaration granting Syria independence must, 'from the standpoint of international law, be regarded as provisional, since the Free French movement had no international status and no power to negotiate the termination of the Mandate'.[17]

Churchill held that France could preserve its interests by signing postwar treaties with Syria and Lebanon, in the mould of the Anglo-Iraqi Treaty of 1930, which was implemented in 1932.[18] Yet de Gaulle and the Free French Committee were suspicious of Churchill's intentions in the Levant. They believed that he was seeking to consolidate 'British leadership in the whole Middle East', with foreign policy endeavours to 'sometimes stealthily and sometimes harshly replace France at Damascus and at Beirut'.[19] Thus, while he recognised the right of both states to independence, de Gaulle had no intention of 'abolishing the principle' of French authority during the war, as he feared that to do so would amount to France being replaced by the British.[20]

Both the Free French and the British had misread the political climate in the Levant, as many of them failed to realise the growing strength of Arab nationalism during the war. However, one close friend of Churchill did appreciate it. That was Sir Edward Louis Spears, who,[21] regardless of de Gaulle's persistent appeals to Churchill not to appoint him,[22] had become Britain's Minister in the Levant in 1942. Spears viewed himself in the Lawrence of Arabia mould and based his pro-Arab policy on the premise that Britain had underwritten the Free French declarations of independence. While his political instincts proved correct, his handling of de Gaulle and the French Committee resulted in a serious clash between the allies over the Levant states. Spears surely dreamt of replacing French influence in the region, but Churchill would not hear of it 'under any circumstances'.[23] The premier told Spears that the French could retain the same position as the British in Iraq, 'no more, no less', emphasising and re-emphasising the fact that his 'entire policy was based upon working in the closest touch with [US] President Roosevelt', who did not share Spears's colonial aspirations.[24]

Of course, the withdrawal of the French was not wholly Spears's work, but he did everything within his power to hasten their departure. He opposed Catroux and bolstered the Arab nationalist leaders until Churchill, apparently putting Anglo-French relations before loyalty to an old friend, forced his return to London in 1944.[25] General de Gaulle later contended that: 'In every domain, every day, everywhere, there was interference from our allies, multiplied by an army of uniformed agents'.[26] It was in this atmosphere that an embattled France clung to her imperial possessions, while an intercommunal Christian–Muslim coalition emerged to challenge them and bid for Lebanon's independence with the help of Spears.

FACING THE ARAB WORLD

During the Mandate years Lebanon had become polarised over the form of independent state the country should eventually have. Initially there were three schools of thought in the debate regarding Lebanon's future.

Eddé and Khoury led the first, advocating a Greater Lebanon, arguing that it was the only way of ensuring a politically and economically viable state. The second favoured a smaller, Christian Lebanon, but most viewed this as politically impractical. The third, promoted by the Arab nationalist leaders, Riad Solh and Abd al-Hamid Karame, sought a united Arab state that would include both Syria and Lebanon.

In the late 1920s a struggle had begun between the two principal Christian politicians, Eddé and Khoury, for political leadership and dominance within the Maronite community.[27] By the 1930s the two men were the figureheads of the two main Christian parties, the National Bloc and the Constitutional Bloc, respectively.[28] Ironically, neither of these politicians was traditional *Zu'ama*, their French colonial masters having promoted them to positions of prominence.

Eddé was a Francophile Lebanese nationalist, and his political philosophy was as attractive to the idiosyncratic Maronites of the mountain as it was repellent to the Arab nationalists of the coastal cities. He espoused a particularistic strand of Lebanese politics that was overtly pro-French and covertly pro-Zionist,[29] shunned close ties with the Arab world, and nurtured an isolationist view of Lebanese history.[30] Eddé believed in a Lebanon culturally, economically and politically tied to France and the West, and was sceptical about retaining the parts of Greater Lebanon with large Muslim populations.[31] While he was not at all opposed to independence and had contributed greatly to the creation of the state, he believed that Lebanon was not yet ready for self-government in 1943.[32]

Khoury, who had also previously supported the French, had by the early 1940s been converted to the idea of breaking Lebanon's ties with France and reconciling its relationship with the Arab world. His relationship with the French had broken down over their continued support for his rival, Eddé, so his conversion was as pragmatic as it was principled. The essential ingredient in Khoury's political success was that his realistic view of Lebanese politics left him more open to compromise than Eddé, who was extremely unpopular with mainstream Muslims, having constantly denounced Arab nationalism and the notion of Greater Syrian unification.[33] Fundamentally, Beirut was Khoury's source of influence, as he was at the heart of the city's Christian–Muslim intellectual and socio-economic elite and was strongly backed by political and economic thinkers such as Michel Chiha and Henri Pharaon, whose 'convivialist ideals' provided the ideological framework for a Lebanese consensus to emerge.[34]

By 1932 rivalry between the two Christian blocs had become so intense that Eddé backed a Muslim presidential candidate, Sheikh Muhammad al-Jisr, in order to provoke a political crisis. His plan succeeded, prompting the French to intervene, dissolve Parliament and postpone the forthcoming elections. When they were finally held, at the end of 1935, Eddé was elected President, beating Khoury by just one vote. Eddé quickly signed a treaty regarding independence with France, providing Britain and France with the use of Lebanese territory in the event of war. This caused grave discontent within the Muslim community, particularly among the Sunnis, as it reinforced French influence and fixed Lebanon's present borders.

At the time most Muslims rejected the idea of a Greater Lebanon and strove towards unity with Syria in a larger united Arab state. They viewed the idea of Greater Lebanon as a French colonial vehicle for dividing the Arab peoples, in contradiction to secular Arab nationalist principles. However, the Muslims were also divided over the direction of their nationalism and its political purpose.[35] One group promoted Arab nationalism and a Greater Syrian state, while another group, the secretive Arab National Party (ANP), championed unionism from within Lebanon. Their conflicting political ideologies were fashioned at a series of meetings promoting Arab union, which became known as the Conference of the Coast.

The unionist split was a consequence of the divergence between the interests of the Sunni elite in Beirut and those of their co-religionists in Tripoli and Sidon. Solh emerged as the leader of the ANP unionists in Beirut, opposed largely by Karame, who led the Greater Syrian nationalists in Tripoli. As Beirut was the growing centre of cross-communal economic transactions, the interests of the Sunni community in the capital lay with their Christian counterparts. This was where they diverged from the Arab nationalists in Tripoli, who had no such political or economic ties. In Tripoli Sunni economic interests lay squarely in full union with Syria, as partition meant that Beirut would become the natural trading centre for Damascus, Homs and Hama at their expense. These arguments held true for the Christian Orthodox community as well, for their interests were in line with Greater Syrian nationalism as opposed to Lebanese nationalism.

At the conference in 1936 the Syrian nationalists still called for nothing short of total independence and union with Syria, while Solh began to argue that this position would only push the Lebanese nationalists into a corner and further into the French camp. He argued that the nationalist movement must concentrate on removing the French and gaining Lebanese independence before pursuing pan-Arab ambitions. The following year, in response to the unionists, France forged a coalition between Eddé and Khoury, which excluded the important Sunni leaders and isolated them from their Christian counterparts. Yet circumstances changed and, as tension mounted in Europe over war, the French suspended the Constitution. For the first time Christian nationalists and Muslim unionists found common cause in seeking the removal of the Mandate. A new centrist movement emerged, composed of convivialists and political converts from both the Christian and Muslim camps. By 1943 the leaders of this movement, Khoury and Solh, were winning the argument for a Lebanon that was both independent of France and part of the Arab world.

In March 1943 the Free French reinstated the Constitution and agreed to elections in August. These took place amid great acrimony: the Free French interfered to produce favourable results and halt Khoury's presidential campaign, and the British threatened not to recognise a government brought into being by malpractice and corruption.[36] By then Catroux had been replaced by the less resourceful Free French Ambassador, Jean Helleu, granting Spears more scope to influence the electoral process. Outraged by Spears's actions, the Free French accused the British of interfering in the elections and displaying outright opposition to their preferred candidate, Eddé.[37] Spears clearly had control over the situation, as he announced to the Lebanese deputies that without authorisation from London he 'would not recognise a government headed by Eddé'.[38]

Much to the delight of Spears, the presidential vote left Khoury and Eddé evenly matched. This enabled Spears to endorse Camille Chamoun as a compromise candidate, pushing the two rivals to accept his candidacy, while outwitting Helleu. The idea of the pro-British Chamoun becoming President horrified the Free French so much that, fearing he might win enough support in Parliament, they dropped Eddé and threw their weight behind Khoury.[39] Spears then gladly lent him full British support, but the Free French, having spent every ounce of their influence trying to get Eddé elected, had made an enemy out of Khoury.[40] Spears would have preferred Chamoun, his clandestine role in getting Khoury elected was central to his success in outmanoeuvring the Free French and allowed him to take full credit for Khoury's electoral success.[41] Due to Spears' machinations, rifts within the National Bloc[42] and the failure of the Free French to secure their preferred candidate, on 21 September Khoury was elected President, in the absence of Eddé and seven of his supporters, by forty-four votes to none with three spoiled ballots.[43] He then appointed Solh as Prime Minister, and Solh formed his first cabinet on 26 November.[44]

Spears was also instrumental in Solh's appointment. He favoured the Sunni leader because he was coordinating his independence strategy with the Syrian government. Spears viewed Solh's leadership as fundamental to harmonising the policies of the two governments against the Free French. In fact, as Meir Zamir points out, Khoury's key allies, Pharaon and Chiha, were strongly opposed to Solh's appointment, and French accusations that Spears had imposed Solh on Khoury were indeed well founded.[45] Spears was unsure of Khoury's reliability in steering a pro-British course and in a personal letter to the British Minister of State in Cairo, Richard Casey, he declared that:

> The appointment of Riad al-Solh's ministry means that everything
> has ended infinitely more satisfactorily than I ever dared hope for.
> I have felt all along as if I were building a house of cards and that
> each additional card was likely to bring down the whole structure.
> Yet until the last tier was in position, nothing had been achieved.[46]

In response the Free French tried to maintain military bases in the
Levant under new treaties that they hoped to negotiate with the new
Lebanese and Syrian governments. Churchill had clearly indicated his
position on this, maintaining that the Free French (and thus post-war
France) must be on the same footing as Britain in Iraq, and that British
independence pledges 'to Syria and Lebanon are serious and must be
made good'.[47] Of course this was logical, for if Britain had allowed
Lebanon and Syria to sever all ties with France, it would have reflected
very poorly on the British position in Egypt and Iraq.

Khoury and Solh then spelled out the nature of their agreement in
post-election speeches on 21 September and 7 October. They spoke of
how Lebanon was to be governed by a Christian–Muslim coalition based
on fair representation of the communities, and how its independence
would be founded upon the principle of neutrality, with Christians for-
going western influence and Muslims giving up on Arab unity. Solh
declared: 'My government will found these relations on a solid basis,
safeguarding for the Lebanon its independence and complete sovereignty as well as its present boundaries, since the Lebanon is a nation with
Arab character looking westward for its culture'.[48]

On the one hand, Solh sacrificed Arab nationalist goals in order to
convince Christians that this new power-sharing formula was in their
interests; while on the other, Khoury relinquished the French role in
Lebanon in order to make the new republic more attractive to Muslims.
French was dropped as the second national language and Lebanon was
proclaimed to have an Arab face while remaining regionally and internationally independent. In fact, it was to be detached from pan-Arab ideas
and inter-Arab disputes, neutrality in foreign policy forming the corner-
stone of the compromise. Real change was also taking place in Khoury's
constituency, as one British diplomat commented: 'The French have
made such a public mess of their cuisine that countless Lebanese of predominantly French culture, who had never thought in national terms
before, were now doing so with enthusiasm'.[49]

The Free French, however, held out for the acquisition of treaties
before granting any more concessions on Lebanese or Syrian independence.[50] There was little doubt in de Gaulle's mind that they would have
secured these if the British had not stood in their way.[51] The French
Committee issued a communiqué in early November denying the right of
the Lebanese President to 'act unilaterally to dissolve the Mandate'.[52] On

8 November, in response to the French Committee's position, the Chamber of Deputies tabled a constitutional amendment removing all French privileges and, in effect, denouncing the Mandate. This was passed in the Chamber and subsequently signed by Khoury.[53] On 11 November the President, the Prime Minister and all but two government ministers were arrested in the middle of the night and imprisoned by Free French troops, on the orders of Helleu.[54] Khoury was dragged from his bed in front of his wife, while his son 'was driven into a cellar with blows of rifle-butts' to 'cries of "Son of a dog, son of an Englishman"'.[55]

The same morning Helleu issued a decree appointing Eddé as the new President. This provoked widespread criticism, with Spears labelling Eddé a 'complete French stooge',[56] and demanding the government's immediate release and reinstatement. Catroux asserted that Helleu had acted without instructions from Algiers, yet he refused to say when the politicians would be released, as he was not going to accept a British 'ultimatum'. Spears concluded that there was little doubt that 'Helleu's *coup d'état* was carried out under the direct orders of General de Gaulle'[57] and that Catroux was going to use 'Helleu's totally inexcusable action as a bargaining counter to extract promises from the Lebanese before releasing the ministers'.[58] In other words, the French would release the prisoners if they agreed to go back to the Mandate system or sign an international treaty. Helleu claimed that he was acting on de Gaulle's orders, as he had no more authority to arrest the ministers without instructions from Algiers than he did to release them, as it soon transpired.[59]

In response de Gaulle stated that the French Committee's position was that, while Helleu's actions had been excessive, they were 'perfectly justifiable'[60] and 'the Mandate could not be legally terminated during the war'.[61] Conversely, Churchill stressed that: 'the Mandate disappeared both *de facto* and *de jure* from the day on which the French and British governments recognised the independence of Syria and Lebanon'.[62] Further, Spears reminded the French that in a published letter to the head of the Syrian government, dated 23 June 1941, 'Catroux stated categorically that the "Syrian peoples might immediately adopt any constitution they chose"'.[63] However, in the North African press de Gaulle described it as 'no more than an incident', while the Paris papers accused Britain of trying to usurp France's role in the Levant, and de Gaulle and the French Committee of being at their beck and call.[64]

However, directives from the British Foreign Office highlighted the view that Britain 'should work for the release of the ministers and *not* their immediate restitution as a government' [original emphasis] so that Britain could act as 'honest brokers' between the two parties.[65] London's response was not the foregone conclusion that Spears's reaction had suggested. Casey contended that if it had not been for their virulent protests from Beirut, 'the Foreign Office would have let it go at release – and the fort would have been sold'.[66] Catroux ominously declared that the situation was 'another Fashoda',[67] concluding that the lack of good Anglo-French relations had allowed the Lebanese to play the allies off against each other.[68]

This action caused the Christians and Muslims of Lebanon to rise as one against their flailing colonial masters, and Spears called for martial law to be imposed.[69] As a result Britain called the French Committee's bluff, delivering Catroux an ultimatum to either release the ministers or see British martial law installed.[70] The ink was still drying on the posters declaring British rule when the Free French, unprepared for the military confrontation that the British seemed ready to contemplate, finally backed down.[71] On 22 November Khoury, Solh and the ministers were finally released, and Lebanon's independence was marked as they arrived in Beirut to a heroes' welcome.[72]

A CHRISTIAN–MUSLIM PACT

It was during the course of the Second World War that Arab nationalists began to view Free French colonial weakness and mounting Anglo-French rivalry as an opportunity to achieve independence. The bulk of the Sunni leadership came to accept and support the idea of an independent Lebanon, a state acceptable to the Maronites, in return for the abolition of the French Mandate. On the other hand, the Christian socio-economic elite in Beirut had been sufficiently alienated by the French and carried enough influence in the mountainous hinterland for them to endorse a political settlement based on confessional power-sharing within an independent state.[73] In fact, the continued French presence finally forced reasonableness and conciliation upon Solh's Arab unionists and Khoury's Lebanese nationalists. Like many other Arab leaders, Solh recognised that the only way in which Arab unity could ever be realised was through a process of decolonisation: the formation of independent Arab states was a prerequisite to collective Arab self-determination. Solh had moderated his nationalist stance in order to win Christians over to Greater Arab nationalism, arguing that 'nationalists should be willing to make great sacrifices by placing the interest of the nation above and beyond any other regional interests', and that unity could be achieved only through consent.[74]

Solh's leadership was crucial at this stage, as he was the only Muslim leader in Lebanon with the wider Arab credibility and legitimacy to argue for the partition of Lebanon from Syria without his rivals capitalising on such a compromising stance.[75] The Sunni reading of the political situation was founded on the premise that Christians could be converted to this nationalism, which would take precedence over any Lebanese identity in the future. However, this was in spite of the fact that many Maronites did not view themselves as Arabs at all, for their Lebanese or Phoenician identity was contradictory to any such sentiments.

Many Maronite leaders had also moved towards a conciliatory position in response to French rule. In the mid-1930s the Maronite Patriarch Arida had called for greater autonomy for Lebanon delivering a five-point plan to the French demanding the independence and self-government promised under the Mandate.[76] By the early 1940s enough Christian leaders were prepared to accept the moderate dose of Arab nationalism required to rid Lebanon of colonial rule. By this stage both the National Bloc and the Constitutional Bloc had declared themselves ardent defenders of Lebanese independence.[77] The Christian interpretation of the political climate was founded upon the premise that any future Lebanese Arab nationalism would echo its secular origins and, more importantly, that Arab nationalism or Arab identity would be a force within an independent Lebanese state. The fundamental problem, which was ignored in order to attain independence, was that, while Sunnis viewed the Christian–Muslim agreement as a temporary necessity on the road to Arab unity, the Christians – especially the Maronites – saw it as a permanent solution to Lebanon's national question.

Crucially, Khoury and Solh subsequently came to share a common understanding: that Anglo-French rivalry would lead to the defeat of the French in the Levant sooner rather than later. Further, it was clear to Solh that a similar sea change had occurred in Syria by the early 1940s. Many leaders of the Syrian National Bloc, of which he was a member, had become far more anxious to achieve Syrian independence than to create a greater Arab state that included Lebanon.[78] This shift in Syrian Arab nationalism helped to forge a centre ground in Lebanese politics. It allowed enough Christians and Muslims to take a moderate stance, under the rubric of a Lebanese compromise, and achieve independence.

When the French eventually conceded defeat the groundswell of popular opinion beneath the two champions of Lebanese independence ensured the agreement broad intercommunal endorsement. Yet its formation had little bearing upon the frenetic events that saw Lebanon emerge from the shadow of colonial rule. The communal pact was a pragmatic agreement constructed incrementally over many years. By 1943 Maronite and Sunni interests and political aspirations had momentarily converged to the extent that an interconfessional political coexistence had become viable. It was in this contentious yet ultimately conciliatory climate that the consociational arrangement came into being.

In sum, this meeting of minds was primarily due to four events: first, the common external threat of French imperialism to both Christians and Muslims; second, the weakening of French power and the presence of the

British through Spears; third, the changing currents within Arab nationalism, whereby independent states took precedence over a unified Arab
entity, with Syrians and Lebanese working together against the French;
and, fourth, Christian willingness to share power in order to achieve an
economically viable 'Greater' Lebanon. The overlapping effects of these
local, regional and international factors enabled the Lebanese agreement
to be forged. Without these positive external variables neither independence nor a power-sharing agreement could have been achieved. These
favourable circumstances allowed the Lebanese to gain inter-Arab legitimacy for their independence and consolidate their government with
British support.

THE MYTH OF THE NATIONAL PACT

What the Lebanese National Pact became in later decades was far
removed from the compromise that was brokered by Khoury and Solh
in 1943. Their agreement was certainly not a national power-sharing
accord, designed to set confessional politics in stone on a proportional
basis between Lebanon's various religious communities. It was actually
a *realpolitik* compromise undertaken by the dominant Maronite and
Sunni leaderships to rid themselves of the French, facilitated by positive
regional and, more importantly, international variables. In many ways
the National Pact, as it came to be thought of and nostalgically written
about, was a myth. It did not actually come into existence in 1943 and
no radically new consociational agreement emerged between Lebanon's
communities. Rather, the Pact was a reformulated continuation of an
interconfessional political administration that had developed under the
Ottoman *millet* system and the French Mandate,[79] and temporarily sidestepped Lebanon's contradictory ideological differences in order to gain
independence. Thus, the accord was very much a creature of its time,
rather than a clearly thought-out programme for government; yet it subsequently evolved into an integral part of the national constitutional
framework. Just as regional and international factors had defined its creation, and marked its development, similar variables consistently tested
its robustness and finally caused its collapse. Therefore, in order to
understand the formation, meaning and durability of the National Pact,
the local, regional and international variables that brought it about must
be examined and understood.

The Constitution of 1926 had granted the President strong executive
powers and it had long since been established that the post was a
Maronite preserve. Therefore the Muslim elites needed something to
offer to their constituency in the ideological debate over independence in
1943. This was where the unwritten confessional side to the new consti-

tutional formula developed and the Christian–Muslim compromise came to be underwritten by two constitutional equations: the official, written Constitution of 1926 and the unofficial, unwritten agreement of 1943. The latter was something of an unknown quantity at the time, especially on the details of the structures that were to govern the country. These were not so important at the time, quite simply because Solh and Khoury's primary concern was to take advantage of the wartime situation to gain Lebanon's freedom:[80] the intricacies of power-sharing could be worked out later. Thus, some Lebanese politicians came to talk about the Pact with hindsight as if it was a concrete constitutional entity, but it became so only after it faced its first big crisis during Camille Chamoun's presidency, in 1958.[81]

In fact, the phrase 'National Pact' was not even part of Lebanese political language in 1943 and did not become so until much later. This was part of the myth of the Pact. The trick that Khoury and Solh played was to appear to have agreed a grand Lebanese internal compromise, sell it on the wave of independence and emerge triumphantly as Lebanon's joint national leaders. In reality, parts of the Pact had been specified in the 1930s, when it became the custom that the President would be a Maronite and, after 1937–38, that the Prime Minister would be a Sunni. It was not until 1947 that it became firmly established that the office of the Speaker was a Shi'a preserve, after the appointment of a Christian provoked Shi'a outrage.[82] Until then custom had not been firmly established as to who would hold the Speaker's position, and it had alternated among the Shi'a, Greek Orthodox and Greek Catholic communities. It became a customary part of the unwritten pact because of this crisis.

Not only were these parts of the Pact unwritten in 1943, but they were also unspoken and, arguably, unagreed. They developed through intercommunal bargaining. Further, they were founded upon the local and regional political forces that bolstered and guaranteed them. Thus, from its inception the agreement, and therefore Lebanese power- sharing, were open to bargaining, custom, personality and extra-constitutional compromise within a regional context. Antoine Messarra argues that: 'The Lebanese national pacts (not to be confused with the specific National Pact of 1943) are not constitutional anomalies, nor are they anachronic facts, but rather [they] belong to a general historical category'.[83]

Therefore the power-sharing system evolved, since it was never rubber-stamped or constitutionally entrenched. The pact of Lebanese coexistence developed into a see-saw equilibrium, with the internal dynamics of power-sharing on one side, and the external balance of eastern and western orientations on the other. If either side lost balance or became top-heavy, then the Lebanese system and, in effect, the dual constitutional formula came under pressure. This was to be the First Republic's most enduring feature.

Consociational tensions became exacerbated when external events altered the equilibrium, events such as the creation of the state of Israel, which posed a challenge to Lebanon's foreign policy symmetry. Yet the Pact was not seriously contested until opposition to Chamoun had grown. Muslims were outraged by his approach to the Baghdad Pact of 1955, his refusal to break off diplomatic relations with Britain and France in 1956 after Suez, and, most importantly, his signing up to the Eisenhower Doctrine in 1957. Further, Nasserism challenged the National Pact in the sense that, after Suez, many Muslims looked to Nasser as their national leader and reviled Chamoun as the only Arab leader to have signed up to the Eisenhower Doctrine, in contravention of the principles of 1943. Thus, as the foreign policy equilibrium of the Pact became strained, the gulf between the two communities became increasingly salient.[84]

Chamoun's presidential term also raised questions over whether Lebanon had a presidential system or a consociational power-sharing one. In times of crisis, such as 1958, some Christians argued that it was the written Constitution that really mattered and that the Pact of 1943 was simply an accord between two politicians. On the other hand, Muslims contended that the Constitution was not amended in 1943 in order to guarantee the Christian position in Lebanon and the region as a whole. They argued that they had accepted the unwritten Pact only as part of this compromise, so its power-sharing provisions were equally, if not more, constitutionally valid.

This dispute over executive presidential government as opposed to intercommunal power-sharing – written Constitution versus unwritten – highlighted the interconfessional differences that existed after 1943 over what exactly the Lebanese constitution was, and how its duality should be interpreted and implemented. Of course, it is not surprising that this was most prominent in times of national crisis, as the agreement was seen as being merely transitional, rather than as the embodiment of the political system that it was to become for the remainder of the twentieth century.[85] In fact, this duality in Lebanese politics became pertinent relatively soon after independence, as Khoury used the presidency autocratically, and Solh was weakened after the execution in 1948 of Antoine Sa'adeh and was himself assassinated in 1951.

Did the Pact ever actually exist as a political partnership? It appears to have existed as just that, as a 'contract of association' between pragmatic politicians based on immediate interests and motives.[86] It is unlikely that Solh and Khoury imagined in 1943 that their agreement would last for decades. Yet once they were locked into the pact, it remained in the political and economic interests of those in power to work and maintain the power-sharing system.

One long-term effect this had on Lebanon was that politics and government based on the agreement failed to foster and produce national

leaders. Solh and Khoury were national leaders, but only national leaders of the movement of 1943. They brokered the Pact to become the
founding fathers of Lebanon's independence and their subsequent split
resulted in the unhealthy precedent of the Prime Minister representing
the Sunni Muslims, and the President the Maronite Christians, in the new
state. What a country as divided as Lebanon needed most was a national
figure, but after the compromise had served its purpose its leaders
retreated to their confessional positions. This had as much to do with the
pre-war communal system of traditional notables as with the interethnic
division that the Pact consolidated.

In sum, on an internal level the National Pact was primarily an agreement between Solh and Khoury to achieve independence. The very fact
that the two men detested each other, or at least did not get on well, politically or personally, is indicative of the Maronite–Sunnite ideological gulf
that they bridged and that successive future leaders would have to overcome in conjunction with their political and economic interests, under the
rubric of the Pact. It was changes in the international environment and
regional Arab nationalist developments that brought these leaders to cap-
italise on their socio-economic commonalities. The sanctity of the Pact
came much later.

A REGIONAL SETTING FOR INDEPENDENCE

Solh's role in attaining independence deserves considerable credit, for his
weight as an Arab nationalist leader and his pragmatic vision of how the
region would take shape after the Second World War enabled him to
deliver the Muslim side of the Lebanese equation. He was able to distance himself sufficiently from Greater Syrian nationalism, while retaining the political authority to employ Syria, Egypt and Iraq to provide the
Arab legitimacy that Lebanon needed to attain its independence. Along
with Khoury he made visits to Egypt to argue Lebanon's case for independence. As a result both Egypt and Iraq pressured the leadership of the
Syrian National Bloc into accepting and supporting Lebanese independence and promoting the Muslim–Christian agreement. This accord
hinged very much on the Lebanese first getting rid of the French, and
then settling their differences with Syria and the Arab world.

If Britain was the international guarantor of Lebanon's independence,
then Egypt and Syria were its regional sponsors.[87] It has even been argued
that Egypt went as far as to create and cement the partnership between
Solh and Khoury, who until 1943 were not allies.[88] Solh read the Syrian
political situation correctly: he knew that its national leaders were
prepared to forgo union with Lebanon, provided that they could achieve
unity among the divided Syrian regions.[89] If Syria had to be divided, par-

tition from Lebanon was the lowest common denominator its leaders could possibly accept. Pragmatically, Solh also knew that it was better to be the leader of 'the Muslims in Lebanon than a Muslim leader in a Greater Syria'.[90] Therefore, rather than being an impediment to Lebanese independence, and despite the fact that many Syrian leaders were still pressing for union, Syria, in seeking to maintain its own unity and gain its independence, acquiesced in the formation of the Lebanese National Pact under the strong influence of Britain, Egypt and Iraq.[91] The support of these countries and the blessing of the Saudis was crucial, as they were in competition for leadership over the emerging Arab world.

From the Christian perspective Egypt also played a very significant role. Egyptian acceptance of, and support for, Lebanese independence, and the internal Christian–Muslim alliance that enabled it to emerge, allowed Khoury to accept, support and sell Lebanon's Arabic face and relinquish his ties with France. Instead of having a French-dominated state, Khoury supported an independent and shared Lebanon that was part of and friendly to the Arab world. This setting was integral to the success of the Pact and the achievement of independence. The Arab face allowed the Christians to give something to the Muslims, but exactly what that face meant for Lebanon was not clearly spelled out in the Pact's foreign policy dimension. Consequently, many questions remained unresolved. What was Lebanon's role to be in the Arab world? Just how could it remain neutral in respect of inter-Arab conflicts? What would happen if a Zionist state was set up bordering Lebanon?

The creation of Israel in 1948 quickly brought these questions to the surface, as the Pact was founded on the premise of the Arab balance of power and regional stability as of 1943. The creation of a Zionist state was not considered in the 1943 equation. Many Lebanese leaders feared that what really threatened the agreement was the birth of a Jewish state bordering Lebanon,[92] while others actually lobbied for it.[93] In effect, all the leaders involved knew that the Pact was going to be weak and probably did not expect it to last very long, underlining their foresight in seizing the moment when local and international variables created the motives and incentives for them to do so.

Finally, another important regional factor was that a major incentive for the Lebanese to forge agreement was the extremely favourable economic developments in the 1930s regarding the oil trade and Lebanese banking in the Middle East. Lebanon had seen a boom in its relations with the oil-producing countries, and the political stability and economic prosperity that this had entailed was a strong facilitating factor in the events of 1943. The economic relationship with Syria also played a role, as the two countries agreed to maintain an economic union while forming two separate states. Crucially, overarching these local and regional political and economic variables was the imperial struggle over the Middle East.

THE END OF EMPIRE

In 1943 the long-running Anglo-French rivalry in the Middle East came to a head in Lebanon, creating the crucial exogenous pressure for the Lebanese to achieve independence.[94] The Lebanese took advantage of these externally favourable circumstances, and rightly so, as the regional environment rarely favoured Lebanon again in its modern history. Contrary to almost every statement made by the British on the French position in the Levant during the war, Spears and, to a lesser extent, Churchill were clearly engaged, with the support of the US, in a mission to reduce French colonial influence in the Middle East. Having installed the Free French, Britain fostered Arab nationalism in Lebanon and Syria, as it had in Egypt and Iraq. It soon became apparent to the Arabs which power was in the ascendancy, since Britain was conducting the war effort economically, strategically and logistically through a grand communications network centred on Cairo. This heightened Egypt's aspirations to become the leading Arab state. The effect of this was that French colonial decline became increasingly obvious to the Levant states and that Britain became just as obviously the power to be dealt with. This led Christians such as Khoury and Chiha, who had never really taken the idea of independence without French help seriously, to move to the centre ground and work with Britain to get rid of their old masters.

There remains, however, much confusion as to what exactly British policy on the French position in the Levant actually was. This revolves around the differing positions of Churchill, Spears and the British Foreign Office. Britain's official policy was contradictory. It had underwritten both Lebanese and Syrian independence, while also committing itself to restoring France's pre-war position and securing the Levant for the war effort. Officially, Britain had 'no desire to undermine or weaken the French position in the Levant', nor had it 'any ambition whatever to succeed the French position of prominence there'.[95] However, General de Gaulle highlighted contrary British actions in the Levant to Churchill, stressing that: 'The constant interventions of the representatives of the British Government ... are not compatible with the political disinterestedness of Great Britain in the Lebanon and Syria ... and the pressure of your representatives is harmful to the war effort of the Allied nations'.[96]

Spears's task was to interpret this contradiction but, above all, to help the war effort by calming the situation, which was of course Britain's primary concern. By 1943 this was something that the British Foreign Office considered Spears utterly incapable of doing.[97] It accused Spears of 'taking too much a pro-native and anti-French line', whilst Churchill reprimanded him, stating that: 'you are going further than I wish and anyone can see you have become bitterly anti-French'.[98]

Even as late as November 1943 it was Foreign Secretary Anthony

Eden's view that Spears should do everything in his power to force the Lebanese and the French to come to an amicable settlement that would last until the end of the war.[99] Eden argued that, 'although the French had behaved abominably, he did not want them to be humiliated further'.[100] Fundamentally, the Foreign Office took the view that Britain should be an honest broker between the two parties, as far as was possible. At the same time, while the last thing Britain wished to do was fight the French, the War Office had detailed full plans and printed martial-law proclamation posters to be used if the French did not comply.[101] In fact, if the Foreign Office had got its way, this would not have been the case. The ministers might not have been reinstated and the British would have then had to deal with a Lebanese uprising as well as the Free French.[102]

The common thread throughout was that Spears acted beyond his instructions from London and, in particular, those from the Foreign Office. From the stark lack of information in the British archives on the formation of the Lebanese government in September 1943, as well as the Spears Papers, it appears that the Foreign Office was unaware of the intrigues behind Spears's success in securing pro-British electoral candidates at the expense of the Free French. Further, Spears often complained about 'being up against the Foreign Office' to the Prime Minister, who replied that he was 'well aware of the situation with them'.[103] It is presumed that Spears remained in office for so long, against the constant protestations of de Gaulle,[104] solely because of his close friendship with Churchill. (Ironically, it was de Gaulle whom Churchill actually attempted to remove from office in 1941, only to be overruled by the War Cabinet.[105])

Of course, this explanation was extremely convenient from the Foreign Office's perspective, as it rid itself of its main rivals in the region and kept the Axis Powers at bay. On the one hand, Britain appeared to have removed the Free French from the Levant by employing the legendarily overzealous Spears and then using him as a scapegoat, as he was happy to play upon Britain's contradictory pledges in order to undermine de Gaulle. However, on the other hand, the Foreign Office would undoubtedly have taken a long-term view of the situation, and would not have wanted to destroy the French position since it envisaged a post-war anti-colonial stance from the US. It may well have believed that the British and the French could make a post-war stand together to protect their interests in the region, whereas Spears clearly had other ideas.

A closer look at the situation reveals that there was in fact little difference between Spears's actions in the Levant and the policies advocated by Churchill. In a letter addressed to President Roosevelt the day after the French arrested Khoury and Solh, Churchill stated that:

> If it be established that de Gaulle was responsible for giving orders to arrest the President and Ministers and carry out this *coup d'état*,

we should decline to renew our relations with the French Committee while he is head or a member of that body. This is probably the last chance of getting rid of this infant Mussolini ... for I assure you there is nothing this man will not do if he has armed forces at his disposal.[106]

The Foreign Office appears to have disagreed with these positions: it did not send this version of Churchill's letter to Roosevelt, instead drafting a much tamer response to the situation.[107]

There can be no doubt, however, that, while Spears greatly accelerated the French withdrawal, he was certainly rebuked by Churchill when he suggested that the British should replace the French in the Levant.[108] Spears was a man on a mission against de Gaulle – this much is clear – but the French undoubtedly assisted him through their conduct in 1943. It is certain that by the time Spears was forced to resign British actions in the Levant had rendered the French position untenable, with de Gaulle having been forced into a humiliating retreat over the arrest of the Lebanese government. The constant fear of the Free French leaders that Britain was out to replace their influence in the region,[109] given Spears' interpretation of his remit and his endeavours to do just that, was hardly paranoia.[110] To this the British consistently responded that the official policy of His Majesty's Government was not to weaken the position of the French in the Levant, but to insist on the French guaranteeing independence to Lebanon and Syria.[111] The contradiction in this policy was highlighted by Churchill's assertion to de Gaulle, when discussing these matters at 10 Downing Street on 28 September 1942, that 'You claim to be France! You are not France! I do not recognise you as France'.[112] Thus, the paradoxical nature of British policy in the Levant was not lost on the French, the Lebanese or the Syrians.

In contradiction to the Foreign Office's view, Spears believed that British interests justified replacing the French in Lebanon and Syria, but, crucially, the fact remains that he held his position there until the damage was already done and the French were close to collapse. It seems that Spears had the leeway to override the Foreign Office when it mattered and it was only after the French climb-down that he was replaced. Either Churchill overlooked his old friend's behaviour, or he was quietly content to see de Gaulle's position eroded and have someone capable of doing it at hand. Given Churchill's own leanings towards keeping the Free French in subordination and his total contempt for their leader, the latter is the more convincing explanation.

Moreover, it was not just the British who were acting against the French and eroding their position in the region, as US Minister of Legation, George Wadsworth, acted alongside Spears in undermining the

Free French and fostering Arab nationalism.[113] Of course, US–French rivalry in the Levant was nothing new: the US had pressured the French to uphold their commitments to deliver independence under the Mandate through the King–Crane Commission, which had been set up in 1919.[114] General de Gaulle concluded that 'Spears's action in Syria and Lebanon corresponded to the general policy Great Britain tended to pursue in the Middle East during the war's final phase'.[115]

On the French side there was also a failure to deal with Lebanon and Syria in a pragmatic fashion, and ratify treaties and security arrangements with them as the British had in Egypt and Iraq. While this had much to do with internal French politics and the failure to nurture independence movements in the region, by the time the French again attempted this in 1944 their position was so weak, and Lebanese determination so strong, that they left with almost nothing.[116] The French were, of course, playing for time. They hoped to avoid granting independence in the unfavourable circumstances of war in order to negotiate treaties with the Levant states from a position of strength. This was something of which the Lebanese and Syrian governments were well aware.[117]

In sum, Lebanese independence and the emergence of the National Pact were facilitated by three crucial factors. First, there was a convergence of Christian and Muslim aspirations to achieve independence from France. Second, there was a regional push to create Arab states in lieu of wider nationalist aspirations, which was fostered by the British. Third, there was the crucial international rivalry that culminated in the eclipse of the French in the Levant and the emergence of an interconfessional independence movement.

THE INTER-CONFESSIONAL COMPROMISE

The unwritten compromise of 1943 went on to become Lebanon's National Pact, a power-sharing agreement between Christians and Muslims that dealt with the two most pressing issues in Lebanese politics: foreign policy in the new Arab world and the distribution of political power between Lebanon's communities. First, the external compromise of the Pact involved finding the middle ground over what form Lebanon's foreign policy would take. The Maronite elite became more reconciled with the Arab world, the Muslims with an independent Greater Lebanon. The new republic was to be neither eastern nor western, rather an independent state within the Arab world. Internally, the Pact retained the constitutional confessional system of the Mandate, changing only the parts regarding France. Implicitly, the powerful position of the presidency remained the preserve of the Maronites and the office of prime minister that of the Sunnis. Seats in Parliament were allocated on a

Christian–Muslim ratio of six to five, with a cabinet reflective and representative of all the communities.

Externally the Arab face was a problem-solving device. Lebanon was not seen purely as an Arab country, in accordance with Christian demands, but rather as a country with an Arab outlook in line with Muslim aspirations. The Pact did not detail what Arabism was or what Lebanon's role in the Arab world would be. In fact, foreign policy decisions by the Arab League were formally binding on all member states, which obviously heightened Christian apprehensions. What the Muslims gained from this part of the bargain was that France would have no military base in Lebanon after withdrawal. Solh thus ensured that Lebanon's independence was confirmed and accepted in Arab circles, while Khoury made sure that the Christians denied the French their privileged connection. The crucial aspect of this understanding between the two leaders was that, if there was any inter-Arab conflict, Lebanon would remain neutral. The problem arose in 1948 as to whether Lebanon should remain neutral in Arab–Israeli conflicts, something that was to strain the pact until the outbreak of civil war in 1975. Increasingly after 1948 the Christians, particularly the Maronites, viewed neutrality as being inclusive of Arab–Israeli conflicts, while the Muslims, particularly the Sunnis, took the opposite view. Here lay Lebanon's foreign policy weakness. The Pact remained static while the political dynamics of the Arab world fluctuated dramatically. After the radicalisation of Arab politics in the 1950s what it meant to be Arab and have an Arab face was very different from what it had meant in 1943. Thus, the Pact's major problem externally was that, as the world changed, the Pact had to adapt, but there was only so far it could go without breaking.

The Pact became an all-important annex to the Constitution that was referred to in times of crisis, when internal and external events threatened stability. It was a rudder to guide the political leaders and an anchor to hold government in place. In terms of constitutional duality, internally the Pact boosted the Muslim position, in the sense that it privileged the role of the Prime Minister, was founded upon partnership and installed sectarian quotas throughout the administration. Without such arrangements the Christians would naturally have dominated, as they were educationally and politically more advanced than their Muslim counterparts.

The Pact underwrote independence, and the leaders who followed Solh and Khoury were reliant on it for their positions. In this sense Lebanon was unique in the region and without an interconfessional agreement Lebanese independence would have taken a very different form. L. Abul-Husn argues that these 'concessions produced a national settlement that explicitly rested on the assumption that both blocs had abandoned their loyalties to external powers in favour of an independent and sovereign Lebanese state'.[118] It was not, however, a national settlement in any sense. It was primarily an accord between the Maronite Christian and Sunni Muslim elites, a consequence of their converging political and economic interests. Moreover, it did not resolve the existing contradictory ethno-national aspirations, nor did it rest on the assumption that both blocs had abandoned them. Rather, both blocs agreed to disagree and work towards their national goals from the strength of an independent Lebanon.

The Pact did cement the Christian–Muslim dichotomy that preceded 1943 and established unnatural political lines that were more Maronite–Sunni than Christian–Muslim. For example, the Greek Orthodox did not have Maronite Christian interests, while the Druze, whose interests from the *Règlement* until the Mandate period lay firmly with the Maronites, quickly became politically 'Muslim' as the Maronite–Sunni alliance was established. The Shi'a accepted a multicommunal Lebanon, as it safeguarded and recognised their position for the first time as a separate community, but to say that their interests were symmetrical to those of the Sunnis would be a gross oversimplification. They were still economically, politically and religiously disadvantaged and underdeveloped in the region, so their political orientation was radically different from that of their urban Sunni counterparts.[119] The National Pact did not simply set Christians and Muslims apart, it heightened the intracommunal divisions that had existed before 1943 and at the same time made these groups implicitly reliant on each other within the interconfessional system.

Abul-Husn goes on to argue that the Pact was meant to pave the way towards integration and nation-building, but both the Pact and the Constitution, as Theodor Hanf correctly argues, politically, socially and culturally institutionalised the segregation and autonomy of the different religious communities.[120] The paradox of the Pact was that, while there could have been no national independence without it, it prevented national leaders emerging and stunted any nation-building programme, as it merged and papered over so many different national aspirations. Many of the founders of the Constitution and the Pact certainly intended convivialism and power-sharing to be an integrative and syncretistic nation-building programme,[121] but any suggestion that both political elites and national blocs truly believed in this is without foundation. The two blocs simply held the conflicting interpretations of the Pact that their leaders sold to them. While there was nothing in it that restricted future constitutional reform, it contained no provision for dealing with demographic shifts and was implemented in the strictest proportional sense along Christian–Muslim lines. It ensured that power-sharing politics developed into a balancing act between Lebanese and Arab national identities. The legitimacy of the First Lebanese Republic was therefore in question from its very inception. Many Sunnis supported the agreement purely as a means of removing the French, with their hearts set on supporting Syrian irredentism at a later date. Conversely, Maronite Lebanese nationalism prevented many Muslims from supporting or identifying with the new republic. In order to succeed, Lebanon's new regime had to counter opposing external and internal nationalist forces, and provide an inclusive stable government that both Christians and Muslims could support.

Here lay the inherent weakness of such consociational arrangements. The Pact was not an agreement born out of any overarching desire among both Christians and Muslims to coexist; rather, it was initially seen as a short-to-medium-term compromise for securing the long-term goals of both communities. Farid el-Khazen argues:

> The National Pact was based on two faulty assumptions: an internal one based on the belief that elite consensus reflected grassroots communal support; and an external one derived from the assumption that the balance of power in the region would remain unchanged in the sense that it would always reflect the value system of the first-generation pro-western Arab nationalists.[122]

Thus, on the one hand, Christians remained frightened of increasing Muslim input into the system and their tendency to follow calls for pan-Arabism at the expense of Lebanese sovereignty, while, on the other, most Muslims thought that the Christians, especially the Maronites, were disloyal to pan-Arab causes and isolationist, in contradiction to their Arab roots.[123] Externally, how could an accord created to achieve independence have predicted or accounted for changes in the Arab world, such as the creation of a Zionist state or the radicalisation of Arab politics? These negative exogenous pressures were to be the root causes of Lebanon's conflicts throughout the remainder of the twentieth century.

Intercommunal consensus was certainly often achieved in the post-independence period, but the nature of the National Pact and its confessional party system prevented a syncretistic Lebanese national identity from ever developing. The Chamber of Deputies continued to be made up of *Zu'ama*, whose electoral successs depended upon their constituencies remaining traditional in their political outlook and thus solely dependent upon them. As a result the election of independent politicians and electoral blocs, whose politics were zero-sum, provided little incentive for policies of an interconfessional nature to be tabled or fostered in government, as had often been the case during the *Règlement* period.

The National Pact also provided a big swing away from the traditional power-holders in the Lebanese mountains, first towards the urban Maronite bankers and merchants, and then to the Sunnis of the coastal cities. Therefore the Druze lost second place in the Lebanese political system to their Sunni counterparts, who vastly outnumbered them in the new republic. The Druze position before and after 1943 illustrated the explicit zero-sum confessional struggle of Lebanese politics. Before 1943 the Druze had not been seen and had not seen themselves as a Muslim community, but after 1943, when it became politically expedient to be part of the Muslim bloc, their leaders shifted to this position.[124] (To even raise this debate within the Druze community today, or suggest that their interests lie once again with the Maronites, is to cause an outrage). Pragmatically, they were prepared to live with this political demotion as long as their position on Mount Lebanon was safe and their strong standing in the army was secured under the Pact.

While the Druze got their confessional recognition, the real political losers under the agreement were the Shi'a community, who remained badly underrepresented. This was in direct contradiction to demographic shifts, as the Shi'a were Lebanon's fastest growing community after 1943. As population statistics were contested by all sides, no official census was taken after 1932 and all other figures are estimates (see Tables 10 and 11). It is difficult to ascertain exactly how fast the Shi'a population was growing, but it is certain that their increased political representation underestimated their demographic advances in alignment with the interests of those who brokered the National Pact. While the figures are not completely reliable and the size of the Shi'a community varies greatly depending on the source, some conclusions can be drawn from them. It is obvious that, while the Christian majority decreased throughout the First Republic, there was a relatively even Christian–Muslim split. Therefore no single ethnic group held anything like a majority and, whether it was Christians or Muslims who held an overall majority, it was always a very slim one.

One observation that stands out when analysing the estimated demograhic changes between 1932 and 1973 is that the two communities whose population share decreased significantly in comparison with the others were the two principal brokers of the National Pact. The Maronite stake in these estimated figures fell by 5 per cent, and that of their Sunni counterparts by 7 per cent, while the Shi'a community rose by 9 per cent (see Table 11). Therefore, as a consequence of the National Pact having been drawn up between Christians and Muslims on the basis of the census of 1932, it remained in the interests of those in power that no provision for demographic change be incorporated into its conditions. As time went by, due to different birth rates and other socio-economic factors, the governing coalitions grew increasingly unrepresentative of the changing Lebanese population.[125]

The Pact institutionalised confessional politics within the Lebanese system, solidified the Maronites' political ascendancy and preserved the Maronite–Sunni status quo: it was a pact of regulation rather than reso-

TABLE 10: Religious communities as a percentage of 1932 Census

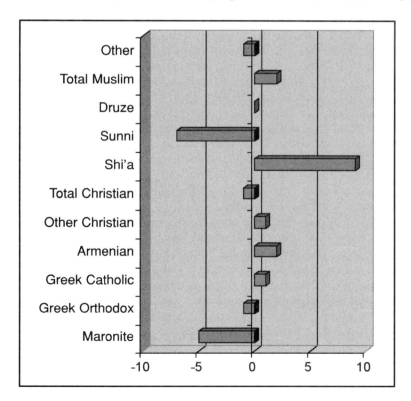

TABLE 11: Estimated changes in resident citizens by religious affiliation between 1932 and 1973 (%)

lution. As such it failed on two counts. First, it lacked flexibility and scope for internal constitutional and political reform. Second, it failed to address the question of Lebanon's medium-to-long-term international political position, as neutrality was an unrealistic short-term policy. Given that it was an elite agreement, however, it was understandable that the Maronite and Sunni leaders did little to change it, as it entrenched their political supremacy.

Since the National Pact was based upon the first and only official census to date, no leeway for demographic change was envisaged within the constitutional electoral arrangements. The continuation of the Maronite–Sunni ascendancy, however, led to the strictest proportional implementation of the Pact along inter rather than intra-confessional lines. Instead of leading to integration and convivialism, as leaders such as Chiha had hoped, the Pact set in stone the confessional and interethnic nature of the first republic.[126] Zamir contends that these elites were largely motivated by economic and personal political interests as opposed to being zealous convivialists proselytising a syncretic Lebanese nationalism.[127] The swift breakdown of the Solh–Khoury alliance after 1943 bears out this argument.

The Pact also meant that every significant post, from the head of government to the clerks in the civil service, was distributed not according to merit, but according to religious creed (based on the figures from 1932) provided that the communities had people equipped to fill the jobs. This distribution of seats and jobs meant that when the socio-political environment changed in Lebanon the administration failed to change with it. Instead of facilitating political reform and socio-economic modernisation, the Pact ensured that change was rarely in the governing elites' interest, thus causing long-term widespread social discontent and mismanagement throughout the country. Consequently, while the Maronites, or the Christians as a group, were not much better off than other communities,[128] their special political position gave the impression that they were and was in stark contradiction to Lebanon's changing demographic make-up (see Table 11).

Further, none of the elite leaders involved in the brokering of the agreement, or their constituents, had any neutral feelings about what Lebanon's position should be in the Middle East. Indeed, the possibility of a country as small as Lebanon remaining neutral in the Middle East was, at best, remote. The National Pact did not consider the effects that a changing regional and international environment might have on Lebanon in the near or distant future. Its rigidity failed to provide the leeway and scope to manage an international environment that was anything but stable. Initially, the agreement was not meant to, as its brokers sought primarily to get rid of the French, so that in the event of the ejection of the imperial power they were left with a very narrow political system. Of course, their interests still merged, but the *raison d'être* of their coalition had been achieved. Independence was accomplished through the National Pact, but it was unclear how long the politicians could agree upon what form it should take. With the French gone, it was only a matter of time before some form of constitutional crisis arose that the Pact was unable to deal with, bringing to a head the ethno-national tensions that had been temporarily soothed in order to rid Lebanon of colonialism.

Without provisions for internal constitutional change, such as those that the *Règlement* had contained, or an external guarantee of regional stability, such as the European colonial powers had provided until the First World War, the National Pact was always going to be fragile. It lacked provisions for re-negotiation, and the elites that brokered it lacked the motivation to undertake such a process. It was a short-to-medium-term mode of conflict regulation initiated by a concurrent majority of Maronite and Sunni leaders whose long-term goal of independence had finally become attainable with British help. The distinction between this and the *Règlement* lies in the difference between the imperial conflict regulation imposed upon Mount Lebanon under the *millets*, and the self-imposed, elite-led democratic consociational government engineered under the National Pact. The National Pact's power-sharing government did not reinforce the Lebanese state after independence; instead, it left it vulnerable to a series of internal and external political crises that it could not manage. In stark contrast, the *Règlement's* pillars of consociationalism, underwritten by the European powers, had constitutionally strengthened and politically regulated a region that was as prone to civil war in the late nineteenth century as it became in the twentieth.

CONCLUSION

It could be argued that Lebanese independence could or should have been guaranteed or imposed after the Second World War by the British and the Americans, or that it simply was far from ready for it. This had been the key to the success of the *Règlement*, under which the people of the mountain were no less free or autonomous than when Lebanon was finally independent, arguably more so. Further, if there had been some form of international stabilising force, it might have then been possible to renegotiate the agreement in accordance with democratic and political changes, as had occurred under the *Règlement*. However, the Pact held and was tested over the years by such exogenous pressures. As the French threat was removed, the inherent deficiencies within the Pact haunted Lebanon through a succession of constitutional crises. As a consociational agreement, it ignored demographic changes, and disproportionately favoured the Maronite and Sunni communities. Further, it failed to create a Lebanese national identity, fostered confessional instability and state weakness, and provided no mechanisms for socio-political change.

In sum, independence was achieved only in 1943 because of factors that were beyond the control of the Lebanese. However, it was most definitely the Lebanese who took advantage of these positive external variables to snatch independence, while the international environment favoured and sponsored it. Without the regional and international forces pushing Lebanon towards independence the Lebanese elites would have struggled to turn their common socio-economic interests and diverging national aspirations into a national pact.

CHAPTER SIX

Lebanisation

If regional conflicts are not settled, this does not necessarily bother the great powers. The term Lebanisation has finally come to mean an insoluble matter.

Farid el-Khazen[1]

In 1975 the National Pact finally collapsed with the outbreak of civil war in Lebanon. From the outset of this violence there were internationally sponsored efforts to end the fighting and regulate the escalating conflict. The war created a political vacuum in the Middle East, which was quickly filled by different external protagonists, as Lebanon succumbed to the dynamics of the Arab–Israeli conflict. Negative international variables further destabilised the country and prevented national reconciliation. This chapter examines the various attempts to reconstitute the state of Lebanon, which culminated in the negotiation of the Ta'if Agreement in 1989. It argues that these regulatory endeavours were all largely beyond the control of the Lebanese and that the roles played by the different communities quickly became secondary to those played by the exogenous actors who had an interest in Lebanon. Before examining how and why the Ta'if Agreement was successfully negotiated, a brief overview of the collapse of the National Pact, the outbreak of civil war and the subsequent regional and international attempts to regulate the conflict is required.

THE PACT COLLAPSES

Between 1920 and 1975 Lebanon suffered internally from four major problems: the refractory question of national identity that divided Lebanon's communities; the consociational conflict over the allocation of power among the confessional elites; the shifting demographic proportions among the communities; and the growing socio-economic gaps among the different classes. These problems dominated political life in Lebanon, as the traditional elites consistently failed to meet the challenges of modernisation and political reform facing Lebanon in the 1960s and 1970s.

The growing call for radical political change from the emerging counter-elite of the Progressive Socialist Party (PSP) under its leader, Kamal Jumblat, made the corruption of President Suleiman Frangieh's government increasingly salient. Appealing for widespread social and political reforms, Jumblat and the intercommunal PSP attacked the outdated confessional allocation of power under the National Pact, highlighting Lebanon's socio-economic imbalance and political corruption. It was not simply that the National Pact was at fault, but that the traditional elites were unwilling to reform the agreement and therefore incapable of managing the demands of a modernising society. In fact, the Pact had survived an equal if not stronger challenge in 1958, when Nasser had taken the region by storm and Chamoun's acceptance of the Eisenhower Doctrine in 1957 had torn Lebanon between East and West. Conversely, there was far less discord among the political elites concerning domestic matters in 1975 than there had been in 1958, when a full-scale civil war was actually averted.[2]

While demands for radical political and social reform certainly heightened tensions and challenged the government, in themselves they were not enough to provoke the outbreak of civil war. However, the growing voice of opposition to the government and the National Pact strengthened the perception within certain communities, especially the Sunnis and the Shi'a, that they were politically disadvantaged within the wider Lebanese community due to political 'Maronitism', the perception that the Maronites had *de facto* control over the political system. Whether they were significantly disadvantaged vis-à-vis any of their counterparts was not the issue; rather, it was this increasing perception that was an important internal catalyst in the outbreak of war.

Theodor Hanf argues that Christian dominance existed mainly on paper. He contends that key decisions needed the consent of both the President and the Prime Minister, and, crucially, the 'Christian majority in Parliament had been qualified by an electoral *modus operandi* that made far more Christian deputies dependent upon Muslim voters than vice versa'.[3] No one outside the Maronite camp believed this, and due to the perceived Christian dominance and the Pact's exclusivity in the face of shifting demographic realities, the movement for political reform was often voiced in terms of reform against political Maronitism. This rekindled Christian fears of being dominated by the Muslim community, which, after 1975, came increasingly to be voiced in sectarian terms.

Externally, the Palestinians were undoubtedly the catalyst for Lebanon's civil war, for armed conflict initially broke out between them and the Maronites. The PLO was not, however, merely a foreign actor, and it soon became an extension of the Sunni community in the absence of a Lebanese Sunni militia that could match the Christian forces. After 1975 Sunnis largely came to view the Palestinian presence as a matter of 'our cause is their cause and theirs ours'.[4] This new dichotomy in

Lebanese politics exacerbated the already raw tensions over political reform that had existed among the different ethno-national groups for many years.

This in turn led to the weakening of Lebanese sovereignty under the Cairo Agreement, signed on 3 November 1969, which granted the PLO freedom of action against Israel from within Lebanon and limited the possibility of the government exercising a purely Lebanese foreign policy.[5] The Melkart Protocols, signed on 18 May 1973, attempted to explain and re-interpret the failing Cairo Agreement, which had attempted to define and regulate the PLO's presence in Lebanon. However, as it resulted in the PLO effectively acting as a state within a state, it set the Lebanese on a collision course with their Arab guests and, consequently, one another. The PLO's institutionalised political strength quickly became Lebanon's political weakness. By 1975 it had attained such a degree of influence that the cabinet split over the issue of sending the army to the south to halt the PLO's attacks on Israel. Officially, Lebanon supported the Palestinian cause, in line with the Arab League, but, unlike in states such as Jordan, which had faced similar threats to its sovereignty, Lebanon's fragile Christian–Muslim balance rendered the regime too weak to manage the challenge. Further, compared to Jordan's army, which was one of the most professional in the region, Lebanon's was not a potent force.

The Christians primarily wanted to halt the PLO's attacks in order to prevent Israeli reprisals against the state, while many of the Muslim leaders, who were relying on the PLO to help to force Christian concessions on political reform, were either unable or unwilling to control its actions. The presence of the PLO thus antagonised Israel, facilitated foreign interference in Lebanese affairs, and dragged Lebanon into the Arab–Israeli conflict and, increasingly, the Cold War. After 1975 Syria attempted to control both the Lebanese and the Palestinian positions in the regional struggle with Israel, while the Israelis by 1978 had begun moves to eliminate the PLO from Lebanon altogether.[6] By 1975 Lebanon was completely divided over the Palestinian question. The army had split, its symbolic neutrality giving way to the Muslim perception that it was a Christian and anti-Palestinian force. At the same time Jumblat was entertaining the possibility of seizing control of Lebanon with Palestinian support. This undermined the state's sovereignty, allowing both Israel and Syria to exploit internal divisions further.[7]

The external variables, however, should not overshadow the underlying issues of internal political reform that illustrated both the need to amend the National Pact, and the government's inability and unwillingness to tackle the constitutional issues that threatened the status quo. The administration had also failed to absorb the growth of the Shi'a community, which, under the leadership of Musa Sadr, had become a serious political force in Lebanon by 1975.[8] Sadr's Movement of the Disinherited accounted for another large section of Lebanese society that felt excluded by the National Pact. Moreover, by 1975, his modernised and politicised community was arguably Lebanon's largest.

No one knows whether a Lebanese civil war would have broken out without the armed presence of the Palestinians, but this variable undoubtedly pushed the National Pact to breaking point over the army's neutrality. By 1975, even without the presence of the PLO, it would have taken a considerable overhaul of the political system and a radical governmental confessional realignment to prevent armed conflict with Jumblat's opposition. Frangieh's administration did not look capable of delivering any sweeping political changes or of dealing with the socio-economic imbalance within the state. If civil war among the Lebanese was unavoidable, or if it had been simply among them and no one else, then it is unlikely that it would have lasted fifteen years, only to culminate in a return to the pre-war status quo. Aside from the fact that Ta'if was a written document, there was, arguably, no great constitutional difference between the agreement of 1943 and that of 1989. If a reformulated National Pact was the most acceptable solution to civil war, then perhaps it was simply war within Lebanon that was unavoidable? The Lebanese peace process began not long after the outbreak of the war, so to examine this question an analysis of the different attempts to regulate the conflict and how they culminated in agreement in 1989 is required.

Between 1975 and 1989 Lebanon witnessed a variety of attempts to regulate its ethnic conflict and restore power-sharing democracy to its institutions. These took place amid consistent attempts by the warring factions to impose victory upon their enemies, with goals ranging from the imposition of deconfessionalisation/secularisation to the establishment of a Christian state. Until the deputies met at Ta'if and an accord was externally imposed in 1989, each round of mediation ended in failure to achieve any comprehensive settlement, due to both internal and external factors. Internally, each side believed that it could succeed in achieving its aims militarily; externally, those locked into the Arab–Israeli conflict played the different sides off against each other and took the timing of the conclusion of the conflict out of Lebanese hands. The most important of these attempts were the National Dialogue Committee in 1975, the Constitutional Document of 1976, the Agreement of 17 May 1983 and the Tripartite Agreement of 1985.

NATIONAL DIALOGUE COMMITTEE

After the outbreak of the war in April 1975 the Syrian Foreign Minister, Abdel Halim Khaddam, initiated a National Dialogue Committee,[9] which was made up of both moderate and militant Christian and Muslim leaders. This followed the rejection of political reforms by some Christian leaders, who refused to deal with them before Lebanon's security issues had been addressed. The Syrians feared the creation of a Christian state, as it would naturally become allied to Israel, prompting them to seek an end to the fighting through a dialogue that enforced a modified return to the National Pact. Syrian policy in Lebanon at the start of the war was, however, two-pronged and seemingly contradictory.[10] On the one hand, Syria was facilitating the mediation process, but, on the other, Assad was arming the Palestinians, who were subsequently supplying Jumblat and his leftist Lebanese National Movement (LNM). Syria was therefore consciously fuelling the very conflict that it appeared to be trying to stop: it had thus begun implementing a divide-and-rule policy in respect of the warring factions.[11] Further, the US Secretary of State, Henry Kissinger, had undertaken a 're-evaluation' of Syria's position in the conflict and accepted that it had a 'role to play'.[12]

The Committee met nine times[13] between September and October, and enjoyed international support from France and the Vatican. It attempted to draft a working paper on national reconciliation through the traditional elites, but the chances of a successful regulation were very limited, for three reasons. First, sectarian conflict was breaking out all over the country, with 'identity card' massacres and militia street battles stunting moves towards a consensus.[14] Second, the elites came nowhere near agreement on a national compromise. On the one hand, the Christians were moving from a defensive position vis-à-vis the Palestinians towards seeking a smaller Christian state,[15] illustrating their total resistance to any modification of the status quo. On the other hand, Jumblat was demanding political reform extending to deconfessionalisation and secularisation,[16] while the former Prime Minister, Abdallah Yafi, called for Lebanon to be constitutionally defined as an 'independent Arab country'.[17] Finally, due to these conflicting aspirations, the elite solidarity that had held Lebanon together since 1943 had collapsed and with it had gone the overriding belief that the old system was the best way to regulate intercommunal differences. The National Dialogue Committee never stood any serious chance of bringing an early halt to the escalating civil war. However, this initial mediation did illustrate the dynamics of what sort of solution there could be to the Lebanese crisis. It also raised questions over whether the solution would be Lebanese, Syrian, Arab or international.

This aspect was to prove crucial in the timing and success of any future Lebanese settlement. Any Arabisation of the solution to Lebanon's civil war was a direct threat to Syria's strategy to control Lebanon and the Palestinian movement in the regional conflict, especially in the wake of what Syria perceived as Egypt's betrayal over its Sinai Agreement with Israel in 1975.[18] It was clear that any regulation of the conflict was going to be one that suited Syrian national interests before Lebanese; and it was no coincidence that the war erupted in Lebanon at a time when Egypt was disengaging from the Arab–Israeli conflict, leaving Syria to face the Israelis alone, as envisaged by Kissinger.

THE CONSTITUTIONAL DOCUMENT

The Constitutional Document[19] of 1976 was Syria's first US-backed attempt[20] to impose a settlement on the Lebanese. This marked a decisive shift in Syrian foreign policy, from external mediation to coordinated internal political and military action in line with Syrian President Hafiz al-Assad's Greater Syria strategy.[21] The escalation of the civil war following the failure of the National Dialogue Committee resulted in a *de facto* partitioning of the country – exactly what Syria wanted to avoid. This made it clear to Syria that intervention was the most advantageous policy to pursue. Khaddam spelled this out by announcing in January 1976 that 'Syria would not accept any partitioning of Lebanon; in this event, Syria would annex Lebanon, in its view historically part of Syria'.[22]

On 14 February 1976, President Franjieh announced the Programme for National Action. It was a limited reform of the National Pact that he and Khaddam had agreed upon, and that would enable him to continue his term, with the agreement of many of Lebanon's confessional leaders, in the hope that Syria would support his conservative government as opposed to the LNM. Karim Pakradouni, then an activist in the Lebanese Forces (LF), claims that Assad himself found the constitutional loophole that was necessary for the amendment to be made.[23] The political deal was that the Muslims would accept a reduced Palestinian influence in Lebanon by reactivating and applying the Cairo Agreement under Syrian sponsorship, while the Christians would accept political reforms and a 'privileged relation' between the two countries.[24] The outcome of this was the continuation of the interconfessional system, but it marked some significant departures from 1943.

The Constitutional Document declared Lebanon a 'sovereign Arab state' and, for the first time, guaranteed in writing that the posts of President, Prime Minister and Speaker were preserves of the Maronite, Sunni and Shi'a communities, respectively. As a concession to moderate Muslim demands, the Prime Minister was to be elected by a simple majority of the deputies, rather than appointed by the President, and the President was to be elected by a minimum of 55 per cent of the parliamentarians. Further, the size of the Parliament was to be increased from 99 to 110 deputies, the remaining seats to be divided equally between Christians and Muslims. Proportionality was to be dropped from appointments to government jobs, except at the highest levels of the civil service. By emphasising the Arab identity of Lebanon and enhancing the position of the Sunni Prime Minister, the reform granted traditional Muslim leaders some of their more moderate demands, while ensuring the Christian position within Lebanon and reaffirming Maronite control over the presidency, the army and the civil service.

With the exception of Pierre Gemayel, militant Christians were content to accept the agreement, but Jumblat and his coalition rejected it, as it further cemented the confessional system and ignored almost all their demands. The agreement held out no prospect of deconfessionalisation and therefore offered Jumblat no means of achieving his political aspirations. It cemented the exclusion of the Druze from high office as laid down (unwritten) in the old National Pact. Finally, the Cairo Agreement and the Melkart Protocols were to be respected, so the PLO would lose most of its military gains, as Syria, in its new role as guarantor, sought to further curtail its activity and compromise its status as a free military agent within Lebanon.[25]

In sum, the Constitutional Document failed for two reasons. First, it did not address the concerns of the Lebanese parties that demanded radical political reforms; second, Syria actually lacked the capacity in Lebanon to control the PLO. Jumblat acted on the final disintegration of the Lebanese army, which had until that stage, much to the frustration of many Christian leaders, kept out of the interethnic fighting that was erupting across the country. It eventually split with the formation of the Lebanese Arab Army, which took up arms alongside the LNM and the PLO.

Jumblat did everything he could to persuade Assad that a military settlement was the only way to settle the conflict. Assad tried to convince him otherwise, indicating that it was not feasible and emphasising 'that the political solution was the alternative'.[26] In June 1976, Jumblat's rejection of the agreement and his attempt to take control of Lebanon, with the PLO's assistance, prompted a swift military intervention by the Syrians and his assassination in 1977, probably at their hands.[27] Fundamentally, the Lebanese had already devised most of the compromises that were to be realised in 1989, but the internal and external stalemate in 1976 rendered one side incapable of making any meaningful concessions and the other incapable of accepting any. The dynamics of this struggle remained intractable until after the Israeli invasion of Lebanon in 1982 and the formulation of a US policy to regulate the Arab–Israeli conflict.

THE AGREEMENT OF 17 MAY

On 17 May 1983, the US sponsored a Lebanese–Israeli accord[28] through Amin Gemayel, who had become President on 20 September 1982 following the assassination of his brother, President Bashir Gemayel, on 14 September. US intervention had assured Amin Gemayel's candidacy[29] and he felt compelled to negotiate an agreement in an attempt to rid Lebanon of the foreign forces that had occupied the country since the Israeli invasion earlier in 1982.[30] He attempted to walk a tightrope between the two poles in the hope that US intervention, with a commitment from President Ronald Reagan,[31] would bring the removal or curtailment of Syria and Israel, and enable him partially to reconstitute Lebanese sovereignty.[32] The US linked the withdrawal of both Israeli and Syrian troops from Lebanese soil to the Arab–Israeli peace process. Lebanon's sovereignty became secondary to both positions, with Amin Gemayel being forced to choose the lowest common denominator – a deal with Israel.

Gemayel wanted an Israeli withdrawal at the minimum political price vis-à-vis his relations with the Arab world, while the Israelis pushed to maximise their gains, having fought a costly war in Lebanon. They sought a peace treaty with full 'normalisation' in all but name. As for the Syrians, the then US Special Envoy to the Middle East Morris Draper contends that Khaddam told him in Washington before the negotiations began that the Syrians would 'fully cooperate with any agreement that successfully brought the Israelis out of Lebanon' – and in late 1982 they were in no position to refuse.[33] Conversely, Gemayel maintains that the Soviet Union determined to confuse the US in Lebanon and that the Soviet Ambassador, Alexander Soldatov, told him: 'We won't let the US get out safely from this Lebanese swamp'.[34]

The driving force behind the Agreement was the Reagan Plan and the Israelis' desire to establish permanent security in southern Lebanon, as they needed to legitimise their invasion of Lebanon domestically.[35] The Israelis agreed to a withdrawal if the Syrians followed suit. After arduous Israeli negotiation and mounting pressure on Gemayel, on the one hand from the US and Israel, and on the other, from Syria, the Soviet Union and Iran,[36] he agreed on 17 May, with the full backing of his cabinet, to a security agreement granting Israel full diplomatic relations and conceded *de facto* sovereignty in the south. The deal was to come into effect after the simultaneous withdrawal of Syria's troops, a stipulation added in a US–Israeli side letter to the agreement. Syria balked at this equation, as the Christians had invited it into Lebanon in the first place and the Arab League had legitimised its presence in 1976. Yet it was happy that the Agreement gave Damascus a *de facto* veto over implementation and, in effect, over the Reagan Plan.[37] Syria did not reject the

Agreement until the negotiations had matured, raising the temperature in the struggle for Lebanon and holding the Lebanese government hostage in the middle.[38]

The US sought to renegotiate the Agreement after it had been signed,[39] but it underestimated Syria's strength and Assad's resolve to block a regional settlement that reduced his influence. Reagan's Secretary of State, George Shultz, later admitted that the Americans got their timing wrong over the Agreement. By the time it was brokered the Soviet Union had rearmed the Syrians, whereas in September/October 1982 they had still been reeling from the Israeli offensive in Lebanon and were in no position militarily to challenge an accord.[40] Syria thus destroyed the Agreement by testing US–Israeli resolve to remain in Lebanon through exacerbating the Christian–Druze conflict in the Chouf, where the Israelis were stationed. This called the Israelis' bluff over the Agreement and they quickly retreated, leaving the US under fire from the Druze in the mountains, who had also been armed by the Soviets.[41] The last straw for Reagan came when suicide bombers blew up the US and French headquarters in Beirut, killing hundreds of soldiers. In Beirut US Vice President George Bush Sr declared that the Reagan administration would 'not let a bunch of terrorists shape the foreign policy of the US',[42] but Congress restricted Reagan's freedom of action and prompted a swift troop withdrawal.

This outcome further confirmed Lebanon's subordinate role in the Arab–Israeli conflict and the Cold War. The remainder of Amin Gemayel's presidency was spent trying to conserve a veneer of legitimacy on Lebanon's democratic institutions, and to maintain a government trying to function in the stark absence of both political and territorial sovereignty.[43] Assad and the Soviet Union sent a clear message to Israel and the US that Syria could not be overlooked in any agreement concerning Lebanon or a broader political process. Thus the Agreement of 17 May was made at a time when Israel was domestically in turmoil over the aims and consequences of its invasion, while Assad knew that there was a limit to the extent to which US military action would bolster its diplomacy. Shultz conceded that 'the crucial combination of diplomacy and strength was not available'.[44] The US solution to this debacle was to withdraw from Lebanon, and allow Syria to fill the vacuum once again and initiate the Tripartite Agreement of 1985.[45] The contradictions and inconsistencies in the Reagan administration's foreign policy in Lebanon are illustrated by Casper Weinberger, then US Secretary of Defense, in his aptly titled analysis *Fighting for Peace*.[46] Due to this US inconsistency, Gemayel was abandoned and left to struggle alone with Syria for the rest of his term.

The Tripartite Agreement

In 1985 Saudi Arabia helped Syria to initiate another attempt to end the fighting by bringing the warring factions together through its envoy, Rafic Hariri.[47] However, this time they excluded Gemayel's dysfunctional Lebanese government, aiming to regulate the conflict with an agreement solely between the three main militia leaders – Elie Hobeika of the LF, Walid Jumblat of the PSP and Nabih Berri of Amal – and at the same time to redefine Lebanese–Syrian relations. On 28 December they signed the Tripartite Agreement with no representation of the Sunnis, who had no militia.[48]

The Tripartite Agreement sought to impose a political reform of the National Pact that was far more binding at the level of deconfessionalisation/secularisation of the system than previous compromises would have been.[49] This, and the proposed creation of a second legislative tier, encouraged Jumblat, as it would allow the Druze leader the senior governmental position he craved. The other major internal reform, which later came through at Ta'if, was that power should be taken from the President and vested in the cabinet. However, none of the militias signed the Tripartite Agreement out of any genuine conviction. They did so primarily because no one was challenging Syria in Lebanon at that time and it controlled the balance of forces in the war.

The external side of the Agreement was a firm policy marker of Syria's intentions and ambitions in Lebanon, and a foretaste of the authority that it would seek to impose under Ta'if. This relationship was outlined by the 'strategic complementarity' that was to exist between the two countries, on the basis that the expression of true Lebanese Arabism could be achieved only through the country's distinctive relationship with Syria.[50] More specifically, it bound Syrian and Lebanese foreign policy, pledging to rehabilitate the Lebanese army with Syrian assistance.

The importance of the Tripartite Agreement was that it reflected Syrian confidence in Lebanon after the Agreement of 17 May and, was, in fact, the very opposite of it. While the Agreement of 17 May attempted to end the Israeli–Lebanese war to Israel's advantage, the Tripartite Agreement attempted to regulate the whole conflict to the advantage of Syria. The Agreement of 17 May had been a US-brokered Lebanese–Israeli accord that went through the legal channels and ignored the Syrians, while the Tripartite Agreement was a Syrian-enforced deal between the militias that bypassed those legal institutions and lacked solid international support. Pakradouni warned Syria that the Agreement would fail without legal national legitimisation and that Gemayel would reject it. Khaddam replied that Gemayel was coming to Damascus to discuss the Agreement and would be convinced to support it, stressing that 'either he goes or he goes' – either with the Agreement, or from the presidency.[51]

However, the failure of the Triparte Agreement illustrated the fact that any successful Lebanese deal needed to fall somewhere between these two poles, and highlighted the requirement for it to be underpinned by both regional and international support. In fact, this accord would have legitimised militia rule, increased the division of the country into pockets of confessional control and further weakened internal consensus, as the traditional forces of government would never have accepted it.[52] If it stood no chance of being implemented, why was the Triparite Agreement signed? First, 1985 saw the lowest point in the war for the Christians, who had lost the battle for the mountain and suffered the assassination of Bashir Gemayel; their leaders now wanted to proceed very slowly towards any proposed settlement. Conversely, Assad was in a hurry to get an agreement signed and used division within the Christian community as a means to 'weaken Amin Gemayel's stand'.[53] Opposing him was the LF, whose strategy was simply a containment policy of Syrian intervention based on the hope of future western support, without any real political project or long-term thinking.[54] It was the second part of the agreement, concerning relations with Syria, that was flatly rejected by the Christian militias, the Lebanese army and President Gemayel.

Hobeika signed the Agreement hoping to end the war, grant political reforms to Muslims in a continuation of the process started in 1976, choose the Syrian option over Israel and firmly establish himself as the leader of his community. As a result his LF rival, Samir Geagea, switched sides and forged an alliance with Gemayel to delay the Syrian takeover of Lebanon. Hobeika was then ousted from East Beirut after the LF split and the Agreement was terminated.[55] It is likely that this was the sole reason for the immediate failure of the Agreement, as the Christian leaders were not all against it until US opposition to it became clear at a later stage.[56] It is equally unlikely that in 1985 Syria was acting alone in Lebanon: it had probably secured a measure of US support for the accord. The conundrum for the US was whether granting Syria control over Lebanon at this stage would enhance Assad's willingness to move towards a regional settlement.

The Triparite Agreement marked Assad's second attempt to impose a regulation of the civil war in Lebanon. However, it lacked internal consensus and positive external sponsorship, for the regional situation did not favour a settlement. Most Arab states did not want to see a purely Syrian solution and the US kept its distance after Reagan's failed intervention in 1983.[57] While the US had accepted Syria's hegemony in Lebanon by 1985, it was happy to see its control curtailed in lieu of an overall settlement. As one of the signatories emphasised, 'the regional circumstances did not favour it [the Agreement] in any way – also, you could not have an agreement without a major component of the population, the Sunnis'.[58]

THE STRUGGLE TO END THE WAR

After the failure of the Tripartite Agreement the years preceding the end of Gemayel's presidency in 1988 saw Lebanon divided further, with no obvious end to the conflict in sight. As time ran out for the beleaguered President, he travelled to Damascus on his last day in office to try to renew his mandate, only for Assad to reject him.[59] In turn, the Christian community rejected the Syrian-nominated presidential candidate, Mikhail Dyer, who would adhere to the Tripartite Agreement. In response to the US–Syrian ultimatum of 'Mikhail Dyer or chaos' – a phrase ascribed to the US Assistant Secretary of State, Richard Murphy,[60] based on the precedent set in 1952 when Khoury appointed a cabinet under General Fouad Chehab[61] – Gemayel appointed General Michel Aoun as head of a transitional military administration. This immediately plunged Lebanon further into a military and constitutional crisis, and resulted in the formation of two rival governments. Murphy denies ever saying the phrase, however, and contends that the Syrians told him it was either 'Dyer, or there would be no election', adding that if they gave the Lebanese the choice, 'they would choose chaos'.[62]

Hanf argues that there is no doubt about the legality of Gemayel's appointment under Lebanese constitutional law.[63] However, as far as the Muslim community was concerned, it broke the National Pact and prompted the formation in West Beirut of a rival administration led by Salem al-Hoss, which also claimed the legitimacy of the state.[64] This situation raised tension in Lebanon and in the Middle East as a whole, with Syria and Iraq stepping up hostilities. Syria backed Hoss, while Iraq armed both Aoun and his rivals in the LF, seeking to weaken Syria through an alliance with its enemies.[65] Other than opposition to Syria, one of the core reasons for this crisis was the division over who was going to lead the Christian community. This was similar to the conflict in 1985, but in 1989 it was purely a struggle for power between Aoun and Geagea, who had been left out of Aoun's provisional administration, and lacked even the semblance of ideological difference that Hobeika's Syrian venture had provided.[66] Ideologically they both still sought to delay the Syrian takeover, while harbouring dreams of partition and the attainment of the presidency. As events transpired, they had no practical or coherent strategy to support such visions; yet, if they had been united, it is likely that they would have posed a considerable threat to Syrian designs in Lebanon.

On 12 January 1989 the Council of Ministers of the Arab League responded to this crisis by appointing a commission of six states to address the crisis, excluding Syria, and with Kuwait as its chair. This aimed to bring together the Lebanese parties, internationalise the conflict and prevent Syria from annexing Lebanon. The meetings in Tunis and

Kuwait took place in three stages: first, with Aoun, Hoss and Speaker Hussein Housseini; second, a round with all the surviving former presidents, prime ministers and speakers; and, finally, with all the religious leaders and political movements in Lebanon.[67] While the commission failed to come to any solid conclusions, Syria shelled East Beirut in response to its pressure. However, it was a building block in the process towards a settlement, upon which the Lebanese were able to present their vision of internal reforms. As the conflict took place in Beirut, dialogue between Muslim and Christian leaders culminated in an agreement on which internal reform should be implemented. Housseini, Hoss, Maronite Patriarch Sfeir and Khaddam produced a document on national reconciliation, the culmination of years of mediation, dialogue and explanation among all the different facets of Lebanese society, upon which consensus had been reached by April 1989.[68]

These developments led to the creation of the Tripartite High Commission, or the Troika as it became known, at the Casablanca Summit, which was held between 23 and 26 May 1989. The Troika comprised three Arab heads of state: King Hassan II of Morocco, King Fahd of Saudi Arabia and President Chadli Benjedid of Algeria. Lakhdar Ibrahimi of the Arab League, who chaired the commission, announced that its mandate was to 'liberate Lebanon from all regional hegemony and restore its national sovereignty'.[69] The scene was set for the Ta'if Conference, as internal reforms were agreed by Housseini, Hoss and Sfeir,[70] and the will of the Arab world and the international community merged to put an end to the Lebanese war, and in doing so, conceded Syria the major role in its regulation.

Casablanca spelt the end of the war in Lebanon. Internally, all the players knew that Lebanon was trapped in a vicious cycle and that no one side could ultimately triumph. Externally, the US saw Lebanon as a dangerous source of regional instability and a threat to Israeli security at the end of the Cold War. The US had continuing concerns over the rise of political Islam and the spread of terrorism, from which, of course, states in the Middle East were by no means immune.[71] Syria set about positioning itself for the acceptance of the proposed accord. Having little ideological attachment to the Soviet Union, Assad viewed the end of the Cold War as an opportunity to consolidate his position in Lebanon, and move into the western camp. Due to the convergence of these positive regional and international factors, the consociational reformulation was preordained at Casablanca, well before Ibrahimi called the surviving deputies of the Parliament elected in 1972 to convene at Ta'if.

Before these developments took place, Aoun had launched the first of his two wars attempting to consolidate his position in the segregated Christian area and destroy Geagea. He announced the closure of Lebanon's illegal ports in February 1989, thereby challenging his enemy, who gained much of his revenue and his unpopularity, through illegal taxation. This move also answered Aoun's pressing economic problems, as he needed capital to fund his war, operate his government and run his part of the Christian sector, his official financial resources having been blocked by the dual governmental crisis.[72]

A month later, on 14 March, Aoun declared a war of liberation against Syria's occupation of Lebanese territory. His actions against the Syrians and the LF quickly made the Christian masses adore him. His leadership and platform were, however, founded upon ideology without strategy, and his lack of political acumen led his community to disaster and Lebanon to further destruction. His actions resulted in full-scale war, which culminated in Syria blockading and shelling Beirut. The Troika issued ultimatums to Iraq and Syria to stop arming the rival Christian factions, and to lift the siege on Beirut. Aoun believed that he could provoke a western intervention that would seal off his area from the Syrians and allow him to consolidate his control of it. In a more dramatic style than Gemayel, his aim was to force military intervention through conflict with Syria, thereby limiting its influence. It is also possible, however, that by that stage Aoun believed that he could defeat Syria militarily, or at least position himself for the presidency of the republic through this stand-off. The fact that Aoun's populist policies shifted so often and lacked any long-term strategic scope makes an analysis of his true intentions somewhat difficult, but, given the scale of his ambitions and the military actions undertaken, he clearly believed that at least one of the above objectives was attainable.

While Ibrahimi was making progress within Lebanon over internal political reform, the Troika invited the deputies to meet outside Lebanon to discuss a framework of national reconciliation and the resuscitation of the state. Syria blocked all efforts to this effect and increased its stranglehold on East Beirut. The Syrian message to the Troika was to concentrate on ending the war by regulating internal political reforms and forget about the question of Lebanese sovereignty. The Troika tried again and on 13 September it called the deputies to convene at Ta'if in Saudi Arabia for a conference. Having moved considerably towards the Syrian position by abandoning linkage between internal reform and withdrawal of Syrian troops, the Troika conceded that no agreement could be made without Assad's support. Subsequently, no efforts were made to block it except by Aoun, who demanded Syrian withdrawal as a precondition to any agreement over political reform by the deputies,[73] having unsuccessfully tried to prevent many of those in his area from attending the conclave.

On 1 October the deputies met at Ta'if, where they were presented with a first draft for negotiation drawn up by the Troika,[74] loosely based on the Glaspie Papers and taking into account all shades of Lebanese opinion as solicited by the US.[75] The sixty-two deputies gathered at Ta'if all delivered inaugural addresses before a Committee of Seventeen was formed from the different communities, with Housseini as its chairman. While they had not been elected to Parliament since 1972, these men were the last representatives of the only remaining Lebanese political institution, and their legitimacy lay in their communal and geographical reflection of the Lebanese population. However, the Committee did not want to negotiate on the basis of the international community's draft, as it took into consideration all the Lebanese perspectives and was too close to the Tripartite Agreement for its liking.[76] The Committee of Seventeen insisted instead on Housseini's draft, which was a product of consultations among Lebanon's traditional elites as opposed to its militias, very much along the lines of the Constitutional Document of 1976.[77]

The framework of everything in the Troika's draft had already been agreed before Ta'if, but the minutiae of the constitutional reforms had still to be bargained over in the Committee of Seventeen. It appears that either the international community was unaware that there was a Lebanese draft, as some of the chief Lebanese negotiators contend,[78] or it was putting pressure on the Lebanese to reach agreement by giving them something to negotiate away from. The latter seems the more likely scenario, as the international community knew that no deal could be done that was not between the moderates, and clearly favoured such an option anyway. This provided further incentive for the deputies to agree, as they actually had no power in Lebanon, and Ta'if presented them with an opportunity to break the dominance of the militias and return to government under the National Pact.

Negotiations got under way within the Committee of Seventeen, which was divided into two groups, one mostly Christian and the other mostly Muslim, but both together reflecting the broad array of Christian–Muslim interests. The parliamentarians were in daily contact with the different factions within Lebanese society that were absent from Ta'if, but whose political representation and consent on internal reform was vital.[79] The parliamentarians also had regular access to the media based nearby, but they used this access as much to re-launch their political careers as to inform the public of proceedings.[80]

The Ta'if negotiations were divided into two sections, internal and external, which were facilitated by the Saudis through their Foreign Minister, Saud al-Faisal, and Hariri. They also represented the US, and acted as intermediaries between Syria and the other parties.[81] While there was no official Syrian presence at Ta'if, its interests were well accounted for by those Muslim and Christian deputies whose constituencies fell within the Syrian-controlled zone of Lebanon.[82] The major points of contention still to be finalised concerned the reallocation of presidential powers to the Council of Ministers and the relationship with Syria over the future redeployment or withdrawal of its troops from Lebanon.

Following Aoun's policy not to accept any amendment to the Constitution before fixing an agreement linking it to the withdrawal of Syrian forces, many of the Christian deputies held out for a timetable for withdrawal,[83] while the Muslims rejected even partial withdrawal without the prior departure of Israeli forces, reorganisation of the army and, of course, political reforms. It became evident that the external part of the Agreement was non-negotiable when Ta'if came to a standstill, and Faisal and Hariri travelled to Damascus. Without Lebanese representation, they presented a draft and argued the Lebanese position. Assad removed the offending sentences tying the Troika as a guarantor to a Lebanese–Syrian security agreement, in effect the opposite of what the Christians had sought.[84] The only concession he made was over the increase in parliamentary seats, to 108 as opposed to 128.[85] This was the lowest common denominator for Christian–Muslim parity in the chamber. However, this was of no great importance to Assad for, if it had been, he would have insisted on 128.[86] The US intervened in the form of its envoy, David Satterfield, in an attempt to try to speed things up, much to the annoyance of the Saudis, who did not want anything to shatter the illusion that Ta'if was an exclusively Arab solution.

Faced with a *fait accompli*, financial incentives that many claim were bribes and the chance to regain power over their country, fifty-six of the sixty-two deputies present at Ta'if approved the Agreement with four abstentions.[87] The remaining two were in favour on the condition that a later date for withdrawal was set.[88] Aoun rejected the accord when it became clear that he had no chance of becoming President and René Moawad, who had good relations with Syria, emerged as the US–Saudi candidate.[89] On 4 November, in a vain attempt to scupper the ratification of the Agreement, Aoun announced the dissolution of Parliament,[90] only to see ratification achieved the following day, with nine reservations, when the deputies met at an airfield in Koleyat, in Syrian-controlled northern Lebanon.[91] At the same meeting Moawad was elected President on the second ballot, with six abstentions, only to be assassinated days later by a car bomb and replaced by the more compliant pro-Syrian candidate, Elias Hrawi.

This marked the beginning of the dereliction of Ta'if, which culminated in the removal from power of Housseini, 'the father of Ta'if', and of Hoss, in effect the two principal political leaders who had made the agreement. However, the Aoun factor also contributed to the non-implementation of the Ta'if Agreement. If he had accepted Moawad and the Agreement, Syria would not have been able to interpret and implement Ta'if exactly as it saw fit. A troika of Moawad, Hoss and Housseini might have led to a Lebanese execution of Ta'if, whereas Aoun's intransigence broke the internal and external equilibrium upon which implementation depended.

Crucially, in the year between Ta'if and the defeat of Aoun the local, regional and international situation changed. Externally, the Gulf War in 1991 allowed Syria to join the US-led coalition, resulting in Lebanon being dropped from the region's priorities along with the Troika's promises. Internally, the Lebanese army and the LF destroyed each other, disrupting the political and military balance among the different communities, while Syria laid siege to Beirut. Any hope the Lebanese had of reconstituting their sovereignty and implementing Ta'if in its letter and spirit was shattered by these events. Just as positive exogenous forces had ended the war with a reformulated consociational pact, negative external shifts looked set to scupper its implementation. Jumblat reflects that Assad admitted to him during the conflict with Aoun that he had come to realise that Jumblat's father, Kamal, had been correct after all: 'a military settlement is a must'.[92]

As events unfolded, Ibrahimi tried to convince Aoun to accept Ta'if and take his place in the new government.[93] As he did so, Syria shelled the palace in an attempt to prevent the meeting.[94] Aoun became further isolated when Geagea accepted Ta'if and allowed the LF to join Hoss's administration.[95] Syria did not simply get the green light from the US to remove Aoun due to its military contribution to the allied forces against Iraq: other factors influenced this as well. Aoun antagonised the Americans by forcing the closure of their embassy in East Beirut and continuing to support Iraq throughout the Gulf War. From that moment Lebanon's chance of becoming master of its own destiny faded, as the interpretation and implementation of Ta'if were left entirely in Syrian hands.

Assad realised that the Soviet Union was no longer going to sponsor Syria and act as a counterbalance to US power in the region. When Syria's interests coincided with those of the US during the Gulf War Assad allied himself with the US and Saudi Arabia. Syria's reward was a 'green light' from the US to remove Aoun from his perch in East Beirut, and to stabilise and control Lebanon in the process. After bringing a war to the capital that cost more than 1,000 lives, Aoun finally sought refuge in the French Embassy and then fled to France.

Pakradouni contends that Aoun had been badly misguided by himself, public opinion and, to a certain extent, the French, who were struggling to maintain their influence in Lebanon against the regional agenda of the US and its support for Geagea.[96] After Aoun's siege of the US Embassy in Beirut the Americans openly encouraged Geagea to attack him, while the French provided reassurances that the West would not allow his defeat in Beirut. Regardless of whether the French were telling him the whole story or not, Aoun should have realised that Lebanon was completely shattered by war, and that the regional and international coalition supporting Ta'if meant that something was taking place with or without him. Instead, Anoun continued his war against Geagea, which forced his rival to accept Ta'if in order to gain protection from him and, as a result, further weakened the Christian position. It appears that the US then made a secret deal with the Syrians, indirectly, through the Saudis, probably to remove Aoun from East Beirut. Evidence for this comes through an analysis of the Kissinger Agreement regarding Lebanon and its international dynamics. Israel controlled the sea and the air, whereas Syria controlled the land. Only the US could have guaranteed Syria air cover to bomb Aoun out of Beirut with no fear of Israeli reprisal. Syria joined the international coalition against Iraq, Aoun was removed from the Ta'if equation, and Syria's policing role was at last fully legitimised and supported by the US.

CONCLUSION

Like the Tripartite Agreement, Ta'if's three aims were to end the war, institute political reforms and define Syrian–Lebanese privileged relations. Yet, unlike the militia agreement, Ta'if was imposed by Syria and the US through Saudi Arabia, and agreed by the traditional Lebanese politicians in the spirit of 1976. In 1976 the Christians and Muslims had been divided over two key issues, the Palestinians and internal political reform. Lacking this external catalyst, a revised National Pact was easier to come by than it had been at the outbreak of war. However, before analysing the implementation of Ta'if and its consequences, an evaluation of exactly what was agreed at the Saudi summit is required.

CHAPTER SEVEN

The Ta'if Agreement

Michael Kerr: 'Why did the US not push Syria to implement Ta'if in the letter and spirit of the agreement?'
Dr Vincent Battle, US Ambassador to Lebanon: 'The Lebanese government didn't ask us to'.[1]

In 1989 the Ta'if Agreement ended a civil war that had divided and engulfed the state of Lebanon for fifteen years. It attempted to amend and reinstate the power-sharing formula that had functioned between 1943 and 1975, and to constitutionally legitimise Lebanon's position in the regional conflict under Syrian tutelage. Such a conclusion to the Lebanese civil war raises questions as to whether the international community actually intended Ta'if to be a new start for Lebanon. It is also uncertain what influence the Syrians would have had in Lebanon if the Gulf War had not drawn them into the US coalition against Iraq, thereby granting them unfettered control over the country. Moreover, the return to the political status quo suggests that the Lebanese would not have had such a long and protracted civil war if it had not been for regional and international factors.

The purpose of this chapter is to analyse the internal and external elements of the Agreement, its regional and international ramifications, and its interpretation and implementation by Syria. With Ta'if the Lebanese continued to be victims of their own divisions and competing geopolitical interests in the Middle East, as they had often been under the National Pact and during the long years of civil war. It was safe to conclude long before 1989 that any internal solution to the problems of Lebanese interconfessional coexistence would always come second to the dynamics of regional power struggles. Thus, the timing of the Agreement had little to do with the Lebanese, nor was it a symbol of Lebanon's capacity to transform its yearning for peace into a political settlement.

Ta'if ushered in a new era of internationally legitimised and unfettered Syrian hegemonic control in Lebanon. It was this external variable, backed by regional and international support, that ended the civil war and brokered a return to power-sharing. While Ta'if constructed a consociational realignment of the consensus of 1943 and subsequently amended Lebanon's Constitution, it failed to redress seriously political and social inequality, as Syrian interests defined the interpretation of political reform. Lebanon reverted to the old system of political custom and tradition that had created many of the grievances that led to civil war in 1975. It is difficult to judge Ta'if on its merits, as its Syrian interpretation left it very much unimplemented and untested.

The Ta'if Agreement bore considerable resemblance to the National Pact, reaffirmed Lebanon's acceptance of the old confessional system and marked the culmination of a political process that began with the Constitutional Document just after the start of the civil war. Essentially, what Ta'if brought to the National Pact was further inclusiveness. It was a power-sharing agreement among all of Lebanon's communities, as opposed to the predominant Maronite–Sunni accord of 1943. Furthermore, it underlined a desire for future deconfessionalisation, but again in keeping with 1943, reinforced the sectarian system that had governed Lebanon before the civil war. In its compromise Ta'if marked no radical break with the past: this in itself was how compromise was achieved. While there were certainly some communities that gained or compromised more than others, it avoided an all-out Christian defeat, upholding the Lebanese maxim of 'no victor, no vanquished'. Nevertheless, this does not necessarily mean that it fundamentally changed the unwritten National Pact, or even attempted to replace it. It also differed fundamentally from the National Pact in ways that were not intrinsically related to its consociational structure. It brought an end to a civil war; it defined Lebanon as an Arab state; it imposed and Arabised the regulation of the Agreement; it legalised Syrian political and military ascendancy in the country; and it was a written document.

At the conclave only the parts of the Agreement relating to domestic reform were actually negotiated by the Lebanese deputies, and most of that had already been negotiated and agreed beforehand.[2] Ta'if allowed the Lebanese deputies of 1972 to return to Lebanon, arm in arm, with a new document of national reconciliation. Whether or not the circumstances would allow them to implement it was a gamble they took to end the war, regain power and limit the dominance of the militias in any settlement. As for the sections regarding Lebanese–Syrian relations they were non-negotiable, underlining Syria's *de facto* veto over the whole process. In fact, the main beneficiary at Ta'if was undoubtedly Syria, rather than any of the Lebanese communities, but to exactly what extent was not clear in 1989. On Lebanese–Syrian relations, Ta'if did bear a great deal of resemblance to the Tripartite Agreement,[3] which had outlined this new order, and left the extension of Lebanese sovereignty that it said so much about clearly linked to Syria's foreign policy and the wider Arab–Israeli conflict. To evaluate Ta'if these internal and external aspects of the Agreement need to be dealt with separately.

INTERNAL RELATIONS

In the confessional gains, losses and compromises that were exchanged at Ta'if, the Shi'a were the clear winners, gaining a share of power that was more proportionate to their demographic strength for the first time. In practice, the Muslim community as a whole certainly benefited from Ta'if at the expense of the Christians, especially the Sunnis vis-à-vis the Maronites. In fact, on paper, all the non-Maronite communities made political gains at the expense of the Maronites. Yet, given the demographic realities in Lebanon, the Christians, who were in fact the stronger negotiators at Ta'if,[4] maintained a position disproportionate to their demographic strength, holding the Maronite presidency and retaining Christian–Muslim parity in the Parliament. The Sunnis also maintained their position, despite the rapid growth of the Shi'a community, benefiting greatly from the transfer of power and prerogatives from the Maronite President to the Council of Ministers. In spite of their demographic strength the Shi'a gained only three of the nine new seats allocated to Muslims at Ta'if, merely bringing them into line with the smaller Sunni community (see Table 12). The reason they maintained their strong position in government had a lot to do with Saudi influence in keeping the old equilibrium, the Saudis having viewed themselves as the guardians of the Sunni in Lebanon since before independence.[5] To a similar extent the Syrians elevated the Shi'a closer to their rightful position, demographically speaking, but were careful not to raise them politically above the Maronites or the Sunnis, in order to keep the old balance.

The most significant constitutional change that came out of Ta'if was the shift in power from the President to the Council of Ministers. The

TABLE 12: Confessional representation in the Lebanese Parliament, 1972–92

	1972	1989 (Ta'if Accord)	1990 (Vacancies)	1992
Christian				
Maronite	30	30	12	34
Greek Orthodox	11	11	4	14
Greek Catholic	6	6	0	6
Armenian Orthodox	4	4	0	4
Armenian Catholic	1	1	1	2
Protestant	1	1	0	1
Other	1	1	0	3
Subtotal	54	54	17	64
Muslims				
Sunni	20	22	5	27
Shi'a	19	22	3	27
Druze	6	8	5	8
Alawite	0	2	0	2
Subtotal	45	54	13	54
Total	99	108	30	128

prime ministership, which remained a Sunni preserve by custom, in prac- tice gained the most from this political redistribution of power.

What these changes amounted to was a move away from presidential government to cabinet collegiality, with the President's role becoming more that of a grand arbitrator between Parliament and the executive. While the office remained a Maronite preserve in practice, the Presi- dent's position became that of a ceremonial figurehead, a presidency in name only, with most of his powers reallocated to the cabinet. He could no longer dissolve Parliament, appoint or dismiss the Prime Minister, control the Lebanese army, head the government or even chair cabinet meetings. His main function was to oversee the application of the Con- stitution after Ta'if, although he could still preside over the Council of Ministers when he chose to attend its meetings. As his status had been reduced to that of referee, he retained neither voting nor veto rights. Before Ta'if the President could veto legislation by refusing to promul- gate it, whereas afterwards this power was reduced to a fifteen-day delay on any legislative decisions taken by the Council of Ministers. However, a one-third blocking veto was introduced to force the government to resign if it could not gain two-thirds support for its legislation, something the Christians viewed as a gain.[6]

One of the ideas behind these reforms was to put some of the cus- tomary relations between the President and the Prime Minister into the text: the President could not make any decisions without consulting the Prime Minister. Therefore, theoretically, Muslim rights were taken from the unwritten Pact and put into the text of the Constitution for the first time. In essence, Ta'if tried to amalgamate the text with the practice of Lebanese constitutional duality by giving old practices the power of the new text.

However, this transfer of presidential power was certainly not some- thing that was just implicitly given to the Muslims, but something that all communities represented in the cabinet would gain from: for example, the Greek Orthodox would gain a constitutional power-sharing role that they did not have before. This was not written into the text, but was implied in Article 95 of the new Constitution. These reforms meant that Ta'if attempted to shift governmental responsibility from the presidency to the cabinet so that the President could no longer impose his will on the Prime Minister and the Speaker, thus for the first time giving all the communities a more tangible power-sharing role. It was not intended that the Prime Minister would replace the President as the most impor- tant figure, as is often suggested, but custom, text and implementation in Lebanon remained three different things.

As the head of a new Council of Ministers the Prime Minister's role was greatly enhanced. Having been appointed by the President after binding parliamentary consultation, he could be dismissed only by the deputies, rather than by the President. The Prime Minister thus became the head of government and was charged with forming the executive after non-binding parliamentary consultations. He was to control its agenda, chair cabinet meetings and sign all legislative decrees, with the exception of the one appointing him. The executive would completely control the legislative process, the administration, the army and the appointment of leading civil servants. Decisions in cabinet would be taken by consensus but, when this proved impossible, the two-thirds-plus majority would prevail.

However, on the question of cabinet formation there was major disagreement between the Sunni and Shi'a communities over a proposed mechanism for resolving conflict between the President and the Prime Minister if they failed to come to an understanding over cabinet formation. Some Shi'a deputies on the Committee of Seventeen suggested that, if the President did not agree to the Prime Minister's cabinet list and the government's policy after thirty days, then the premier should resign. If the same thing happened again with a new Prime Minister, it should then go to Parliament for a vote.[7] The Sunnis,[8] led by Saeb Salam, and some of the Christians, rejected this, as it would have enhanced the Speaker's role in government, forcing the Shi'a negotiators to concede.[9] Ta'if therefore provided no mechanism for resolving this potential problem, the Maronites retained a veto on cabinet formation by default and the old Maronite–Sunnite alliance retained its position in the confessional balance.

The real problem for the Christians here was that, by giving up Maronite presidential prerogatives, they had conceded what many of them viewed as the crucial Christian constitutional guarantees in Lebanon and the Middle East in general. So why did they not refuse? The simple answer to that question is that, having lost the war, the Christians had no choice. Joseph Maila argues that the transfer of executive power to the Council of Ministers signalled a clear Muslim victory in this debate, as the Christians had long argued for any re-division of these powers to be between the President and the Prime Minister.[10] On the other hand, some Muslims were arguing that, since in 1943 the population had been about 6:5 Christian–Muslim and 6:5 was taken as the parliamentary divide, whereas in 1989 it was at least 6:5 in favour of the Muslims, why should this not be reflected in the Lebanese Parliament?[11]

At Ta'if the Christian negotiating position was that they would forgo Maronite presidential prerogatives only in return for a fixed date for a Syrian withdrawal, which would be overseen by the Troika. However, lacking political or military strength, they were unable to secure this *quid pro quo*.[12] Consequently, the Christians conceded, as refusal would have meant continuation of the war, the continuation of Aoun and a further weakening of their negotiating position. However, in an aside to the

accord the Troika gave an unwritten promise to oversee Syria's redeployment, while the five permanent members of the UN Security Council
pledged that they were 'determined to support … the restoration of the
full sovereignty of Lebanon over the whole of its territory'.[13]

Practically speaking, then, it was the Maronite community that made
the most concessions at Ta'if, with the Sunni and Shi'a communities
equalling them in political influence for the first time, and the Orthodox
and Druze making marginal gains. The Maronite position was blurred,
however, by the amount they had to give up and by the non-implementation of the Agreement. Theodor Hanf argues that: 'The fundamental
difference between the new coexistence pact of Ta'if and the National
Pact of 1943 lay in the distribution of power. The old Pact was a matter
between two communities, the new one was between all communities on
the basis of parity between Christians and Muslims'.[14] Yet, in reality, some
Christians and Muslims remained more equal than others.

The Shi'a having long called for political representation to be accord-
ed to them vis-à-vis their apparent demographic status as Lebanon's
largest community, had the Speaker's term of office effectively extended
from one year to a four-year renewable tenure. In the first draft it had
been set at two years, but at Housseini's insistence it was changed to four,
in line with the prime ministerial and presidential terms.[15] The Speaker's
influence was greatly enhanced by this change, as he could play a key role
in the formation of government, become presidential king-maker and
oversee government activity, without being open to the political pressures
and bargaining to which a one-year mandate had left him susceptible.[16]
However, it could be interrupted after two years if ten or more deputies
signed a petition and two thirds of the Parliament voted against him. In
practice, given a strong bloc in the chamber, the new Speaker virtually
had a 'job for life'.[17] Conversely, while this strengthened the Shi'a position in government, it severely weakened Lebanese parliamentary
democracy, as the Speaker no longer needed to consider the positions of
the different parties in Parliament every year. As the Deputy Speaker, Elie
Ferzli, put it, 'Why should he care if he has got four years?'[18] Of course,
these concessions fell far short of the old Shi'a demands for deconfessionalisation of the political system.[19] Housseini created this new role but,
ironically, it ended up consolidating Amal's position in government, as
Housseini did not have a strong following in Parliament and his position
subsequently fell to Berri. The power of the Speaker's new role did not
just come with his enhanced position, but through the strength of his parliamentary bloc.

When the Muslims arrived at Ta'if they were largely happy with the
initial draft, whereas the Christians, having lost the war and shrunk
numerically since 1975, compensated their losses with the maintenance of
the Maronite presidency and 50:50 parity in Parliament. The Muslims

were, however, mindful that it was not in their interests to further weaken the beleaguered Christian community, so no one wanted to go far beyond the internal boundaries of the National Pact. Fundamentally, avoiding any grand constitutional change was in almost everyone's interests.

To meet one of the aspirations of the Druze community Ta'if contained provisions for the creation of a Senate, after the election of the first non-confessional Lebanese Parliament. This was as uncertain and as unlikely to be enacted as the provisions for deconfessionalisation that it depended upon, and was therefore not taken very seriously.[20] Further, Jumblat lacked representation at Ta'if, with only one Druze deputy being in attendance, and, due to demographic shifts, he was faced with an ever-decreasing slice of the Muslim segment.[21]

Jumblat compensated for this by cleverly positioning himself during the pre-Ta'if negotiations. He was not against Ta'if, but, lacking numbers and political strength, he gave the impression that he was by making reservations about the Agreement and, in doing so, situated himself alongside the Syrians in order to guarantee himself and his community a role in the new system in return for his compliance.[22] Knowing that the Syrians were not 100 per cent happy with Ta'if, he tactically linked his position to theirs in order to benefit from their implementation, as and when they finally agreed it.[23] As a result the Druze managed to get two of the nine new Muslim seats in Parliament, while the numerically superior Shi'a got only three (see Table 12).

As far as the small communities were concerned, on the one hand the expansion of Parliament to 108 seats decreased their influence, while on the other, the transfer of power from the President to the executive could enhance or decrease it, depending on the size of the cabinet. For example, where the Druze had customerily had three ministers in a cabinet of sixteen headed by the President, after Ta'if they had three in a cabinet of thirty that had inherited the President's constitutional powers.

The Greek Orthodox benefited from the extension of the Speaker's term, as this reform also applied to the post of Deputy Speaker, which they occupied by tradition along with the post of Deputy Prime Minister. However, at Ta'if the Greek Orthodox deputies attempted to introduce some definitive powers for the Deputy Prime Minister, yet no consensus on this emerged and a decision on the matter was postponed.[24] All this, of course, was not written into the Ta'if Agreement, but was understood at Ta'if in the Committee of Seventeen.

While Ta'if delayed deconfessionalisation, it also avoided cementing it in the fashion that the Constitutional Document had proposed. However, as the proposals of 1976 had envisaged, it did abolish confessional allocation beneath the senior ranks of the civil service. Most Lebanese leaders argue that there was no renewal of the unwritten National Pact, so theoretically the Parliament could elect a non-Maronite President, for nowhere in Ta'if does it say that he has to be a Maronite. Arguably, Ta'if is a step away from confessionalism, as it sets up a formula to institutionally rid Lebanon of it. The problem is that deconfessionalisation would, perhaps, remove the unwritten side to Lebanese politics, the communal balances that hold the political system together, so no one really expected deconfessionalisation to happen, as it was not in anyone's short-to-medium-term interests. It remained an aspiration for many, but no one sect was actually ready to put it into effect, with the exception of the Shi'a, who, while being the biggest community demographically, were also unable to hold the office of President or Prime Minister under the National Pact system.

Instead of deconfessionalisation, Ta'if actually re-established parity of political representation in the Chamber of Deputies between Christians and Muslims, and replaced the 6:5 Christian bias with 50:50 proportionality. To enable this change the number of parliamentary seats was increased from 99 to 108, the minimum number needed to achieve this provision. This led to the debate over how these seats, and others vacant due to natural death and assassination, would be filled. This was settled through a one-off nomination process, on Syrian insistence. This violated the very principles of democracy and electoral representation that Ta'if was attempting to reconstitute, allowing Syria to influence and shape the formation of the new political establishment in its own image.

As it was a constitutional reform document, the Ta'if Agreement did not go into explicit detail about electoral reform, an issue that was not discussed in depth at Ta'if. However, it stipulated that a new electoral law would be established that ended the use of small electoral districts (*qada'*), redrawing the boundaries into six large provinces (*mohafazat*). This was to make them more heterogeneous and ensure coexistence between all the communities in each province. Ta'if also specified that the judicial system should be completely independent from the government, to prevent electoral manipulation. Further, the idea of returning to the *mohafazat* was to have electoral districts that served as large decentralised governmental units, thereby amalgamating electoral and administrative boundaries.

However, Ta'if actually avoided consociational decentralisation and failed to grant autonomy to the ethnic communities on a regional or federal basis in any meaningful way. In fact, it underlined the 'strong central' nature of Lebanese government even as it referred to the future establishment of assemblies aimed at creating 'local participation'. Maila argues that everything in the document indicates the opposite of any decentralisation of administrative power within Lebanon: the whole thrust of Ta'if revolves around the restoration of Lebanese sovereignty and the shoring up of multiethnic authority through the executive body of central government.[25]

In 1943 the Lebanese had a written Constitution that satisfied the Christians and an unwritten pact that created an equilibrium with the Muslims. In 1989 they both gained a written Constitution and a reformed unwritten National Pact. With the non-implementation of both these political arrangements, it is very difficult to tell exactly what the National Pact now is, or even what it was meant to be after 1989. Moreover, while Lebanon was under Syrian control, both parts of the reformulated Pact remain in limbo, with the government being dependent on personalities and confessional bloc strength in parliament vis-à-vis Syria. While Ta'if has not been implemented by the Lebanese, it is difficult to ascertain exactly what powers each of the three heads of government would have had if it had been, but there is no doubt that tradition and custom would have played a central role.

Fundamentally, 1989 changed the equation to a certain extent in its attempt to solve the question of national identity. The National Pact gave Lebanon an Arab face whilst keeping its western orientation. In an attempt to resolve this contradiction Ta'if stated that Lebanon was now an Arab country with an Arab identity, but that the Lebanese state was its definitive final form.

In summary, the Ta'if Agreement did not replace the National Pact, it was merely a redefinition of it. The unwritten National Pact remains in effect, with the three main positions of power in Lebanon still being reserved for the three main communities. However, the powers of these positions shifted to reformulate the equilibrium within Lebanese politics that collapsed in 1975. Nowhere in Ta'if does it say that the President must be Maronite, the Prime Minister Sunni and the Speaker Shi'a. The difference between the interpretation of the text and practice remains at the hub of Lebanese politics.

EXTERNAL RELATIONS

Sections II and IV of the Ta'if Agreement dealt with the issues of restoring Lebanese sovereignty and Lebanese–Syrian relations. These parts were non-negotiable and were submitted only following Syrian approval.[26] One deputy likened the role of Lebanon's politicians at Ta'if to appearing 'in a film', as they had 'no influence' over Parts II and IV of the Agreement, and substantively contributed 'nothing' to their negotiation.[27] The restoration of Lebanese sovereignty was to take place under the new government by progressively extending the state's authority with the use of the Lebanese army. The obvious contradiction was that, by legally constituting Syrian political and military ascendancy in Lebanon, Section IV limited Lebanese sovereignty. It did, however, present a solution for dissolving the Lebanese and non-Lebanese militias. The Lebanese militias were all to be disarmed and many of their regular troops incorporated into the Lebanese army; as for the non-Lebanese militias, it was clear that their fate would be more closely linked to Syrian foreign policy goals than to the restoration of Lebanese sovereignty.

Ta'if left Lebanon under *de facto* Syrian control and very much again at the mercy of the Arab–Israeli conflict. It provided Syrian forces in Lebanon with the role of restoring Lebanese sovereignty and re-establishing the state's territorial integrity. The Lebanese deputies accepted the compromise on the basis of political realism. Their choice was either to submit to the return of old-style power-sharing under Syrian tutelage, in the hope of regaining sovereignty at a later date, or to continue a civil war that they had no control over and nothing to gain from. There was no reference in the Agreement to a date when Syria would actually withdraw its troops from Lebanese territory. Rather, it stated that there would be a 'redeployment' of Syrian troops two years after the domestic political reforms had been implemented. This redeployment was to be overseen and guaranteed by the Troika, which gave unwritten promises to this effect. When many of the Christians disagreed and protested about the exclusion of a time frame from the Agreement, Prince Faisal spelt the situation out to them: 'You either take it, or you break it'.[28] This left the Syrians in the privileged position of being legally able to station part of their army in Lebanon for the security of its territory, given the Israeli occupation of the south, which did not end until May 2000. Before Ta'if the Syrian presence was not legal, as its mandate under the ADF had expired on 27 July 1982.[29] Ominously, the US and the West in general seemed to find little discomfort in entrusting the resuscitation of Lebanese democracy to a dictatorship.

The Ta'if Agreement inextricably bound Lebanon to its Arab brother and neighbour, Syria. There can be little doubt that the redefinition of the relationship after the civil war was exactly the sort of association the Christians strove to avoid when forging the National Pact in 1943 and, in this sense, they lost the most at Ta'if. Their Muslim counterparts, however, also lost in terms of sovereignty. While they would have largely welcomed such a Lebanese–Syrian relationship in 1943, the debate over Lebanese nationalism had largely been resolved as a by-product of the war, with most Muslims in Lebanon viewing themselves as Lebanese and holding a strong sense of allegiance to the state. At Ta'if many of the Muslim deputies agreed with and shared the fears of their Christian counterparts over the Syrian position in Lebanon, but they were too frightened to speak up, in fear for their lives.

When the Lebanese arrived at Ta'if, the joke was that the Agreement they were about to negotiate had been translated from English into Arabic just in time for the conference.[30] The deputies who were unaware that the war was about to end probably realised it after hearing this quip.

It was well known that this was an agreement between, and managed by, the US and the Syrians through the Saudis. While there were other regional and international interests being played out during the negotiations, every actor knew the solution had to be a Syrian one, yet almost all wanted to dilute Syria's influence and Arabise the arrangements as much as possible. However, as the force on the ground in Lebanon, Syria was well aware that the US needed it to implement any agreement. Accordingly, Assad distanced himself from the proposed accord and flexed his muscles militarily until any serious linkage between Syrian troop withdrawal and political reform was dropped.

The US wanted to clear up the Lebanese crisis at the end of the Cold War, as it had become a running sore, spreading tension throughout the region. US–Syrian relations were not great at that time, but the Americans used Ta'if to improve them, as Syria was too important in the regional scene to remain in isolation forever. One imagines that the US did not know that it was going to fight the Gulf War at this stage, but this marked the start of the process that saw Syria enter the US-led alliance against Iraq. Further, Israeli security concerns vis-à-vis Hizballah and Iran deeply worried the US.[31] It has been argued that, before the emergence of Hizballah, Lebanon could well have been excluded from the regional peace deal, for the US and Israel wanted them safely under Syrian regulation.[32]

In 1989 Saudi Arabia wanted to limit Syrian dominance in Lebanon, position itself as the second Arab power vis-à-vis Syria, gain a role as peace broker in the Middle East and reinstate the traditional elites to power in Lebanon, particularly the Sunni community, whose position had been hijacked by Syria during the war. As for Morocco and Algeria, they had little interest in Lebanese affairs and, being detached from the conflict, brought an air of neutrality to the arbitration. While they lacked the military might of Syria, the Saudi's strength lay in their financial power and their close ties with the US. At Ta'if the Saudis promised massive monetary aid through Hariri, with the Troika making sincere pledges to oversee the implementation of the Agreement and the rehabilitation of the country, if not for the sake of the Lebanese, then certainly to stunt Syria's dominance.

By invading Kuwait Saddam Hussein undermined the Troika's reconstruction work and the regional equilibrium that was crucial for any resuscitation of Lebanese democracy.[33] The Syrians joined the US-led alliance against Iraq, and the Arab world's pledges of investment and support for Lebanon vanished. Whether the US ever had any intention to follow through on Ta'if and enforce a Syrian withdrawal is difficult to ascertain. The Gulf War changed everything, after the US Ambassador to Iraq, April Glaspie, apparently misled Saddam, or Saddam misled himself, as to US approval of his aspirations in the Gulf.[34] This prompted a major US intervention in the Middle East, and any hope that Ta'if had fashioned for the reconstitution of Lebanese sovereignty disappeared. Although officially the US's policy remains that it supports the full implementation of Ta'if, it has not pushed the Syrians to install it in its true format because the Lebanese government has never asked it to do so.[35] To understand why that is a particularly contrived and cynical position, an analysis of the Syrian interpretation and implementation of Ta'if is necessary.

'TA'IF PLUS'

There is no doubt that the Gulf War changed the outcome of the Ta'if process in favour of Syria achieving its primary goals in Lebanon. Equally, Aoun's intransigence shattered any chance the Lebanese had of controlling their own reconciliation. It was ironic that Aoun called the Ta'if Agreement a mechanism for Syrian domination within Lebanon, when his own rejection of it and his stalling of its implementation helped to ensure that the international community allowed Syria to fill the power vacuum that Aoun had helped to create. In fact, he fully came out against Ta'if only when he realised that there was no hope of either the Lebanese deputies or the international community supporting him as a presidential candidate.[36] Therefore, not only did the US allow Syria to take charge of Lebanon, it gave its full approval. Syria, which had been distant from the Ta'if process from the beginning, became prepared to work the accord, albeit in its own interests and according to its own interpretation. The Gulf War had, on the one hand, turned Assad into a temporary ally of the US and, on the other, isolated Aoun. Hrawi and Hoss were, of course, in no position to deal with Aoun and disarm the militias without Syrian assistance, so from the beginning the first Ta'if government was completely dependent on Lebanon's neighbour, for both its birth and its conservation.

The true nature of this new partnership was evident from the first steps towards the implementation of the Ta'if Agreement. Hoss quickly demanded the powers due to him as Prime Minister under the new Constitution, but Hrawi, who acted like a President of the old republic due to his close relationship with Syria, rebuffed him.[37] Hanf argues that 'Constitution and constitutional reality began to diverge at a very early stage of the Second Republic'.[38] Thus, Hrawi, whose role it was to implement the new constitution, consulted alone with Damascus about the make-up of the administration and ignored Ta'if's new amendments. Hoss resigned in protest and Omar Karami formed a government of national unity, which included the militias. In addition to posts for each of their leaders, Amal, LF, Kataeb and the PSP received two cabinet seats each, while Hizballah, Aoun's supporters, Chamoun's National Liberal Party and the Communists were all excluded.

Karami's cabinet was so large that it provided no possibility of ever using the one-third blocking abstention that was required for a veto on legislation: other than the LF and Kataeb ministers, the government was composed of pro-Syrian figures. Consequently, while the administration was divided equally between Christian and Muslim ministers, the cross-communal consociational element was hollow, for the majority of Christians were not represented by the pro-Syrian Christian ministers in cabinet, something that was to become a common trend in Lebanese politics.

With the militia leaders safely on board, the government set about the daunting task of disarming their organisations. This was successfully achieved through a programme of assimilating around 20,000 militiamen into Lebanon's various security and civil services.[39] Unlike the militias, the Palestinians had no political incentive to disarm, but were successfully forced to do so by the Lebanese army, with Syrian support. As for Hizballah, it remained intact and was on hand when it became expedient for Syria to use southern Lebanon as a battleground against Israel.

Syria had allowed the Lebanese government to reconstitute itself and regain control over most of the state. In return, on 22 May 1991 the government signed a Treaty of Brotherhood, Cooperation and Coordination with Syria, as stipulated at Ta'if.[40] This treaty bound Lebanon and Syria to 'seek the highest levels of cooperation and coordination in all fields' (Article 1), while emphasising the 'interconnectedness between the security of both countries', stressing that 'Lebanon should not be a source of threat to Syria's security and viceversa under any circumstances', so much so that Syria would 'not allow any action that would constitute a threat or danger to Lebanon's security' (Article 3).

The Treaty also reaffirmed the time frame of two years after ratification of Ta'if for the 'redeployment' of Syrian troops to the Bekaa. However, it was very clear from the tone of the text that this was not a partnership agreement between equals, rather it was a legitimisation of Lebanese subordination in return for Syria's role in reconstituting the state. Syria was simply cashing in its chips after the Ta'if card game, only the price for ending the civil war was to be paid in Lebanese sovereignty rather than pounds. It looked set to be much more costly than the Lebanese gamblers had banked on. The Christians protested, but dissent and opposition in Lebanon, as in most authoritarian regimes, had little impact. Respect for civil liberties and freedom of expression – democratic principles clearly outlined in Ta'if – were soon threatened by newspaper censorship[41] (often self-imposed) and frequent unwarranted arrests of Aoun's supporters. In the Second Republic democracy became exactly how the pre-war generation remembered it: a thing of the past.

The government filled the empty seats in Parliament by selecting forty deputies, thirteen of whom were cabinet ministers, meaning that 'almost half the government elected themselves to Parliament'.[42] The eighteen newly created seats were divided equally between the Christian and Muslim communities, and many of them were allocated to loyal supporters of Damascus. This was clearly illustrated when the tiny Alawite community was given its first ever seats, in Tripoli and Akkar.

Early elections were called in 1992, as the Syrians were keen to have a compliant Parliament in case they came under international pressure to redeploy troops after the two-year deadline passed.[43] The cynicism and brashness with which the Syrian and Lebanese governments swept away the democratic foundations and principles enshrined in Ta'if for the reconstruction of the state and national reconciliation were an ominous indication of how Lebanon was to be governed. The new electoral law, passed on 16 July 1992, ignored Ta'if's recommendations, with the government opting instead for a system based on flagrant gerrymandering. Lists of pro-Syrian candidates, which resulted in an almost total Christian boycott, further undermined Ta'if.[44] The new law expanded the Parliament to 128 seats, with a heavily uneven regional distribution favouring the peripheral areas closer to Syria, as opposed to the densely populated cities. Seats were again shared evenly between Christians and Muslims, further weakening the influence of smaller sects. The Druze failed to benefit this time from the Muslim segment, as the Sunnis and the Shi'a received half each (see Tables 12 and 13). Further, the new law determined the sizes of the constituencies in the new provinces with the election of pro-Syrian candidates in mind, rather than creating the desirable situation of constituencies where the election of a deputy might require cross-communal voting, as it had under previous electoral systems since the mid-nineteenth century.

Hanf argues that the new electoral law undermined the consociational proportional representation of the two communal blocs underpinned by the shift to 50:50 at Ta'if. Under the old system the Christian dominance in Parliament had been equalised by the *modus operandi* under which many more Christians were reliant on Muslim votes to be elected than vice versa. With the new system of equal representation not only did this Christian dependence increase, but the law actually ensured that there would not be enough Christian deputies elected by Christian majorities to constitute a blocking minority of one third in the chamber.[45]

If further proof of Syria's intentions for Lebanon was necessary, Khaddam duly delivered it straight after the elections by announcing a new linkage between the partial withdrawal of Syrian troops and the implementation of deconfessionalisation.[46] These elections marked the end of the whole Ta'if process and the Lebanese politicians who had agreed it. The last of its linchpins, Housseini, fell from government and

TABLE 13: Confessional Distribution of Parliamentary Seats, 1992 (%)

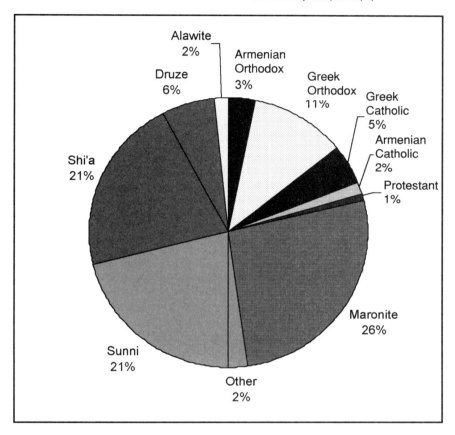

his rival, Berri, became the new Speaker. If a troika of Moawad, Hoss and Housseini had headed a real government of national reconciliation, it is impossible to judge how much of Ta'if they would have managed to implement. However, what is unquestionable is that they would not have been anywhere near as compliant as Hrawi, Hariri and Berri, for the primary interests of the former were Lebanese and interconfessional while those of the latter were Syrian, Saudi and then Lebanese.

The role played by Housseini in brokering Ta'if's internal agreement was instrumental, so his political demise was a benchmark in the Syrian takeover. The very fact that none of these three took office in the 'Ta'if plus' era is indicative of the potential they had to steer the Constitution closer to the letter and spirit of the Agreement, and thereby hamper Syrian control. This marked another dramatic shift in the unwritten National Pact. While Ta'if was an inclusive agreement, it certainly did not

envisage the militias superseding the traditional elites, which is exactly
what began to happen after the elections. Therefore 'Ta'if plus' not only
deviated from the written word of its constitutional amendments and the
National Pact, but fundamentally eluded those who had negotiated and
agreed it.

By holding elections before 1994 Syria also ensured a very low
turnout, as most of those who had fled during the civil war had not
returned, and most of the displaced in Lebanon were ineligible to vote.
Many of those overseas were Christians and, under the new law, they
were denied the right to vote from abroad. In response, Christian leaders organised a massive boycott, turning the elections into a vote of no
confidence in the government and the legitimacy of the Syrian-dominat-
ed system, in the hope that the elections would be cancelled. The boycott
failed and the elections took place anyway with only 5 per cent of
Christians voting in Beirut and 20 per cent in the north where it was least
effective. One consequence was to deprive moderate Muslims of seats
they would have won with Christian support, making way for Hizballah
and Amal to enter Lebanese politics. More importantly, it ensured that
any real opposition to the government would be extraparliamentary, at
least during the government's next term. This was a grave mistake by the
Christians, illustrating that leaders such as Aoun and Geagea were still
blind to the reality of Lebanon's new equilibrium: the Syrian equilibrium.[47] The Christians made a grand gesture over the lack of legitimacy and
democracy in the new system, but the West paid little attention to their
predicament and the newly elected Lebanese government got on with its
business without them.

So, from the beginning, the consociational elements of the Ta'if
Agreement were rendered hollow through Syrian manipulation. Syria's
interpretation of the Agreement was the one being imposed and accepted by the majority of the deputies, and the weakened Christian community could do almost nothing about it. The implementation of Ta'if made
a mockery of the very consociational principles that it sought to preserve
and redefine in the hope that they would provide the political fabric for
an independent and democratic 'Second Republic'. Instead of ushering in
a new era of democratic coexistence in Lebanon, the elections consolidated Syrian dominance in the Lebanese Parliament, as the effects of the
new electoral law blunted the PR system, favouring the Muslims at the
expense of their Christian counterparts. The implementation of Ta'if
totally failed to provide a power-sharing government that commanded
mutual acceptance, confidence or allegiance among its citizens. Nor did
its interpretation underscore any of the consociational democratic principles designed to regulate societies that are ethnically divided.

As text and practice are always two different things in Lebanon, it is first
of all both difficult and unfair to judge Ta'if on its Syrian implementation,

and it is safe to say that the verdict remains open on the untried Ta'if Agreement. However, forgetting for a moment its non-implementation, Ta'if still suffered from many of its predecessor's defects. In fact, its distinct lack of difference justifies this re-examination of what was wrong with the National Pact in the first place, as it is anything but a demographically proportionate redistribution of political power. Despite having significantly shrunk in proportion to the overall population, the Maronites and Sunnis both maintained their prominent positions in government at the expense of the Shi'a. Moreover, the smaller communities became, arguably, more insignificant with the increase in the number of parliamentary seats from 99 to 128 and with the large cabinets negating any real influence they had previously enjoyed in the Lebanese system. Of course, this is only partly the fault of the Ta'if Agreement. More importantly, most of the calls for political reform from the left stemmed from the perception that one community held power well above its demographic weight. In practice, Ta'if simply swapped this around. Previously, the Maronite Christians had held more power on paper than was due to them proportionally; after Ta'if the Sunni Muslim community became disproportionately dominant.

Ta'if was also as inflexible as the National Pact, in the sense that it contained no provision for future restructuring of intercommunal parliamentary representation in accordance with demographic shifts. In fact, there was no mention of the delicate issue of census figures anywhere in the Agreement. While Ta'if aspired to abolish political confessionalism, it actually enshrined communal privilege and religious segregation by its continuation of unwritten customs.

It has been argued that Ta'if was 'successful in resolving the Lebanese conflict because it restored consociationalism to the management of its multicommunal structure'.[48] Was the mismanagement of consociationalism to blame for the civil war and, if so, has Ta'if solved it? Unfortunately, the non-implementation of Ta'if restored the mismanagement of consociationalism to Lebanese politics. Given the failure to restore the consociational model to the management of Lebanon and a reallocation of powers that made little difference to the various communities, it is hard to believe that it was a similar inequality of power in 1975 that led to the outbreak of civil war.

The very fact that Ta'if was a politically redistributive revision of the National Pact suggests that the internal solution to Lebanese political coexistence is relatively simple: finding that narrow piece of common ground where nobody is happy but where everyone can live, as in many other ethnic conflicts. However, it is finding the internal and external will and coincidence of political circumstances that would foster inter-ethnic coexistence that is problematic. There was a glimmer of hope for the Lebanese at Ta'if to regain control of their state but, as so often in the past, their own divisions meant that they failed to seize the moment and external political events conspired against them, allowing Syria to consolidate its position. If Ta'if had been implemented as intended by the Troika, Lebanon might well have regained much of its sovereignty under the Trioka's supervision. Instead, the Lebanese were forced to settle for uncertain stability under Syrian hegemony.

If it had not been for the Gulf War and Aoun's political adventure in East Beirut, the international community might have given Lebanon's elites the incentive they lacked to come together and rework the National Pact. However, these are very big 'ifs'. Lebanon remained at the beginning of the twenty-first century, as it was in 1989, a helpless captive of the Arab–Israeli conflict. The Gulf War signalled realignment in regional and global alliances, as it was the first major international crisis following the end of the Cold War. However, while the lack of bipolar rivalry in the Middle East boded well for the initiation of an Arab–Israeli peace process, it also gave Syria the push it needed to play the lead role in the implementation of Ta'if. Thus, the deputies of 1972 gambled at Ta'if in the hope that the Trioka would regulate Syria's role and, subsequently, restore Lebanese sovereignty.

What changed, and what did the Lebanese learn from their civil war and, for the time being at least, the loss of their sovereign state? For one thing, the debate over national identity had changed dramatically by 1989, as all communities viewed themselves as Lebanese. Ironically, this was often voiced through their mutual dislike for the Syrians, the Palestinians and the Israelis. However, this is not quite the same as the debate over national self-determination. While the vast majority of Lebanon's citizens want to belong to an independent sovereign Lebanese state, either the Christians want it more than the Muslims or the Muslims are too frightened to say otherwise. Some argue that the Muslims are just being pragmatic, but their public absence from the mainly Christian extraparliamentary opposition is stark.

L. Abul-Husn argues that, 'for the time being at least, the accord has restored legitimacy to the concept of multicommunalism and efficiency to consociational management'.[49] A more critical look at the realities of Lebanese politics today paints a very different picture. The accord did not restore legitimacy to the concept of multicommunalism in Lebanon at all. In fact, it did the exact opposite, as the Christian population felt totally underrepresented by a government that many viewed as illegitimate and it was difficult to find a Muslim leader who will openly voice dissent on such matters. The violation of the consociational principles laid out in Ta'if made a mockery of the serious efforts of many Lebanese during the war years to try to guide the country back to prosperous, harmonious coexistence. Moreover, efficient consociational management did not exist in Lebanon's post-Ta'if governments, unless one defines efficient management as Syria making all the important and not so important decisions, and a compliant Lebanese government administering them.

Many Lebanese continue to call for the abolition of the confessional system, as if this would be a panacea for all Lebanon's political and social ailments. If the similarity between the National Pact and the Ta'if Agreement is anything to go by, however, then no other form of government can be expected in Lebanon, even in the distant future. Future deconfessionalisation was also called for in 1943, but Lebanon has a long way to go before it is back to the position it was in at independence, when it was unquestionably an independent state. Perhaps the Lebanese simply use this issue as a political scapegoat because the truth as to where their conflict lies is too awful to face: if only the answer to Lebanon's problems lay in an ideological realignment within a new party system. In a similar fashion, many Lebanese very often avoid the 'S' word in public conversation, apportioning blame all over the place while tucking the Syrian question neatly at the back of their minds.

Between 1989 and 2005, the Ta'if Agreement remained largely unimplemented, with the vast majority of Christians, and many Muslims also, feeling excluded from the political process or, at least, underrepresented in government. Syria did engage in troop redeployment in April 2002, however, the action was meaningless, as Damascus had long since consolidated its political control over Lebanon. This remained the major source of animosity within the Christian community, especially among the Maronites and among the surviving deputies of 1972, of all religious persuasions until 2005.[50] As a result national reconciliation will not, and cannot, take place until Ta'if is implemented in the letter and the spirit of the Agreement, and the Syrian question is resolved.

Of course, none of this will happen without a successful regulation of the regional Arab–Israeli conflict, meaning the sort of major shift in US foreign policy that does not appear likely, even after 9/11. The loss of Lebanese sovereignty during the civil war can only be rectified if radical political changes in the regional environment occur. While the events of 9/11 were radical and might to some extent change western thinking on the Middle East, it would take an overdose of wishful thinking to imagine that Lebanon, with its veneer of democracy and national reconciliation, will suddenly re-emerge as a gateway of understanding between East and West.

Abul-Husn argues further that 'resolution of the conflict became possible when the problems of power and authority in the social structure were addressed', and that of all the attempts to resolve the war Ta'if 'has been the most successful in taking into account those issues primarily responsible for the perpetuation of conflict in Lebanon'.[51] First, under the Syrian interpretation and implementation of Ta'if exactly the same problems of power and authority exist, and are even more salient in Lebanon today than they were before the outbreak of the civil war. The government is more corrupt, the communal balance is increasingly untenable, and there is a growing perception within certain communities that they are under-represented in the administration and unfairly treated within the system.

Second, Ta'if differed very little from any of the previous attempts to stop the bloodshed and it basically consolidated what was agreed in 1976. It was successful, however, in addressing the issues that perpetuated the conflict externally, as Syria came to control the state. Further, Ta'if presupposed that a national consensus existed in Lebanon at the end of the war, and that it was consecrating it with Syria as the godfather overseeing this process. So, in effect, Ta'if was based on the false premise that national reconciliation had occurred. Ironically, the violation of Ta'if prevented any such reconciliation process from taking place. However, the Palestinian catalyst for war, which had provoked stalemate in the 1970s, was missing and it was this factor that helped to facilitate agreement in 1989.

CONCLUSION

The implementation of Ta'if circumnavigated the four fundamental pillars of consociational democracy. Its electoral law established a government that favoured one community over the others, making parity of interconfessional representation a numerical veneer. The electoral system of proportional representation in multiethnic constituencies envisaged at Ta'if was corrupted through widespread gerrymandering and pro-Syrian electoral lists. This blocked the one-third-minority veto on government decisions and, in the chamber, deprived Lebanon's communities of the essential mechanism for jamming legislation of a constitutional or national nature. Finally, it delivered the exact opposite of devolution and autonomy to the different ethnic communities; rather, it centralised government and maximised power in the hands of the few.

However, internally and on paper, Ta'if was an inclusive elite-led agreement that differed from the exclusive nature of the Tripartite Agreement and the National Pact. Like Khoury and Solh's ulterior motive of getting rid of the French, the Lebanese agenda behind Ta'if was about ending a civil war and restoring sovereignty to a shattered multiethnic state. It contained many of the same contradictions, and appeared to be just as inflexible and unsustainable. However, the National Pact had one great advantage in the fact that the Lebanese agreed and worked it, whereas Ta'if is strictly a Syrian creature. The Syrians have begun to bring the Lebanese together in opposition to foreign rule, as the French did during 1943.

CHAPTER EIGHT

Imposing power-sharing

'Consociationalism is a heroic program because it aims to maintain imperial coexistence without the imperial bureaucrats and without the distance that made those bureaucrats more or less impartial rulers'.

Michael Walzer[1]

Did the imposition of consociation create overarching national identities in Northern Ireland or Lebanon, or did power-sharing actually reinforce the ethnic boundaries in these two societies? Does the initial failure of consociation in Northern Ireland and Lebanon enhance the potential for future collapse, or does its reimposition signify that no other form of conflict regulation is possible? Were the success and failure of consociation in Northern Ireland and Lebanon determined entirely by external forces, or could domestically constructed consociational initiatives have been possible? If they were primarily externally driven, what does this tell us about the use of consociation to regulate societies divided by ethno-national conflict?

In order to answer these questions and draw comparative lessons from the different consociational experiments, an evaluation of the implications of the power-sharing experiences in Northern Ireland and Lebanon is required. This chapter examines and contrasts these different consociational agreements, analysing their impact on national identity, self-determination and intercommunal reconciliation. It evaluates the imposition and implementation of these agreements, their internal and external dynamics, and the limitations of coercive consociationalism on both external and domestic elites. It concludes that the scope for the implementation of successful consociation in the long term can only be seriously enhanced by the existence of stable exogenous environments that facilitate or maintain intercommunal power-sharing equilibriums.

COMPARATIVE CONSOCIATIONS

The purpose of this book has been to explore the similarities and differences among the agreements that have led to the application and imposition of consociational government in Northern Ireland and Lebanon.

The first thing to note is that, of the four agreements, only Lebanon's National Pact was not entirely externally engineered, although its establishment was heavily influenced and facilitated by positive exogenous pressures. In contrast, the Ta'if Agreement and both of Northern Ireland's power-sharing accords were imposed by external regional powers, but imposition in these three cases took radically different forms.

Sunningdale was primarily an exclusive agreement, in that there was no question of opening the consociation to non-compliant or extremist sections of the unionist political elite, nor to republican or loyalist paramilitaries. The Agreement was designed to isolate them by establishing a political centre-ground where consociational government could be facilitated through such exclusion. In that sense the GFA was the exact opposite of Sunningdale. It was agreed on the premise of inclusivity, being open to all the major political representatives of both communities; the only segments that were excluded were those that refused all overtures to participate. The British had come to realise that Northern Ireland's conflict could not be regulated by a military solution, nor in simply unionist or nationalist terms. This thinking had a lot to do with Northern Ireland's regional situation. Lebanon, in contrast, being caught in the middle of the Arab–Israeli conflict, never found itself in such fortunate circumstances after 1975. As Adrian Guelke emphasises, in comparison to Lebanon, Northern Ireland 'is fortunate in being a backwater in strategic terms'.[2] This predicament was illustrated at Ta'if, where the Lebanese were given a choice between Syrian hegemony or chaos. The reality of this *fait accompli* was that Syria determined whether Lebanon was to have political or military regulation of its conflict. Assad had backed away from a military solution in the 1970s and had been prevented from achieving one in 1985, but in 1990 the Gulf War paved the way for an international arrangement that facilitated Syrian military control.

In contrast, Northern Ireland's GFA was imposed to a far lesser extent than Sunningdale or Ta'if and, initially, acquired broad-based political legitimacy through referendums in Northern Ireland and the Republic, gaining crucial support from majorities of both populations. Yet, the extent to which it was imposed is highlighted by the multiple suspensions of its power-sharing arrangements. Since 1998 the British government has repeatedly exercised its sovereignty over Northern Ireland in order to maintain the GFA. This became apparent through its attempts to implement the agreement with the Irish government by providing various incentives and motives to the parties at different junctures. By imposing political sanctions and implementing the Agreement in stages it coerced some of Northern Ireland's elites into maintaining the initiative that brought about the Agreement. The British government used the threat of reinstating direct rule through the Secretary of State, returning to the AIA and moving towards some form of joint authority, to coerce parties initially to live up to their commitments. It also initially withheld progress on its commitments to army withdrawal, demilitarisation and normalisation, as the paramilitaries failed to disarm. Thus, many parts of the GFA were negotiable or renegotiable and the governments used many issues as bargaining tools to keep the agreement functioning. However, their inability to sustain the momentum of the GFA for any substantial length of time illustrates the limitations of imposing consociation in a democratic environment. The stumbling block was decommissioning. The two governments refused to punish Sinn Féin for their intransigence over the issue of IRA arms. This left David Trimble with the political conundrum of constantly attempting to coerce a democratic party, the UUP, into maintaining its position in a power-sharing administration with a party using both democratic and undemocratic negotiating methods. Tony Blair broke his promises to the UUP leader because he valued maintaining the British government's security pact with Sinn Féin above implementing the GFA's power-sharing arrangements at Stormont through the moderate parties. This seriously damaged the process in the short-term and undermined the credibility of the Agreement in the eyes of the Unionist electorate.

While there are questions as to exactly how well the description of 'external imposition' fits the GFA, no such queries could be raised regarding the Ta'if Agreement. Not only were its provisions reinterpreted and imposed by Syria, but its implementation was exclusive, in the sense that the traditional leaders who negotiated it were largely replaced by pro-Syrian figures in government. This process left most of the old elite in the extraparliamentary opposition after the elections in 1992. Having boycotted those elections, the Christians were themselves partly to blame for their exclusion, but they merely hastened a process that Syria intended to undertake anyway. The cynical decisiveness with which Syria swept away the consociational principles enshrined at Ta'if illustrates the extent to which the new Lebanese agreement was imposed and raises questions as to whether Lebanon has actually been a consociation since 1989.

Just as the DUP and UKUP had excluded themselves from Northern Ireland's substantive negotiations, Aoun isolated himself from the Ta'if process. Geagea's exclusion came after he challenged the government over the absence of the one-third consociational veto in the cabinet, and he was imprisoned for crimes committed during the civil war. This was in contrast to Lebanon's more compliant confessional warlords, who remained part of the Ta'if process. The similarity here is that the self-exclusion of the two unionist parties led to a settlement in Northern Ireland, which the pro-Agreement parties subsequently failed to sell to the unionist community. Equally, if Lebanon's Christians had unified, with Aoun taking his place in a post-war government, the power-sharing administration of the Second Republic might have been a very different creature. As in Northern Ireland, it was intrasegmental instability and rivalry that allowed the agreement to take the form it did. It was these intracommunal divisions that resulted in the majority of unionists and of Lebanese Christians subsequently perceiving themselves as the losers in their respective settlements, alienated and isolated from the political process.

Conversely, while the National Pact was not imposed in a similar fashion to Sunningdale or Ta'if, it was no less an exclusive arrangement, as its power-sharing formula regarding communal representation was reflective of each segment's political strength in relation to the others – and their standing and links within the Middle East itself – as opposed to their demographic strength within the state. For example, the politically underdeveloped Shi'a community did not gain a position in government that followed a strict application of proportional representation based on census figures. Nor did any of the other communities. In this sense, Ta'if marked a change from the old system, as the allocation of parliamentary seats and the reallocation of government powers reflected the strength of the communities in Lebanon vis-à-vis their external backers, as opposed to their demographic weight. For example, the Christians retained the 50:50 proviso in government and Parliament, despite demographic losses, while the minuscule Alawite community gained two seats, due to its links with the Alawite ruling elite in Syria.

Given its long-term success in regulating Lebanon's ethno-national conflict, one of the most interesting observations regarding the National Pact is that it was never meant to last. Similar observations can be made about Sunningdale, in that it was primarily an arrangement to reduce political violence. With hindsight it seems unlikely that either the British government or the Irish government actually expected Sunningdale, to work, or had any real enthusiasm for the concept of power-sharing itself. Like the National Pact, Sunningdale appeared to be a temporary arrangement aimed at filling a political vacuum, reducing the potential for ethno-national violence and containing the conflict to Northern Ireland. Unlike Lebanon, however, Northern Ireland's leaders had no history of power-sharing nor intercommunal motivation to engage in it. What has changed, then, as far as the reimposition of consocation is concerned in either case?

First, Ta'if was similar to the National Pact in that the Lebanese elites were able to take advantage of favourable external pressures, which engineered a return to power-sharing and ended the war. It was thus primarily an agreement to regulate the conflict and the exogenous variables acted to facilitate its reformulation. In contrast, by 1989 the traditional Lebanese elites had long since agreed the general parameters of a National Pact compromise and they were largely realistic in sharing the view that no other form of government was viable. As in 1943, a majority of Lebanon's traditional elites were willing to re-engage in consociation without being forced into it by outside powers. However, even if the exogenous variables changed – such as the Syrian departure of 2005 – allowing Ta'if to be properly implemented in the future, Lebanon would still suffer from many of the same internal confessional problems that hampered its agreement in 1943 and would remain susceptible to similar negative external influences. In that sense Lebanese politics had not changed by 1989 and Ta'if reflected its continuity. Each Lebanese community still followed linkage policies with external powers, and accordingly each community still held privileged links with external governments and political forces. Further, the fact that Syria's military withdrawal was actually precipitated by the assassination of one of Ta'if's most pivotal figures on 14 February 2005, Rafic Hariri, illustrates the ultimate fragility of the political situation in Lebanon.[3]

In Northern Ireland the GFA's signatories believed it to be an arrangement that would lead to a variety of contending outcomes, some provisional and some permanent, from a unitary Irish state to a strengthening of the union with Great Britain. The internal and external constitutional reforms that it entailed, its strict adherence to equality and consociational constructs, and the exogenous foundations that underpinned it strongly indicated that its brokers seriously expected, or at least hoped, that it would regulate the conflict in the short to medium term. What it did ensure, however, was that, once the decommissioning issue had been settled, the struggle between unionism and nationalism would be fought out on a constitutional political basis – or at least that is what its architects had hoped. Compared to 1973, even those in opposition had, by 1998, largely accepted that they could not simply ignore the GFA or have it replaced. In fact, they implicitly accepted that, even if they did manage to destabilise it critically, any replacement agreement would inevitably be of a similar nature to its predecessor. By 2004 they were scrambling to steal the clothes of the pro-Agreement parties and engage in a form of government that they had spent their entire political careers rejecting.

Turning to questions concerning the intended longevity of these pacts, or whether their real function was merely to stop or contain ethnonational violence, one ironic difference between the two cases is drawn out by an examination of their external environments and their proximity to democratic regimes. While the majority of Lebanon's traditional elites sought a return to the old form of power-sharing, the success or failure of their endeavours was determined by external factors. Conversely, while there was little concrete desire for political coexistence among Northern Ireland's elites, there was also a stark lack of any tradition of accommodationist politics and a declining enthusiasm for power-sharing within the two communities. In spite of this the positive external parameters of strong Anglo-Irish relations, the stabilising environment of the EU and the good offices of the US government boosted its prospects of success immensely.

So does a history of consociation actually matter in this sense? As far as Lebanon is concerned, a history of power-sharing, stretching back centuries, failed either to prevent the outbreak of ethno-national conflict or safeguard consociation in the long term. As for Northern Ireland, even in the absence of a successful history of power-sharing the antagonistic blocs were prepared to engage in political coexistence as a means to further their long-term political goals when continuation of the conflict proved unproductive. The external factors were crucial in directing the behaviour of the domestic elites and forging a power-sharing agreement, even in the absence of many of Arend Lijphart's favourable internal variables. In assessing whether history mattered in Northern Ireland or Lebanon, one crucial difference emerges between the two cases as a result of a history of power-sharing: changes occurred in how the Lebanese perceived themselves in an ethno-national sense, changes derived from their experience of consociational government and protracted civil war.

SHIFTING NATIONAL IDENTITIES?

Does power-sharing in societies divided by ethno-national conflict facilitate a form of syncretistic identity or loyalty to the state that overarches or supersedes antagonistic national identities? Did the use of consociation in Northern Ireland and Lebanon facilitate such changes? Or did it do the exact opposite, as many contend?[4] In Northern Ireland, while the GFA stopped the violence, or put an end to a phase in its conflict, inter-communal tension and antagonism clearly rose in the years that proceeded the signing of the accord. Moreover, extremist parties on both sides of the divide were boosted by strong electoral performances as a consequence of the GFA and its political fallout. While Sinn Féin and the DUP had pro-Agreement agendas after 1998, they both used the symbolic successes and defeats, for nationalism and unionism respectively, to varnish over those agendas. Sinn Féin had accepted partition and the IRA's military failure, and the DUP leadership had grasped that there was no alternative to a power-sharing government with republicans in Northern Ireland.

As for the question of diluting unionist or nationalist identities, creating loyalties to the institutions of the state, and establishing intercommunal harmony and reconciliation, the post-Agreement phase proved more politically divisive electorally between 1998 and 2005 than the ethno-national conflict had been over the preceding 25 years. So how has

Northern Ireland's ethnic conflict actually changed since Sunningdale's collapse? On the surface there appeared to have been no great movement in the conflicting political positions, at least officially speaking, as far as most of the party leaders were prepared to admit. However, Trimble's talk of a pluralist Northern Ireland for a pluralist people was in stark contrast to the majoritarian rhetoric of his anti-Sunningdale days.[5] A majority of unionists came to accept that Northern Ireland was not an entity that could be governed by unionists alone within the UK and that a future of political coexistence with nationalists was a political fact of life. Trimble put an end to the regressive politics of opposition that had misrepresented the unionist community for decades. He began a process of political reengagement that was designed to make the distinction of being both Irish and British a valuable addition to the United Kingdom.

Republicans, on the other hand, had set aside their demands for the immediate unification of the island of Ireland. They came to accept that working within a Northern Ireland framework was the only way that they could ever realistically achieve this national aspiration. This step-by-step approach, however, does not mean that they have any newfound loyalty to the institutions of the administration, or to the concept of a plural Northern Ireland as an entity in itself. This was clearly illustrated after 1998 by the republican movement's involvement in weapons procurement, the conviction of republicans for the training of guerrillas in Colombia, illegal intelligence-gathering at Stormont, the 2005 Northern Bank robbery and the IRA's continued paramilitary activity.[6] After the signing of the GFA Sinn Féin argued that Irish unity would be achieved following referendums on Northern Ireland's constitutional status, as soon as the Catholic population reached 51 per cent. This rhetoric, however, seems to have been largely for internal consumption and Sinn Féin dropped this position soon after the results of the Census of 2001 were published. Yet these were the arguments with which Sinn Féin had sold the Agreement to its constituency, in the full knowledge that it had set aside any realistic prospect of Irish unity in the near future.

In the same way that Ta'if freed the Lebanese from the depredation of their civil war, the GFA paved the way for Northern Ireland's elites to emerge from their uncompromising and destructive political and military stalemate. Engaging in consociation enabled both sets of paramilitaries to wind down their military campaigns and, in return, collect the political rewards that constitutional politics offered. Many commentators believed that republicans would never disarm, as it was against their tradition to do so. Yet, at the negotiating level the decommissioning issue was about Sinn Féin maximising its gains through its security *quid pro quo* with the British government, strengthening its election position vis-à-vis the SDLP and dividing unionism over the issue. A similar assessment could be made regarding Hizballah and Amal in Lebanon. While Ta'if provided none of their preferred solutions to the conflict and they both opposed a return to power-sharing in principle, they soon reversed their positions in the light of the political benefits on offer for making the transition from paramilitarism to politics.

By 1989 the dynamics of Lebanon's ethno-national tension had radically changed in some respects. Before 1975 intercommunal divisions among the Lebanese were exacerbated as the consociational system failed to deal with the challenges of modernisation and political reform. After the civil war, however, there was more agreement on what it was to be Lebanese and on the view that a return to the Pact was the only way for the country to be governed. While some Christian leaders still harboured thoughts of an independent Christian state, most realised that, whether they liked it or not, all Lebanese had to live together. Most significantly, members of the Muslim communities had largely come to view themselves as Lebanese, or had at least formed a strong attachment to the state of Lebanon. For example, the formerly dispossessed and disinherited Shi'a community not only became politically mobilised and organised within Lebanon, but was actually prepared to go into battle to maintain the integrity of the state. While it was not just fighting for Lebanon, it was the Shi'a community that made the Israeli occupation of the south unsustainable. Before 1943 few Muslims would have volunteered to defend Greater Lebanon's borders. Moreover, the Sunni and Shi'a communities at Ta'if realised that their future remained with their Christian counterparts, and made no attempts to further destabilise their position, despite the fact that they had lost the war. This was also in keeping with the regional thinking and exogenous influences behind the Agreement. Joseph Maila makes an interesting comparison, pointing out that after Ta'if the three main communities had all participated in the making of modern Lebanon: the Maronites in 1920, the Sunnis in 1943 and the Shi'a in 2000, when the Israelis finally withdrew.[7] However, the lack of substance in this argument regarding the Shi'a position bacame apparent in 2005 when the Syrians were under pressure to withdraw from Lebanon. How deep their loyalty to Damascus is, hoewever, remains to be seen.

From these internal changes can some equation or correlation be made between instability encouraging intercommunal intransigence – driving parties to push forward with mutually antagonistic ethno-national aspirations – and stability facilitating and promoting compromise? The internal and external instability of the Sunningdale period on the one hand encouraged the majority of unionist leaders to reject any notion of compromise and on the other prompted republicans to escalate their campaign of violence. In fact, if an overarching syncretistic Lebanese identity existed after 1989, it was not clear whether it was a result of the shared experience of consociation or of the shared trauma of civil war. The latter seemed the more likely at the time as, if such a thing had existed even at elite level in 1975, the outbreak of violence as a consequence of foreign intervention might have been avoidable. It was, after all, not out of any sense of stability that the Lebanese agreed a compromise in 1989, but because domestic chaos and international pressure left them with no alternative.

In Northern Ireland it was the strong unity of purpose that had developed between London and Dublin that led its parties to a settlement and facilitated its transition from violence to consociational government. Conversely, the National Pact emerged amid the chaos of the Second World War, and at the height of Anglo–French rivalry in the Levant. Yet Lebanon's elites were able to forge an agreement that lasted decades and withstood the contractions of successive Arab–Israeli wars. The National Pact must surely be seen as the high watermark of consociation under such volatile circumstances. If Lebanon had enjoyed a democratic environment such as Switzerland's, it would almost certainly have avoided the collapse of power-sharing and the slide into civil war, and perhaps easily consolidated a national identity. It would have dealt with socio-economic and political reform in the absence of exogenous incursions such as the intercommunal fissure brought about by the presence of the PLO. So does this indicate that reconciliation can take place only in plural societies in a democratic environment that are not divided by ethno-national conflict? Is the development of a syncretistic national identity in societies divided by ethno-national conflict possible?

NATIONAL RECONCILIATION AND SELF-DETERMINATION

The very fact that there was an ongoing debate over national reconciliation in Lebanon before and after Ta'if indicates that there had been considerable movement towards a widespread acceptance of the nation state since the days of Greater Syrian nationalism and Christian separatism before independence. The Ta'if Agreement was, however, supposed to be a document of national reconciliation and understanding, something that was ultimately sidestepped during the Syrian dereliction of Ta'if. Yet the fact that such a debate was going on indicates that those engaged in it believed that there was at least a possibility of resolving the ethno-national conflict, or that it had been resolved to some extent before Lebanon's consociational weaknesses encouraged others to conduct the Arab–Israeli conflict on its soil.

In contrast, no serious elite level debate took place during Northern Ireland's recent troubles, or even after the signing of the GFA. Any such debate would have been before its time, as politics in Northern Ireland actually became increasingly zero-sum after the signing of the GFA. So far behind the Lebanese were Northern Ireland's elites that, while Sinn

Féin implicitly accepted the principle of consent in signing up to the GFA, it continued to view the unionist community as a significant minority within the Irish nation as a whole, as opposed to a separate ethnonational bloc. The unionist community itself, had either hardened to the idea of sharing power with Sinn Féin after the GFA or had not fully grasped what its implementation would entail before it was agreed. Either way, national reconciliation was not on the agenda.

It does seem safe to assume that, if the Lebanese have learned one lesson from the war, it is that they cannot allow such circumstances to divide them again. After 1989 most Lebanese came to accept that foreign influences had undermined their state and that its future could only be secured by putting Lebanese coexistence above pan-Arab causes or Christian separatist dreams. Muslim leaders came to view their support of the Palestinians in the late 1960s and the early 1970s as a mistake, and most Christian leaders realised that a Christian state was an unviable and unrealistic aspiration. Yet after Ta'if Lebanese power-sharing continued to be influenced by external forces just as much as at the outbreak of the civil war. The conflict in Lebanon did not erupt in 1975 because of Greater Syrian nationalism or Christian separatism, but because the state was too weak to deal with the conflicting internal and external challenges that faced it. As a consequence of Lebanon's continuing status as a hostage in the regional power struggle, national reconciliation failed to occur. National reconciliation is a realisable goal for the Lebanese, but it can come about only under the rubric of a new consociational arrangement following Syria's 2005 withdrawal. So, if the Lebanese need stable consociational government to coexist and fully reconcile their differences, do the people of Northern Ireland need consociation to be apart? If consociation is not aimed at, or has no chance of, bringing Northern Ireland's ethnic blocs to some form of reconciliation, is it just a method of short-to-medium-term conflict regulation?

The consociational experiences in Northern Ireland and Lebanon have had differing effects on claims and counter-claims about self-determination as a result of the paradoxical origins of power-sharing in both societies. The debate over self-determination was successfully sidelined due to the proactive engagement of a majority of the Lebanese elites in power-sharing. As a majority of Northern Ireland's elites never actually had the desire to engage in power-sharing and were coerced into these arrangements by the British and Irish governments, this partly explains the intractability of their conflict regarding self-determination and why it was fudged through a consociational deal in 1998. Rather than initiating any major shifts in this debate, consociation merely sidelined this problem, in much the same way as the National Pact temporarily dealt with Lebanon's contradictory identities, but in the absence of any solid domestic enthusiasm for political coexistence. While Northern Ireland remained divided over the same issues after the GFA, to a similar extent the debate over the future of the Lebanese state remained open after Ta'if. The Ta'if Agreement declared Lebanon an Arab country, while underlining its finality as a nation state within which the Lebanese would coexist. Lebanese citizens did not, however, legitimise this equilibrium or any of its declarations in any way and the accord itself lacked the broad-based domestic support that referendums in Northern Ireland and the Republic of Ireland conferred on the GFA.

Who defined what it meant to be Lebanese or Arab? The Lebanese certainly were not asked such questions. The constitutional legitimacy of the Ta'if settlement was highly questionable for a number of other reasons. While the deputies of 1972 were the last remaining symbols of Lebanon's pre-war institutions and its consociational era, they scarcely represented the Lebanese people and held no electoral mandate to renegotiate a constitutional settlement on their behalf. Further, the fact that very little was actually negotiated at Ta'if, the Syrian veto over both internal and external aspects of the accord leaving it largely non-nego-tiable, meant that many of the questions at the heart of Lebanon's conflict remained unresolved.

The GFA significantly differed from Ta'if in three ways. First, nothing was agreed in the negotiations between the parties and the governments until everything was agreed, and there were various trade-offs between the different strands, on both internal and external issues. Second, the design of the negotiating system meant that, even without the presence or the approval of almost half the unionist electorate, the parties negotiating the Agreement had a mandate to broker a settlement, the result of which was then further legitimised through referendums. Third, the external or confederal aspects of the Agreement were not designed to retain sovereignty or remove it from Northern Ireland's elites. Conversely, the motives and incentives entailed in the GFA were aimed at satisfying contradictory claims to self-determination by devolving power to Northern Ireland vis-à-vis internal and external institutions. The alternative to this formula was either a return to direct rule or some form of joint authority. This was quite the opposite of Syria's intentions regarding Lebanon under Parts II and IV of the Ta'if accords, and the subsequent Treaty of Brotherhood. These aspects were clearly designed to restrain and limit the Second Republic's sovereignty. The implementation of Ta'if was therefore in direct contradiction to 1943, as the Lebanese had rejected France in order to gain independence during the Second World War, whereas at Ta'if they conceded state sovereignty and accepted Syria. In contrast, it was the promise of devolved institutions and the first real opportunity since 1974 for Northern Ireland's domestic elites to get their hands on power that helped motivate them to engage in consociation.

The four agreements illustrate how external variables can both obstruct and facilitate consociational settlements. Like the GFA, the National Pact's power-sharing provisions were formulated over time by the Lebanese elites in the tradition of the consociational governments that had existed under the French Mandate and the *Règlement*. Yet it was the positive international and regional environment that allowed such a deal to be reconstructed. Subsequently, sufficient leeway existed between the Lebanese after independence to facilitate new pacts and to consolidate what became known as the National Pact. As with the GFA, there was a narrow piece of ground where compromise could be reached between the Lebanese parties, with the external actors helping to shape their compromise. Sunningdale and Ta'if offer the opposite experience from the perspective of internal and external relationships. At the conclaves where agreement was reached, large segments of those who represented different parties were absent. While those absent from Ta'if were kept informed of what was taking place, the Agreement was a *fait accompli* by the Arab states and the US, and their input was negligible. At Sunningdale the bulk of the unionist leadership were excluded or had excluded themselves, along with the republican and loyalist paramilitaries. Both these agreements were publicised as having been negotiated by the representatives of the different communities, yet that was far from being the whole truth. Consequently the litmus test of a general election saw both agreements rejected. Lacking broad based interconfessional popular legitimacy, the internal and external foundations of these agreements were weak. Accordingly, they failed to deal in any meaningful way with the ethno-national problems that they set out to confront, or to offer a compromise over self-determination that satisfied either community. Does this mean, then, that an imposed consociation has a very limited time span, or one that is reliant on the coercive external pressures that facilitated its development?

IMPLEMENTING CONSOCIATION

The limitations of imposed consociations are apparent from these four agreements, which illustrate how different degrees of coercion and legitimacy influenced the prospects of power-sharing in Northern Ireland and Lebanon in the long term. Gaining independence gave the National Pact's brokers the legitimacy to ensure that power-sharing became established as Lebanon's mode of government until the civil war period. Regardless of how good the Ta'if Agreement might have been for the Lebanese people, or how progressive its consociational modifications were, its non-implementation and corruption under Syrian rule left it lacking the sort of popular legitimacy the National Pact had enjoyed. It is safe to conclude that before true reconciliation can actually take place

Ta'if must be replaced by a new Lebanese pact or, at the very least, be properly implemented in order to gain genuine support from the different communities. The problem with the latter suggestion is that after the Syrian implementation the circumstances that brought about the compromise at Ta'if no longer exist and a new equilibrium may be required following the Syrian's military withdrawal.

In the case of the GFA, even with the best of intentions to regulate the conflict even-handedly, the British and Irish governments suffered consistent setbacks in its implementation. The fact that during the negotiations the British government felt it necessary to conceal its intentions over the decommissioning issue, among others, in order to bring the majority of the two communities to an initial compromise, ensured a heavy political fall out when it came to the actual implementation process. Even with all the resources of the British and Irish states the two governments failed to convince majorities in both communities to support the consociational idea, and cross-community enthusiasm for the Agreement diminished in the following years. While they arguably got the constitutional balance of the GFA as close to satisfying the contradictory claims to self-determination as possible, they and Northern Ireland's pro-Agreement parties failed to psychologically prepare the different communities for the realities and sacrifices that consociation entailed, particularly in the unionist segment. The failure of anti-Agreement unionism caused convulsions within the Protestant community, as the DUP was forced to become a pro-Agreement party on an anti-Agreement platform. Its triumph in the Westminster general election in 2005 left it with nine seats in the House of Commons, and marked the end of the Trimble project. The fact, however, that Trimble's rivals publicly accepted the GFA in its entirety under the guise of the Comprehensive Proposals underlined the great distance Trimble had carried unionism.

There can be little doubt, then, that the external forces determined an end to the latest spell of ethnic conflict and imposed peace settlements in both societies, but the actual implementation and imposition of these two accords could not have been more different. Northern Ireland's settlement was imposed by two liberal democracies that held a joint interest in the regulation of ethnic conflict and the maintenance of stability in their region. While the external impact on stability and regulation in the Lebanese case was similar, external influence was neither liberal, nor democratic nor positive. Syrian domination after Ta'if meant that the political destiny of the Lebanese continued to play a secondary role to the Arab–Israeli conflict and Syria's regional aspirations. Therefore, different limitations and constraints affect those powers engaging in coercive consociational engineering in democratic and non-democratic environments. The illegality (in the eyes of many observers) of the US-led invasion of Iraq and the subsequent attempts to speedily install a democratic power-sharing administration in the absence of inter-ethnic popular support bears out this point.

Having learned the lessons of Sunningdale, the British and Irish governments attempted to coerce the Northern Ireland parties into a settlement by providing incentives for them to support power-sharing. The abject failure of the two goverments to punish or sanction parties that failed to live up to their pledges under the GFA undermined the implementation process and further polarised the two communities. There were, however, certainly limitations as to how far they could pressurise the domestic elites, as the GFA was set up with the language and pretensions of being a democratic arrangement, and this is what the public expected. Suspending the Northern Ireland Assembly reinforced the zero-sum nature of post-Agreement politics in Northern Ireland, as power-sharing was something that could, to a certain extent, be enforced and very definitely be removed. If nothing else, this emphasised the impermanence of the political arrangements to the participants. So where did this leave the British and Irish governments? Were they the masters of this consociational relationship, or had they become trapped within the dimensions of the conflict regulation initiative that they had created?

On one level the governments were certainly constrained within the consociational relationship that they had manufactured, and the 2005 election results support this view. This became more apparent as the security elements of the GFA overshadowed and undermined the democratic transition process that Northern Ireland was supposed to be undertaking. Yet from a long-term perspective this may well have been inevitable. In stark contrast to 1974, the two governments had invested far too much in the political process to allow it to collapse. Yet their interests were not the same as those parties attempting to work the GFA. This posed a problem for democratic governments such as Britain's and Ireland's in that they had to play by their own rules, or at least be seen to do so. They set the GFA up as an inclusive open political playing field, within which the different communities could coexist, yet they failed to create an environment within which this consociation could come to fruition, as it subsequently lacked the backing and legitimacy of majorities in both communities and the support of the two governments implementing it.

Imposing consociation in the absence of reconciliation or broad-based public support creates serious problems for the success of consociation in the long term. This is regardless of whether the imposition comes from a democratic regime or not, or in fact whether the external pressures are positive or not. Sunningdale, Ta'if and the GFA were all political bargains concluded without national or interethnic reconciliation: in fact, they were agreements forced through despite the absence of reconciliation. Further, the last two agreements were unlike the Dayton Peace Accord in

Bosnia–Herzegovina, signed in 1995, which sought to bring war criminals to trial. In Northern Ireland, all prisoners affiliated to a party that had signed up to the GFA were subsequently released and their paramilitary representatives had an equal opportunity to take their place in the government if they won enough seats in the Assembly. In Lebanon the military combatants who had taken part in the civil war were also rewarded with seats in government, while those who rejected the system due to the corruption of Ta'if were excluded. This illustrates the limitations to imposing inclusive consociation. Those whom the general public, or certain segments of the population, viewed as largely responsible for the exacerbation of the conflict were subsequently rewarded by the external powers for engaging in consociation and leaving violence behind. The contradictions this posed within the democratic framework under which consociation was set up in Northern Ireland resulted in serious implementation problems. Such difficulties were less evident in Lebanon between 1989 and 2005, due to the consolidation of Syrian political and military control. This illustrates the different levels of consociational control available to the exogenous powers as a result of how democratic they were. The consequence of these democratic paradoxes is that the state tends to forget the past while the people do not, and the contradiction between what people expect from democratisation based on reconciliation and the reality of imposed consociation quickly becomes apparent. This is not to say that there were better alternatives to Ta'if or the GFA as inclusive processes, but the contradiction inherent in selling such agreements to the public as a means for democratic political reconciliation is clear.

DOES HISTORY MATTER?

It should be easy to evaluate exactly what the different communities and their elites have learned from their consociational experiences, but the fact that the failure of consociation in either Lebanon or Northern Ireland could lead directly to renewed ethno-national conflict clouds the picture considerably. Is there a broad-based popular political culture of power-sharing in either society? Could such a culture supersede ethno-national identity in either Northern Ireland or Lebanon? Is there even a culture of democracy in either society? The short answer to each of these questions is probably no, but there are big differences between the two cases. A political culture of intercommunal coexistence simply did not exist at the time the GFA was signed and, as with the Ta'if Agreement, inter and intra-confessional hostilities were at a peak during the political process that led to the DSD in 1993. The dominance of extremist parties in Northern Ireland and the polarisation of the two communities after 1998 supports this argument. In contrast, a culture of power-sharing certainly existed in Lebanon before 1975, and it had developed steadily as a consequence of the successful institutionalisation of consociation and the tradition of political coexistence. The negative aspect here was that, in spite of this culture, the Lebanese state had been plunged into internecine violence and, ironically, the task of restoring this democracy and rehabilitating this consociational culture was left to Syria. Paradoxically, a country that is not a democracy, and one that took every opportunity to use consociation as a means to divide and rule the Lebanese since 1975, was trusted by the US and the Arab states to reconstitute consociational democracy in Lebanon, and uphold its interconfessional compromise. Thus, in that sense, it was doomed to failure.

The Lebanese have, however, undergone a collective learning process, as most of their politicians now accept and recognise that reliance on external backers for their own idiosyncratic ethno-national goals had huge costs for the Lebanese state. Both the Christian and the Muslim communities blame the Syrians, the Israelis and the Palestinians for the collapse of their state. While this is short-sighted, given that most of them were allied to at least one of these foreign forces during the war, it indicates a collective belief that future stability can come about only through intercommunal coexistence. Whether the civil war has finally embedded this in the national psyche, granted that such a thing exists, is something only time will tell. Yet, given the instability of the exogenous environment, it is a question that will certainly be addressed at some time in the future.

In view of the problems the Lebanese have encountered, even with a well-established culture of consociation, is the development and establishment of such a culture possible in Northern Ireland? Again, given a stable external environment and a long incubation period, such a culture could be successfully nurtured in Northern Ireland. However, the counter argument to Lijphart's comment about the ability of democracies to shed consociation in favourable circumstances remains true. Northern Ireland and Lebanon could still easily shed consociation for civil war if the external stanchions supporting power-sharing in either society break down. What might prevent this occurring and instead prompt a similar transition to democracy, as Lijphart predicted for some of his plural societies, would be the long-term stabilisation of the exogenous environment. In this sense there is actually reason to be optimistic about the future of consociation in Northern Ireland.

CONFEDERAL AND EXTERNAL ASPECTS

All four of the consociational agreements hinged on external relations with either patron states or the international and regional environment within which they existed. The crux of the National Pact, which allowed the internal equilibrium to be realised, was that Lebanon would be neither eastern nor western, but a neutral part of the Arab world. Conversely, the rejection of Sunningdale's external dimensions facilitated its collapse, in that the anti-Agreement unionists rejected any Irish dimension, while republicans continued to oppose any internal settlement to the conflict. However, things had significantly changed when Northern Ireland and Lebanon returned to the consociational model at the end of their ethno-national conflicts.

Maila highlights two major shifts in the consociational framework during the negotiations at Ta'if.[8] First, the Ta'if accords bound the reconstruction of Lebanon to policy coordination with Syria in all fields. Second, it consolidated consociation, or the new National Pact, in the sense that it constituted a Lebanese logic or law of power-sharing as the supreme political norm. It set in place a principle of coexistence as a political and national imperative in government, in that any legislation that departed from it, or in fact contradicted Ta'if, would lack any legal efficacy and be unconstitutional. Thus, in principle Ta'if established a law above the law, or a foundation beneath the foundation, in its attempt to ensure that the reformulated principles of consociation were untouchable and politically infallible. The violation of these principles in the years following Ta'if is well documented and has already been elaborated on.[9] The Lebanese equation, therefore, had a tightly bound consociational formula for the re-establishment of a confessional administration, but only after the sovereignty of the state had been compromised through the external sections of the Agreement. At Ta'if the rehabilitation of consociation was a *quid pro quo*: the Lebanese were assisted in the re-establishment of their pact of coexistence and in return conceded an unknown quantity of state sovereignty to Damascus. From the Christian perspective the crucial linkage between accepting political reform and the withdrawal of Syrian troops was missing.

The GFA addressed the question of sovereignty in quite an opposite sense. All those who held paradoxical claims to self-determination had their demands addressed by the GFA in various different ways. The nationalists achieved an Irish dimension, while the unionists curtailed it by binding it to the Northern Ireland Assembly. Further, provisions were laid down for future constitutional changes in Northern Ireland's status to be based upon the principle of consent. Thus, while Ta'if aimed to finalise and consolidate interethnic coexistence with a law above the law through the concession of state sovereignty, the GFA sought to devolve power to internal and external administrative bodies, linking the existence of consociation to the rival claims to self-determination and, in effect, allowing for its own future collapse. The provisions laid down for future referendums on a united Ireland or, in fact, acceptance of the position of Northern Ireland within the UK implicitly amounted to an acceptance that coexistence was not possible and, arguably, that the GFA is just a temporary solution to regulate the conflict.

A cynic might say that the GFA provides the combatants in the zero-sum game of ethnic conflict the tools for deconstructing the accord at a later date. It is not an attempt at national reconciliation, but a device for short-to-medium-term interethnic stabilisation. The GFA has been more successful than its predecessor, as it addressed the dual claims over Northern Ireland's sovereignty[10] while facing and accepting the realities and constraints of ethnic conflict regulation. Essentially, it is a realist agreement. Unlike Ta'if, the GFA does not try to do more than regulate the conflict. It is not that consociation in this case is inherently divisive, or that it aims to separate and compartmentalise the different segments, but that its idiosyncratic formulation in Northern Ireland was due to the particular dynamics of the political situation, rather than the consociational model itself.[11] The desire that many Lebanese leaders maintained for coexistence throughout their conflict was simply lacking across the majority of Northern Ireland's elites and large segments of their communities. Further, their mutually antagonistic aspirations remained intact and they collectively viewed consociational practices as a temporary phase in their ongoing political struggle. Consequently, only a long incubation period of externally managed consociation in Northern Ireland could produce a culture of coexistence similar to the one that has existed in Lebanon since independence.

On a more optimistic note, such an incubation period or transition period is certainly possible in Northern Ireland, especially given its favourable exogenous environment. However, at best, the GFA marked the beginning of such an incubation phase. In retrospect, the years of violence in Northern Ireland between Sunningdale and the GFA were a period of reflection and reconciliation between the British and Irish governments, which culminated in an interim constitutional settlement. Moreover, the Northern Ireland parties were only at the beginning of a potential phase of reflection and reconciliation in 1998, and remained largely reliant on positive exogenous forces to facilitate any future domestic transition. As consociation was set up under the zero-sum dynamics of the ethno-national conflict in Northern Ireland, the course it takes in politics may be highly reflective and indicative of the violent path that was its alternative. A positive incubation period is not impossible, as Anglo-Irish relations look set to maintain their steady cordial pace as their interests converge both domestically and within the EU. The two communities, however, lack any of the shared grievances and fears that held the Lebanese together before the civil war. Yet the fact that the Lebanese experienced colonial rule together did not prevent each community looking abroad for the security and privileged links that a foreign sponsor might add to their domestic strength or weakness.

Unlike the GFA, Ta'if attempted in its communitarian re-equilibrium to set in stone again the parameters of consociation, through a reinstitution of the traditional moderate confessional Lebanese representatives. It failed to do this in any meaningful way due to Ta'if's external linkage to Syria and Assad's implementation of a very different power-sharing framework than had been envisaged, one where Damascus delegated power to a new, compliant Lebanese elite. This extinguished any possibility of a successfully reconstructed consociational Lebanon with a government of national reconciliation. The GFA recognised the parameters of political power within Northern Ireland's ethnic conflict, attempting regulation through consociation within a framework that included both moderates and extremists. Many commentators hoped that, through engaging in consociation, moderate parties would outflank the extremists and create a centre ground wherein a culture of coexistence could be nurtured. As consociation was imposed in the stark absence of reconciliation, with the political fudges the British and Irish governments needed to finalise the accord, and, arguably, lacking democratic legitimacy and broad-based popular support despite the two referendums, such a moderate centre ground rapidly collapsed. In fact, the only way such a thing could come about would be if the exogenous forces finally manage to deal with the democratic contradictions inherent in consociation. This might go some way towards dragging consociational politics back from the zero-sum nature of the conflict that it regulates.

CONCLUSION

There are clearly limits to how successful imposed consociations can be, and the case studies of Northern Ireland and Lebanon illustrate this distinctly in various different ways. The comparative analysis of these four agreements has shown both the necessity of externally imposed consociation if conflict is to be regulated by power-sharing, and the drawbacks and difficulties for the external elites in advancing such initiatives. While the possibility of a successful conclusion to the consociational method of conflict regulation clearly exists in both these cases, it is hard to imagine that their dependence on external forces will not continue to define the success or failure of these experiments. In sum, the internal and external equations determined the prospects of successful power-sharing in both Northern Ireland and Lebanon in the twentieth century. Only through the establishment of a stable and unthreatening contiguous environment can consociation positively regulate ethnic conflict in these divided societies in the long term.

Conclusion

Drawing together the analysis of these four agreements, and their negotiation, interpretation and implementation, it seems clear that the relationship, between exogenous and endogenous variables, and external and domestic elites, were the determining factors when weighing up the causes and consequences of consociational success and failure in both Northern Ireland and Lebanon. Addressing the question as to whether power-sharing can be used to regulate ethno-national conflict in the long term, these changing relationships defined the life span of consociation in these countries. Power-sharing was used in all four agreements primarily to regulate conflict, but it was the nature of the external forces and the stability of the immediate environment that initially facilitated or obstructed the implementation of consociation. It was external intervention that either strengthened or undermined the foundations of consociation, depending on whether its influence was positive or negative.

Another key feature in this debate, greatly influencing consociation in both cases, was proximity to democratic regimes. The circumstances of Northern Ireland's and Lebanon's agreements illustrate this point, highlighting the limitations of coercive consociation, both in a democratic environment and in a region where the majority of the regimes are authoritarian. The consociational debate largely revolves around which democratic criteria and favourable variables are essential for the successful implementation of consociation. Yet, even with many of the key favourable conditions for consociation, the Lebanese equilibrium was constantly at the mercy of an increasingly negative regional environment, while, despite lacking most key variables for power-sharing, its implementation in Northern Ireland was to some degree successful, as a result of highly positive external stabilising and coercive pressures.

The experiences of power-sharing in Northern Ireland and Lebanon illustrate the fact that the relationship is certainly not one-dimensional. The long-term success of consociation hinges upon how the internal–external relationship is managed. This external supervision is largely defined by the political circumstances and options at the disposal of the exogenous elites. Thus, in Northern Ireland many of the implementation problems arose out of the democratic culture that restricted the imposition of consociation by the British and Irish governments, and conversely, their own unwillingness to abide by that democratic culture. At the same time democracy provided many of the GFA's strengths, as its legitimacy was derived from popular support. However, the intractability of intrasegmental rivalry, particularly within Unionism, clearly illustrates the limitations of coercive consociational engineering within the Anglo-Irish democratic framework. If the external nature of this Anglo-Irish framework changes, its effects will be felt within Northern Ireland and have a dramatic influence on its future stability.

In contrast, Lebanese consociation in the 1990s lost the essence of agreed interconfessional equilibrium and consociational realignments at Ta'if, as Syria had no democratic constraints placed upon its imposition or interpretation of the accord. With a free hand to reconstruct consociation primarily in its own interests, as opposed to those of the Lebanese communities, Syria consigned Ta'if to history before it was even tested. Therefore, for consociation to be successful in regulating ethno-national conflict in the long term, the external actors with an interest in the divided society must also hold an interest in regulating the conflict for the benefit of that society itself. While there is clearly the need for some form of coercive imposition of consociation in these cases, its mishandling or selfish interpretation quickly deprives the formula of the legitimacy it needs for long-term success. This is a lesson that US policy-makers in Iraq should take note of.

What is interesting in these cases is that, while both Ta'if and the GFA were externally imposed agreements, the relationship between the external and domestic elites changed through consociation. In Northern Ireland, given the positive nature of the relationships, a higher level of interdependence developed among all the parties involved in the consociation, including the external elites. The British and Irish governments had a stake in maintaining consociation in Northern Ireland, and as it suited their mutual interests in regulating the conflict, they had to make it work. There can be no doubt that this bodes well for the future of power-sharing in Northern Ireland. On the other hand, the relationship between Syria and Lebanon vis-à-vis the Arab world, was a more complex one. The paradox of the minority Alawite government running an authoritarian state in Damascus and a fig-leaf consociational democracy in Beirut was extraordinary. Yet this arrangement did influence and affect Syria, albeit less visibly than the impact regulating Northern Ireland's conflict through consociation had on Britain and Ireland. From a purely cynical perspective, Syria stuck with the Lebanese consociational system, as it made government easier for Syria to control. The communities remained divided and lacked any serious unified Christian–Muslim opposition to Syrian hegemony, right up until the assassination of Hariri. However, the free-market environment of Beirut and the interdependence of the two countries' economies had the potential to allow Syria to quicken the sort of political and economic liberalisation that Assad employed in the 1980s. It would be unduly optimistic, however, to expect this to have any impact on Syrian–Lebanese relations without an overall settlement of the Arab–Israeli conflict.

What is conclusive in the application of conflict regulation through consociation in Northern Ireland and Lebanon is that its success or failure is dependent on the maintenance of positive exogenous variables. These constitute a factor that has been seriously underestimated in the literature to date. If such proactive and beneficial influences continue to buffer and stabilise consociation in Northern Ireland, then the prospects for power-sharing remain reasonably good, despite the fact that the moderate centre ground has now been marginalized. Conversely, if the Middle East remains the focal point of global tension, and Syria maintains a pivotal role in the Arab–Israeli conflict, then a true Lebanese pact of consociation will remain a thing of the past.

Endnotes

INTRODUCTION

1. See Adrian Guelke, *Northern Ireland: The International Perspective* (New York: St. Martin's Press, 1988), pp. 174–94; Frank Wright, *Northern Ireland: A Comparative Analysis* (Dublin: Gill & Macmillan, 1987).
2. See Arend Lijphart, *Democracy in Plural Societies* (New Haven, CT: Yale University Press, 1977); John McGarry and Brendan O'Leary, *Explaining Northern Ireland* (Oxford: Blackwell, 1995), pp. 320–53.
3. Anthony Coughlan, 'A Unitary Irish State', in John McGarry and Brendan O'Leary (eds), *The Future of Northern Ireland* (Oxford: Oxford University Press, 1990), pp. 48–68.
4. See David Miller, *Queen's Rebels: Ulster Loyalism in Historical Perspective* (Dublin: Gill and Macmillan, 1973); Michael Gallagher, 'Do Unionists have a Right to Self-Determination?', *Irish Political Studies*, 5 (1990), 11–30; A. T. Q. Stewart, *The Narrow Ground: Patterns of Ulster History* (Belfast: Blackstaff Press, 1977). See also Arthur Aughey, *Under Siege: Ulster Unionism and the Anglo-Irish Agreement* (Belfast: Blackstaff Press, 1989); Terence O'Neill, *Autobiography* (London: Rupert Hart-Davis, 1972).
5. *McGimpsey and McGimpsey* v. *Ireland*, High Court, 29 July 1988; *McGimpsey and McGimpsey* v. *Ireland*, Supreme Court, 1 March 1990.
6. See McGarry and O'Leary, *Explaining Northern Ireland*, Chapters 2 and 4.
7. Brendan O'Leary and John McGarry, *The Politics of Antagonism: Understanding Northern Ireland* (London: Athlone Press, 1996), p. 139.
8. See McGarry and O'Leary, *Explaining Northern Ireland*, Chapter 5.
9. Richard Rose, *Governing Without Consensus* (London: Faber & Faber, 1971), pp. 248.
10. See Donald Akenson, *God's Peoples: Covenant and Land in South Africa, Israel, and Ulster* (Ithaca, NY: Cornell University Press, 1992); Brian Mawhinney and Ronald Wells, *Conflict and Christianity in Northern Ireland* (Berkhamsted: Lion Publishing, 1975).
11. Brendan O'Leary and Paul Arthur, 'Introduction' in McGarry and O'Leary (eds), *The Future of Northern Ireland*, pp. 1–49; O'Leary and McGarry, *The Politics of Antagonism*, pp. 142–3.
12. See John Whyte, *Interpreting Northern Ireland* (Oxford: Clarendon Press, 1990); McGarry and O'Leary, *The Future of Northern Ireland*; McGarry and O'Leary, *Explaining Northern Ireland*, pp. 311–82; Paul Mitchell, 'Futures', in Paul Mitchell and Rick Wilford (eds), *Politics in Northern Ireland* (Boulder, CO: Westview Press, 1999), pp. 265–84.
13. McGarry and O'Leary, *Explaining Northern Ireland*, pp. 311–53; Lijphart, 'The Northern Ireland Problem: Cases, Theories and Solutions', *British Journal of Political Science 5* (1975), 83–106; Brendan O'Duffy, 'British and Irish Conflict Regulation from Sunningdale to Belfast: Part I: Tracing the Status of Contesting Sovereigns, 1968–1974', *Nations and Nationalism*, 5:4 (1999), 523–42, and 'Part II: Playing for a Draw, 1985–99', *Nations and Nationalism*, 6:3 (2000), 399–435.
14. Richard English, 'Challenging Peace', *Fortnight*, 1997, 362, 24–5; Paul Dixon, 'Paths to Peace in Northern Ireland (I): Civil Society and the Consociational Approaches', *Democratization*, 4:2 (Summer 1997), 1–27, '(II): The Peace Processes 1973–74 and 1994–96', *Democratization*, 4:3 (Autumn 1997), 1–25; Rupert Taylor, 'Consociation or Social Transformation?' in John McGarry (ed.), *Northern Ireland and the Divided World* (London and New York: Oxford University Press, 2001), pp. 37–52.
15. Dixon, 'Paths to Peace in Northern Ireland (I)', 16–22.
16. Paul Bew and Henry Patterson, 'Scenarios for Progress in Northern Ireland', in McGarry and O'Leary (eds), *The Future of Northern Ireland*, pp. 206–18.

17. Ibid., p. 217.
18. Dixon, 'Paths to Peace in Northern Ireland (I)', 16.
19. Rick Wilford, 'Women and Politics' in Mitchell and Wilford (eds), *Politics in Northern Ireland*, p. 216.
20. Taylor, 'Consociation or Social Transformation?', pp. 37–52.
21. Ibid., p. 46.
22. Ibid., p. 47.
23. Joseph Ruane and Jennifer Todd, *The Dynamics of Conflict in Northern Ireland: Power, Conflict and Emancipation* (Cambridge: Cambridge University Press, 1996), pp. 290–316.
24. O'Duffy, 'British and Irish Conflict Regulation from Sunningdale to Belfast', (I), 526; John McGarry, 'Political Settlements in Northern Ireland and South Africa', *Political Studies*, 46:4 (1998), 853–70.
25. Joseph Ruane and Jennifer Todd (eds), *After the Good Friday Agreement* (Dublin: UCD Press ,1999), pp. 1–29 and 144–169.
26. See McGarry and O'Leary, *Explaining Northern Ireland*, pp. 207–11 and 363–66.
27. Interview with Denis Loretto (founder member of the Alliance Party, 1970), Leatherhead, 12 Dec. 2000.
28. McGarry and O'Leary, *Explaining Northern Ireland*, pp. 320–6.
29. Brendan O'Leary, 'The Limits to Coercive Consociationalism in Northern Ireland', *Political Studies*, 37 (1989), 562–88.
30. See Chapter 2.
31. O'Leary, 'The British–Irish Agreement' in McGarry (eds), *Northern Ireland and the Divided World*, pp. 54–69.
32. See Eric Nordlinger, *Conflict Regulation in Divided Societies* (Cambridge, MA: Harvard University Press, 1972).
33. Paul Mitchell, 'Conflict Regulation and Party Competition in Northern Ireland', *European Journal of Political Research*, 20 (1991), 67–92. See also Nordlinger, *Conflict Regulation in Divided Societies*.
34. Mitchell, 'Conflict Regulation and Party Competition in Northern Ireland', pp. 82–8.
35. Ibid., 83.
36. O'Duffy, 'British and Irish Conflict Regulation from Sunningdale to Belfast (I)', 523.
37. O'Duffy, 'British and Irish Conflict Regulation from Sunningdale to Belfast (II)', 399.
38. O'Duffy, 'British and Irish Conflict Regulation from Sunningdale to Belfast (I)', 524.
39. Harvey Cox, 'Managing Northern Ireland Intergovernmentally: An Appraisal of the Anglo-Irish Agreement', *Parliamentary Affairs*, 40:1 (1987), 97.
40. Ibid., 97.
41. Guelke, *Northern Ireland: The International Perspective*, p. 18.
42. Ibid., p. 174.
43. Ibid., p. 194.
44. See Liam Kennedy, 'Repartition', in McGarry and O'Leary (eds), *The Future of Northern Ireland*, pp. 137–61.
45. Ibid., pp. 159–60.
46. Claire Palley, 'Towards a Federal or Confederal Irish State', in McGarry and O'Leary (eds), *The Future of Northern Ireland*, pp. 68–99.
47. Brendan O'Leary, 'The Limits to Coercive Consociationalism in Northern Ireland', *Politics Studies*, 37:4 (1989), 585–7.
48. O'Leary and McGarry, *The Politics of Antagonism*, pp. 294–5.
49. Kemal Salibi, *A House of Many Mansions: The History of Lebanon Reconsidered* (Berkeley, Los Angeles and London: University of California Press, 1988), pp. 200–16.
50. See Benjamin Braude and Bernard Lewis (eds), *Christians and Jews in the Ottoman Empire*, 2 vols (London: Holmes & Meier Publishers, 1982), pp. 69–88; J. Spagnolo, *France and Ottoman Lebanon, 1861–1914* (London: Ithaca Press, 1977), Chapter 2.
51. Salibi, *A House of Many Mansions*, p. 201.
52. If the Maronites are descended from the Phoenicians then this strengthens their natural ties with the Jews, as the Phoenician language was, like Hebrew, a dialect of Canaanite: see M. Bernal, *Black Athena: The Afroasiatic Roots of Classical Civilization*, Vol. I (London: Free Association Books, 1987). Schulze argues that they originated from northern Syria: Kirsten Schulze, *Israel's Covert Diplomacy in Lebanon* (New York: St. Martin's Press, 1997), p. 13._

53. W. Phares, *Lebanese Christian Nationalism* (Boulder, CO: Lynne Rienner Publishers, 1995), p. 31.
54. Salibi, *A House of Many Mansions*, p. 41.
55. Michael Hudson, *The Precarious Republic: Political Modernisation in Lebanon* (New York: Random House, 1968), pp. 87–105.
56. Michel Chiha, 'A Jewish Story – 26 Sept. 1945' in Michel Chiha, *Palestine* (Beirut: Editions du Trident, 1966), translation by Michel Hartman, 2002, unpublished.
57. Farid el-Khazen, *The Breakdown of the State in Lebanon, 1967–76* (London: I. B. Tauris, 2000), p. 20.
58. L. Abul-Husn, *The Lebanese Conflict* (Boulder, CO: Lynne Rienner Publishers, 1998), p. 38.
59. Theodor Hanf, *Coexistence in Wartime Lebanon: The Decline of a State and the Rise of a Nation* (London: I. B.Tauris, 1993), p. 71.
60. Ibid., p.140.
61. Guelke, *Northern Ireland: The International Perspective*, p. 178.
62. Interview with Basim al-Jisr (Lebanese academic and journalist), Beirut, 4 April 2002; see also Basim al-Jisr, *Mithaq, 1943: Limaza Kan wa-Limaza Saqat* (Beirut: Dar al-Nahar Lilnashr, 1978); Abul-Husn, *The Lebanese Conflict*.
63. Hanf, *Coexistence in Wartime Lebanon*, pp. 71–4; Farid el-Khazen, *The Communal Pact of National Identities: The Making and Politics of the 1943 National Pact* (Oxford: Centre for Lebanese Studies, 1991); Elizabeth Picard, *Lebanon: A Shattered Country* (New York: Holmes & Meir, 1996), pp. 63–76; Eyal Zisser, *Lebanon: The Challenge of Independence* (London: I. B. Tauris, 2000), pp. 57–68.
64. Khazen, *The Command Pact of National Identities*, p. 5.
65. Ibid., p. 6.
66. Hanf, *Coexistence in Wartime Lebanon*, p. 70; see also Michel Chiha, *Visage et présence du Liban* (Beirut: Cénacles Libanais, 1964).
67. Hanf, *Coexistence in Wartime Lebanon*, p. 73.
68. Picard, *Lebanon: A Shattered Country*, pp. 68–9.
69. Ibid., p. 63.
70. Ibid., p. 71.
71. Zisser, *Lebanon: The Challenge of Independence*, p. 58.
72. See Braude and Lewis, *Christians and Jews in the Ottoman Empire*, Vol. 1, pp. 69–88; J. Spagnolo, *France and Ottoman Lebanon*, Chapter 2; J. Spagnolo, 'Constitutional Change in Mount Lebanon, 1861–1864', *Middle Eastern Studies*, 7:1 (1971), 25–48.
73. Zisser, *Lebanon: The Challenge of Independence*, p. 58.
74. Ibid., p. 63.
75. Ibid., p. 66.
76. See Marius Deeb, *The Lebanese Civil War* (New York: Praeger, 1980); Hanf, *Coexistence in Wartime Lebanon*; Hudson, *The Precarious Republic*; Walid Khalidi, *Conflict and Violence in Lebanon: Confrontation in the Middle East* (Cambridge, MA: Harvard University Press, 1979); Khazen, *The Breakdown of the State in Lebanon*; Kamal Salibi, *Crossroads to Civil War: Lebanon, 1958–76* (London: Ithaca Press, 1976); Charles Winslow, *Lebanon: War and Politics in a Fragmented Society* (London: Routledge, 1996).
77. Michael Hudson, 'Why Consociationalism Failed', in N. Shehadi and D. Mills (eds), *Lebanon: A History of Conflict and Consensus* (Oxford: Centre for Lebanese Studies, 1988), pp. 224–39.
78. Hudson, *The Precarious Republic*, pp. 87–105 and 325–31; Hudson, 'Why Consociationalism Failed', pp. 230–1.
79. R. Dekmejian, 'Consociational Democracy in Crisis: The Case of Lebanon', *Comparative Politics*, 10:2 (1978), 251–66.
80. Hudson, 'Why Consociationalism Failed', pp. 230–1.
81. Ibid., p. 238.
82. Michael Hudson, 'A Case of Political Development', *Journal of Politics*, 29:4 (1967) 821–37.
83. Interview with Farid el-Khazen (Chairman and Professor of Political Science, American University of Beirut), Beirut, 10 June 2002.
84. Interview with Joseph Maila (Lebanese academic), Beirut, 23 April 2002.
85. Khazen, *The Breakdown of the State in Lebanon*, p. 18.
86. Ibid., p. 6.

204 Imposing Power-Sharing

87. Interview with Farid el-Khazen, Beirut, 10 June 2002.
88. Khazen, *The Breakdown of the State in Lebanon*, p. 7.
89. Ibid., pp. 361–78.
90. Deeb, *The Lebanese Civil War*, pp. 139–42.
91. Abul-Husn, *The Lebanese Conflict*, p. 122.
92. See Hanf, *Coexistence in Wartime Lebanon*; Joseph Maila, *The Document of National Understanding: A Commentary* (Oxford: Centre for Lebanese Studies, 1992); Albert Mansour, *Al-Inqilab ala al-Ta'if* (Beirut: Dar al-Jadid, 1993).
93. Abul-Husn, *The Lebanese Conflict*, p. 91.
94. Ibid., p. 123.
95. Hanf, *Coexistence in Wartime Lebanon*, pp. 583–90.
96. Ibid., pp. 621–36.
97. Ibid., p. 622.
98. Ibid., p. 623.
99. Picard, *Lebanon: A Shattered Country*, pp. 156–7.
100. Ibid., p. 157.
101. Maila, *The Document of National Understanding*, p. 3.
102. Ibid., p. 53.
103. Ibid., pp. 53–62.
104. Ibid., p. 58.
105. Ibid., pp. 92–3.
106. Interview with Joseph Maila, Hamra, 23 April 2002.
107. Leonard Kerr, (ed.), in, Binder, M. *Politics in Lebanon* (London: J. Wiley & Sons, 1966), p. 211.

CHAPTER ONE

1. Antoine Messarra, 'Between Good Luck and Bad: How is Lebanon to be Independent?', *Beirut Review*, 6 (1993), 7–14.
2. Eric Nordlinger, *Conflict Regulation in Divided Societies* (Cambridge, MA: Harvard University Press, 1972), p. 4.
3. *Oxford English Dictionary* (Oxford: Oxford University Press, 2001).
4. Brendan O'Leary, 'Consociation: What We Know or Think We Know and What We Need to Know', paper presented at the Conference on National and Ethnic Conflict Regulation at the University of Western Ontario, 8–10 Nov. 2002.
5. Arend Lijphart, *Democracy in Plural Societies* (New Haven, CT: Yale University Press, 1977), p. 1.
6. See M. Bogaards, 'The Favourable Factors for a Consociational Democracy: A Review', *European Journal of Political Research*, 33 (1998), 475–96.
7. See Introduction; see also Brian Barry, 'The Consociational Model and its Dangers', *European Journal of Political Research*, 3 (1975), 393–413 and 'Review Article: Political Accommodation and Consociational Democracy', *British Journal of Political Science*, 5:4 (1975), 477–505.
8. O'Leary, 'Consociation', p. 26.
9. Adriano Pappalardo, 'The Conditions for Consociational Democracy: A Logical and Empirical Critique', *European Journal of Political Research*, 9:4 (1981), 365–90.
10. John McGarry and Brendan O'Leary, *Explaining Northern Ireland* (Oxford: Blackwood, 1995), pp. 338–44.
11. See Paul Mitchell, 'Conflict Regulation and Party Competition in Northern Ireland', *European Journal of Political Research*, 20 (1991), 67–92.
12. Antoine Messarra, 'Between Good Luck and Bad', *Beirut Review* 6 (1993), p. 9.
13. Lijphart, *Democracy in Plural Societies*, p. 1.
14. Ibid., p. 43.
15. Arend Lijphart, 'Consociational Democracy', *World Politics*, 21 (1969), 219.
16. Messarra, 'Between Good Luck and Bad', 14.
17. O'Leary, 'Consociation', p. 3.
18. Antoine Messarra, 'A Problematic Approach to the State of Lebanon: A Debate', *Panorama of Events*, 12:51 (1988); Norton, A. R., 'Lebanon after Ta'if: is the civil war over?' *Middle East Journal*, 45:3 Summer 1991, 457–73.

19. O'Leary, 'Consociation', 2003, pp. 5–19.
20. Lijphart, *Democracy in Plural Societies*, p. 53.
21. Ibid., p. 52.
22. Ibid., p. 137.
23. O'Leary, 'Consociation', p. 40.
24. Lijphart, *Democracy in Plural Societies*, pp. 65–70.
25. O'Leary, 'Consociation', p. 41.
26. Antoine Messarra, 'A Consociative Approach to Lebanon's Political System', *Panorama of Events*, 24 (1981).
27. O'Leary, 'Consociation', 2003, p 41.
28. See Brendan O'Duffy and Brendan O'Leary, 'Political Violence in Northern Ireland, 1969 to June 1989' in John McGarry and Brendan O'Leary, (eds), *The Future of Northern Ireland* (Oxford: Oxford University Press, 1990), pp. 318–41.
29. See Chapters 2 and 3.
30. O'Leary, 'Consociation', p. 42.
31. M. Bogaards, 'The Favourable Factors for Consociational Democracy: A Review', *European Journal of Political Research*, 33 (1998), 486.
32. See Chapter 8.
33. Brendan O'Leary, 'The Limits to Coercive Consociationalism in Northern Ireland', *Politics Studies*, 37:4 (1989), 574.

CHAPTER TWO

1. Interview with Sir Ken Bloomfield (Secretary of the Northern Ireland Executive 1974), Craigavad, 23 Aug. 2001.
2. *Northern Ireland Constitutional Proposals* (Belfast: HMSO, 1973).
3. Ibid., p. 13.
4. *The Future of Northern Ireland* (Belfast: HMSO, 1972).
5. *The Northern Ireland Act, 1973* (London: HMSO, 1973).
6. PREM15/486, Meetings between the Prime Minister and Mr Lynch, Doc. 14, 3 Sept. 1971.
7. FCO33/1611, Meetings between the Prime Ministers of the UK and the Republic of Ireland, Gregson to Graham, 31 March 1971.
8. Interview with James Molyneaux (MP for South Antrim 1970–83 and Lagan Valley 1983–97; UUP Leader 1979–95), Westminster, 30 Jan. 2001.
9. See Terence O'Neill, *Autobiography* (London: Rupert Hart-Davis, 1972); Brendan O'Leary and John McGarry, *The Politics of Antagonism: The Politics of Northern Ireland* (London: Athlone Press, 1997), pp. 162–71.
10. Alliance Party, Independent Unionists, Loyalist Coalition, Official Unionists and Vanguard Unionists.
11. Private conversation with John Taylor (Assembly Member for Fermanagh and South Tyrone 1973–74; MP for Strangford 1983–2001), Westminster, 19 July 2000.
12. Brian Faulkner, *Memoirs of a Statesman* (London: Weidenfeld & Nicolson, 1978), p. 195.
13. Sydney Elliott and W. D. Flackes, *Northern Ireland: A Political Directory, 1968–1999* (Belfast: Blackstaff Press, 1999), p. 533.
14. Interview with Oliver Napier (Alliance Party Leader 1972–84; Minister for Law Reform 1974), Holywood, 29 Dec. 2000; interview with James Molyneaux, Westminster, 30 Jan. 2001.
15. Garret FitzGerald, *All in a Life* (London: Macmillan, 1991), p. 238.
16. Ibid., p. 198.
17. See William Whitelaw, *The Whitelaw Memoirs* (London: Aurum Press, 1989), pp. 115–22; Faulkner, *Memoirs of a Statesman*, pp. 203–25.
18. *Irish Times*, 17 Sept. 1973.
19. Robert Fisk, *The Point of No Return* (London: André Deutsch, 1975), p .42.
20. *Irish Times*, 3 Nov. 1973.
21. Whitelaw, *The Whitelaw Memoirs*, pp. 110–14.
22. *Irish Times*, 29 Nov. 1973.
23. *Northern Ireland Assembly Debates*, 27 Nov. and 5 Dec. 1973.
24. *Northern Ireland Assembly Debates*, 5 Dec. 1973.
25. Interview with Sir Ken Bloomfield, Craigavad, 23 Aug. 2001.
26. FitzGerald, *All in a Life*, p. 215.

27. Interview with Dermot Nally (Irish diplomat at Sunningdale), Dublin, 10 May 2001.
28. *Irish Times*, 7 Dec. 1973.
29. O'Leary and McGarry, *The Politics of Antagonism*, p. 200.
30. Interview with Garret FitzGerald (Irish Foreign Minister 1973–77; Taoiseach 1981–82 and 1982–87), Dublin, 12 Sept. 2001.
31. FitzGerald, *All in a Life*, pp. 219–22.
32. *Financial Times*, 12 Dec. 1973.
33. *Irish Times*, 15 Dec. 1973.
34. Governor Robert Lundy betrayed the Protestant community at the Siege of Londonderry/Derry in 1690.
35. *Northern Ireland Assembly Debates*, 14 Dec. 1973.
36. O'Leary and McGarry, *The Politics of Antagonism*, p. 200.
37. *Irish Times*, 16 Jan. 1974.
38. Elliot and Flackes, *Northern Ireland: A Political Directory*, pp. 537–8.
39. Faulkner, *Memoirs of a Statesman*, pp. 251–60.
40. *Northern Ireland Official Debates*, Jan.–April 1974.
41. *Irish Times*, 14 March 1974.
42. *Financial Times*, 2–5 April 1974. See also Merlyn Rees, *Northern Ireland: A Personal Perspective* (London: Methuen, 1985), pp. 49–52.
43. Fisk, *The Point of No Return*, pp. 24–8.
44. Interview with Glen Barr (Assembly Member for Londonderry/Derry 1973–74; Chairman of the UWC), Londonderry/Derry, 22 Aug. 2001.
45. Interview with John Taylor, Westminster, 15 Feb. 2001.
46. *Financial Times*, 18 April 1974.
47. *Financial Times*, 25-26 April 1974.
48. Interview with Robert Fisk (journalist, *Independent*), Beirut, 13 May 2002.
49. *The Financial Times*, 12 May 1974.
50. Interview with Major C. T. Hogg (UDR member 1972–2000), Belfast, 1 Nov. 2001.
51. BBC Radio, *A Modern Rebellion*, 14 May 1984; interview with Major C.T. Hogg, Belfast, 1 Nov. 2001.
52. Rees, *Northern Ireland*, pp. 66–7.
53. D. Mullan, *The Dublin and Monaghan Bombings* (Dublin: Wolfhound Press, 2000), pp. 131–45.
54. Interview with Oliver Napier, Holywood, 29 Dec. 2000.
55. Interview with Glen Barr, Londonderry/Derry, 22 Aug. 2001.
56. *Financial Times*, 22 May 1974.
57. *Hansard*, 21 May 1974.
58. FitzGerald, *All in a Life*, p. 237.
59. Interview with Austin Currie (SDLP politician and Minister for Housing, Planning and Local Government 1974), Dublin, 5 Jan. 2001.
60. Fisk, *The Point of No Return*, p. 159.
61. *Hansard*, 23 May 1974.
62. Harold Wilson, *Final Term: The Labour Government 1974–76* (London: Weidenfeld & Nicolson, 1979), pp. 68–76. Wilson claims that he helped Faulkner by unblocking roads and providing essential services, but fails to explain why he waited fourteen days. On the British government's confusion and inaction see also Rees, *Northern Ireland*, pp. 65–90.
63. Interview with Oliver Napier, Holywood, 29 Dec. 2000; interview with Ken Bloomfield, Craigavad, 23 Aug. 2001.
64. Fisk, *The Point of No Return*, p. 192.
65. Rees, *Northern Ireland*, p. 76.
66. Faulkner, *Memoirs of a Statesman*, p. 275.
67. Interview with Denis Loretto, Leatherhead, 12 Dec. 2000.
68. For full text of Wilson's speech see Fisk, *The Point of No Return*, pp. 252–4.
69. Ibid., pp. 201–2.
70. J. Bardon, *A History of Ulster* (Belfast: Blackstaff Press, 1992), p. 707; Paul Bew, Peter Gibbon and Henry Patterson, *Northern Ireland, 1921–1994* (London: Serif, 1995), p. 199.
71. Interviews with Ken Bloomfield, Craigavad, 23 Aug. 2001; Austin Currie, Dublin, 5 Jan. 2001; John Hume MP (Minister for Commerce 1974; Deputy Leader of the SDLP 1973–79 and Leader 1979–2001), Londonderry/Derry, 13 Sept. 2001; Basil McIvor (Unionist and

Minister for Education 1974), Spa, 24 Aug. 2001; Oliver Napier, Holywood, 29 Dec. 2000; Leslie Morrell (Unionist and Minister for Agriculture 1974), Belfast, 4 Jan. 2001.

72. *Fortnight*, 21 May 1973, p. 7. The poll, conducted by Carrick James Market Research, involved a sample of 950 voters, drawn from six areas: two groups from Belfast; two from Antrim and Down; and two from Tyrone, Fermanagh, Armagh and Londonderry/Derry. The samples were representative of religion, gender, age and class.

73. The concept of a 'New Ireland' came from the SDLP's joint authority proposals in *Towards a New Ireland*, Sept. 1972.

74. Interview with Austin Currie, Dublin, 5 Jan. 2001.

75. *Belfast Telegraph*, 19 April 1974. Unionists East of the Bann might have been expected to be more liberal.

76. NOP survey conducted between 31 March and 7 April 1974.

77. Paul Dixon, 'Paths to Peace in Northern Ireland (I): Civil Society and Consociational Approaches', *Democratization*, 4:2 (1997), p. 1.

78. T. Hennessy, *A History of Northern Ireland, 1920–96* (London: Macmillan, 1997), p. 222.

79. Brendan O'Duffy, 'British and Irish Conflict Regulation from Sunningdale to Belfast: Part I: Tracing the Status of Contesting Sovereigns, 1968–1974', *Nations and Nationalism*, 6:3 (1999), 533.

80. FCO33/1606, Political Relations between the Republic of Ireland and Northern Ireland, Diplomatic Report No. 226/71, 6 April 1971.

81. Interview with Ken Bloomfield, Craigavad, 23 Aug. 2001.

82. Interview with Dermot Nally, Dublin, 10 May 2001.

83. Interview with Garret FitzGerald, Dublin, 12 Sept. 2001.

84. Interview with Edward Heath (British Prime Minister 1970–74), London, 4 April 2001.

85. Interview with Garret FitzGerald, Dublin, 12 Sept. 2001.

86. Ibid., Sept. 2001.

87. Interview with John Hume, Londonderry/Derry, 13 Sept. 2001.

88. Interview with Robin Butler (Private Secretary to Edward Heath 1972–74), Oxford, 9 Oct. 2001.

89. Interview with Basil McIvor, Spa, 24 Aug. 2001.

90. PREM15/486 Doc 14, British Policy on Northern Ireland, 3 Sept. 1971.

91. Interview with Jim Gibney (republican activist in the 1970s), Belfast, 11 April 2001.

92. Interview with Ken Bloomfield, Craigavad, 23 Aug. 2001.

93. CJ3/25, Relations with the Irish Republic, 1970 NIO, Woodfield to Crawford, 24 Nov. 2001.

94. Interview with Glen Barr, Londonderry/Derry, 22 Aug. 2001.

95. Interview with Austin Currie, Dublin, 5 Jan. 2001.

96. Interview with Mitchell McLaughlin (republican political activist in the 1970s), Londonderry/Derry, 4 Jan. 2001.

97. Interview with Leslie Morrell, Belfast, 4 Jan. 2001.

98. Interview with James Molyneaux, Westminster, 30 Jan. 2001.

99. CJ4/48, NIO Tripartite Talks, Meeting between Faulkner and Heath at Chequers, 26 Sept. 1971.

100. Interview with Leslie Morrell, Belfast, 4 Jan. 2001.

101. Interview with Oliver Napier, Holywood, 29 Dec. 2000.

102. Interview with John Hume, Londonderry/Derry, 13 Sept. 2001.

103. Interview with Mitchell McLaughlin, Londonderry/Derry, 4 Jan. 2001.

104. Brendan O'Leary, 'The Limits to Coercive Consociationalism in Northern Ireland', *Politics Studies*, 37:4 (1989), 571.

105. Interview with Garret FitzGerald, Dublin, 12 Dec. 2001.

106. Hennessy, *A History of Northern Ireland*, p. 225.

107. Interview with John Taylor, Westminster, 15 Feb. 2001.

108. Interview with Basil McIvor, Spa, 24 Aug. 2001.

109. Interview with James Molyneaux, Westminster, 30 Jan. 2001.

110. Interview with John Taylor, Westminster, 15 Feb. 2001.

111. Interview with Glen Barr, Londonderr/Derry, 22 Aug. 2001.

112. Bardon, *A History of Ulster*, pp. 711–14.

113. Interview with Glen Barr, Londonderry/Derry, 22 Aug. 2001.

114. Interview with Robin Butler, Oxford, 9 Oct. 2001.

115. Interview with James Molyneaux, Westminster, 30 Jan. 2001.
116. Interview with Glen Barr, Londonderry/Derry, 22 Aug. 2001.
117. Interview with Major C. T. Hogg, Belfast, 1 Nov. 2001.
118. Interview with John Taylor, Westminster, 15 Feb. 2001.
119. BBC Radio, *A Modern Rebellion*, interview with Bill Craig and Billy Kelly, transmitted on 14 May 1984.
120. PREM15/487, Tripartite meeting at Chequers between Prime Minister, Jack Lynch and Brian Faulkner, 13 Oct. 1971.
121. Interview with Robert Fisk, Beirut, 13 May 2002.
122. Interview with Major C. T. Hogg, Belfast, 1 Nov. 2001.
123. Interview with Ken Bloomfield, Craigavad, 23 Aug. 2001.

CHAPTER THREE

 1. Interview with Lord Butler, (Private Secretary to Margaret Thatcher 1982–85), Oxford, 9 Oct. 2001.
 2. Adrian Guelke, 'British Policy and the International Dimensions of the Northern Ireland Conflict', *Regional Politics and Policy*, (1991), 140–60; Brendan O'Leary and John McGarry, *The Politics of Antagonism: Understanding Northern Ireland* (London: Athlone Press, 1997), pp. 176–216.
 3. *Anglo-Irish Agreement* (London: HMSO, 1985).
 4. *Agreement between the Government of the United Kingdom of Great Britain and Northern Ireland and the Government of Ireland* (London: HMSO, 1998).
 5. *Joint Declaration* (London: HMSO, 1993).
 6. F. Cochrane, *Unionist Politics and the Politics of Unionism since the Anglo-Irish Agreement* (Cork: Cork University Press, 2001), pp. 126–31.
 7. *Irish Times*, 11 Nov. 1985.
 8. *The Times*, 15 Nov. 1985.
 9. O'Leary and McGarry, *The Politics of Antagonism*, pp. 220–41; Brendan O'Leary, 'The Limits to Coercive Consociationalism in Northern Ireland', *Politics Studies*, 37:4 (1989) 579–85.
10. See Arthur Aughey, *Under Siege: Ulster Unionism and the Anglo-Irish Agreement* (Belfast: Blackstaff Press, 1989); Harvey Cox, 'Managing Northern Ireland Intergovernmentally: An Appraisal of the Anglo-Irish Agreement', *Parliamentary Affairs*, 40:1 (1987), 80–97; Tom Hadden and Kevin Boyle, *The Anglo-Irish Agreement: Commentary, Text and Official Review* (London: Sweet & Maxwell, 1989).
11. O'Leary and McGarry, *The Politics of Antagonism*, p. 223.
12. Margaret Thatcher, *The Downing Street Years* (London: HarperCollins, 1993), pp. 402–15.
13. Guelke, 'British Policy and the International Dimensions of the Northern Ireland Conflict', 145.
14. Interview with Robin Butler, Oxford, 9 Oct. 2001.
15. Thatcher, *The Downing Street Years*, p. 402.
16. Ibid., p. 403.
17. Ibid., pp. 404–6.
18. Interview with Robin Butler, Oxford, 9 Oct. 2001.
19. Ibid.
20. Interview with Dick Spring (Environment and Energy Minister, and Tánaiste, 1982–87), Dublin, 6 Sept. 2001.
21. FitzGerald, *All in a Life*, p. 496.
22. Ibid., p. 497.
23. Ibid., pp. 500–1.
24. Ibid.
25. Ibid., p. 519.
26. Interview with Dick Spring, Dublin, 6 Sept. 2001.
27. Cochrane, *Unionist Politics*, pp. 122–33.
28. Interview with Robin Butler, Oxford, 9 Sept. 2001.
29. See *Sinn Féin Ard-Fheis* (Dublin: Sinn Féin, 1986).
30. See *Scenario for Peace* (Dublin: Sinn Féin, 1987) and *Towards a Lasting Peace in Ireland*

(Dublin: Sinn Féin, 1992).
31. Interview with Gary McMichael (UDP negotiator), Lisburn, 8 May 2001; see also *Common Sense* (Belfast: Ulster Political Research Group, 1986).
32. O'Leary, 'The Limits to Coercive Consociationalism in Northern Ireland', 585.
33. Interview with John Hume, Londonderr/Derry, 13 Sept. 2001.
34. Interview with Jim Gibney, Belfast, 11 April 2001.
35. Interview with Denis Haughey (assistant to John Hume), Stormont, 8 May 2001.
36. *The Times*, 4 Nov. 1989.
37. *Financial Times*, 10 Nov. 1990.
38. Adrian Guelke, 'British Policy and the International Dimensions of the Northern Ireland Conflict', p. 140.
39. *The Times*, 3 Dec. 1993.
40. Interview with Peter Brooke (Secretary of State for Northern Ireland 1989–92), London, 6 July 2001.
41. Antony Seldon, *Major: A Political Life* (London: Phoenix, 1998), p. 264; Eamonn Mallie and David McKittrick, *The Fight for Peace: The Secret Story of the Irish Peace Process* (London: Heinemann, 1996), p. 106.
42. John Major, *The Autobiography* (London: HarperCollins, 1999), p. 442.
43. Interview with Martin Mansergh (special adviser to Albert Reynolds 1992–94), Dublin, 10 Sept. 2001.
44. Interview with Albert Reynolds (Taoiseach 1992–94), Dublin, 20 Sept. 2001.
45. Interview with Martin Mansergh, Dublin, 10 Sept. 2001.
46. *Irish Times*, 16 Dec. 1993.
47. Interview with Patrick Mayhew (Secretary of State for Northern Ireland 1992–97), Westminster, 17 July 2001.
48. Brendan O'Leary, 'The Conservative Stewardship of Northern Ireland, 1979–97: Sound-bottomed Contradictions or Slow Learning?', *Irish Political Studies*, 45:4 (1997), 667.
49. Interview with Patrick Mayhew, Westminster, 17 July 2001.
50. Interview with David Blatherwick (British Ambassador to Ireland 1991–95), London, 25 July 2001.
51. Ibid.
52. Interview with Patrick Mayhew, Westminster, 17 July 2001.
53. Interview with Albert Reynolds, Dublin, 20 Sept. 2001.
54. O'Leary, 'The Conservative Stewardship of Northern Ireland', 671.
55. Interview with Father Gerry Reynolds (mediator involved through Clonard Monastery in talks with Sinn Féin), Belfast, 25 Aug. 2001.
56. Conor O'Clery, *The Greening of the White House* (Dublin: Gill & Macmillan, 1996), pp. 43–53.
57. Interview with Sean O hUiginn (senior Irish diplomat involved in negotiating the DSD), Dublin, 6 Aug. 2001.
58. Interview with Robin Butler, Oxford, 9 Oct. 2001.
59. Interview with David Adams (loyalist activist and UDP negotiator), Lisburn, 9 May 2001.
60. Interview with Gary McMichael, Lisburn, 8 May 2001.
61. Interview with Robin Eames (mediator in secret talks with loyalists), Armagh, 3 Aug. 2001.
62. Interview with Roy Magee (mediator between Irish government and UDA Army Council), Dundonald, 5 Sept. 2001.
63. Interview with Albert Reynolds, Dublin, 20 Sept. 2001.
64. Interview with Robin Eames, Armagh, 3 Aug. 2001.
65. Interview with Patrick Mayhew, Westminster, 17 July 2001.
66. Interview with Jeffery Donaldson, Lisburn, 14 Aug. 2001.
67. Interview with David Blatherwick, London, 25 July 2001.
68. Interview with Dermot Nally (senior Irish diplomat involved in negotiating the DSD), Dublin, 10 May 2001.
69. Major, *The Autobiography*, p. 442.
70. Interview with David Blatherwick, London, 25 July 2001.
71. Ibid.
72. O'Clery, *The Greening of the White House*, pp. 89–100.
73. Interview with Albert Reynolds, Dublin, 20 Sept. 2001.
74. Interview with Conor O'Clery (Washington correspondent, *Irish Times*), Dublin, 22 Aug. 2002.

75. See Mallie and McKittrick, *The Fight for Peace*, pp. 232–40.
76. *The Times*, 25 July 1994.
77. Seán Duignan, *One Spin on the Merry-Go-Round* (Dublin: Blackwater Press, 1996), pp. 118–28.
78. Interview with Sean O hUiginn, Dublin, 6 Aug. 2001.
79. *Irish Press*, 19 Nov. 1993.
80. Interview with Robin Butler, Oxford, 9 Oct. 2001.
81. Interview with Patrick Mayhew, Westminster, 17 July 2001.
82. Private conversation with James Molyneaux.
83. *Irish Times*, 1 Sept. 1994.
84. *The Times*, 12 Sept. 1994.
85. *The Times*, 4 Oct. 1994.
86. Interview with Roy Magee, Dundonald, 5 Sept. 2001; Brian Rowan, *Behind the Lines: The Story of the IRA and Loyalist Ceasefires* (Belfast: Blackstaff Press, 1995), pp. 75–8.
87. Interview with David Adams, Lisburn, 9 May 2001; Rowan, *Behind the Lines*, pp. 110–23.
88. Interview with David Ervine (loyalist activist and PUP negotiator), Stormont, 9 May 2001.
89. Interview with Gary McMichael, Lisburn, 8 May 2001; see also Gary McMichael, *An Ulster Voice* (Boulder, CO: Roberts Rinehart, 1999), pp. 55–63.
90. *The Times*, 19 July 1994.
91. Interview with Dick Spring, Dublin, 6 Sept. 2001.
92. See *A Framework for Accountable Government in Northern Ireland* (London: HMSO, 1995); *A New Framework for Agreement: A Shared Understanding between the British and Irish Governments to Assist Discussion and Negotiation Involving the Northern Ireland Parties* (London: HMSO, 1995).
93. O'Leary and McGarry, *The Politics of Antagonism*, p. 336.
94. O'Duffy, 'British and Irish Conflict Regulation from Sunningdale to Belfast: Part II', 416.
95. *The Times*, 26 June 1997.
96. The *Mitchell Commission Report* is available at http://www.psr.keele.ac.uk/docs/mitch.htm
97. Interview with David Kerr (personal assistant to David Trimble during the talks process), Stormont, 5 Sept. 2001.
98. George Mitchell, *Making Peace* (New York: Alfred Knopf, 1999), p. 110.
99. Private conversation with Senator Mitchell, House of Lords, Westminster, 15 Nov. 2004.
100. *Propositions on Heads of Agreement* (London: HMSO, 1998).
101. Mitchell, *Making Peace*, p. 159.
102. *Belfast Telegraph*, 7 April 1998.

CHAPTER FOUR

1. Interview with Dick Spring, Dublin, 6 Sept. 2001.
2. Rickhard Rose, *Governing Without Consensus* (London: Faber & Faber, 1971), pp. 447–73.
3. *The Belfast Agreement* (London: HMSO, 1998), pp. 11–12.
4. See Brendan O'Leary, 'The Nature of the British–Irish Agreement, *New Left Review*, 233 (1999), 95–6; Brendan O'Leary, 'The British–Irish Agreement' in John McGarry (ed.), *Northern Ireland and the Divided World* (London and New York: Oxford University Press, 2001), pp 69–81.
5. *The Belfast Agreement*, pp. 14–21.
6. Ibid., pp. 22–5.
7. O'Leary, 'The Nature of the British–Irish Agreement', *New Left Review*, 233 (1999), pp. 80–1.
8. O'Leary, 'The British–Irish Agreement', p. 60.
9. Ibid., p. 61.
10. CJ3/25, Relations with the Irish Republic 1970 NIO, Woodfield to Crawford, 24 Nov. 1970.
11. Interview with Dermot Nally, Dublin, 10 May 2001.
12. On the impact of the Cold War on the peace process see Adrian Guelke, 'The International System and the Northern Ireland Peace Process', *Working Papers in British–Irish Studies*, 21 (2002); Michael Cox, 'Bringing in the International: The IRA Ceasefire and the End of

the Cold War', *International Affairs*, 73:4 (1997), 671–93.
13. Interview with Conor O'Clery, Dublin, 22 Aug. 2002.
14. Ibid.
15. Interview with Sean O hUiginn, Dublin, 6 Aug. 2001.
16. Interview with Conor O'Clery, Dublin, 22 Aug. 2002.
17. O'Clery, *The Greening of the White House*, pp. 43–54.
18. See O'Leary, 'The Nature of the British–Irish Agreement', 66–96.
19. Interview with John Alderdice (Alliance Party leader 1987–98; Assembly Speaker 1998–2004), Stormont, 24 Aug. 2001.
20. Interview with Paddy Teahon (senior Irish negotiator in the substantive negotiations), Dublin, 31 Oct. 2001.
21. Interview with Martin Mansergh, Dublin, 10 Sept. 2001.
22. Ibid.
23. Interview with Paddy Teahon, Dublin, 31 Oct. 2001.
24. Interview with Mark Durkan (Deputy First Minister of Northern Ireland 2001–2; SDLP leader from 2001), Londonderry/Derry, 14 Sept. 2001.
25. Interview with David Campbell (UUP talks delegate 1996–98), Stormont, 11 Sept. 2001.
26. *Belfast Telegraph*, 19 Nov. 1999; see also Deaglán de Bréadún, *The Far Side of Revenge: Making Peace in Northern Ireland* (Cork: Collins Press, 2001), pp. 294–5.
27. Interview with Denis Haughey (SDLP politican; junior minister from 1999), Stormont, 8 May 2001.
28. Interview with Mark Durkan, Londonderry/Derry, 14 Sept. 2001.
29. Interview with Albert Reynolds, Dublin, 20 Sept. 2001.
30. Interview with Martin Mansergh, Dublin, 10 Sept. 2001.
31. Interview with David Kerr, Stormont, 5 Sept. 2001.
32. Interview with David Campbell, Stormont, 11 Sept. 2001.
33. Interview with Mark Durkan, Londonderry/Derry, 14 Sept. 2001.
34. Interview with Sean O'Callaghan, (former head of the IRA's Southern Command), London, 18 Oct. 2004.
35. Interview with Jim Gibney (Sinn Féin negotiator 1996–98), Belfast, 11 April 2001.
36. Interview with Mitchell McLaughlin (Sinn Féin Party Chairman from 1998), Londonderry/Derry, 4 Jan. 2001.
37. Interview with Sean O'Callaghan, London, 18 Oct. 2004.
38. Interview with Jim Gibney, Belfast, 17 Sept. 2004.
39. See Adrian Guelke, 'The Peace Process in South Africa, Israel and Northern Ireland: A Farewell to Arms', *Irish Studies in International Affairs*, 5 (1994), 93–106, and (2002) 3–4.
40. Interview with David Kerr, Stormont, 5 Sept. 2001.
41. Interview with Jeffery Donaldson (UUP talks delegate 1996–98; MP for Lagan Valley from 1997), Lisburn, 14 Aug. 2001.
42. Interview with David Kerr, Stormont, 5 Sept. 2001.
43. Interview with David Campbell, Stormont, 11 Sept. 2001.
44. The AIA institutionalised an Intergovernmental Conference at Maryfield in Belfast and the unionists had long since called for its removal.
45. Interview with David Campbell, Stormont, 11 Sept. 2001.
46. Interview with David Kerr, Stormont, 5 Sept. 2001.
47. Interview with Denis Rogan (UUP Leader in the House of Lords from 2001), Belfast, 5 Jan. 2001.
48. Interview with Jeffery Donaldson, Lisburn, 14 Aug. 2001.
49. Interview with David Kerr, Stormont, 5 Sept. 2001.
50. Interview with Denis Rogan, Belfast, 5 Jan. 2001.
51. Interview with John Taylor, Westminster, 15 Feb. 2001.
52. See *Proposals by the British and Irish Governments for a Comprehensive Agreement*, 8 December 2004 (London: HMSO, 2004).
53. Interview with Jeffery Donaldson, Lisburn, 14 Aug. 2001.
54. Brendan O'Duffy, 'British and Irish conflict regulation from Sunningdale to Belfast: Part II', 422.
55. Interview with Paddy Teahon, Dublin, 31 Oct. 2001.
56. Interview with Denis Rogan, Belfast, 5 Jan. 2001.
57. Private conversation with David Trimble, Westminster, 17 Nov. 2004. See Michael Kerr,

Transforming Unionism: David Trimble and the 2005 Election (Dublin: Irish Academic Press, 2006) Chapter 7.
58. Interview with Martin Mansergh, Dublin, 10 Sept. 2001.
59. Interview with Paddy Teahon, Dublin, 31 Oct. 2001.
60. Interview with Peter Mandelson (Secretary of State for Northern Ireland 1999–2001), Westminster, 2 June 2001.
61. Data from http:// www.nisra.gov.uk/census/start.html (19 Dec. 2002).
62. John McGarry and Brendan O'Leary, *Explaining Northern Ireland* (Oxford: Blackwell, 1995), pp. 341–4.
63. Ibid., pp. 347–8.
64. PriceWaterhouseCoopers' survey of 1,173 unionist voters conducted for the UUP on 23–26 March 2001. The base for this question was 371: those unionist voters determined to vote for an anti-Agreement candidate in the forthcoming general election of 2001.
65. Interview with David Burnside, London, 25 May 2005.
66. O'Leary, 'The British–Irish Agreement', p. 66.
67. Ibid., p. 67.
68. Interview with Martin Mansergh, Dublin, 10 Sept.r 2001.
69. O'Leary, 'The British–Irish Agreement', p. 68.

CHAPTER FIVE

1. GB165-0269 Box II File 6, Spears Papers, Notes on Conversation with General de Gaulle, 12 March 1942.
2. See D. Fromkin, *A Peace to End all Peace* (London: André Deutsch, 1989), pp. 188–99; G. Antonius, *The Arab Awakening* (London: Hamish Hamilton, 1938), pp. 244–63.
3. Antonius, *The Arab Awakening*, pp. 243–75.
4. N. Ziadeh, *Syria and Lebanon* (London: Ernest Benn, 1957), p. 47.
5. Meir Zamir, *Lebanon's Quest: The Road to Statehood, 1926–1939* (London: I. B. Tauris, 2000), pp. 1–28.
6. Ibid., p. 45.
7. M. Suleiman, *Political Parties in Lebanon* (Ithaca, NY: Cornell University Press, 1967) pp. 263–79.
8. Zamir, *Lebanon's Quest*, pp. 186–7.
9. Ziadeh, *Syria and Lebanon*, pp. 62–74.
10. Docs 229, Agreement Concerning the Collaboration between the British and Free French Authorities in the Middle East, de Gaulle, 1955, pp. 201–3; Andrée Pierre-Viénot, 'The Levant Dispute: The French Case', *World Affairs*, (Oct. 1945), 220–2.
11. Doc. 369, Telegram from General de Gaulle to General Catroux, Beirut, 31 Oct. 1941, in Charles de Gaulle, *The Call to Honour: Documents* (London: Collins, 1955), pp. 307–8. See also Martin Mickelsen, 'Another Fashoda: The Anglo-Free French Conflict over the Levant, May to September 1941', *Revue Française, d'histoire d'Outre-Mer*, 63:230 (1976) ,75–100; Pierre-Viénot, 'The Levant Dispute: The French Case', 219–28; E. Atiyah, 'The Levant Dispute: The Arab Case', *World Affairs*, (Jan. 1946), 336–47.
12. de Gaulle, *The Call to Honour*, p. 188.
13. Doc. 378, Letter from General de Gaulle to the Secretary General of the League of Nations, London, 29 Nov. 1941, in de Gaulle, *The Call of Honour*, pp. 321–2.
14. Edward Spears, *Fulfilment of a Mission* (London: Seeley, Service & Cooper, 1977), pp. 96–8; Mickelsen, 'Another Fashoda', pp. 76–81.
15. de Gaulle, *The Call to Honour*, pp. 188–9.
16. Ibid.
17. GB165-0269 Box II File 4, Spears Papers, Note of a Meeting between the Prime Minister, the Minister of State and General de Gaulle, 1 Oct. 1941.
18. PREM3/422/13 Doc. 502, Lebanon and Syria, Churchill to Foreign Minister, 15 July 1943.
19. de Gaulle, *The Call to Honour*, p. 188.
20. Charles de Gaulle, *Unity* (London: Weidenfeld & Nicolson, 1959), p. 25.
21. A. Gaunson, *The Anglo–French Clash in Lebanon and Syria, 1940–45* (London: Macmillan, 1987), p. 190.
22. Doc. 402, Telegram from General de Gaulle, London, to General Catroux, Beirut, 8 April 1942, in de Gaulle, *The Call to Honour*, pp. 339–41.

23. GB165-0269 Box II File 7, Spears Papers, The Prime Minister's Directive to Spears, 27 June 1943.
24. Ibid.
25. FO366/1402, Resignation of Sir Edward Spears, 30 Nov. 1944.
26. de Gaulle, *Unity*, p. 26.
27. Zamir, *Lebanon's Quest*, pp. 84–179.
28. Suleiman, *Political Parties in Lebanon*, pp. 250—60.
29. K. Schulze, *Israel's Covert Diplomacy in Lebanon* (New York: St. Martin's Press, 1997), pp. 11–25.
30. See Salibi, *A House of Many Mansions*, pp. 166–81.
31. Zamir, *Lebanon's Quest*, pp. 69–76.
32. Interview with Carlos Eddé (National Bloc Leader), Ashrafieh, 4 Dec. 2001.
33. Khazen, *The Communal Pact of National Identities*, p. 29.
34. Interview with Michel Khoury (son of President Khoury and Minister of Defence 1965–66), Ashrafieh, 23 May 2002.
35. See R. Solh in N. Shehadi and D. Mills, (eds), *Lebanon: A History of Conflict and Consensus* (Oxford: Centre for Lebanese Studies, 1988), pp. 149–65.
36. FO660/36 Doc. 86, Beirut to Algiers, 26 Aug. 1943.
37. FO660/36 Doc. 118, Foreign Office to Spears, 30 Sept. 1943.
38. See Meir Zamir, 'New Light Shed on the Making of the National Pact', Parts I and II and in *Al-Hayat* (Nov. 1999).
39. GB 165-0269 Box III File 4, Spears Papers, Review of the Year in the Lebanon, 1 Feb. 1944.
40. FO660/36 Doc. 115, Spears to Algiers, 21 Sept. 1943.
41. See Zamir, 'New Light Shed', Part I.
42. *Palestine Post*, 23 Sept. 1943.
43. FO660/36 Doc. 116, to Algiers, 21 Sept. 1943; *Palestine Post*, 22 Sept. 1943.
44. *Palestine Post*, 27 Sept. 1943.
45. Zamir, 'New Light Shed', Part II.
46. Ibid.
47. PREM3/422/13 Doc. 501, Prime Minister to Foreign Minister, 15 July 1943.
48. *Palestine Post*, 10 Oct. 1943.
49. FO660/36 Doc. 129, Lascelles to Foreign Office, 14 Oct. 1943.
50. FO660/36 Doc. 132, Spears to Algiers, 22 Oct. 1943.
51. de Gaulle, *Unity*, p. 200.
52. Richard Casey, *Personal Experience, 1939–46* (London: Constable, 1962), p. 143.
53. *The Times*, 12 Nov. 1943.
54. *Palestine Post*, 12 Nov. 1943.
55. GB165-0269 Box III File 3, Spears Papers, Spears to Foreign Office, 11 Nov. 1943.
56. Ibid.; see also *Palestine Post*, 12 Nov. 1943.
57. GB 165-0269 Box II File 4, Spears Papers, Memorandum on de Gaulle, 14 April 1954.
58. GB 165-0269 Box III File 3, Spears Papers, Spears to Foreign Office, 17 Nov. 1943.
59. *Palestine Post*, 17 Nov. 1943.
60. de Gaulle, *Unity*, pp. 200–1.
61. GB 165-0269 Box III File 3, Spears Papers, Makins to Spears, 12 Nov. 1943; see also *Palestine Post*, 14 Nov. 1943.
62. GB 165-0269 Box III File 3, Spears Papers, British Embassy Cairo to British Legation Beirut, 11 Nov. 1943.
63. GB 165-0269 Box III File 3, Spears Papers, Spears to Foreign Office, 13 Nov. 1943.
64. GB 165-0269 Box III File 4, Spears Papers, Review of the Foreign Press, Series F, France and the French Empire, 13 Nov. 1943.
65. GB 165-0269 Box III File 4, Spears Papers, Extracts from Diary of Richard Casey, 17 Nov. 1943; Casey, *Personal Experience*, p. 145.
66. GB 165-0269 Box III File 4, Spears Papers, Extracts from Diary of Richard Casey, 27 Nov. 1943.
67. GB 165-0269 Box III File 4, Spears Papers, Extracts from Diary of Richard Casey, 19 Nov. 1943; Mickelsen, 'Another Fashoda', 75–81. The Fashoda incident marked French humiliation at the hands of the British as they vied for hegemony in the Middle East and Africa in 1898.
68. Casey, *Personal Experience*, p. 144.
69. PREM3/421 Doc. 359, Lebanon and Syria, Cairo to Foreign Office, 11 Nov. 1943.
70. FO195/2478 Doc. 224, British Embassy Andorra No. 224, Cairo to Ambassador in

Andorra, 20 Nov. 1943.
71. PREM3/421 Doc. 351, Churchill to General Wilson, 12 Nov. 1943.
72. PREM3/421 Doc. 265, Beirut to Foreign Office, 23 Nov. 1943.
73. FO660/36 Doc. 129, Political: Syria and Lebanon Part II, Lascelles to Foreign Office, 14 Oct. 1943.
74. Khazen, *The Communal Pact of National Identities*, p. 15.
75. Interview with Farid el-Khazen, Beirut, 10 June 2002.
76. Khazen, *The Communal Pact of National Identities*, pp. 6–11.
77. *Palestine Post*, 6 Sept. 1943.
78. Interview with Farid el-Khazen, Beirut, 10 June 2002.
79. See J. Spagnolo, 'Constitutional Change in Mount Lebanon, 1861–1864', *Middle Eastern Studies*, 7:1 (1971), 25–48; and J. Spagnolo, *France and Ottoman Lebanon, 1861–1914* (London: Ithuan Press, 1977), pp. 41–7.
80. Casey, *Personal Experience*, pp. 143–8.
81. Interview with Basim el-Jisr, Beirut, 4 April 2002.
82. Interview with Michel Khoury, Ashrafieh, 23 May 2002.
83. Antoine Messarra, 'National Edification through Pacts and National Contrition', *Panorama of Events*, 47 (1987), Summaries 36.
84. See M. Agwani (ed.), *The Lebanese Crisis, 1958* (London: Asia Publishing House, 1965), pp. 1–54; see also Theodor Hanf, *Coexistence in Wartime Lebanon: The Decline of a State and the Rise of a Nation* (London: I. B. Tauris, 1993), pp. 111–8.
85. Interview with Michel Khoury, Ashrafieh, 23 May 2002.
86. See al-Jisr, *Mithaq 1943*.
87. Khazen, *The Communal Pact of National Identities*, pp. 17–18.
88. Interview with Fawaz Traboulsi (member of the Communist Party and academic at the American University of Beirut), Hamra, 8 April 2002.
89. Interview with Monah Solh (historian), Hamra, 2 May 2002.
90. Ibid.
91. Interview with Monah Solh, Hamra, 18 April 2002.
92. Interview with Farid el-Khazen, Beirut, 10 June 2002; see also Michel Chiha, 'A Jewish Story', 26 Sept. 1945, 'Palestine'.
93. Schulze, *Israel's Covert Diplomacy in Lebanon*, pp. 11–25.
94. Khazen, *The Communal Pact of National Identities*, pp. 17–23.
95. GB 165-0269 Box III File 1, Spears Papers, Record of a Meeting held in the Secretary of State's Room, Foreign Office, 14 July 1943.
96. de Gaulle, *Unity*, pp. 26–7.
97. FO660/36 Doc. 150, Casey to Spears, 28 Oct. 1943.
98. GB 165-0269 Box II File 7, Churchill to Spears, Spears Papers, 13 Oct. 1943.
99. CAB122/810 Telegram 7977, Lebanon Dispute 1943–44, Eden to Halifax, 18 Nov. 1943.
100. GB 165-0269 Box III File 3, Spears Papers, A Meeting in Cairo with Eden, Macmillan, Cadogan, Killearn, Casey, Croft, Makins, and Lascelles, 7 Dec. 1943.
101. WO201/982, Nov. Crisis Lebanon: Miscellaneous Papers – Operation Orders, 20 Nov. 1943.
102. GB 165-0269 Box III File 4, Spears Papers, Extracts from Diary of Richard Casey, 27 Nov. 1943; Casey, *Personal Experience*, p. 148.
103. GB 165-0269 Box II File 7, Spears Papers, Minutes of Meeting with Churchill, 9 Dec. 1943.
104. Doc. 402, Telegram from General de Gaulle, London, to General Catroux, Beirut, 8 April 1942, de Gaulle, *The Call to Honour*, pp. 339–41.
105. Mickelsen, 'Another Fashoda', 94–6.
106. PREM3/421 Doc. 347, Lebanon and Syria, Draft Letter from Churchill to Roosevelt, 12 Nov. 1943.
107. PREM3/421 Doc. 345, Churchill to Roosevelt, 13 Nov. 1943.
108. GB 165-0269 Box II File 7, Spears Papers, The Prime Minister's Directive to Spears, 27 June 1943.
109. de Gaulle, *The Call to Honour*, p. 188.
110. PREM3/422/13 Doc 513, Spears to London, 5 July 1943.
111. FO 660/35 Doc. 54, Political: Syria and Lebanon Part I, Foreign Office to Lascelles, 21 July 1941.

112. de Gaulle, *Unity*, p. 38.
113. Interview with Monah Solh, Hamra, 2 May 2002.
114. Interview with Michel Khoury, Ashrafieh, 23 May 2002.
115. de Gaulle, *Unity*, p. 199.
116. FO226/266, 1944 Franco-Lebanon-Syrian Treaty Negotiations.
117. FO 660/36 Doc. 142, Spears to Algiers, 28 Oct. 1943.
118. Abul-Husn, *The Lebanese Conflict*, p. 78.
119. A. R. Norton, *Amal and the Shi'a: The Struggle for the Soul of Lebanon* (Austin: University of Texas Press, 1987), pp. 1–12.
120. Hanf, *Coexistence in Wartime Lebanon*, p. 73.
121. Ibid., p. 70.
122. Khazen, *The Communal Pact of National Identities*, p. 39; see also Khazen, *The Breakdown of the State in Lebanon*, pp. 87–128.
123. Salibi, *A House of Many Mansions*, p. 198.
124. Interview with Farid Salman (political philosopher and former journalist), Beirut, 24 April 2002.
125. Suleiman, *Political Parties in Lebanon*, p. 45.
126. Hanf, *Coexistence in Wartime Lebanon*, pp. 70–4.
127. Zamir, *Lebanon's Quest*, pp. 179–239.
128. Hanf, *Coexistence in Wartime Lebanon*, pp. 97–110.

CHAPTER SIX

1. Antoine Messarra, 'A Problematic Approach to the State of Lebanon', 12:51 (1988).
2. Theodor Hanf, *Coexistence in Wartime Lebanon*, p. 558.
3. Ibid., p. 555.
4. Interview with Muhieddin Chehab (former Mourabitoun combatant and Sunni major, Beirut), Beirut, 28 Nov. 2001.
5. Interview with Fouad Boutros (Minister of Foreign Affairs 1976–82), Ashrafieh, 6 Dec. 2001; see also Khazen, *The Breakdown of the State in Lebanon, 1967–76*, pp. 140–75.
6. Patrick Seale, *Asad: The Struggle for the Middle East* (Berkeley, Los Angeles and London: University of California Press, 1996), pp. 267–89; Avi Shlaim, *The Iron Wall: Israel and the Arab World* (London: Allen Lane, 2000), pp. 384–423.
7. See W. Goria, *Sovereignty and Leadership in Lebanon, 1943–76* (London: Ithaca Press, 1985), pp. 204–31.
8. A. R. Norton, *Amal and the Shi'a*, pp. 37–58.
9. N. Weinberger, *Syrian Intervention in Lebanon* (London: Oxford University Press, 1986), pp. 165–71.
10. Moshe Ma'oz, *Assad: The Sphinx of Damascus* (London: Weidenfeld & Nicolson, 1988), pp. 126–7.
11. R. Avi-Ran, *The Syrian Involvement in Lebanon Since 1975* (Boulder, CO: Westview Press, 1991), p. 20.
12. Interview with US Ambassador Richard Murphy, on Al-Jazeera Television, *War of Lebanon*, Part 4 (2001).
13. For committee minutes see *al-Tariq* (1–8 Jan.–Aug. 1976).
14. Hanf, *Coexistence in Wartime Lebanon*, p. 327. Hundreds of Christians and Muslims were slaughtered by rival factions on the basis of the identity cards they carried bearing their confidential details.
15. Interview with Assad Chaftari (Lebanese Forces negotiator with Hobieka), Hamra, 19 Nov. 2001.
16. Interview with Walid Jumblat (PSP leader from 1977), Hamra, 9 April 2002.
17. Hanf, *Coexistence in Wartime Lebanon*, p. 209.
18. Seale, *Asad*, pp. 267–89.
19. For excerpts see Walid Khalidi, *Conflict and Violence in Lebanon: The 1975–76 Civil War* (London and New York: Oxford University Press, 1986), pp. 189–91.
20. N. Weinberger, *Syrian Intervention in Lebanon: The 1975–76 Civil War* (London and New York: Oxford University Press, 1986), pp. 184–92; Goria, *Sovereignty and Leadership in Lebanon*, p. 218.
21. On Assad's policy on Lebanon see Seale, *Asad*, pp. 267–89; Ma'oz, *Assad*, pp. 123–34.

216 *Imposing Power-Sharing*

22. Hanf, *Coexistence in Wartime Lebanon*, p. 212.
23. Interview with Karim Pakradouni on Al-Jazeera Television, *War of Lebanon*, Part 4 (2001).
24. Interview with Karim Pakradouni (Kataeb leader), Ashrafieh, 15 May 2002.
25. Hanf, *Coexistence in Wartime Lebanon*, p. 213.
26. Interview with George Hawi, Lebanese Communist Party, on Al-Jazeera Television, *War of Lebanon*, Part 4 (2001).
27. Interview with Walid Jumblat, Hamra, 9 April 2002.
28. For full text see CEDRE (eds), *Lebanese–Israeli Negotiations* (Beirut: CEDRE, The Lebanese Centre for Documentation and Research, 1984), pp. 297–311.
29. Interview with US Ambassador, Morris Draper, on Al-Jazeera Television, *War of Lebanon*, Part 11 (2001).
30. Elie Salem, *Violence and Diplomacy in Lebanon: The Troubled Years, 1982–88* (London: I. B. Tauris, 1995), pp. 68–128.
31. Interview with Amin Gemayel (Lebanese President 1982–88), Sin al-Fil, 2 Dec. 2001.
32. George Shultz, *Turmoil and Triumph* (New York: Macmillan, 1993), pp. 196–234.
33. Interview with Morris Draper on Al-Jazeera Television, *War of Lebanon*, Part 11.
34. Interview with Amin Gemayel, Sin al-Fil, 2 Dec. 2001; interview with Amin Gemayel on Al-Jazeera Television, *War of Lebanon*, Part 11.
35. W. Quandt, 'Reagan's Lebanon Policy: Trial and Error', *Middle East Journal*, 38:2 (1984), pp. 237–54; Hanf, *Coexistence in Wartime Lebanon*, pp. 264–6.
36. Interview with Amin Gemayel, Sin al-Fil, 2 Dec. 2001.
37. Caspar Weinberger, *Fighting for Peace* (London: Michael Joseph, 1990), p. 108.
38. W. Haddad, *Lebanon: The Politics of Revolving Doors* (New York: Praeger, 1985), pp. 84–115.
39. Interview with Morris Draper on Al-Jazeera Television, *War of Lebanon*, Part 11.
40. Shultz, *Turmoil and Triumph*, p. 232.
41. Interview with Walid Jumblat, Hamra, 9 April 2002.
42. Interview with George Bush Sr on Al-Jazeera Television, *War of Lebanon*, Part 11.
43. Interview with Amin Gemayel, Sin al-Fil, 4 Dec. 2001.
44. Shultz, *Turmoil and Triumph*, p. 233.
45. Interview with Karim Pakradouni, Ashrafieh, 15 May 2002.
46. See Weinberger, *Fighting for Peace*; see also Weinberger, *Syrian Intervention in Lebanon*, pp. 94–122.
47. Interview with Rafic Hariri (Prime Minister of Lebanon 1992–98 and 2000–4), Beirut, 26 June 2002.
48. Ibid.
49. Interview with Joseph Maila, Beirut, 23 April 2002; Salem, *Violence and Diplomacy in Lebanon*, pp. 189–219; Hanf, *Coexistence in Wartime Lebanon*, pp. 306–12; Joseph Maila (under pseudonym Sami Dilali), 'L'Accord Tripartite', *Les Cahiers de l'Orient*, 1986.
50. *Middle East Reporter*, 49:439 (1985), 21.
51. Interview with Karim Pakradounion on Al-Jazeera Television, *War of Lebanon*, Part 12, (2001).
52. Interview with Hussein Housseini (Speaker of the Lebanese Parliament 1972–92), Raouche, 24 June 2002.
53. Interview with Walid Jumblat, Hamra, 9 April 2002.
54. Interview with Karim Pakradouni, Ashrafieh, 15 June 2002.
55. Interview with Elie Karame (Kataeb leader 1984), Ashrafieh, 23 Nov. 2001.
56. Interview with Assad Chaftari, Hamra, 19 Nov. 2001.
57. Interview with Amin Gemayel, Sin al-Fil, 4 Dec. 2001.
58. Interview with Walid Jumblat, Hamra, 9 April 2002.
59. Interview with Rashid Solh (Prime Minister of Lebanon 1974–75 and 1992), Beirut, 9 May 2002.
60. Interview with Patriarch Nasrallah Sfeir (Maronite Patriarch from 1986), Bkirke, 23 June 2002.
61. Interview with Amin Gemayel, Sin al-Fil, 4 June 2001.
62. Interview with Richard Murphy on Al-Jazeera Television, *War of Lebanon*, Part 14, (2001).
63. Hanf, *Coexistence in Wartime Lebanon*, p. 592.
64. Interview with Salim Hoss (Prime Minister of Lebanon 1976–80, 1987–90 and 1998–2000), Ashibakar, 3 Dec. 2001.

65. Interview with Charles Chartouni (Lebanese Forces), Ashrafieh, 12 June 2002.
66. Interview with Assad Chaftari, Hamra, 19 Nov. 2001.
67. Interview with Khalid Kabbani (senior Lebanese judge and Sunni political adviser at Ta'if), Beirut, 13 June 2002.
68. Interview with Hussein Housseini, Raouche, 18 June 2002.
69. Hanf, *Coexistence in Wartime Lebanon*, p. 579.
70. Interview with Patriarch Sfeir, Bkirke, 23 June 2002.
71. Interview with Vincent Battle (US Ambassador to Lebanon from 2001), Aoukar, 14 June 2002.
72. Interview with Assad Chaftari, Hamra, 19 Nov. 2001.
73. Statement by General Michel Aoun on Al-Jazeera Television, *War of Lebanon*, Part 15 (2001).
74. Interview with Bechara Manassa (academic, Christian adviser at Ta'if), Ashrafieh, 30 May 2002.
75. Salem, *Violence and Diplomacy in Lebanon*, pp. 275–9.
76. Interview with Hussein Housseini, Raouche, 18 June 2002.
77. Interview with Khalid Kabbani, Beirut, 13 June 2002.
78. Ibid.
79. Interview with Dory Chamoun (National Liberal Party leader), Ashrafie, 30 Nov. 2001.
80. Interview with Nicholas Nassif (*al-Nahar* reporter), Hamra, 28 June 2002.
81. Interview with Rafic Hariri, Beirut, 26 June 2002.
82. Interview with Mahmoud Ammar (Shi'a deputy for Baabda 1972; Minister of Information 1974; negotiator at Ta'if 1989), Hasmieh, 25 April 2002.
83. Interview with Pierre Daccache (Maronite deputy for Matn 1972; negotiator at Ta'if 1989), Beirut, 8 April 2002.
84. See Mansour, *Al-Inqilab ala al-Ta'if*.
85. Interview with Chafic Badre (Maronite deputy for Aley 1972; negotiator at Ta'if 1989), Hamra, 22 April 2002.
86. Interview with Rashid Solh, Beirut, 9 May 2002.
87. *Avenire*, 15 March 1990.
88. Hanf, *Coexistence in Wartime Lebanon*, p. 590.
89. Interview with Nayla Moawad (Maronite deputy for Zahorta, widow of assassinated Lebanese President René Moawad), Beirut, 5 Dec. 2001.
90. Statement by General Michel Aoun on Al-Jazeera Television, *War of Lebanon*, Part 15 (2001).
91. Hanf, *Coexistence in Wartime Lebanon*, pp. 592–3.
92. Interview with Walid Jumblat on Al-Jazeera Television, *War of Lebanon*, Part 15 (2001).
93. Interview with Samir Frangie (Maronite opposition figure), Hamra, 22 Nov. 2001.
94. Interview with Lakhdar Ibrahimi on Al-Jazeera Television, *War of Lebanon*, Part 15.
95. Ibid.
96. Interview with Karim Pakradouni, Ashrafieh, 15 May 2002.

CHAPTER SEVEN

1. Interview with Vincent Battle, Aoukar, 14 June 2002.
2. Interview with Hussein Housseini, Raouche, 18 June 2002.
3. See Mansour, *Al-Inqilab ala al-Ta'if*.
4. Interview with Talal Housseini (Shi'a adviser at Ta'if), Hamra, 28 May 2002.
5. Interview with Riad Rayyes (publisher and journalist), Hamra, 7 May 2002.
6. Interview with Nasri Maalouf (Greek Catholic deputy for Beirut 1972; Minister of Finance 1956–57; Committee of Seventeen at Ta'if), Ashrafieh, 26 April 2002.
7. Interview with Ali Khalil (Shi'a deputy for Tyre 1972; Minister of Finance 1979–82; negotiator of Ta'if 1989), Beirut, 17 June 2002.
8. Interview with Boutros Harb (Maronite deputy for Batrun 1972; Minister of Public Works and Education 1979; member of Committee of Seventeen at Ta'if), Ashrafieh, 11 June 2002.
9. Interview with Rafic Hariri, Beirut, 26 June 2002.
10. Joseph Maila, *The Document of National Understanding: A Commentary* (Oxford: Centre for Lebanese Studies, 1992), p. 45.
11. Interview with Nasri Maalouf, Ashrafieh, 26 April 2002.
12. Interview with Bechara Manassa, Ashrafieh, 30 May 2002.

13. Statement by the Five Permanent Members of the UN Security Council, New York, 31 Oct. 1989.
14. Hanf, *Coexistence in Wartime Lebanon*, p. 587.
15. Interview with Ali Khalil, Beirut, 17 June 2002.
16. Maila, *The Document of National Understanding*, pp. 18–19.
17. Interview with Rashid Solh, Beirut, 7 May 2002.
18. Interview with Elie Ferzli (Deputy Speaker of the Lebanese Parliament from 1992), Lebanese Parliament, Beirut, 2 May 2002.
19. Interview with Ali Khalil, Beirut, 17 June 2002.
20. Interview with Walid Jumblat, Hamra, 9 April 2002.
21. Ibid.
22. Interview with Hussein Housseini, Raouche, 24 June 2002.
23. Interview with Talal Salman (editor of *al-Sifr*), Hamra, 20 June 2002.
24. Interview with Ali Khalil, Beirut, 17 June 2002.
25. Maila, *The Document of National Understanding*, p. 63.
26. Interview with Edmond Rizk (Maronite deputy for Jazzine 1972; Minister of Justice and Information 1989–92; negotiator at Ta'if 1989), Ashrafieh, 26 May 2002.
27. Interview with Najah Wakim (Sunni deputy for Beirut 1972; negotiator at Ta'if 1989), Beirut, 13 May 2002.
28. Confidential sources.
29. Maila, *The Document of National Understanding*, p. 83.
30. Interview with Jubran Toak (Maronite deputy for Bshara 1972; negotiator at Ta'if 1989), Lebanese Parliament, Beirut, 8 May 2002.
31. Interview with Vincent Battle, Aoukar, 14 June 2002.
32. Interview with a senior European diplomat, 30 May 2002.
33. Interview with Lakhdar Ibrahimi on Al-Jazeera Television, *War of Lebanon*, Part 15 (2001); see also Amatzia Baram, 'The Iraqi Invasion of Kuwait: Decision-making in Baghdad' and Barry Rubin, 'The United States and Iraq: From Appeasement to War', in Amatzia Baram and Barry Rubin (eds), *Iraq's Road to War* (Basingstoke: Palgrave, 1996), pp. 5–36 and 255–72.
34. Interview with senior European diplomat, Beirut, 30 May 2002; see also Baram in 'The Iraqi Invasion of Kuwait', pp. 5–36.
35. Interview with Vincent Battle, Aoukar, 14 June 2002.
36. Interview with Pierre Helleu (Maronite deputy for Alley 1972; negotiator at Ta'if 1989; Minister without Portfolio 2000–3), Beirut, 23 April 2002.
37. See Mansour, *Al Inqilab ala Ta'if*.
38. Hanf, *Coexistence in Wartime Lebanon*, p. 614.
39. See 'Plan for the Incorporation of Militiamen into the State', *Beirut Review*, Lebanon Documents (1991), p. 119.
40. For the full text of the agreement see *Beirut Review*, Lebanon Documents, (1991) pp. 115–19.
41. Interview with Farid Salman, Beirut, 24 April 2002.
42. Hanf, *Coexistence in Wartime Lebanon*, p. 619.
43. Elections were due to take place in 1994.
44. For a detailed analysis of the election results see Richard Norton and Jillian Schwedler, 'Swiss Soldiers, Ta'if Clocks and Early Elections' in D. Collings (ed.), *Peace for Lebanon?: From War to Reconstruction* (Boulder, CO: Lynne Rienner Publishers, 1994), pp. 45–65.
45. Hanf, *Coexistence in Wartime Lebanon*, p. 628.
46. Ibid., p. 636.
47. Interview with Karim Pakradouni, Ashrafieh, 15 May 2002.
48. Abul-Husn, *The Lebanese Conflict*, p. 119.
49. Ibid., p. 122.
50. See documents of 'The Meeting for the Charter and the Constitution: A Conference on the Fate of the Ta'if Accord – Reminding and Requesting the Fulfilment of Promises', Beirut, 14 Dec. 2001.
51. Abul-Husn, *The Lebanese Conflict*, p. 123.

CHAPTER EIGHT

1. Michael Walzer, *On Toleration* (New Haven, CT: Yale University Press, 1997), p. 22.

2. Adrian Guelke, *Northern Ireland: The International Perspective* (New York: St. Martin's Press, 1988), p. 195.
3. BBC, 14 Feb. 2005: http://www.news.bbc.co.uk/1/hi/world/middle_east/1263893.stm
4. Rupert Taylor 'Consociation or Social Transformation?' in John McGarry (ed.Δ), *Northern Ireland and the Divided World* (London and New York: Oxford University Press, 2001), pp. 36–52.
5. Joseph Ruane and Jennifer Todd, *After the Good Friday Agreement* (Dublin: UCD Press, 1999), pp. 144–69.
6. See *Reports* 1, 2 and 3, *Independent Monitoring Commission*, (London: Belfast, 2004).
7. Lecture given by Joseph Maila at St-Joseph's University, Beirut, 18 April 2002.
8. Ibid.
9. See Chapter 7 and also Hanf, *Coexistence in Wartime Lebanon*, pp. 621–35
10. Brendan O'Duffy, 'British and Irish Conflict Regulation from Sunningdale to Belfast: Part II', pp. 399–435
11. Brendan O'Leary, 'The Nature of the British-Irish Agreement', *New Left Review*, 233 (1999), 66–96.

Bibliography

NORTHERN IRELAND

Interviews

David Adams (former UDP negotiator 1996–98), Lisburn, 9 May 2001

Lord Alderdice MLA (Speaker of the Northern Ireland Assembly 1998–2004), Stormont, 24 Aug. 2001

Glen Barr (Assembly Member for Londonderry/Derry 1973–74; Chairman of the UWC), Londonderry/Derry, 22 Aug. 2001

Alderman Roy Beggs (UUP MP for East Antrim 1983–2005), Westminster, 8 June 2005

Sir David Blatherwick (British Ambassador to Ireland 1991–95), London, 25 July 2001

Sir Ken Bloomfield (Northern Ireland Executive Secretary 1974; Head of the Northern Ireland Civil Service 1984–91), Craigavad, 23 Aug. 2001

Lord Brooke (Secretary of State for Northern Ireland 1989–92), London, 6 July 2001

David Burnside MLA (UUP MP for South Antrim 2001–5), London, 25 May 2005

Lord Butler (Private Secretary to Edward Heath 1972–74; Private Secretary to Margaret Thatcher 1982–85), Oxford, 9 Oct. 2001

David Campbell (UUP negotiator 1996–98), Stormont, 11 Sept. 2001 and 8 June 2005

Former Chief Superintendent from Londonderry/Derry, (name withheld) RUC, 8 July 2002

Austin Currie TD (Minister for Housing, Planning and Local Government 1974), Dublin, 5 Jan. 2001

Jeffery Donaldson MP (UUP negotiator 1996–98; MP for Lagan Valley from 1997), Lisburn, 14 Aug. 2001

Mark Durkan MLA (Deputy First Minister 2001–2, SDLP Leader from 2001, MP for Foyle 2005–), Londonderry/Derry, 14 Sept. 2001

Lord Archbishop Dr Robin Eames (Church of Ireland Primate), Armagh, 3 Aug. 2001

David Ervine MLA (PUP Leader), Stormont, 9 May 2001

Dr Sean Farren MLA (SDLP; Minister of Higher and Further Education 1999–2001), Belfast, 15 May 2001

Robert Fisk (journalist, *Independent*), Beirut, 13 May 2002
Garret FitzGerald (Irish Foreign Minister 1973–77; Taoiseach 1981–1982, 1982–87), Dublin, 12 Sept. 2001
Jim Gibney (Sinn Féin negotiator 1996–), Belfast, 11 April 2001 and 17 Sept. 2004
Denis Haughey (SDLP junior minister 1999–2001), Stormont, 8 May 2001
Sir Edward Heath (British Prime Minister 1970–74), London Victoria, 7 Feb. 2001
Lady Sylvia Hermon (MP for North Down, 2001–), Westminster, 7 July 2005
Major C. T. Hogg (retired UDR major), Belfast, 1 Nov. 2001
John Hume MP (Minister for Commerce 1974; Deputy Leader of the SDLP 1973–79 and Leader 1979–2001; MEP 1979–2004, MP for Foyle 1985–2005), Londonderry/Derry 13 Sept. 2001
David Kerr (former personal assistant to David Trimble), Stormont, 5 Sept. 2001
Lord Kilclooney (UUP MP for Strangford 1983–2001 and Assembly Member for Fermanagh and South Tyrone 1973–74; MEP 1979–89), Westminster, 19 July 2000 and 15 Feb. 2001
Denis Loretto (former Alliance Party Chairman), Leatherhead, 12 Dec. 2000
Anne McCann (Women's Coalition), Stormont, 25 Sept. 2001
Basil McIvor (UUP Education Minister 1974), Spa, 24 Aug. 2001
Mitchell McLaughlin MLA (Sinn Féin Chairman from 1998), Londonderry/Derry, 4 Jan. 2001
Gary McMichael (former UDP Leader), Lisburn, 8 May 2001
Reverend Dr Roy Magee (Fitzroy Presbyterian Church), Dundonald, 5 Sept. 2001
Peter Mandelson (Secretary of State for Northern Ireland 1999–2001), Westminster, 2 July 2001
Dr Martin Mansergh (adviser to the Taoiseach from 1997), Dublin, 10 Sept. 2001
Lord Mayhew (Secretary of State for Northern Ireland 1992–97), Westminster, 17 July 2001
Lord Molyneaux of Killead (MP for South Antrim 1970–83 and Lagan Valley 1983–97; UUP Leader 1979–95), Westminster, 30 Jan. 2001
Leslie Morrell (UUP Agriculture Minister 1974), Belfast, 4 Jan. 2001
Dermot Nally (senior Irish diplomat), Dublin, 10 May 2001
Sir Oliver Napier (Alliance Party Leader 1972–84 and Minister for Law Reform 1974), Holywood, 29 Dec. 2000
Sean Neeson MLA (Alliance Party Leader 1998–2001), Stormont, 8 May 2001
Reverend Ken Newell (Fitzroy Presbyterian Church), Dundonald, 7 May 2001

Sean O'Callaghan, (former head of the IRA's Southern Command), London, 18 Oct. 2004

Conor O'Clery (journalist, *Irish Times*), Dublin, 22 Aug. 2002

Sean O hUiginn (former Irish Ambassador to the US), Dublin, 6 Aug. 2001

Albert Reynolds (Taoiseach 1992–94), Dublin, 20 Sept. 2001

Father Gerry Reynolds (Clonard Monastery mediator), Belfast, 25 Aug. 2001

Lord Rogan (UUP Leader in the House of Lords after 2001), Belfast, 5 Jan. 2001

Sir John Semple (former Secretary to the Northern Ireland Executive), Helen's Bay, 9 July 2002

Rev. Martin Smyth (UUP MP for South Belfast 1982–205), Westminster, 22 June 2005

Dick Spring (Tánaiste and Foreign Minister 1993–97), Dublin, 6 Sept. 2001

Paddy Teahon (senior Irish negotiator), Dublin, 31 Nov. 2001

Rt. Hon. David Trimble MLA (First Minister of Northern Ireland 1998–2002; UUP Leader 1995–2005, MP for Upper Bann 1990–2005), Westminster, 8 June 2005

Periodicals and television archives

Belfast Telegraph	*Irish Independent*
Financial Times	*Irish Press*
Fortnight	*Irish Times*
Guardian	*The Times* (London)

BBC Northern Ireland Archive, Ulster Folk and Transport Museum, Cultra, County Down: all relevant political data recorded between 1972 and 1998

The National Archives (incorporating the Public Record Office), London

CJ3/25 Relations with the Irish Republic 1970 NIO

CJ4/48 NIO Tripartite Talks

FCO33/1606 Political Relations between Republic of Ireland and Northern Ireland

FCO33/1611 Meetings between the Prime Ministers of UK and Republic of Ireland

PREM15/486 Meetings between Prime Minister and Mr Lynch

PREM15/487 Tripartite meeting at Chequers between Prime Minister, Mr Faulkner and Mr Lynch

Offical publications

Anglo/Irish Relations: August 1969 to October 1971 (Dublin: Government Information Bureau, 1972)

The Future of Northern Ireland (Belfast: HMSO, 1972)

Northern Ireland Constitutional Proposals (Belfast: HMSO, 1973)

The Northern Ireland Act, 1973 (London: HMSO, 1973)

Cosgrave Liam, *Text of Opening and Closing Statements at Sunningdale: 6–9 December 1973* (Dublin: Government Information Services 1973)

Text of Opening and Closing Statements at Sunningdale, 6–9 December 1973 (Dublin: Government Information Bureau, 1973)

Northern Ireland Assembly Official Report of Debates, Vols. 1–3, July 1973 – May 1974 (Belfast: HMSO)

Hansard Parliamentary Debates, 1973–74 (London: HMSO)

Anglo-Irish Agreement (London: HMSO, 1985)

Joint Declaration (London: HMSO, 1993)

A Framework for Accountable Government in Northern Ireland (London: HMSO, 1995)

A New Framework for Agreement: A Shared Understanding between the British and Irish Governments to Assist Discussion and Negotiation Involving the Northern Ireland Parties (London: HMSO, 1995)

Hansard Parliamentary Debates, 1997–98 (London: HMSO)

Propositions on Heads of Agreement (HMSO London 1998)

Agreement between the Government of the United Kingdom of Great Britain and Northern Ireland and the Government of Ireland (London: HMSO, 1998)

Independent Monitoring Commission: Reports 1–5 (London: HMSO, 2005)

Jack Lynch's Speeches and Statements on Irish Unity and Northern Ireland (Dublin: Government Information Bureau)

Proposals by the British and Irish Governments for a Comprehensive Agreement, 8 December 2004 (London: HMSO, 2004)

Political memoirs

Bloomfield, Kenneth, *Stormont in Crisis* (Belfast: Blackstaff Press, 1994)

Devlin, Paddy, *Straight Left: An Autobiography* (Belfast: Blackstaff Press, 1993)

Duignan, Séan, *One Spin on the Merry-Go-Round* (Dublin: Blackwater Press, 1996)

Faulkner, Brian, *Memoirs of a Statesman* (London: Weidenfeld & Nicolson, 1978)

FitzGerald, Garret, *All in a Life* (London: Macmillan, 1991)

Heath, Edward, *The Course of My Life* (London: Hodder & Stoughton, 1998)

Hume, John, *Personal Views: Politics Peace and Reconciliation in Ireland* (Dublin: Town House, 1996)

McMichael, Gary, *An Ulster Voice* (Boulder, CO: Roberts Rinehart, 1999)

Major, John, *John Major: The Autobiography* (London: HarperCollins, 1999)

Mitchell, George, *Making Peace* (New York: Alfred Knopf, 1999)

O'Brien, Conor Cruise, *Memoir: My Life and Themes* (Dublin: Poolbeg Press, 1999)

O'Neill, Terence, *Autobiography* (London: Rupert Hart-Davis, 1972)

Rees, Merlyn, *Northern Ireland: A Personal Perspective* (London: Methuen, 1985)

Thatcher, Margaret, *The Downing Street Years* (London: HarperCollins, 1993)

Trimble, David, *To Raise up a New Northern Ireland: Articles and Speeches 1998–2000* (Belfast: Belfast Press, 2001)

Whitelaw, William, *The Whitelaw Memoirs* (London: Aurum Press, 1989)

Wilson, Harold, *Final Term: The Labour Government, 1974–76* (London: Weidenfeld & Nicolson, 1979)

Secondary sources

Akenson Donald, *God's Peoples: Convenant and Land in South Africa, Israel, and Ulster* (Ithaca: Cornell University Press, NY, 1992)

Arthur, P., *Special Relationships: Britain, Ireland and the Northern Ireland Problem* (Belfast: Blackstaff Press, 2000)

Aughey, Arthur, *Under Siege: Ulster Unionism and the Anglo-Irish Agreement* (Belfast: Blackstaff Press, 1989)

Bardon, J., *A History of Ulster* (Belfast: Blackstaff Press, 1992)

Bew, Paul, Gibbon Peter and Henry Patterson, *Northern Ireland, 1921–1994* (London: Serif, 1995)

de Bréadún, Denglán, *The Far Side of Revenge: Making Peace in Northern Ireland* (Cork: Collins Press, 2001)

Cochrane, F., *Unionist Politics and the Politics of Unionism since the AIA* (Cork: Cork University Press, 2001)

Cox, Harvey, 'Managing Northern Ireland Intergovernmentally: An Appraisal of the Anglo-Irish Agreement', *Parliamentary Affairs*, 40:1, (1987), 80–97

Cox, Michael, 'Bringing in the International: The IRA Ceasefire and the End of the Cold War', *International Affairs*, 73:4 (1997), 671–93

Dixon, P., 'Paths to Peace in Northern Ireland (I): Civil Society and the Consociational Approaches', *Democratisation*, 4:2 (1997), 1–27
'Paths to Peace in Northern Ireland (II): The Peace Processes, 1973–74 and 1994–96', *Democratization*, 4:3 (1997), 1–25

Dixon, P., *Northern Ireland: The Politics of War and Peace* (New York:

Palgrave, 2001)

Elliott, Sydney, and W. D. Flackes, *Northern Ireland: A Political Directory, 1968–99* (Belfast: Blackstaff Press, 1999)

English, Richard, 'Challenging Peace', *Fortnight*, 362, 1997, 24–5

Fisk, Robert, *The Point of No Return: The Strike that Broke the British in Ulster* (London: André Deutsch, 1975)

Gallagher, Michael, 'Do Unionists have a Right to Self-Determination?', *Irish Political Studies*, 5 (1990), 11–30

Godson, D., *Himself Alone: David Trimble and the Ordeal of Unionism* (London: HarperCollins, 2004)

Guelke, Adrian, *Northern Ireland: The International Perspective* (New York: St. Martin's Press, 1988)

Guelke, Adrian, 'British Policy and the International Dimensions of the Northern Ireland Conflict', *Regional Politics and Policy*, (1991), 140-160

Guelke, Adrian, 'The Peace Process in South Africa, Israel and Northern Ireland: A Farewell to Arms', *Irish Studies in International Affairs*, 5 (1994), 93–106

Guelke, Adrian, 'The International System and the Northern Ireland Peace Process', *Working Papers in British–Irish Studies*, 21 (2002)

Hadden, Tom, and Kevin Boyle, *The Anglo-Irish Agreement: Commentary, Text and Official Review* (London: Sweet & Maxwell, 1989)

Hadfield, B., *The Constitution of Northern Ireland* (Belfast: SLS, 1989)

Hennessy, T., *A History of Northern Ireland: 1920–96* (London: Macmillan, 1997)

Kennedy, L, *Two Ulsters: A Case for Repartition* (Belfast: Queens University Belfast, 1986)

Kerr, Michael, *Transforming Unionism: David Trimble and the 2005 Election* (Dublin: Irish Academic Press, 2005)

Mawhinney, Brian and Ronald Wells, *Conflict and Christianity in Northern Ireland* (Berkhamstead: Lion Publishing, 1975)

McGarry, John, 'Political Settlement in Northern Ireland and South Africa', *Political Studies*, 46:4 (1998), 53–70

McGarry, John, (ed.) *Northern Ireland and the Divided World* (London and New York: Oxford University Press, 2001)

McGarry, John, and Brendan O'Leary, *The Future of Northern Ireland* (Oxford University Press, 1990)

McGarry, John and Brendan O'Leary, *Explaining Northern Ireland* (Oxford: Blackwell, 1995)

Mallie, Eamonn and David McKittrick, *The Fight for Peace: The Secret Story behind the Irish Peace Process* (London: Heinemann, 1996)

Mallie, Eamonn and David McKittrick, *Endgame in Ireland* (London: Hodder & Stoughton, 2001)

Millar, Frank, *David Trimble: The Price of Peace* (Dublin: Liffy Press, 2004)

Miller, David, *Queen's Rebels: Ulster Loyalism in Historical Perspective* (Dublin: Gill & Macmillan, 1973)

Mitchell, Paul, 'Conflict Regulation and Party Competition in Northern Ireland', *European Journal of Political Research*, 20 (1991), 67–92

Mitchell, Paul and Rick Wilford (eds), *Politics in Northern Ireland* (Boulder, CO: Westview Press, 1999)

Mullan, D., *The Dublin and Monaghan Bombings* (Dublin: Wolfhound Press, 2000)

O'Clery, Conor, *The Greening of the White House* (Dublin: Gill & Macmillan, 1996)

O'Duffy, Brendan, 'British and Irish Conflict Regulation from Sunningdale to Belfast: Part I: 'Tracing the Status of Courting Sovereigns, 1968–1974', *Nations and Nationalism*, 5:4 (1999), 523–42, and 'British and Irish Conflict Regulation from Sunningdale to Belfast: Part II: Playing for a Draw, 1985–1999', *Nations and Nationalism*, 6:3 (2000), 399–435

O'Leary, Brendan, 'The Limits to Coercive Consociationalism in Northern Ireland', *Politics Studies*, 37:4 (1989), 562–88

O'Leary, Brendan, 'The Conservative Stewardship of Northern Ireland, 1979–97: Sound-bottomed Contradictions or Slow Learning?', *Political Studies*, 45:4 (1997), 663–76

O'Leary, Brendan, 'The Nature of the British–Irish Agreement', *New Left Review*, 233 (1999), 66–96

O'Leary, Brendan and John McGarry, *The Politics of Antagonism: Understanding Northern Ireland* (London: Athlone Press, 1996)

Rose, Richard, *Governing Without Consensus* (London: Faber & Faber, 1971)

Rowan, Brian, *Behind the Lines: The Story of the IRA and Loyalist Ceasefires* (Belfast: Blackstaff Press, 1995)

Ruane, Joseph and Jennifer Todd, *The Dynamics of Conflict in Northern Ireland: Power, Conflict and Emancipation* (Cambridge: Cambridge University Press, 1996)

Ruane, Joseph and Jennifer Todd (eds), *After the Good Friday Agreement* (Dublin: UCD Press, 1999)

Schulze, K., 'The Northern Ireland Political Process: A Viable Approach to Conflict Resolution?' *Irish Political Studies*, 12 (1997), 92–110

Stewart, A. T. Q., *The Narrow Ground: Aspects of Ulster, 1609–1969* (Belfast: Blackstaff Press, 1977)

Whyte, John, *Interpreting Northern Ireland* (Oxford: Clarendo Press, 1990)

Wright, F., *Northern Ireland: A Comparative Analysis* (Dublin: Gill & Macmillan, 1987)

LEBANON

Interviews

Mahmoud Ammar (Shi'a deputy for Baabda 1972; Minister of Information 1974; negotiator at Ta'if 1989), Hasmieh, 25 April 2002

Mohamed Baalbaki (President of Lebanese Press Syndicate from 1984), Beirut, 12 June 2002

Chafic Badre (Maronite deputy for Alay 1972; negotiator at Ta'if 1989), Hamra, 22 April 2002

August Bakkos (deputy for Matn 1972; negotiator at Ta'if 1989), Dawra, 10 April 2002

Dr Vincent Battle (US Ambassador to Lebanon 2001–4), Aoukar, 14 June 2002

Dr Ahmad Baydoun (academic), Hamra, 27 Nov. 2001

Fouad Boutros (Minister of Foreign Affairs 1976–82), Ashrafieh, 6 Dec. 2001

Assad Chaftari (former Lebanese Forces intelligence officer and senior negotiator for Elie Hobieka), Hamra, 19 Nov. 2001

Dr Rafic Chahine (Shi'a deputy for Nabatien 1974; Minister for Labour and Social Affairs 1969–70; negotiator at Ta'if 1989), Beirut, 17 April 2002

Dory Chamoun (National Liberal Party Leader from 1990), Ashrafieh, 30 Nov. 2001

Charles Chartouni (Lebanese Forces), Ashrafieh, 12 June 2002

Muhieddin Chehab (former Mourabitoun combatant and Sunni major in Beirut), Hamra, 28 Nov. 2001

Dr Pierre Daccache (Maronite deputy for Matn 1972; negotiator at Ta'if 1989), Beirut, 8 and 29 April 2002

Nadim Dimechkie (Lebanese Ambassador to US 1958–62), Hamra, 1 June 2002

Carlos Eddé (National Bloc Leader), Ashrafieh, 4 Dec. 2001

Elie Ferzli (Greek Orthodox Deputy Speaker from 1992), Beirut, 2 May 2002

Robert Fisk (journalist, *Independent*), Beirut, 13 June 2002

Former Senior Amal leader, Raouche, 25 June 2002

Samir Franjieh (Maronite opposition leader) Beirut, 22 Nov. 2001

Amin Gemayel (President of Lebanon 1982–88), Sin al-Fil, 4 Dec. 2001

Timor Goksel (UNIFIL senior political spokesman from 1982), UNIFIL headquarters, Naqoura, 26 Nov. 2001

Amin Haffez (Prime Minister of Lebanon April 1973 to June 1973), Beirut, 5 June 2002

Boutros Harb (Maronite deputy for Batrun 1972, Minister of Public Works and Education 1979; negotiator at Ta'if 1989), Ashrafieh, 11 June 2002

Rafic Hariri (Prime Minister of Lebanon 1992–98 and 2000–4), Quoriten, Beirut, 26 June 2002

Pierre Helleu (Maronite deputy for Aley 1972, negotiator at Ta'if 1989; Government Minister 2000–3), Beirut, 23 April 2002

Dr Salim al-Hoss (Prime Minister of Lebanon 1976–80, 1987–90 and 1998–2000), Ashibakar, Beirut, 3 Dec. 2001

Hussein al-Housseini (Speaker of Lebanese Parliament 1972–92; Shi'a deputy for Baalbeck-Hermal; Chairman of Committee of Seventeen at Ta'if 1989), Raouche, 24 Nov. 2001, and 18 and 24 June 2002

Talal Housseini (Shi'a adviser and drafter at Ta'if), Hamra, 22 Nov. 2001 and 28 May 2002

David Hurst (former *Guardian* correspondent in Lebanon), Beirut, 13 April 2002

Basim al-Jisr (political adviser, academic and journalist), Beirut, 4 April 2002

Walid Jumblat (President of the PSP from 1977), Beirut, 9 April 2002

Khalid Kabbani (senior judge and Sunni adviser at Ta'if), Justice d'état, Beirut, 13 June 2002

Mohammad Kabbani (Sunni deputy for Beirut from 2000), Hamra, 1 and 7 Dec. 2001

Rashid el-Kadi (Housseini's press officer during Ta'if period), Beirut, 17 April 2002

Abdullah Kaffir (Shi'a deputy for Tripoli, Hizbollah, from 2000), Lebanese Parliament, Beirut, 20 Nov. 2001

Dr Elie Karame (Kataeb Leader 1984), Ashrafieh, 23 Nov. 2001

Dr Ali Khalil (Shi'a deputy for Tyre 1972; Minister of Finance 1979–82; negotiator at Ta'if 1989), Beirut, 17 June 2002

Zaher el-Khatib (Shi'a deputy for the Chuf 1972; National Front; negotiator at Ta'if 1989), Beirut, 28 May 2002

Dr Farid el-Khazen (Chairman and Professor of Political Science, American University of Beirut), Beirut, 10 June 2002

Michel al-Khoury (Bashara al-Khoury's son; Minister of Information and Defence 1965–66), Ashrafieh, 23 May 2002

Nasri Maalouf (Greek Catholic deputy for Beirut 1972; Minister of Finance 1956–57; negotiator at Ta'if 1989), Ashrafieh, 26 April 2002

Dr Joseph Maila (academic), Beirut, 23 April 2002

Dr Bechara Manassa (Christian adviser at Ta'if) Ashrafieh, 30 May 2002

Maronite Bishop Paul Mattar, Ashrafieh, 31 June 2002

Nayla Moawad (Maronite deputy for Zghorta; former President's widow), Beirut, 5 Dec. 2001

Dr Albert Monsour (Greek Catholic Deputy 1972; Minister of Defence 1989–92; negotiator at Ta'if 1989), Beirut, 15 April 2002

Bhraim el-Moussawi (former Hizballah spokesman), Hamra, 26 April 2002

Nicholas Nassif (*an-Nahar* reporter), Hamra, 28 June 2002

Karim Pakradouni (Kataeb leader), Ashrafieh, 15 May 2002

Riad el-Rayyes (publisher and journalist), Hamra, 7 May 2002

Hassan Rifi (Sunnite deputy for Baalbeck-Hermal 1972), Beirut, 27 May 2002

Edmond Rizk (Maronite deputy for Jazzine 1972; Minister for Justice and Information 1989–92; negotiator at Ta'if 1989), Ashrafieh, 26 April 2002

Antoine Saad (Lebanese Forces, Geagea), Ashrafieh, 19 April 2002

Farid Salman (political adviser and writer), Beirut, 24 April 2002 and 23 May 2002

Talal Salman (editor of *el-Sifr*), Hamra, 20 June 2002

Nasrallah Sfeir (Maronite Patriarch from 1986), Bkirke, 23 June 2002

Elie Skaff (Greek Catholic deputy), Baabda, 19 April 2002

Monah el-Solh (historian), Beirut, 18 April 2002 and 2 May 2002

Rashid Solh (Prime Minister of Lebanon 1974–75 and 1992), Beirut, 7 and 9 May 2002

Dr Jubran Toak (Maronite deputy for Bsharreh 1972; negotiator at Ta'if 1989), Beirut, 8 May 2002

Dr Fawaz Traboulsi (Communist Party), Beirut, 8 April 2002

Ghassan Tuéni (former editor of *an-Nahar* Permanent Representative of Lebanon to the UN 1977–82), Ashrafieh, 30 April 2002

Gibran Tuéni (publisher of *an-Nahar*; associate of Aoun), Hamra, 20 Nov. 2001

UN press officer (Hasan), Naqoura, 29 Nov. 2001

Najah Wakim (Sunnite deputy for Beirut 1972; negotiator at Ta'if 1989), Beirut, 13 May 2002

Periodicals and television archives

Avenire
Beirut Review (including commentary by Antoine Messarra)
Daily Star (Beirut)
Independent (London)
Middle East Insight
Middle East Reporter
Monday Morning
Palestine Post
Panorama of Events (including commentary by Antoine Messarra)
al-Tariq
The Times (London)

Al-Jazeera Television, DVD, *War of Lebanon: So That History Doesn't Repeat Itself!*, Parts 1–15 (2001)

The National Archives (incorporating the Public Record Office), London

CAB122/810 Lebanon Dispute 1943–44
FO195/2478 Syria and Lebanon: Political Situation 1943
FO226/266 Treaty Negotiations 1944
FO366/1402 Resignation of Spears
FO660/35 Political: Syria and Lebanon Part I
FO660/36 Political: Syria and Lebanon Part II
FO684/15 Lebanon Political 1944
PREM3/421 Lebanon and Syria
PREM3/422/13 Lebanon and Syria
WO201/982 Crisis Lebanon Nov. 1943

Middle East Centre Archive, St Antony's College, Oxford

File 1 Spears Visit to London July 1943
File 2 English Translation of Spears's *al-Hayat* interview
Files 3 and 4 Lebanese Constitutional Crisis Nov./Dec. 1943
File 6 Relations with the French and British Policy towards the French in
   the Levant 1942–45
File 7 General Spears's Correspondence with Churchill 1941–54
GB165-2069 Box III
GB165-2069 Box II
Spears Papers

Other documents

CEDRE (eds), *Lebanese–Israeli Negotiations: Chronology, Bibliography,
   Documents and Maps* (Beirut: CEDRE: The Lebanese Centre for
   Documentation and Research, 1984)
Statement by the Five Permanent Members of the UN Security Council,
   31 Oct. 1989
The Meeting for the Charter and the Constitution: A Conference on the
   Fate of the Ta'if Accord – Reminding and Requesting the Fulfilment
   of Promises, 14 Dec. 2001

Political memoirs

Casey, Richard, *Personal Experience, 1939–46* (London: Constable 1962)
Chiha, Michel, 'Une histoire juive' in *Palestine* (Beirut: Foundation
   Chiha, 1994), pp. 19–22
de Gaulle, Charles, *War Memoirs*, Vol. I, *The Call to Honour, 1940–42*
   (London: Collins, 1955)
de Gaulle, Charles, *War Memoirs*, Vol. I, *The Call to Honour, 1940–42 –
   Documents* (London: Collins, 1955)
de Gaulle Charles, *War Memoirs*, Vol. II, *Unity, 1942–44* (London:

Weidenfeld & Nicolson, 1959)

de Gaulle Charles, *War Memoirs*, Vol. III, *Salvation* (London: Weidenfeld & Nicolson, 1960)

Schultz, George, *Turmoil and Triumph* (New York: Macmillan, 1993)

Spears, Edward, *Fulfilment of a Mission* (London: Seeley, Service and Cooper, 1977)

Weinberger, Caspar, *Fighting for Peace* (London: Michael Joseph, 1990)

Secondary sources published in English

Abul-Husn, L., *The Lebanese Conflict* (Boulder, CO: Lynne Rienner Publishers, 1998)

Agwani, M. (ed.), *The Lebanese Crisis, 1958* (London: Asia Publishing House, 1965)

Antonius, G., *The Arab Awakening* (London: Hamish Hamilton, 1938)

Atiyah, E., 'The Levant Dispute: The Arab Case', *World Affairs*, (Jan. 1946), 336–47

Avi-Ran, R., *The Syrian Involvement in Lebanon Since 1975* (Boulder, CO: Westview Press, 1991)

Baram, Amatzia and Barry Rubin (eds), *Iraq's Road to War* (Basingstoke: Palgrave, 1996)

Bernal, M., *Black Athena: The Afroasiatic Root of Classical Civilization*, Vol. I (London: Free Association Books, 1987)

Binder, Leonard, *Politics in Lebanon* (London: J. Wiley & Sons, 1966)

Braude, Benjamin and Bernard Lewis (eds), *Christians and Jews in the Ottoman Empire*, vol. 2 (London: Holmes & Meier Publishers, 1992)

Chiha, Michel, *Visage et présence du Liban* (Beirut: Cénacles Libanais, 1964)

Collings, D. (ed.), *Peace for Lebanon? From War to Reconstruction* (Boulder, CO: Lynne Rienner Publishers, 1994)

Deeb, Marius, *The Lebanese Civil War* (New York: Praeger, 1980)

Dekmejian, R., 'Consociational Democracy in Crisis: The Case of Lebanon', *Comparative Politics*, 10:2 (1978), 251–66

Fromkin, D., *A Peace to End all Peace* (London: André Deutsch, 1989)

Gaunson, A., *The Anglo-French Clash in Lebanon and Syria, 1940–45* (London: Macmillan, 1987)

Goria, W., *Sovereignty and Leadership in Lebanon, 1943–76* (London: Ithaca Press, 1985)

Haddad, W., *Lebanon: The Politics of Revolving Doors* (New York: Praeger, 1985)

Hanf, Theodor, *Coexistence in Wartime Lebanon: The Decline of a State and the Rise of a Nation* (London: I. B. Tauris, 1993)

Hourani, Albert, *The Emergence of the Modern Middle East* (London: Macmillan, 1981)

Hudson, Michael, 'A Case of Political Development', *Journal of Politics*,

29:4 (1967), 821–37

Hudson, Michael, *The Precarious Republic: Political Modernisation in Lebanon* (New York: Random House, 1968)

Khalidi, Walid, *Conflict and Violence in Lebanon* (Cambridge, MA: Harvard University Press, 1979)

el-Khazen, Farid, *The Communal Pact of National Identities: The Making and Politics of the 1943 National Pact* (Oxford: Centre for Lebanese Studies, 1991)

el-Khazen, Farid, *The Breakdown of the State in Lebanon, 1967–76* (London: I. B. Tauris, 2000)

Longrigg, Stephen H., *Syria and Lebanon under French Mandate* (London and New York: Oxford University Press, 1958)

Maila, Joseph [Sami Dilali], 'L'Accord tripartite', *Les Cahiers de l'Orient*, 1986

Maila, Joseph, *The Document of National Understanding: A Commentary* (Oxford: Centre for Lebanese Studies, 1992)

Ma'oz, Moshe, *Assad: The Sphinx of Damascus* (London: Weidenfeld & Nicolson, 1988)

Messarra, Antoine, 'A Consociative Approach to Lebanon's Political System', *Panorama of Events*, 24 (1981)

Messarra, Antoine, 'National Edification through Pacts and National contition', *Panorama of Events*, 47 (1987) Summaries 36

Messarra, Antoine, 'A Problematic Approach to the State of Lebanon: A Debate', *Panorama of Events*, 12:51 (1988)

Mickelsen, Martin, 'Another Fashoda: The Anglo-Free French Conflict over the Levant, May–September 1941' *Revue Française, d'histoire, d'Outre-Mer*, 63:230 (1976), 75–100

Norton, A. R., *Amal and the Shi'a: Struggle for the Soul of Lebanon* (Austin: University of Texas Press, 1987)

Norton, A. R., 'Lebanon after Ta'if: Is the Civil War Over?', *Middle East Journal*, 45:3 (Summer 1991), 457–73

Phares, W., *Lebanese Christian Nationalism* (Boulder, CO: Lynne Rienner Publishers, 1995)

Picard, Elizabeth, *Lebanon: A Shattered Country* (New York: Holmes & Meir, 1996)

Pierre-Viénot, Andrée, 'The Levant Dispute: The French Case', *World Affairs* (Oct. 1945), 219–28

Quandt, W., 'Reagan's Lebanon Policy: Trial and Error', *Middle East Journal*, 32:8 (1984), 237–54

Rabinovich, I., 'Israel, Syria and Lebanon', *International Journal*, 45 (Summer 1990), 529–552

Rieck, A., 'A Peace Plan for Lebanon?: Prospects after the Ta'if Agreement', *Aussenpolitik*, 3 (1990), 297–309

Salem, Elie, *Violence and Diplomacy in Lebanon: The Troubled Years, 1982–1988* (London: I. B. Tauris, 1995)

Salibi, Kemal, *Crossroads to Civil War: Lebanon, 1958–76* (London: Ithaca Press, 1976)

Salibi, Kemal, *A House of Many Mansions: The History of Lebanon Reconsidered* (Berkeley, Los Angeles, and London: University of California Press, 1988)

Schulze, Kirsten, *Israel's Covert Diplomacy in Lebanon* (NY: St. Martin's Press, 1997)

Seale, Patrick, *Assad: The Struggle for the Middle East* (Berkeley, Los Angeles and London: University of California Press, 1996)

Shehadi, N. and D. Mills (eds), *Lebanon: A History of Conflict and Consensus* (Oxford: Centre for Lebanese Studies, 1988)

Shlaim, Avi, *The Iron Wall: Israel and the Arab World* (London: Allen Lane, 2000)

Spagnolo, J., 'Constitutional Change in Mount Lebanon, 1861–1864', *Middle Eastern Studies*, 7:1 (1971), 25–48

Spagnolo, J., *France and Ottoman Lebanon: 1861–1914* (London: Ithaca Press, 1977)

Suleiman, M., *Political Parties in Lebanon* (Ithaca, NY: Cornell University Press, 1967)

Weinberger, N., *Syrian Intervention in Lebanon, The 1975–76 Civil War* (London and New York: Oxford University Press, 1986)

Winslow, Charles, *Lebanon: War and Politics in a Fragmented Society* (London: Routledge, 1996)

Zamir, Meir, *The Formation of Modern Lebanon, 1918–1926* (London: Croom Helm 1985)

Zamir, Meir, 'New Light Shed on the Making of the National Pact', Parts I and II, *al-Hayat* (Nov. 1999)

Zamir, Meir, *Lebanon's Quest: The Road to Statehood, 1926–1939* (London: I.B. Tauris, 2000)

Ziadeh, N., *Syria and Lebanon* (London: Ernest Benn, 1957)

Zisser, Eyal, *Lebanon: The Challenge of Independence* (London: I. B. Tauris, 2000)

Unpublished secondary source in French

Maila, Joseph, *The Republic of Ta'if Thirteen Years Later*, lecture given at St-Joseph University, Beirut, 18 April 2002

Secondary sources published in Arabic

al-Jisr, B., *Mithaq 1943: Limaza Kan wa-Limaza Saqat* (Beirut: Dar al-Nahar Lilnashr, 1978)

Monsour, A., *Al-Inqil-ab ala al-Ta'if* (Beirut: Dar al-Jadid, 1993)

El-Rayyes, R., *Lebanon: A History Unspoken Of* (Beirut: El-Rayyes Books, 2001)

CONSOCIATIONAL THEORY

Barry, Brian, 'Review Article: Political Accommodation and Consociational Democracy' *British Journal of Political Science*, 5:4 (1975), 477–505

Barry, Brian, 'The Consociational Model and its Dangers', *European Journal of Political Research*, 3 (1975), 393–413

Bogaards, M., 'The Favourable Factors for Consociational Democracy: A Review', *European Journal of Political Research*, 33 (1998), 475–496.

Butenschøn, N., 'Conflict Management in Plural Societies: The Consociational Democracy Formula', *Scandinavian Political Studies*, 8:1–2 (1985), 85–103

Daalder, H., 'The Consociational Democracy Theme', *World Politics*, 26:4 (1974), 604–21

Halpern, S., 'The Disorderly Universe of Consociational Democracy' *West European Politics*, 9:2 (1986), 181–97

Lembruch, G., 'Consociational Democracy in the International System', *European Journal of Political Research*, 3 (1975), 377–91

Lijphart, Arend, 'Consociational Democracy', *World Politics*, 21:2 (1969), 207–25

Lijphart, Arend, 'The Northern Ireland Problem: Cases, Theories, and Solutions' *British Journal of Political Studies*, 5:3 (1975), 83–106

Lijphart, Arend, *Democracy in Plural Societies* (New Haven, CT: Yale University Press, 1977)

Lustick, I., 'Stability in Deeply Divided Societies: Consociationalism versus Control', *World Politics*, 31 (1979), 325–44

Lustick, I., 'Lijphart, Lakatos and Consociationalism', *World Politics*, 50:1 (1997), 88–117

Messarra, Antoine, 'Between Good Luck and Bad: How is Lebanon to be Independent?', *The Beirut Review*, 6 (1993), 7–14

Nordlinger, Eric, *Conflict Regulation in Divided Societies* (Cambridge, MA: Harvard University Press,1972)

O'Leary, Brendan, 'Consociation: What We Know or Think We Know and What We Need to Know', unpublished manuscript, 2003

Pappalardo, Adriano, 'The Conditions for Consociational Democracy: A Logical and Empirical Critique', *European Journal of Political Research*, 9:4 (1981), 365–90

Rea, D., *Political Cooperation in Divided Societies* (Dublin: Gill & Macmillan, 1982)

Steiner, J., 'The Consociational Theory and Beyond', *Comparative Politics*, (April 1981), 339–54

Walzer, Michael, *On Toleration* (New Haven, CT: Yale University Press, 1977)

Index

Abul-Husn, L., 19, 24–5, 133–4, 176, 177
Adams, Gerry, 77, 82, 83, 91, 92, 96, 102
Adib Pasha, Auguste, 114
Agreement of 17 May (1983), 144, 148–9, 150
Ahern, Bertie, 84–6, 96, 98, 101–3
Akkar, 172
Alawites in Lebanon, 161, 172, 173, 182
Alawites in Syria, 182, 199
Algeria, 153, 169
Alliance Party of Northern Ireland, 11, 13, 45, 47, 53, 63, 65, 74, 93
Amal, 150, 164, 170, 174, 185, 186
Anglo-Irish Agreement (1985), 12–14, 30, 61, 73–7, 81–2, 85, 88, 90, 100, 180
Antrim, County, 57
Aoun, Michel, 153–8, 163, 170, 171, 174, 176, 181
Arab identity of Lebanon, 119, 120, 123, 128, 133, 135, 145–7, 150, 160, 167, 189, 195
Arab-Israeli conflict, 6, 22, 31, 133, 141–9, 160, 168, 176–7, 180, 187, 191, 200
Arab League, 133, 143, 148, 152–3
Arab nationalism, 3, 18, 29, 37, 112–14, 116–20, 122–4, 127–9, 132–5
Arab National Party, 118
Arab states: dictatorships in, 23, 168, 198; independence movements in, 29, 113, 122, 132; Lebanon and, 117, 119, 127, 132, 148, 153, 169, 195; and Palestinians, 19; rivalries among, 22, 128, 133, 135; and Syrian hegemony in Lebanon, 168, 194, 199; and Ta'if Agreement, 24, 153, 190
Aramaic ethnicity, 18
Arida, Antoun (Patriarch), 123
Armagh, North, 57
Armenians in Lebanon, 18, 137, 161, 173
army, British, in Northern Ireland, 51–3, 68–70, 74

army, Jordanian, 143
army, Lebanese, 23, 136, 143–4, 147, 150–1, 156–7, 162–3, 167–8, 171
army, Syrian, 147, 148, 153–5, 163, 164, 168–72, 177, 183, 186, 188, 191, 195
Arthur, Paul, 10
Assad, Hafiz al-, 146–57, 169, 170, 180, 197, 200
Assembly, Northern Ireland: *see under* Northern
Austria, 40

Baghdad Pact (1955), 126
Ballylumford power station, 70
Bann, River, 56, 207
Battle, Vincent, 159
Beirut, 39, 113, 114, 117–18, 122, 149, 151–4, 157–8, 174, 176
Bekaa Valley, 114, 171
Belfast, 51, 65
Benjedid, Chadli, 153
Berri, Nabih, 150, 164, 173
Bew, Paul, 11
Bhutto, Benazir, 12
bill of rights: *see* human rights provisions
Blair, Tony, 84–6, 96–9, 101–3, 109, 110, 181
Bloomfield, Sir Kenneth, 41, 61, 63, 71
Blum, Léon, 115
Boland v. *An Taoiseach* (1973), 49, 68
border, Irish, 45
Bosnia-Herzegovina, 38, 40, 193
Bradford, Roy, 50, 52, 53, 65
British government(s), 31, 37, 39, 41, 112, 196; and Anglo-Irish Agreement, 13, 73–6; Bill Clinton and, 92; coercive pressure of, 29, 188, 192, 198, 199; and colonial empire, 112, 113, 115; discussion paper (October 1972) by, 44; and Downing Street Declaration, 79–83, 90–1; and Good Friday Agreement, 1, 6, 14, 36, 72, 87, 88, 103, 109–11, 180–1, 185, 187, 191, 197; influenced by John Hume, 30; and integrationism, 11;

interest in Northern Ireland of, 77,
   78, 84; and Iraq, 39, 120; and Ireland
   (1801–1922), 10; rivalry in Lebanon
   between French and, 29, 112–24,
   129–32, 139, 187; and Lebanon since
   independence, 126–8; and Northern
   Ireland (1922–72), 10; and peace
   process (1997–98) in Northern
   Ireland, 84–6, 93, 95–7, 99, 100, 104;
   talks between Sinn Féin and, 78,
   82–4; and Sunningdale Agreement, 1,
   4–5, 47, 48, 51, 58–60, 62, 63, 67–9,
   71, 100, 103, 110, 182; White Paper
   (March 1973) by, 42–6, 55, 58, 60
British-Irish Council, 88, 89, 94, 95
Brooke, Peter, 77–8
Brun, Bairbre de, 105
Bruton, John, 84
Bush, George, Sr, 149
Butler, Sir Robin, 62, 73
Byblos, 18

cabinet (Lebanon): *see* Council of
   Ministers
Cairo, 129
Cairo Agreement (1969), 19, 143, 146,
   147
Canary Wharf Tower (London), 84
Casablanca Summit (1989), 153
Casey, Richard, 119, 121
Catholics in Northern Ireland, 10, 11,
   79, 96, 185; opinions of Good Friday
   Agreement among, 107, 108; and
   power-sharing, 35–6; shifting ratio
   between Protestants and, 103; and
   Sunningdale Agreement, 52, 54–7, 71
Catholics, Greek: *see under* Greek
Catroux, Georges, 115, 116, 119, 121,
   122
ceasefires in Northern Ireland, 60, 71,
   74, 79–85, 90, 92, 100, 103
censorship in Lebanon, 171
Chamber of Deputies (France), 115
Chamber of Deputies (Lebanon), 114,
   117–19, 121, 132–3, 135, 142, 147,
   153, 155–6, 161–7, 172–5, 178, 182
Chamoun, Camille, 18, 119, 125, 126,
   142, 171
Chastelain, John de, 85, 102
Chehab, Fouad, 19, 152
Chiha, Michel, 20, 117, 119, 129, 138
Chouf, 149
Christians in Lebanon: and army, 143,
   148; in Chamber of Deputies, 142,
   156, 161–3, 166, 172, 174, 182; and
   civil war, 149, 151, 153, 154, 157–8,
   163, 164, 215; and Constitutional

Document, 146–7; demographic
   decline of, 29–30, 136–8, 164, 182;
   divisions among, 114, 115, 117, 137,
   152–4, 157–8, 181, 182; and Druze,
   16, 18, 149; and France, 20, 114,
   123, 132, 133; and struggle for
   independence, 21, 124, 129, 132; on
   Mount Lebanon, 18, 39; and Muslims,
   1, 5, 16, 21, 112, 116, 118–20,
   122–5, 127, 128, 132–6, 142, 143,
   153, 164–8, 171, 172, 186, 194, 199;
   national aspirations of, 3, 16, 112,
   114, 117, 176, 186–8; and National
   Dialogue Committee, 145; and
   National Pact, 1, 5, 20, 112, 117, 126,
   132–5, 138, 142, 167, 168; and Syria
   148, 151, 152, 168, 171, 174, 177,
   181, 194, 195, 199; and Ta'if
   Agreement, 36, 155, 156, 158, 160–6,
   168, 174, 176, 177, 195; *see also
   specific sects*
church attendance in Northern Ireland,
   10
Churchill, Winston, 115, 116, 120, 129,
   130–1
civic society theory: *see* integrationism
civil rights movement in Northern
   Ireland, 52, 59, 66
civil servants: British, 53, 72, 75, 90;
   Irish, 48, 72, 75, 90; Lebanese, 138,
   147, 163, 165, 171; Northern Ireland,
   64, 69, 70, 72
civil war in Lebanon, 1, 4–6, 16, 18, 24,
   33, 35, 133, 141–63, 168–87, 193,
   194
clans in Lebanon, 115
Clinton, Bill, 82, 91, 92
Cold War, 143, 149, 153, 169, 176
Colombia, 185
colonialism, 3, 31, 38; in Ireland, 7, 9;
   in Lebanon, 16, 21, 112–23, 129,
   139, 196
Combined Loyalist Military Command,
   80–1, 83
Committee of Seventeen (1989), 155,
   163, 165
Commons, House of (Britain), 81, 191
Communist Party (Lebanon), 171
Comprehensive Proposals (Anglo-Irish,
   2004), 99, 103, 109, 191
Conference of the Coast (1936), 118
confessionalism in Lebanon, 22–5, 33,
   114, 122, 124, 132–9, 142–7, 150,
   151, 160–6, 172–8, 193–5, 199
consent, principle of: in Lebanon, 122;
   in Northern Ireland, 59, 60, 71, 76,
   80–4, 88, 111, 188, 195

Conservative Party (Britain), 61, 79
consociation, 1–4, 7, 26–40, 179, 182,
 184, 190, 192–4, 197, 198, 200,
 204–5, 234; in Europe, 21, 22; in
 Lebanon, 5–6, 19–24, 112, 123–6,
 135, 139, 141, 153, 157, 166, 171,
 174, 175, 178, 181, 183–4, 186–9,
 194, 195, 197, 199; in Northern
 Ireland, 6, 10–16, 44, 48, 63, 71, 74,
 83, 86–9, 93, 103, 104, 110–12, 180,
 183–5, 187–9, 191–2, 194, 196, 197,
 199
Constitution, Irish, 8, 48, 49, 58–9, 61,
 75, 76, 84, 88
Constitution, Lebanese: First (1926),
 114, 118, 119, 124–6, 133, 134, 156,
 167; Second (1989), 159, 162, 167,
 170, 173
Constitutional Bloc (Lebanon), 117, 123
Constitutional Convention: *see under*
 Northern Ireland
Constitutional Document (1976), 144,
 146–7, 155, 160, 165
constitutional status of Northern Ireland,
 14–15, 42, 48, 49, 54, 59, 60, 80, 84,
 88, 104, 111, 185, 195
convivialism in Lebanon, 20, 117, 118,
 134, 138
Cooper, Frank, 60
Corish, Brendan, 45
Cosgrave, Liam, 45, 46, 48–52, 61, 62
Coughlan, Anthony, 7
Council of Ireland (proposed 1973),
 41–50, 52, 53, 57, 60–7, 70, 89, 94,
 95, 100, 105, 108
Council of Ministers (Lebanon), 155,
 161–3, 165, 170–1, 175
Council of the Isles (proposed 1998), 64
Cox, Henry, 14
Craig, William, 45, 47, 50, 51, 63, 67, 68
Currie, Austin, 53
Cyprus, 39

Dabbas, Charles, 114
Daher, Mikhail, 30
Dáil Éireann, 42, 49, 50, 77
Damascus, 116, 118, 148, 150, 152,
 156, 170, 172, 177, 186, 195, 197,
 199
Dayton Peace Accord (1995), 40, 192–3
de Gaulle, Charles, 112, 115, 116, 120,
 121, 129–32
decommissioning in Northern Ireland,
 84, 85, 88, 90, 96, 98, 99, 101, 102,
 105, 107–110, 183, 185, 191
deconfessionalisation in Lebanon, 144–7,
 150, 160–6, 172, 175, 177

Deeb, Marius, 23
demilitarisation in Northern Ireland, 96,
 181
democracy and consociation, 27, 33–6,
 40, 187, 191, 193, 194, 198; in
 Lebanon, 21, 23, 24, 166, 171, 178;
 in Northern Ireland, 60, 63, 85, 192,
 193, 197–9
Democratic Unionist Party, 9, 29; and
 Good Friday Agreement, 85, 95, 97,
 99, 100, 101, 103, 106, 109, 181,
 184, 191; and peace process
 (1997–98), 101; and Sunningdale
 Agreement, 48, 67
demographic factors, 27, 37; in Lebanon,
 29–30, 36, 114, 134, 136–9, 141,
 142, 161, 163, 164, 166, 175, 182; in
 Northern Ireland, 29, 63, 96, 103,
 185
deputy prime ministership (Lebanon),
 165
deputy speakership of Chamber of
 Deputies (Lebanon), 165
Devlin, Paddy, 48, 52, 65
d'Hondt electoral system, 88, 93, 94
direct rule over Northern Ireland, 9, 59,
 60, 75, 180, 189
district councils in Northern Ireland, 45
districts, electoral, in Lebanon, 166
Dixon, Paul, 11, 58
Dodds, Nigel, 101
Donaldson, Jeffery, 97, 98, 101
Down, North, 57
Downing Street Declaration (1993), 5,
 74, 78–84, 94, 110, 193
Draper, Morris, 148
Druze, 16, 18, 114, 134, 136, 137, 147,
 150, 161, 164, 165, 172, 173
Dublin, 51–2
Durkan, Mark, 95
Dyer, Mikhail, 152

Eames, Robin (Archbishop), 81, 83
Eddé, Émile, 115, 117–19, 121
Eden, Anthony, 129–30
Egypt, 19, 115, 120, 127–9, 132, 146
Eisenhower Doctrine (1957), 126, 142
electoral law in Lebanon, 166, 172, 174,
 178
elites, 2–4, 7, 26–8, 30–5, 38–40, 193,
 197–9; in Iraq, 39; in Lebanon, 5, 22,
 24, 25, 29, 30, 33–7, 112–13, 115,
 117, 118, 122, 124, 128, 132, 134,
 135, 138–42, 145, 155, 169, 174,
 178, 181–3, 187, 188, 190, 197; in
 Northern Ireland, 5, 10, 13, 14, 29,
 35–6, 57, 58, 68, 71, 86, 87, 104,

109, 110, 112, 180, 183, 185, 187–9, 192, 196, 199; in former Yugoslav states, 38
Empey, Sir Reg, 98, 99
ethnic conflicts, 1–4, 6, 10, 26, 27, 31–5, 38, 40, 179, 191, 193, 199; in Lebanon, 10, 16, 18, 20, 23, 112, 139, 144, 184, 187; in Northern Ireland, 10–13, 87, 88, 185, 196, 197; in former Yugoslav states, 38, 40
Europe, 37, 38, 118, 139
European Union, 39, 90, 184, 196
Executive, Northern Ireland: *see under* Northern
external factors in consociation, 2–4, 6, 7, 26–8, 30–40, 179, 189–91, 193, 194–5, 197–200; in Iraq, 39; in Lebanon, 19, 20, 22–4, 29, 34, 36, 37, 39, 113, 124–33, 135, 138, 139, 141, 143, 144, 147, 157, 167, 176, 182, 183, 186–8, 190, 191, 194–7; in Northern Ireland, 5, 13, 14, 20, 29, 36, 39, 41, 71, 74, 83, 86, 104, 110–12, 180, 181, 183–4, 189, 191, 194, 196, 197; in former Yugoslav states, 38, 40
extradition, 62, 65

Fahd, King, of Saudi Arabia, 153
fair employment policy in Northern Ireland, 43
Faisal, Prince, of Saudi Arabia, 155, 156, 168
Fashoda Incident (1898), 122, 213
Faulkner, Brian, 41, 45–53, 55, 60, 62–8, 70, 72, 100, 109, 206
Ferzli, Elie, 164
Fianna Fáil, 61, 74, 84, 85
Fine Gael, 45, 84
First Republic (Lebanon), 19, 125, 134–5, 136, 138, 170
First World War, 139
Fisk, Robert, 70
Fitt, Gerry, 47, 48, 50, 51, 53, 64–6, 68
Fitzgerald, F. Scott, 1
FitzGerald, Garret, and Anglo-Irish Agreement, 73, 74, 76; and Sunningdale Agreement, 45, 46, 48, 49, 61, 62, 66
Foreign Affairs, Department of (Ireland), 82
Foreign Office (Britain), 64, 121–2, 129–31
foreign policy, 28, 37; of Lebanon, 22, 120, 126, 128, 132, 133, 143, 150; and Northern Ireland, 42; of Syria, 168; of United States, 92

Forum, Northern Ireland: *see under* Northern Ireland
Framework Documents (1995), 84, 93, 102, 110
France, 3, 20, 21, 29, 37, 112–39, 145, 149, 157, 178, 187, 189, 190
Frangieh, Suleiman, 18, 142, 144, 146
Free French Committee, 5, 115, 116, 119–22, 129–32
French language in Lebanon, 120

Geagea, Samir, 151–3, 157–8, 174, 181
Gemayel, Amin, 148–52, 154
Gemayel, Bashir, 148, 151
Gemayel, Pierre, 147
Germany, Nazi, 115
gerrymandering in Lebanon 172, 178
Glaspie, April, 154, 169
Good Friday Agreement (1998), 1, 5, 6, 12–14, 30, 34, 36, 41, 45, 64, 67, 71–3, 85–112, 180, 183–5, 187–93, 195, 197, 199
Government of Ireland Act (1920), 42, 43, 84, 85, 88, 94, 110–11
Greater Lebanon, 5, 21, 114, 117, 118, 124, 132, 186
Greater Syria, 3, 113, 114, 117, 118, 127, 128, 146, 187, 188
Greco-Roman cultural influence in Lebanon, 18
Greek Catholics in Lebanon, 18, 114, 125, 137, 161, 173
Greek Cypriots, 39
Greek Orthodox in Lebanon, 18, 114, 118, 125, 134, 137, 161, 162, 164, 165, 173
Guelke, Adrian, 14–15, 20, 78, 180
Gulf War (1991), 157, 159, 169, 176, 180

Hama, 118
Hanf, Theodor, 19–21, 24, 134, 142, 152, 164, 170, 172
Hariri, Rafic, 150, 155, 169, 183, 199
Hassan II, King, of Morocco, 153
Haughey, Charles, 74, 76, 78, 79, 90
Heath, Edward, 41, 44–53, 59–73, 96, 97, 99, 102
Helleu, Jean, 119, 121
Hennessy, T., 67
Hizballah (Lebanon), 169, 171, 174, 185, 186
Hobeika, Elie, 150–2
Holkeri, Harri, 85
Homs, 118
Hoss, Salem al-, 152, 153, 156, 157, 170, 173

Housseini, Hussein, 153, 155, 156, 164, 172, 174
Hrawi, Elias, 156, 170
Hudson, Michael, 18–19, 22, 23
human rights provisions for Northern Ireland, 42, 43–4, 80, 89–90
Hume, John, 30; and Downing Street Declaration, 80; and Sunningdale Agreement, 46, 48, 49, 53, 60, 62, 65–6; talks between republicans and, 77–79, 90, 91
hunger strikes in Northern Ireland, 75, 77
Hussein–MacMahon Correspondence (1915–16), 113

Ibrahimi, Lakhdar, 153, 154, 157
identity cards in Lebanon, 145, 215
independence: gained by Lebanon, 21, 112, 113, 115–34, 139, 140, 177, 189, 190; gained by Syria, 123, 129, 131, 132; proposed for Northern Ireland, 9, 54, 67
integrationism in Northern Ireland, 9, 11, 12, 15, 16, 54, 58
intelligence, 84, 185
Intergovernmental Conference (Anglo-Irish), 77, 85, 88, 89, 211
internment in Northern Ireland, 48, 49, 52
Iran, 148, 169
Iraq, 32, 34, 39, 191, 199; and Britain, 115, 116, 120, 129, 132; and Lebanon, 19, 127, 128, 152, 154, 157; and Syria, 157–9, 169
Irish Americans, 79, 83, 92
Irish Civil War, 59
'Irish dimension' in Northern Ireland: in Anglo-Irish Agreement, 74, 100; in Good Friday Agreement, 195; poll results concerning, 54, 55; in Sunningdale Agreement, 42, 46, 48, 52, 62, 64, 65, 69, 195
Irish government(s), 8, 31, 37, 39, 41; and Anglo-Irish Agreement, 73–6; relations between British government and, 196; Bill Clinton and, 92; coercive pressure of, 29, 188, 192, 198, 199; and Downing Street Declaration, 79–83, 84, 90–1; and Dublin and Monaghan bombings, 52; and Good Friday Agreement, 1, 6, 14, 36, 72, 87, 88, 103, 109, 111, 180, 181, 187, 191, 197; influenced by John Hume, 30; and integrationism, 11; contacts between loyalists and, 80–1; talks between Northern Ireland

nationalists and, 77, 83; and peace process (1997–98), 85–6, 93–7, 99, 100, 104; and state-building, 10; and Sunningdale Agreement, 4–5, 42–4, 46–9, 58–60, 62, 64–6, 68, 71, 110, 182
Irish Republican Army: and British government, 51, 64, 72, 78–82, 91; ceasefire by, 79, 81, 83–5, 92; decommissioning by, 101, 102, 181; and divisions within Irish nationalism, 7, 46, 64, 66, 79, 83; and Good Friday Agreement, 97; prisoners belonging to, 77; violence of, 8, 48, 63, 68, 73, 75, 77, 78, 184, 185
irredentism, 3; Irish, 8, 9, 68; Syrian, 135
Israel, creation of, 113, 126, 128, 135; and Egypt, 146; and Lebanon, 35, 143, 145, 147–51, 153, 156, 158, 169, 171, 176, 186, 194; and Syria, 22, 146, 171; *see also* Arab-Israeli conflict
Italy, 39

Jabal Amel, 114
Jisr, Sheikh Muhammad al-, 117
Joan of Arc, 112
Jordan, 143
Jouvenel, Henri de, 114
Jumblat, Kamal, 142–5, 147, 157
Jumblat, Walid, 18, 150, 157, 165
justice system: in Lebanon, 166; in Northern Ireland, 88, 90

Karame, Abd al-Hamid, 117, 118
Karami, Omar, 170, 171
Kataeb, 170, 171
Kennedy, Liam, 15
Kerr, Malcolm, 25
Kerr, Michael, 41, 73, 159
Khaddam, Abdel Halim, 145, 146, 148, 150, 153, 172
Khazen, Farid el-, 19, 20, 22–3, 33, 135, 141
Khoury, Beshara al-, 115, 117–30, 133, 138, 152, 178
King, Frank, 69
King, Trevor, 83
King–Crane Commission (1919), 132
Kissinger, Henry, 145, 146, 158
Koleyat, 156
Kosovo, 40
Kurds in Iraq, 39
Kuwait, 152, 153, 169

Labour Party (Britain), 50, 51, 69, 82, 84

Labour Party (Ireland), 45, 76
Labour Party, Northern Ireland (former):
see under Northern
Laird, John, 48
Law Commission Report (United
Kingdom, 1974), 52
League of Nations, 113
Lebanese Arab Army, 147
Lebanese Forces, 146, 150–2, 154, 157,
170, 171
Lebanese National Movement, 145, 146,
147
'Lebanisation', 141
Lebanon, xi–xii, 1–6, 10, 26–33, 35–40,
112–91, 193–200, 201–5, 212–18,
219, 226–33; literature review, 16–25;
map of, 17; compared to Northern
Ireland, 20; as model for Northern
Ireland, 44
Lijphart, Arend, 2, 11, 13, 16, 27, 31–7,
40, 44, 184, 194
Logue, Hugh, 64
London, 84
loyalists in Northern Ireland: ceasefires
by, 74, 80, 83; Bill Clinton and, 92;
and peace process (1997–98), 85, 86,
97, 98, 100, 104; and Sunningdale
Agreement, 57, 60, 71, 180, 190;
talks between British and Irish
governments and, 80; and Ulster
Workers' Council, 51, 53
Lynch, Jack, 44, 45, 49, 59, 61

McCartney, Robert, 85, 101
Macedonia, 38, 40
McGarry, John, 2, 11, 12, 13, 16, 28,
29, 30, 74, 84, 104
McGimpsey, Chris, 8
McGimpsey, Michael, 8, 83
McGuinness, Martin, 77, 78, 96, 102,
105
McMichael, John, 77
Magee, Roy, 80, 83
Maila, Joseph, 22, 25, 163, 166, 186,
195
Major, John, 60, 78–84, 90–1
Mallon, Seamus, 66, 95
Mandelson, Peter, 103
Mansergh, Martin, 78, 80, 93, 103, 111
Maronites in Lebanon: background of,
18, 114, 123, 186, 202; in Chamber
of Deputies, 161, 173; demographic
decline of, 136, 137, 175; divisions
among, 117; and Druze, 136; external
pressures on, 29; and France, 3, 123;
national aspirations of, 114, 122, 132,
135; and National Pact, 124, 134,

136, 138, 139, 142, 160; and
neutrality, 133; and Palestinians, 142;
and presidency, 115, 124, 125, 127,
132, 146, 147, 161–7; and Syria, 113,
177; and Ta'if Agreement, 161, 163,
164, 175
martial law in Lebanon, 122, 130
Marxist views of Northern Ireland, 9
Maryfield, 74, 98
Mason, Roy, 51, 53, 69
Mayhew, Patrick, 81, 84
Meir, Golda, 12
Melkart Protocols (1973), 143, 147
Messarra, Antoine, 30, 37, 125
middle classes in Northern Ireland, 69
Middle East, 18, 37, 38, 153, 177, 200;
Britain and, 113, 116, 128, 129, 132;
France and, 3, 128, 129; Lebanon as
part of, 6, 23, 112, 113, 128, 138,
141, 152, 159, 163, 169, 182; Saudi
Arabia and, 169; Syria and, 176;
United States and, 170
militias in Lebanon, 23, 24, 142, 145,
150, 151, 155, 158, 160, 167–8, 170,
171, 174, 186; see also specific groups
millet system, 16, 21, 39, 124, 139
minorities: consocation and, 13, 39–40,
88; in Ireland as a whole, 188; in
Lebanese Chamber of Deputies, 172,
178; in Lebanon, 18, 114; in
Northern Ireland, 39, 76, 88; in Syria,
199
Mitchell, George, 85, 86, 92–4, 97
Mitchell, Paul, 13–14
Moawad, René, 156, 173
mohafazat, 166
Molyneaux, James, 64, 76, 81
Monaghan, 51–2
Morocco, 153, 169
Mount Lebanon, 16, 18, 21, 39, 113,
114, 117, 122, 135, 139, 151
Movement of the Disinherited
(Lebanon), 144
Mowlam, Mo, 85
Murphy, Richard, 152
Muslims in Lebanon: in Chamber of
Deputies, 133, 147, 156, 161, 163,
165, 166, 172; Camille Chamoun and,
126; and Christians, 1, 5, 16, 21, 112,
116, 119, 120, 122, 123, 127, 128,
134–6, 142, 143, 153, 158, 168, 172,
174; and civil war, 152, 215; on coast,
114, 117; and Council of Ministers,
163, 171; demographic rise of, 136,
137, 163; divisions among, 117, 118;
and Druze, 134, 136, 172; and
France, 20, 118, 123, 132, 133; and

struggle for independence, 21, 132; national aspirations of, 3, 16, 118, 132, 176, 186; and National Dialogue Committee, 145; and National Pact, 1, 5, 20, 112, 123–6, 132–6, 162, 164, 167; and neutrality, 133; and Palestinians, 37, 143, 146, 188, 194; and prime ministership, 146; Riad Solh and, 128; and Syria, 156, 194, 199; and Ta'if Agreement, 153, 155, 156, 161, 162, 164–5, 168, 177; and Tripartite Agreement, 151; *see also specific sects*

Naccache, Alfred, 115
Napier, Oliver, 53
Nasser, Gamal Abdel, 126, 142
Nasserism, 22, 126
National Bloc (Lebanon), 117, 119, 123
National Bloc (Syria), 123, 127
National Dialogue Committee (1975), 144, 145–6
national identity, 184–9
nationalism, Arab: *see under* Arab
nationalists in Northern Ireland, 3, 7–9, 12, 16, 30; and Anglo-Irish Agreement, 74, 76; and Catholicism, 10; Bill Clinton and, 92; demographic shift and, 103; divisions among, 105; and Downing Street Declaration, 79, 80, 84; and Forum, 85; and Good Friday Agreement, 87–9, 105–9, 183–5, 195; and peace process (1997–98), 93, 95, 96, 99, 100, 104; and Sunningdale Agreement, 41, 45, 46, 54, 57, 58, 63, 65–7
National Liberal Party (Lebanon), 171
National Pact (1943), 1, 5, 16, 18–24, 36, 37, 112–47, 150–5, 158–68, 173–8, 180, 182, 186–8, 190, 195
nation-building: in Lebanon, 18, 24, 25, 134; in Northern Ireland, 10, 104
Netherlands, 40
neutrality: Irish, 59; Lebanese, 22, 120, 128, 133, 138, 195
'9/11' (events of 11 September 2001), 177
Nordlinger, Eric, 13, 26, 28
North Armagh, 57
North Down, 57
Northern Bank robbery (2005), 185
Northern Ireland, ix–x, 1–6, 26–32, 35–40, 41–111, 179–94, 197–200, 201–12, 218–19, 220–6; compared to Lebanon, 20; literature review, 7–16; map of, 8
Northern Ireland Assembly (1973–74), 11, 42–5, 51–3, 56, 62, 64–7, 69, 70

Northern Ireland Assembly (proposed 1995), 84
Northern Ireland Assembly (since 1998), 11, 14, 88, 89, 93–6, 100–3, 110, 111, 192, 193, 195
Northern Ireland Assembly Act (1973), 42, 44, 47
Northern Ireland Constitutional Convention (1975), 73
Northern Ireland Executive (1973–74), 42, 43, 46–53, 55, 56, 60, 62, 63, 65, 66, 69–72, 86, 101, 108
Northern Ireland Executive (since 1998), 88, 94, 98, 107, 108, 110
Northern Ireland Forum (1996), 85
Northern Ireland Labour Party (former), 11, 45
North-South Ministerial Council, 85, 88, 89, 93–4, 95, 100, 102, 105

O'Brien, Conor Cruise, 45, 46
O'Clery, Conor, 92
O'Duffy, Brendan, 12, 14, 58, 84, 100
Official Unionist Party, 45, 49, 52, 64, 68, 70
oil trade, 128
Oireachtas, 89
O'Leary, Brendan, 2, 10, 11, 13, 16, 26–30, 33, 37–40, 74, 77, 79, 84, 89, 104, 110–11
O'Neill, Terence, 45
Operation Motorman, 68
opinion surveys relating to Northern Ireland, 54–8, 61, 105–9
Orme, Stanley, 52
Orthodox, Greek: *see under* Greek
Ottoman empire, 16, 18, 21, 25, 39, 113, 114
Oxford English Dictionary, 26

Paisley, Ian: and Good Friday Agreement, 85, 86, 101, 103; and Sunningdale Agreement, 45, 47, 63, 67, 68; and Ulster Workers' Council, 50, 52
Pakradouni, Karim, 146, 150, 157
Palestinians in Lebanon, 19, 23, 37, 142–7, 158, 171, 176, 178, 187–8, 194
Palley, Claire, 16
pan-Arabism: *see* Arab nationalism
Pappalardo, Adriano, 28
paramilitary groups in Lebanon: *see* militias
paramilitary groups in Northern Ireland: Good Friday Agreement and, 71, 90, 181, 185, 193; loyalist, 52, 57, 80, 85; republican, 185; Sunningdale

Agreement and, 180, 190; *see also*
    specific groups
Parliament (Lebanon): *see* Chamber of
    Deputies
Parliament, Scottish, 94
parties, political, 27; in Lebanon, 114,
    115, 135, 164, 177; in Northern
    Ireland, 42, 43, 45, 47, 50, 58, 62,
    67, 70, 74, 87, 88, 92, 99, 102, 110;
    see also specific parties
partition of Ireland, 8, 9, 66, 88
Patterson, Henry, 11
peace process (1997–98) in Northern
    Ireland, 84–6
Pharaon, Henri, 19–20, 117, 119
Phares, W., 18
Phoenicians, 16, 18, 123, 202
Picard, Elizabeth, 20–1, 24–5
'pledged' Unionists (1973), 45, 48, 50, 64
pluralism, 27, 28, 35, 187, 194; in
    Lebanon, 21; in Northern Ireland,
    109, 185
policing in Northern Ireland, 44, 60, 88,
    90, 96, 99
population: *see* demographic factors
Powell, Enoch, 74
power-sharing, 1–3, 4, 6–7, 26–8, 30,
    31, 35, 38, 40, 179, 193, 194, 197,
    198; in Cyprus, 39; in Lebanon, 16,
    18–24, 29, 31, 34, 112, 120–6, 134,
    139, 144, 159, 160, 168, 174, 181–4,
    186–8, 190, 195, 197; in Northern
    Ireland, 5, 13, 29, 31, 34–8, 41–8,
    53–8, 62–8, 70, 71, 75, 87, 95, 96,
    103–8, 112, 180–4, 188, 192, 199; in
    former Yugoslav states, 38, 40
presidency of Lebanon, 25, 114, 115,
    119, 120, 124, 126, 127, 132, 142,
    146–7, 150, 155, 161–7, 170
prime ministership of Lebanon, 125,
    127, 132, 133, 142, 146, 147, 153,
    162–7, 170
Prior, Jim, 73
prisoners issue (Northern Ireland), 88,
    90, 96, 98, 99, 105, 193
Programme for National Action
    (Lebanon, 1976), 146
Progressive Democrats (Ireland), 85
Progressive Socialist Party (Lebanon),
    142, 150, 170
Progressive Unionist Party (Northern
    Ireland), 85, 97, 106
proportionality: in consociational theory,
    27, 28; in Lebanon, 19–21, 114, 124,
    133, 134, 138, 139, 147, 161, 166,
    172, 175, 178, 182; in Northern
    Ireland, 13, 43, 44, 47, 57, 62, 84

*Proposals by the British and Irish
    Governments for a Comprehensive
    Agreement* (2004); *see* Comprehensive
    Proposals
Propositions on Heads of Agreement
    (1998), 85
Protestants in Lebanon, 161, 173
Protestants in Northern Ireland, 7, 10,
    11; and Good Friday Agreement, 105,
    107, 108, 191; and power-sharing,
    35–6; shifting demographic ratio
    between Catholics and, 103; socialists
    among, 9–10; and Sunningdale
    Agreement, 44, 46–8, 50–8, 63, 69,
    71, 72
provinces in Lebanon, 166, 172
Pym, Francis, 48, 50, 60–1

qada', 166

Reagan, Ronald, 148, 149, 151
reconciliation, 11, 179, 187, 192, 193;
    in Lebanon, 23, 24, 141, 145, 153,
    154, 160, 170, 172, 177, 178, 187,
    188, 190; in Northern Ireland, 12, 90,
    184, 188, 196, 197
Rees, Merlyn, 50–3, 69
referendums: on Irish border (conducted
    1973), 45; on changes in Irish
    Constitution (proposed 1973), 61; on
    Good Friday Agreement (conducted
    1998), 36, 45, 72, 87, 88, 90, 104,
    105, 109, 110, 180, 185, 189, 197;
    on a united Ireland (in future), 195–6
Règlement in Lebanon, 16, 21, 134, 135,
    139, 190
Reid, Alex, 79
repartition of Northern Ireland
    (proposed), 15
republicans in Northern Ireland, 8, 9,
    195; ceasefires by, 74, 79, 81–4; and
    Downing Street Declaration, 76–80,
    83, 84; Good Friday Agreement and,
    184, 185; and peace process
    (1997–98), 85, 91, 92, 95–7; and
    Sunningdale Agreement, 43, 48, 49,
    54, 58, 60, 66, 68, 71, 180, 186, 190
Reynolds, Albert, 60, 78–82, 84, 90, 91,
    94
Reynolds, Gerry, 79
Robinson, Peter, 101, 109
Rogan, Denis, 98
Roman Catholics: *see* Catholics
Roosevelt, Franklin D., 116, 130–1
Rose, Richard, 10
Royal Ulster Constabulary, 51, 69, 105
Ruane, Joseph, 12

Sa'adeh, Antoine, 126
Saad, Habib al-, 113
Saddam Hussein, 169
Sadr, Musa, 143–4
Salam, Saeb, 163
Salibi, Kemal, 16–18
Satterfield, David, 156
Saudi Arabia, 1, 5, 19, 24, 37, 128, 150, 153–8, 161, 169, 173
Scottish Parliament, 94
Second Republic (Lebanon), 170, 171, 174, 182, 189
Second World War: Irish neutrality during, 59; Lebanon and, 5, 21, 112, 116, 122, 125, 127, 129, 130, 139, 187, 189
security policy in Northern Ireland, 42, 44–6, 48–50, 59, 60, 62, 66, 68, 69, 71, 73, 75, 181, 185, 192; under Good Friday Agreement, 88, 90, 91, 106, 111; peace process (1997–98) and, 94, 95, 101
self-determination, 179, 188, 190; Arab, 122; Irish, 7–8; Lebanese, 176; in relation to Northern Ireland, 14, 16, 83, 100, 191, 195
Senate (France), 115
Senate (Lebanon), 114, 165
Sfeir, Nasrallah (Patriarch), 153
Shi'a Muslims in Iraq, 39, 114
Shi'a Muslims in Lebanon, 18, 114, 186; in Chamber of Deputies, 161, 165, 172, 173; and deconfessionalisation, 164; demographic rise of, 136, 137, 143–4, 161, 164, 175; and National Pact, 19, 22, 134, 136, 142, 166, 182; and speakership of Chamber of Deputies, 125, 146, 164, 167; and Ta'if Agreement, 161, 163, 164, 175, 186
Shultz, George, 149
Sidon, 18, 118
Sinai Agreement (1975), 146
single transferable vote in Northern Ireland, 42, 43, 45, 88
Sinn Féin, 77, 91; and Anglo-Irish Agreement, 74, 76; and Downing Street Declaration, 77–84; and Good Friday Agreement, 105, 106, 108, 109, 111, 181, 184, 185, 188; and Northern Ireland Executive (since 1998), 94, 98, 101, 103, 105, 106, 108; and peace process (1997–98), 86, 92–7, 102, 104; and Sunningdale Agreement, 44, 50, 66
Smallwoods, Ray, 83
Social Democratic and Labour Party (Northern Ireland), 8, 30; and Anglo-Irish Agreement, 74, 76; and Good Friday Agreement, 106, 185; ; and peace process (1997–98), 92–5, 97, 99, 101, 104; and Sunningdale Agreement, 45–50, 52–4, 56, 62–6, 68, 70; talks between Sinn Féin and, 77, 83
socialists in Northern Ireland, 9–10, 65, 66
Soldatov, Alexander, 148
Solh, Riad, 117–20, 122–8, 130, 133, 138, 178
South Africa, 12, 97
South Tyrol, 39
sovereignty, 24, 40; in Iraq, 34; in Jordan, 143; in Lebanon, 23, 32, 37, 135, 143, 148, 149, 153, 154, 157, 160, 164, 166–8, 170, 171, 176–8, 189, 195; and Northern Ireland, 14, 16, 39, 58, 76, 84, 111, 180, 189, 195, 196
Soviet Union, 148, 149, 153, 157
speakership of Chamber of Deputies (Lebanon), 125, 146, 162–5, 167
Spears, Edward, 112, 116, 119–22, 124, 129–32
spin-doctoring, 72, 100–1
Spring, Dick, 76, 87
State Department (US), 91, 92
Suez crisis (1956), 126
suicide bombers, 149
Sunni Muslims in former empires, 18, 114
Sunni Muslims in Iraq, 39
Sunni Muslims in Lebanon: in Chamber of Deputies, 161, 173; on coast, 114; demographic decline of, 136, 137; divisions among, 118; France and, 118, 122; national aspirations of, 122, 123; and National Pact, 124, 134, 136, 138, 139, 160; and Palestinians, 142; and prime ministership, 125, 127, 146, 147, 162, 167; Saudi Arabia and, 24, 161, 169; and Ta'if Agreement, 161, 162, 163, 164, 167, 175, 186
Sunningdale Agreement (1973), 1, 4–5, 11, 13, 14, 29, 30, 41–72, 112, 180, 182, 183, 185, 186, 190, 192, 195; Anglo-Irish Agreement compared to, 74, 76; Good Friday Agreement compared to, 86–90, 93–7, 99–103, 105, 106, 108, 110; Margaret Thatcher and, 73, 75
Supreme Court (Ireland), 49, 84
Switzerland, 187

Sykes–Picot Agreement (1916), 113
Syria: Britain and, 115, 120, 121, 129, 131, 132; France and, 3, 113–15, 120, 121, 123, 124, 131, 132; and Lebanon, 1, 5, 6, 19, 23–5, 34, 117–19, 122, 127, 128, 135, 143, 145–78, 180–3, 186–91, 193–5, 197, 199–200

Ta'if Agreement (1989), 1, 5–6, 16, 23–5, 30–6, 141, 144, 150, 153–78, 180–3, 185–93, 195–7, 199
Taylor, John, 49, 83, 86, 98, 99
Taylor, Rupert, 12
Thatcher, Margaret, 12, 73, 74, 75, 78, 79, 90
Todd, Jennifer, 12
Treaty of Brotherhood (1991), 171, 189
Trimble, David, 64, 67, 85, 86, 93–103, 109–10, 181, 185, 191
Tripartite Agreement (1985), 144, 149, 150–2, 155, 158, 160, 178
Tripartite High Commission ('Troika'), 153–7, 163, 164, 168, 169, 176
Tripoli, 118, 172
Troika: *see* Tripartite High Commission
Tuéni, Ghassan, 32
Tunis, 152
Turkey, 39
Turkish Cypriots, 39
Tyre, 18

Ulster Defence Association, 50, 77, 80
Ulster Defence Regiment, 69
Ulster Democratic Party, 85, 97
Ulster Unionist Council, 47, 49, 63, 70, 98
Ulster Unionist Party, 8, 9, 29, 181; and Anglo-Irish Agreement, 76; and Downing Street Declaration, 81–3; and Good Friday Agreement, 105, 106, 108–10; and Northern Ireland Executive (since 1998), 94; and peace process (1997–98), 85, 86, 92–101, 102, 104; and Sunningdale Agreement, 45, 47, 64, 67, 100
Ulster Volunteer Force, 50, 80
Ulster Workers' Council, 44, 50, 51–3, 64, 68–72, 99
unionists in Northern Ireland, 3, 7–9, 12, 16, 30, 199; and Anglo-Irish Agreement, 74, 75, 76, 81; East of the Bann, 56, 207; Bill Clinton and, 92; demographic shift and, 103; and Downing Street Declaration, 79, 80,

81; and Forum, 85; and Framework Documents, 84; and Good Friday Agreement, 36, 67, 72, 87–9, 99, 105–6, 108, 109, 111, 181–5, 188, 189, 191, 195; and loyalists, 80; and peace process (1997–98), 85, 93–9, 100–1, 104; and Protestantism, 10; and Sunningdale Agreement, 41, 43–9, 53–5, 57–72, 100, 180, 190, 195
United Kingdom: *see* British government
United Kingdom Unionist Party, 85, 95, 99, 106, 181
United Nations Security Council, 164
United States: and Anglo-French rivalry in Middle East, 129–32; and Gulf War, 157, 159, 169–70; and Iraq, 32, 34, 39, 191, 199; and Lebanon, 1, 5, 24, 139, 145–59, 168–70, 190, 194; and Northern Ireland, 5, 38, 75, 77, 81–3, 91–2, 184
United Ulster Unionist Council, 50, 61, 67, 68, 69
'unpledged' Unionists (1973), 45
Upper Bann, 109

Vanguard, 48, 67
Vatican, 145
veto rights, 13, 27, 28; in Lebanon, 162, 163, 171, 178, 181; in relation to Northern Ireland, 42–4, 63, 64, 70–1, 88, 89; Syrian *de facto*, 148, 160, 189

Wadsworth, George, 131–2
Walzer, Michael, 179
War Office (Britain), 130
Weinberger, Casper, 149
West, Harry, 47, 49–51, 63, 67
Whitelaw, William, 47, 48, 60–3, 67–9
White Paper: *see under* British government
Wilford, Rick, 12
Wilson, Harold, 50–3, 68–70, 101, 206
women in Northern Ireland, 12
Women's Coalition of Northern Ireland, 11, 12
working class, Protestant (Northern Ireland), 10

Yafi, Abdallah, 145
Yugoslav states, former, 38, 40

Zamir, Meir, 19, 119, 138
Zisser, Eyal, 21
Zu'ama, 115, 117, 135